KING OF THE CLUB

KING OF THE CLUB

RICHARD GRASSO AND THE SURVIVAL OF THE NEW YORK STOCK EXCHANGE

CHARLES GASPARINO

COLLINS BUSINESS
An Imprint of HarperCollins Publishers

HarperCollins books may be purchased for educational, business, or sales promotional use. For information please write: Special Markets Department, HarperCollins Publishers, 10 East 53rd Street, New York, NY 10022.

FIRST COLLINS TRADE PAPERBACK EDITION PUBLISHED IN 2008.

Designed by Jaime Putorti

The Library of Congress has cataloged the hardcover edition as follows:

Gasparino, Charles.
  King of the club : Richard Grasso and the survival of the New York Stock Exchange / Charles Gasparino.—1st ed.
    p. cm.
  ISBN 978-0-06-089833-5
  1. Grasso, Richard.   2. New York Stock Exchange—Officials and employees—Biography.   3. Corporations—Corrupt practices—United States—Case studies.   I. Title.

HG4572.G36 2007
332.64'273092—dc22
[B]
                                                                2007042627
ISBN 978-0-06-089834-2 (pbk.)

08 09 10 11 12 DIX/RRD 10 9 8 7 6 5 4 3 2 1

To Gin, for always being there

CONTENTS

CAST OF CHARACTERS

MADELEINE ALBRIGHT: Former U.S. Secretary of State, whom Grasso appointed to the NYSE board in 2003 to fulfill new mandates that called for more board members to be appointed from outside the securities industry. Albright ultimately voted to terminate Grasso as CEO of the exchange.

FRANK ASHEN: Former human resources director of the NYSE. A staunch Grasso loyalist who knew more about Grasso's controversial pay package than any exchange official except Grasso himself. Eliot Spitzer regarded him as a key witness against Grasso and ultimately forced him into a settlement that included testifying in Spitzer's civil case against Grasso over the $139.5 million pay package.

CHARLES BOCKLET: NYSE specialist and board member who was once a Grasso friend—until he provided testimony to Eliot Spitzer for his case against Grasso.

ROBERT BRITZ: Served under Grasso as co-president of the NYSE, and like Catherine Kinney, was considered a likely successor before the pay package controversy.

JAMES "JIMMY" CAYNE: CEO of Bear Stearns and former NYSE compensation committee member who helped blow the whistle on Grasso's large pay package but ultimately voted for Grasso to stay as chairman amid the pay scandal.

RICHARD "BO" DIETL: Former New York City cop, private investigator, and dinner partner with Grasso at Rao's restaurant in East Harlem.

WILLIAM DONALDSON: Chairman of the New York Stock Exchange from 1991 to 1995 and former chairman of the Securities and Exchange Commission. Grasso bristled under his leadership of the stock exchange, unseated him as chairman, and then took the job himself. Donaldson later got his revenge when as chairman of the SEC he started an inquiry into Grasso's pay package.

LAURENCE "LARRY" FINK: CEO of BlackRock and former NYSE compensation committee member. A Grasso supporter who blew the whistle on his pay package.

STANLEY GAULT: Former head of Goodyear and the NYSE compensation committee who devised the various retirement accounts that years later would create so much controversy.

RUDY GIULIANI: Mayor of New York City, 1994–2001. One of the few friends to remain loyal to Grasso even after the pay scandal forced Grasso from his job.

JOSEPH GRANO: Former number two at PaineWebber and a close associate of Grasso who urged him not to appoint former Citigroup CEO Sandy Weill to the board after Weill and the firm were ensnarled in the research analyst investigation.

LORRAINE GRASSO: Richard Grasso's former secretary, later his wife.

RICHARD GRASSO: Chairman, New York Stock Exchange, 1995–2003; resigned from the exchange after the longest tenure of any chairman and a thirty-five-year career at the exchange, amid a scandal over his $139.5 million pay package.

MAURICE "HANK" GREENBERG: Former CEO of American International Group and NYSE board member. Greenberg's constant badgering to get his specialist to bid up shares of AIG stock became legendary inside the exchange and later led to a probe into whether Grasso had improperly interfered with trading.

JOSEPH HARDIMAN: Former chairman and CEO of the National Association of Securities Brokers, which ran the Nasdaq Stock Market, helped the Nasdaq gain market share against Grasso but resigned following a trading scandal.

WILLIAM HARRISON: CEO of JPMorgan Chase, who ultimately voted to have Grasso removed as chairman of the exchange.

PATRICK HEALY: Former marketing executive for the Nasdaq Stock Market and later founder of the Issue Advisory Group helped Grasso bring new listings to the exchange.

MEL KARMAZIN: Former CEO of Viacom; a NYSE board member and Grasso supporter.

BERNARD KERIK: Former New York City police commissioner who worked closely with Grasso during the 9/11 crisis and remained close to Grasso even as Kerik faced his own bout with scandal.

CATHERINE KINNEY: Served under Grasso as co-president of the NYSE and was considered a likely successor before the pay package controversy.

DAVID KOMANSKY: Former chairman and CEO of Merrill Lynch, NYSE board member and supporter, who approved many of Grasso's biggest paychecks.

MICHAEL LABRANCHE: Chairman of LaBranche & Co., the largest independent specialist firm, and a key critic of Grasso among the floor trading community. Aside from Hank Paulson, there was no single person more responsible for rallying support against Grasso.

KENNETH LANGONE: Co-founder of Home Depot, Wall Street financier, and head of the NYSE's compensation committee from 1999 to

2003, who was instrumental in the creation of Grasso's $139.5 million pay package.

SOOJEE LEE: Richard Grasso's loyal secretary who later earned a degree of fame when her own salary was disclosed.

GERALD LEVIN: Former CEO of AOL Time Warner and NYSE board member who supported Grasso until the final days of the pay controversy.

MARTIN "MARTY" LIPTON: Partner at Wachtell, Lipton, Rosen & Katz; legal adviser to the NYSE and Grasso during the pay scandal.

BERNARD "BERNIE" MARCUS: Co-founder of Home Depot who preceded Langone as head of the NYSE compensation committee.

H. CARL MCCALL: Former chairman of the NYSE's compensation committee and former New York State comptroller. Criticized for handling the pay package scandal that led to Grasso's ouster.

ROBERT MICHELS: Daniel Webb's top attorney, who handled many of the interviews that formed the basis of the "Webb" Report into Grasso's pay package.

ROBERT "BOBBY" MURPHY: Longtime floor trader and friend of Grasso who became No. 2 at LaBranche & Co., only to be fired by Michael LaBranche amid the pay controversy.

LEON PANETTA: Former chief of staff to President Bill Clinton and NYSE board member who urged Grasso not to take the money.

HENRY "HANK" PAULSON: Former chairman and CEO of Goldman Sachs and U.S. Treasury secretary. Key opponent of Grasso on issues ranging from the need for more electronic trading at the exchange to Grasso's pay package. Led the charge to depose Grasso and helped transform the NYSE in his own image.

JOHN PHELAN: Chairman of New York Stock Exchange from 1984 to 1990, and Grasso's mentor through his early years at the exchange.

CHRIS QUICK: Former head of Fleet Specialists and former board member of the NYSE. Quick was a key Grasso supporter through the pay package scandal.

CHARLES RAMOS: New York State Supreme Court judge who presided over the Grasso case and, after more than a year of depositions, issued a summary judgment ordering Grasso to repay much of his compensation package. Grasso appealed and released documents showing that Ramos had applied twice to be on the board of the NYSE and been rejected by both Grasso and John Reed.

SUMNER REDSTONE: Chairman of Viacom and, like Hank Greenberg, a persistent thorn in Grasso's side for demanding that his specialist bid up shares of his stock listed on the NYSE.

JOHN REED: Former CEO of Citicorp, co-CEO of Citigroup, and chairman of the NYSE. Took over for Grasso after his ouster, launched an investigation into the pay package, and convinced New York attorney general Eliot Spitzer to investigate.

AVI SCHICK: Former deputy counsel to the New York attorney general and lead counsel on Spitzer's case against Grasso.

ELIOT SPITZER: New York State Attorney General, 1998–2006. Spitzer was regarded as Wall Street's enforcer for his high-profile cases involving mutual funds and Wall Street research. Once a friend and ally of Grasso, he ended up filing a case against Grasso to have him return most if not all of the $139.5 million pay package.

ERIC STARKMAN: Hired by Grasso to handle his public relations after the Spitzer case was filed.

BRENDAN SULLIVAN: Partner at Williams & Connolly and lawyer for Richard Grasso in the case involving his pay package. Known as one of the best attorneys in the country, Sullivan promised an all-out war against Spitzer and the board members who turned their back on Grasso in his time of need.

WILLIAM SUMMERS: Former CEO of McDonald & Co., a Cleveland-based brokerage firm, and a NYSE board member who remained loyal to Grasso even after advising him not to take the pay package.

JOHN THAIN: Former co-president of Goldman Sachs and CEO of the NYSE. His appointment completed the "takeover" of the exchange by Goldman Sachs, and Thain quickly moved the exchange in the direction Hank Paulson desired: to more electronic trading, which led to the demise of the floor trading system, the largest fundamental change in the NYSE's history.

DANIEL TULLY: Former chairman and CEO of Merrill Lynch and NYSE board member. An early Grasso supporter, instrumental in helping him become chairman of the exchange.

DANIEL WEBB: Former federal prosecutor who in private practice was hired by John Reed and the NYSE to investigate Grasso's pay package. He produced a scathing report on the issue, known as the Webb Report, which later formed the basis of Spitzer's civil charge against Grasso and Langone.

SANFORD I. WEILL: Former CEO of Citigroup. The controversy over Grasso's near appointment of Weill to the board of the exchange after Weill was involved in one of Spitzer's high-profile investigations marked the beginning of the end of Grasso's long career at the exchange.

FRANK ZARB: Former chairman and CEO of the NASD. Zarb took over for Hardiman and became one of Grasso's toughest competitors.

ROBERT ZITO: Director of communications and marketing for the NYSE and one of Grasso's closest advisers. Possibly most responsible for creating the NYSE's brand image outside of Grasso.

PROLOGUE

"Mr. Mayor, any positions open at Giuliani Partners?" Richard Grasso asked when he picked up the phone. The chairman of the New York Stock Exchange had just received word from his secretary, SooJee Lee, that Rudolph Giuliani, the former mayor of New York, a Grasso friend and sometime rival, was on the telephone.

It was early in the morning on September 17, 2003. Dick Grasso arrived at work at around 7:00 A.M., early enough to read the morning newspapers and grab some breakfast. It should have been a day filled with celebrations. Exactly two years earlier Grasso and Giuliani had stood on a podium as heroes; the two had reopened the stock exchange less than a week after the 9/11 terrorist attacks occurred.

Fast-forward two years to September 2003, and Grasso was a different man. He was still hard at work; just a few days earlier, the exchange had celebrated the one hundredth anniversary of Harley-Davidson, which had its shares listed to trade on the "Big Board." He had done it in true Grasso fashion with a huge celebration on the floor of the exchange, company officials in leather Harley jackets ringing the opening bell, and one of Grasso's signature publicity stunts, featuring Grasso himself riding a chopper down Broad Street in front of the exchange building with the wife of Harley's CEO seated on the back. "New York Stock Exchange chairmen come and go," he later told one of his aides with a smile on his face, "but hundred-year anniversaries come only once every one hundred years."

Grasso, however, wasn't smiling today. In fact, he remained stoic even as he glanced at the one photo in his office that captured the moment of his greatest triumph: in the picture, he and Giuliani smiled and clapped as they declared the markets open for business following the attacks. Giuliani was now a private security consultant, making a mint off his 9/11 stardom; things were going so well for Giuliani, in fact, that he was considering a run for president.

Giuliani had offered Grasso a chance to work at his firm, but the offer had been made before Grasso's career had imploded in scandal. He was still a friend, however, one of the few Grasso had these days, and Giuliani asked his friend how he was doing. Grasso said he was doing as well as could be expected under the circumstances.

"I'm the only hero of 9/11 who isn't benefiting from being a hero," Grasso muttered to himself as he sat in his office studying the visible evidence of his success: the photos with celebrities, politicians, and world leaders; the shelves stacked with souvenirs from the various companies he had convinced to have their shares listed on the exchange.

What perplexed Grasso the most was how swift his downfall had been. Grasso's office was filled with mementos of his unparalleled reign—the "NYSE Corporate Museum," as he used to call it when he gave tours to everyone from politicians to CEOs of the world's largest companies. In reality it was the Grasso Museum: every square inch was packed with something intended to validate his position as King of the Club.

But a series of missteps over the months leading up to the September 17 anniversary had accomplished what no competitor or terrorist had been able to achieve: Dick Grasso's defeat. That his demise would come in part as the result of his own actions only made the event more tragic. In the summer of 2003, America was still reeling from corporate scandals involving executives run amok: Enron,

WorldCom, and Tyco International, to name just a few. But the litany of stories detailing malfeasance, incompetence, and greed was capped by an extraordinary disclosure: that Grasso wanted to cash in a retirement package worth close to $140 million, including something the press had identified as an unseemly "bonus" of $5 million for working overtime during 9/11. Grasso wasn't stealing the money, of course—in fact, he had been paid the same "special bonus" the previous year—but the revelations had turned him from hero to poster boy for the overpaid chief executive. The same board of directors that had approved his taking the money, 9/11 bonus and all, just a few weeks earlier now wanted him out.

The first staffer to encounter Grasso that morning was his longtime PR man and marketing chief, Robert Zito. All seemed familiar when Zito arrived. The "Hot and Krispy" neon light, a gift from the Krispy Kreme donut company, burned brightly in the chairman's office, as it had since Grasso won that listing two years earlier. But as Zito entered the normally sweltering office—Grasso blasted the heat even during the summer months—he immediately noticed a chill in the air.

"It feels like a morgue in here," Zito thought. And Grasso looked like death. With dark rings under his eyes, he waited a few moments before giving Zito the bad news. Grasso was in mourning. The Club's ruling commission, its board of directors, was getting ready to hand Grasso the ultimate indignity: it was planning to strip him of the only job he had ever really wanted, and one of the few he had ever had.

The problem was bigger than just "that snake" Hank Paulson, the Goldman Sachs CEO who had been calling for his ouster in recent weeks, or longtime critic Michael LaBranche, who ran a powerful "specialist" firm and had rallied opposition to Grasso among the traders who bought and sold stocks on the floor of the exchange, or even that a supporter, Larry Fink, the head of BlackRock, had just crossed to the dark side. Someone the chairman had believed was an untouchable ally was now having second thoughts about his chairmanship: the man he called simply "the lawyer."

The Wall Street superlawyer Martin "Marty" Lipton had been a key adviser to Grasso almost from the moment the pay controversy became front-page news. His advice was simple: there is nothing improper about taking the money as long as the board approved the move, which it did. With Lipton's support, Grasso believed he was unbeatable. But Zito worried that Lipton was conflicted; the lawyer had been dealing too much and for far too long with Grasso's enemies on Wall Street for Grasso to fully trust him. Grasso had ignored Zito's warnings; now he wished he hadn't.

"I guess you were right about the lawyer," Grasso said darkly, according to Zito's recollection. Zito was perplexed for a moment but soon discovered what Grasso was talking about because Lipton had an appointment to meet with Grasso within minutes.

Lipton entered the office and dispensed with pleasantries. As he sat across from Grasso, he announced that after he had spoken to Paulson and several exchange board members, it was his opinion that Grasso should think about resigning. In other words, the board now wanted him out. With a hint of defiance, Grasso summoned his pride and responded, "I'll do what the board wants me to do."

Within a few moments, a plan was set for an emergency board meeting, to be held on a conference call later that afternoon.

All Grasso could think was "How did it come to this?"

Later that afternoon Grasso would, of course, make it official and resign as chairman and chief executive officer of the New York Stock Exchange, ending a thirty-five-year career at the institution known among its members simply as "the Club." If you read the press clippings on Grasso's rise and fall, it's hard to come away feeling good about the man. He's been called imperious, greedy, and spiteful. One story in *The New York Times* compared him to a "ward boss" for his autocratic rule of the exchange. Another likened him to the legendary bandit Jesse James for the manner in which he took his massive pay package.

Like all stereotypes, these contain some element of truth. Grasso was a tough, autocratic boss. He certainly hid his massive retirement package from the public and even from many of the technical owners

of the exchange, the 1,366 "seat holders" who held the exclusive right
to buy and sell stocks on the exchange's trading floor. Fearing a public backlash, Grasso did all he could to take the money out before he
could be denied by a more fearful board. Grasso's obsession with his
enemies at times bordered on paranoia; those who didn't pledge complete loyalty to him and his rule were ostracized. Those who openly
opposed him often suffered a far worse fate.

But to dwell on these shortcomings is to miss the bigger story: the
rise and fall of one of the most remarkable men Wall Street and corporate America has ever seen. Over the past few years, I've had the
opportunity to interview dozens of top executives, including the
CEOs of the biggest Wall Street firms. To a man, they all love to boast
about their rags-to-riches stories. But few of them ever really lived
their Horatio Alger tales. Most of these men (and more recently, a few
women) started off comfortably middle class, attended top colleges,
and then worked their way up the corporate power structure.

Grasso, on the other hand, truly started from the bottom before
rising to the pinnacle of not just his company but Wall Street itself.
He grew up poor, had almost no college education, and would have
happily been earning a middle-class living as a city cop, if only he
could have passed the eye exam. When he didn't, he took an entry-
level job on the stock exchange and thus began one of Wall Street's
most improbable careers. He even succeeded in turning what was
once considered a quasi-governmental job into one that was paid on a
par with the loftiest corporate titans.

Which brings us to a larger matter: the New York Stock
Exchange—the institution Grasso dominated for so long. It is one of
the most important symbols of our country's financial and social success; it plays a critical role in the market economy that makes the
American dream possible. But few people really understand how the
institution works on the inside, particularly from the standpoint of
the people who make it work, men like Dick Grasso and those who
later banished him from the financial business, possibly forever.

1

IT'S GOOD TO BE KING

September 11, 2001, started out as a typical late-summer day in New York. More than 350,000 people filed into the lower Manhattan financial district on a bright, sunny morning when tragedy seemed to be the furthest thing from anyone's mind. Grasso arrived at the office that morning at his usual time, 7:00 A.M., prepared to ring the opening bell with executives from Bergen Brunswig Corporation, a pharmaceutical company that was listed on the exchange, but first he went through the newspapers, and as always he had CNBC on the tube. Company officials were already in the exchange, assembled in the dining hall. By now Grasso had established a certain ritual for all companies he convinced to pay a fee of as much as $500,000 annually to have their shares listed to trade on the New York Stock Exchange; company officials and his senior staff would attend an elaborate breakfast where Grasso would extol the virtues of the world's greatest stock market. From there it was off to ring the opening bell, where companies would be treated to one of the greatest PR stunts in corporate America.

At around 8:50 A.M., Grasso was running late, attending to some housekeeping items in his office and watching CNBC's *Squawk Box* morning show, when he received a call from one of his top officials, deputy enforcement chief David Doherty, whose job it was to make sure trading at the exchange was done legally. Grasso loved to hire former law enforcement officials: his driver was a former cop; his security guards were ex-NYPD vets as well. Doherty had served in the CIA before coming to the exchange a few years earlier to work under enforcement chief Ed Kwalwasser, himself a former SEC attorney. Part of Grasso's recent battle with City Hall had been to get New York City mayor Rudy Giuliani to use city funds to expand the exchange's historic headquarters on the corner of Wall and Broad streets to accommodate all five thousand of its employees and stock traders.

There had been some testy moments in the negotiations. Giuliani had all but accused Grasso of being greedy; Grasso had told Giuliani he was giving the exchange, the anchor of the lower Manhattan economy, short shrift. But Grasso had won concessions from the mayor, and he was in the planning phases of building a new high-rise across the street at 33 Wall. In the meantime, Doherty and his enforcement staff were scattered throughout various locations in downtown Manhattan, including the north tower of the World Trade Center, where Doherty was reporting what looked like a bizarre accident: the Port Authority of New York and New Jersey, the state agency that owned the twin towers, was alerting tenants that a small plane had hit the top floors of the north tower.

Doherty said he wasn't overly concerned. In fact, the word from the authority brass was to stay calm and that under no circumstances should people be evacuated. That's when Grasso noticed something on CNBC. The business station had a remote camera located just across the Hudson River and zoomed into the area of impact. Huge clouds of black smoke and flames could be seen shooting from the top floors of the 110-story edifice. Grasso wasn't an expert on plane crashes, but he knew this was more serious than some hang glider flying into one of the country's and the world's tallest buildings. "Dave," he said with his eyes glued to the screen, "this is no small plane, get them out now."

The exchange had 140 people on the third floor of the north tower.

All of them left promptly except one, a security guard named Oliver Smith, who wanted to make sure a quadriplegic enforcement attorney had made it out alive. Grasso, meanwhile, canceled his listing breakfast and alerted his staff that he was going to walk over to the trade center to see what was happening.

At the corner of Wall and Broadway, Grasso noticed that the sky was filled with white ash, smoke, and flames. He went no further because his chief of security, James Esposito, grabbed him from behind. "Hey, you can't go over there," Esposito said. Esposito is an imposing man with wire-rimmed glasses who had spent most of his career, more than twenty-five years, as an FBI agent. He had just received a report that a second plane had crashed into the south tower. And things were worse, at least according to the reports Esposito had been given. These were no accidents. They were a concerted effort on the part of terrorists.

Grasso now got a clear view of the trade center. It reminded him of a tree that had been chopped with an ax. All four sides of both towers were now blackened with smoke and engulfed in flames. "This ain't no small plane," he repeated to Esposito.

"We've got to get you out of here," Esposito responded.

Grasso and Esposito couldn't believe their eyes; throngs of people, men in their suits and women in their high heels, running for cover as the towers burned. The two hightailed it back to the exchange. Grasso was fifty-five years old, but he ran as if he were twenty-five. By now the word was out on the street—literally—that large jets had crashed into the trade center, and it was an attack by terrorists, probably Muslim extremists. A massive crowd assembled on Broad Street, many of them employees and traders of the exchange, staring in the direction of the trade center, watching the carnage.

As events unfolded that morning inside the trading rooms and on the streets of lower Manhattan, chaos ruled. People watched in horror as bodies began falling from the twin towers. Most, like Grasso, ran for their lives, ducked into stores, or hid under cars and trucks to escape the falling debris. A few looked for ways to make money.

"They're fucking bombing us, sell the S&P! Sell the S&P!"

screamed the legendary stock trader John Mulheren just after the first plane hit. Mulheren was a large, boisterous man with a quick temper and a quick mind when it came to making money in the markets. He had earned fame in the 1980s as a top trader who later attempted to attack the Wall Street swindler Ivan Boesky with a gun after Boesky implicated him in the insider trading scandals. Mulheren was eventually cleared of the insider trading charges, and more recently he had rehabilitated himself by partnering with Bear Stearns and running a big and highly profitable "specialist" firm that made money trading on the floor of the exchange.

Mulheren was in a conference room at his office on 40 Wall Street with one of the best views of lower Manhattan, overlooking the trade center, when the first plane hit. Like most Wall Streeters he knew the area was a prime target for terrorists, particularly after the 1993 bombing of the trade center, which caused limited damage. But Mulheren's bet was that this attack was bigger as he peered out his window, watching the flames and smoke. And if it was bigger the damage to the markets would be bigger as well. That's why he now was "shorting" the market, a trading technique where profits are made when stocks tank. A terrorist attack of a large magnitude would most certainly cause the large-company stocks in the Standard & Poor's 500 index to implode.

Although the stock exchange hadn't opened yet, Mulheren's guys managed to short some futures contracts in the over-the-counter market. Mulheren was a savvy trader, but he was also a nervous man who suffered from the highs and lows associated with a severe case of bipolar disorder. A few moments after placing his trade, he heard on television that the attack might not be so bad—it might have been just a small plane hitting the trade center—and he went into a panic. "Buy the fucking S&P! Buy the fucking S&P!" he screamed, reversing his position.

Mulheren breathed a sigh of relief when he was informed that the second trade had gone through—that is, until he heard another report on television: a second plane had hit the trade center. And these weren't exactly puddle jumpers. They were large jets filled with fuel. The attack, it was later discovered, had been orchestrated by the extremist Osama bin Laden. Soon Mulheren's traders and secretaries began screaming as they watched from the office window as people jumped off the top floors of the trade center.

By now, even the futures markets were shut down, but trading seemed to be the last thing on Mulheren's mind as he issued his last order of the day: "All right, everyone, get the fuck out of here immediately!"

Grasso was now safely indoors—or so it seemed. A rumor began circulating through the floor that the south tower was coming down and the building was collapsing toward the exchange. Grasso had always prided himself on opening the exchange for business, ringing the opening bell to signal the start of trading, no matter how bad the calamity. The opening had survived blizzards, natural disasters, wars, and technology glitches that delayed it for a few hours.

But this was different—he had seen the carnage firsthand and the frenzy in the streets. Grasso had just gotten his breath back as he stood at his control center on the floor of the exchange with his senior staff: Zito, his PR man; Catherine Kinney and Robert Britz, the co–chief operating officers; and Esposito. The exact spot was known as "the ramp" because it was near a ramp that connected the main trading floor to four other rooms that make up the floor. There, Grasso had a PA system he could use to make important announcements, as well as telephone lines connecting him to people of importance, namely Harvey Pitt, the chairman of the Securities and Exchange Commission and his nominal boss, who had just taken the job; Federal Reserve chairman Alan Greenspan; U.S. Treasury secretary Paul O'Neill; and New York City mayor Rudy Giuliani.

Grasso told his staff he was ready to close the place down. No one argued with him. He used the PA system to order people in the exchange's twenty-three-floor edifice out of their offices and onto the floor, just in case the tower crashed directly into the building. He then placed his mandatory call to Pitt and said he was calling it a day. Pitt said that based on everything he had heard, it was a prudent move. Grasso then gave his security chief, Esposito, a special assignment.

About two thousand exchange staffers began filling the five trading rooms that comprise the floor of the stock exchange, joining a couple of thousand traders who hadn't yet fled the building. Grasso ordered Esposito to lock the place down, executing a plan known as "the eye of the needle." No one would be able to leave the exchange, and he wanted Esposito to order everyone—civilians and traders alike—who was watching the catastrophe near the exchange to get indoors.

As it turned out, the south tower didn't fall sideways toward the exchange as feared; instead, at 9:59, it imploded. But whatever relief Grasso and the others at the exchange might have felt was short lived; the exchange was spared the direct impact of the falling building, but the floor was quickly overwhelmed by rumors and fear. The collapse sent a cloud of dust straight at the exchange—and with it, a crowd of people flooded into the building and onto the trading floor in a desperate attempt to escape the chaos in the streets.

Grasso had been used to the frenzy and passion of the trading floor, but the anxiety level now surpassed anything he had ever seen on even the most volatile trading days. As the cloud of smoke and soot filled lower Manhattan, the lights began to flicker and the building darkened. For a few eerie moments, people stood silently, too panicked to speak as they stared at the television sets tuned to CNBC, which reported that the attacks were the result of terrorists.

Soon, wild rumors began spreading among the traders that the dust storm was actually a ball of fire that incinerated anyone in its path. Others said they had heard that bombs that had been placed in cars around the trade center were exploding, adding to the death toll. Inside the exchange, traders were arguing with the security staff, demanding to be allowed to leave the building. Some had sneaked past Esposito's guard and had already made it out the door, running down Broad Street and Broadway to get as far away from the trade center as possible. Then came the news that the Pentagon had been hit with a plane, and the hysteria reached a fever pitch. When another rumor began spreading that armed gangs had attacked lower Manhattan, floor traders, many of them former Marines and Vietnam veterans, began forming groups and vowed to fight the terrorists themselves.

Amid so much anxiety and confusion, Grasso grabbed the microphone of the PA system. "I'm here," Grasso began his first appeal. "Please calm down."

Grasso tried again: "Everything is okay."

But everything wasn't okay. A young man in his early twenties with a Middle Eastern complexion had been swept inside the exchange with the rest of the crowd. He was covered with the white dust that had spread through the streets and had stumbled onto the floor with his knapsack on his back. At one point someone screamed, "He's got a bomb!" With that, a crowd of traders began running for their lives. Amid the chaos, one trader approached the young man and asked pointedly, "What's in the backpack?" The young man was disoriented and began speaking in what appeared to be Arabic. Again the trader asked what was in the bag, but this time he screamed, "Take it off now!" When the young man refused, the trader belted him: a right cross to the chin.

The kid went down, and a crowd surrounded him, kicking him and screaming.

Esposito, the security chief, spotted the melee. He broke up the fight. The exchange's security staff shoved the man against the wall, where he was handcuffed.

"What the hell is going on here?" Grasso asked as he arrived on the scene. The security guard explained the situation as he began searching the bag. Grasso asked the young man his name and what he was doing in the area. As it turned out, he was a college student working for a messenger service. The bag contained only schoolbooks. Grasso breathed a sigh of relief and apologized.

"Get those handcuffs off him," Grasso ordered. "He's a civilian." The young man was taken off the floor, given a drink of water, and kept safely away from the unruly crowd.

Grasso, meanwhile, went back to his desk on the floor of the exchange to determine his next move. Just then he received a call from Salvatore Sodano, the chairman and CEO of the rival American Stock Exchange, just a few blocks south and directly in the line of fire. He told Grasso he was abandoning ship immediately.

But Grasso wasn't ready to send his people running into the streets just yet, not without speaking to his good friend Mayor Rudy Giuliani. Since the battle over building new offices for the exchange, the two had patched things up over lunch. Giuliani wasn't at City Hall when the trouble began; he was trapped inside a building just a few blocks away in downtown Manhattan in direct view of the trade center. He was accompanied by his brain trust: Deputy Mayor Joseph Lhota; Police Commissioner Bernard Kerik; deputy mayor for economic development Robert Harding; and Harding's chief counsel, Dennis Young.

How Giuliani got there is a story in itself. He had been uptown at a breakfast when the attacks began. When he received the first sketchy reports of a small plane crashing into the trade center, he ordered his driver to get him as close to the action as possible. Having a close-up view of the tragedy, Giuliani realized that the event was much bigger than the initial reports suggested. A raging fire engulfed the trade center, and Giuliani witnessed the human carnage firsthand: people jumping out of windows, the street strewn with body parts and debris. Ironically, the city's emergency command center was located at 7 World Trade Center, a building connected to the twin towers. Police Commissioner Bernie Kerik had set up a temporary command post nearby at 75 Barclay Street, which for a few hours would serve, for all intents and purposes, as City Hall. Once inside, Kerik confirmed what the mayor already knew: that the city had been attacked by terrorists.

That's when Giuliani received a call from Grasso. Even before Grasso made contact, Lhota, a former Wall Street investment banker, began making a short list of immediate contacts. Grasso was right at the top. The reason was simple: during the past eight years, the financial system had been one of the primary economic engines of the city. It had helped pump billions of dollars into Giuliani's budget and employed more than 200,000 people, most of them downtown in the financial district. Even though many firms had moved uptown, lower Manhattan remained the hub of finance in New York due to the presence of the New York Stock Exchange. Giuliani and his staff understood that the exchange—and, by extension, the economy of New York City and the country as a whole—were the terrorists' targets. The stock exchange had to be defended at all costs.

Grasso's call to Giuliani was short and to the point: all hell was breaking loose. His member firms, the biggest trading houses on Wall Street, were in disarray. He had already received reports that telephone service and electricity were sporadic and in some cases nonexistent. The situation wasn't good.

Giuliani told Grasso he should be making plans to evacuate. Grasso said he needed an order from the mayor and a plan from City Hall for where to send his people. After all, he couldn't just send thousands of terrified people running through the streets. Giuliani said he would get back to him in twenty minutes.

The first twenty minutes flew by as Grasso received updates about the situation and further confirmation that it was the work of terrorists. Grasso had already canceled the traditional opening of the exchange and announced from his command post that he would soon provide an update about plans to evacuate. His wife, Lori, was in her car stuck on the George Washington Bridge coming into the city when the reports of the attacks started and she frantically called Grasso, who answered the phone and said he had little time to talk. He would be coming home late—or not at all that day. After they hung up, unknown to Grasso, there were scattered reports that the exchange might be a target as well. When Lori heard the news, she knew there was nothing she could do but locate their children, let them know what was happening, and pray.

The mood on the floor was equally tense. A few more traders made it past the security guards and made a run for it through the streets to safety. There was still no call from Giuliani, and Esposito appeared with some troubling news: his sources in the police department said the city had just gone "Code Black," meaning that they had lost all communication with the mayor. That was the official word, Esposito said.

The rumor on the street was that the mayor and his entourage had been killed in the collapse of the south tower. Grasso's heart sank. Giuliani could be nasty and cruel with his opponents. His poll numbers were dropping precipitously, and his personal and political fortunes had already unraveled. There had been an alleged affair with his spokeswoman, a messy divorce from his second wife, and then a series of police brutality cases suggesting that his largely successful war on crime unfairly targeted minorities.

But one thing that no one could deny was Giuliani's management ability. Giuliani had inherited a city in crisis with a massive budget deficit and a soaring crime rate, but in nearly eight years he had reversed both. One reason for that was Giuliani's new style of leadership. He brought a can-do corporate mentality to City Hall. Roads were paved, snow was shoveled, and businesses could cut through red tape and set up shop faster, easier, and more cheaply than at any time in recent history. The crime rate had fallen dramatically under his watch because he used computer analysis to determine hot spots and then held police commissioners accountable for putting bad guys away. The city had become cleaner, safer, and more prosperous under his watch. Grasso knew all this. He knew about the mayor's strengths and his weaknesses, but he also knew there was no one he would rather be stuck in a foxhole with.

Losing Giuliani would be catastrophic, for both the exchange and the city. Grasso frantically began making calls, first to SEC chairman Pitt, then to New York State governor George Pataki, then to anyone else he thought could give him some guidance. Minutes ticked away, but they felt like hours. Esposito began contacting his sources in the federal government, but Washington had been hit as well and communication was difficult. The world seemed to be closing down on them.

At 10:28 A.M. EST, the north tower of the trade center collapsed as well, spreading another cloud of foul-smelling dust over lower Manhattan. No one had ever seen Grasso sweat—he loved the heat so much that Zito remembers that when they traveled to Bangkok in 100-plus-degree weather, Grasso ordered his driver to turn off the air-conditioning—until now. He turned to Esposito and asked if there was any word on Giuliani. Not yet.

By now the floor of the exchange looked nothing like the hub of capitalism seen every day on television: five rooms jam-packed with computers, television monitors, and thousands of traders screaming orders to buy and sell billions of dollars' worth of stocks on a daily basis. Many of the floor traders were like Grasso, street kids from the outer boroughs who had gotten the last job in the financial business where you can make a lot of money without a college education. Even without the pedigree, the floor traders performed possibly the most important function in the financial business: making sure the very essence of capitalism, the ability to buy and sell stocks at a moment's notice, was secure in good times and bad.

But the floor traders had a dark side as well. For generations, investors had complained that the traders were nothing more than well-paid bookies who skimmed profits and inserted themselves between buy and sell orders when they weren't needed. Grasso often referred to them as "the animals" because of their proclivity for practical jokes and unruly behavior. Now he worried that the animals would revolt. The anxiety had calmed a bit, but the tension remained. Traders were grouped in clusters tensely discussing the situation. Grasso monitored them warily.

Grasso knew the floor better than anyone else on Wall Street. He had grown up with many of its top players. He had made many of them rich with order flow and new listings. He had protected them for years from those who pushed electronic trading, yet he had become an increasingly despised figure. Grasso's job in running the exchange was part businessman and part cop. Under federal securities laws, the NYSE was a regulator of all its member firms, including the traders on the floor of the exchange, and traders now openly complained that Grasso had used the threat of enforcement actions to force them to acquiesce to his every whim and maintain his iron-fisted control of the Club.

Grasso had long denied the charge. But now, without the market frenzy to distract and divide them, Grasso feared that the traders would unite against the unreal situation and his authority. They were, for all intents and purposes, wounded prisoners, and Grasso began to worry that many would make a rush at his security staff in a desperate attempt to escape.

A few minutes later the emergency phone rang, jarring Grasso out of his increasingly desperate vision. Howard Germain, a staff assistant, answered it. Germain turned white. Then he handed Grasso the receiver. "It's the mayor," Germain said, his hand shaking.

Given Germain's look and the fact that he didn't refer to Giuliani by name, Grasso was certain that it wasn't Mayor Giuliani but a replacement—whoever that might be. Then he heard the voice. "How you doing?" Giuliani muttered. With that, much of the tension and fear ebbed out of Grasso. For the first time since the action began, his heart beat at a normal rate. Grasso was relieved—so relieved, in fact, that he couldn't help having a little fun at the mayor's expense.

"How are *you* doing?" he shot back.

"No, how *you* doing?" Giuliani teased.

"You're supposed to be dead," Grasso joked.

"Well, I'm not dead," Giuliani said with a slight laugh.

Giuliani had little time for gallows humor. He wanted an update from Grasso. "The building is in lockdown," said Grasso, who loved police terminology. "Eye of the needle," he added.

But Grasso didn't have a full assessment of the damage. Like everyone else that day, and with the added constraint of being barricaded inside the building with his restless charges, Grasso was working with only limited information. If the attacks were anywhere near as large as they seemed, Grasso expected that many of the largest firms that were located near ground zero, such as Merrill Lynch and Lehman Brothers, would be displaced.

More important to both men, and probably the nation and world beyond, Grasso said he had no idea when he could open the exchange again.

Fully apprised, the mayor told Grasso to keep his people indoors until 1:00 P.M. and then evacuate south toward Battery Park. In parting, Giuliani told Grasso that someone wanted to say hello.

"Listen, you little fuck," Police Commissioner Bernie Kerik barked as he got on the line, "aren't you supposed to be dead?"

Both Kerik and Grasso came from a lower-middle-class background, and they both reveled in their outsider status. Kerik was a tough street cop who got to know Giuliani as his driver and bodyguard during his 1993 mayoral election. Just a few years earlier, Giuliani had given Kerik his big break: an important but thankless job as head of the city corrections department. Under Kerik, the department restored order to the city's largest jails, especially Rikers Island, which had become a cesspool of gang violence and corruption. Giuliani was so impressed he made Kerik police commissioner when the job became open.

Grasso chuckled and asked Kerik to be there for him once he got a better assessment of the damage. The police commissioner would have to provide safety to some 350,000 people in what still seemed like a war zone.

Kerik said he would, but he did offer one caveat. Both twin towers had fallen; 7 World Trade Center was ablaze, but that was far enough from the exchange not to be Grasso's most pressing problem. He had just received a report that there was still a chance that One Liberty Plaza, a fifty-four-story building adjacent to the trade center, could fall. If, in the coming days, the building remained upright but failed to pass a stress test, the entire downtown Manhattan financial district would be closed indefinitely.

Grasso's head was filled with emotion. He feared that friends had died in the attack. He feared that he might have lost his own people who were stationed in the trade center. He feared that childhood friends, many of them firefighters, might have died trying to save lives. And he feared that the damage done by the attacks was so great that the terrorists might have inflicted a deadly blow to the economy by shutting down the major Wall Street firms in the area, Merrill Lynch and Lehman Brothers, to name just two, indefinitely and, even worse, crippling the place where they did most of their business: the New York Stock Exchange.

He was, however, calmed by his communication with Giuliani and Kerik. He knew he had backup, and from people he could trust. He then followed Giuliani's orders. At around 1:00 P.M., he opened the doors of the exchange so his people could go home. They were told to head south along Broadway and Broad Street for the first leg of their journey. From there, they were on their own.

With his employees safe, Grasso turned to the even bigger question: How soon could the exchange reopen? And the question wasn't primarily a business concern. It was political—and symbolic. Destroying the World Trade Center was a direct attack on American capitalism. It was an attempt to bring the system to a halt. And the attack would remain a success as long as the exchange stayed closed. In effect, the moment the towers came down, a clock started to tick. And Grasso was the only man with the ability to beat that clock.

Almost as if to prove that point, the phone began to ring. One call came from Elizabeth McCaul, the New York State superintendent of banks. She said her boss, Governor George Pataki, wanted the exchange opened the following day "if only for fifteen minutes."

Knowing that Wall Street was decimated and that trading would be scattershot, with huge fluctuations in prices, Grasso nearly blew his top. "I can open for fifteen minutes or fifteen seconds and you would get the same result," he told her. "Have the governor call me if he wants to discuss this further."

Grasso's challenge was threefold. He needed to rebuild his infrastructure, much of it from scratch; he needed to reassure his own people, who were traumatized by the events of that day; and, perhaps

most important, the crippling of downtown had displaced or damaged many of the most important member firms. The stock exchange,
many people failed to realize, was a human-powered institution.
Without the people on either side of trades—buyers and sellers—the
market could not function.

Grasso understood the symbolism of opening the markets immediately, a grand display that capitalism had trumped terrorism, but
he also had a three-ring circus on his hands. Politicians were of no
use to him.

By early afternoon, Grasso was in communication with Harvey
Pitt, the head of the SEC. Pitt and Grasso had a rapport based on respect. Pitt was Grasso's boss now, but he had recently been a client
when Pitt was in private practice. The two men could talk to each
other honestly.

Pitt told Grasso that the White House wanted stock trading to
start immediately, possibly as early as Wednesday or Thursday. Grasso
told Pitt that an immediate opening of the exchange was out of the
question.

Grasso laid out the problem in no uncertain terms. The Con Edison station that supplied electricity to the trading desks had been destroyed when 7 World Trade Center had caught fire and eventually
collapsed like its bigger neighbors. And the Verizon telephone switching station just yards from ground zero, which provided the valuable
communications connections between the trading desks and the exchange, was now severely damaged by a massive flood.

Grasso's staff, led by co-chief operating officers Kinney and Britz,
had already done wonders in assessing the damage and laying out the
massive obstacles that would have to be overcome to open the exchange. But key members of his staff were still missing. And the rest
of the exchange's workers were not likely to make it to work easily the
next day.

The biggest obstacle by far lay with the exchange's member firms.
Grasso told Pitt that the initial reports about the condition of his
member firms—the major Wall Street outfits that sent trades to the

exchange—were not good. Nearly every firm was affected one way or another by the attacks, even those not in the immediate area. Morgan Stanley's largest New York City brokerage office had been located in the towers. Merrill Lynch, the nation's largest brokerage firm, which pumped more trading volume into the exchange than any other, was located in the World Financial Center, directly across the street from the World Trade Center. The firm had been forced to evacuate. Merrill's CEO, David Komansky, the vice chairman of the exchange, was also on the missing persons list.

Grasso knew Merrill had office space in Jersey City and in midtown Manhattan, but he couldn't say the same for Lehman Brothers. Adjacent to Merrill downtown, the firm had evacuated its employees when the towers fell. But the damage to its building was far more extensive than the damage to Merrill's, Grasso had learned. With no backup, Lehman would need to find new space if it was to open any time soon.

The problems didn't end there. Goldman Sachs was largely untouched by the attacks, but it too was located in downtown Manhattan and would have to find new digs since the city had declared everything south of Houston Street off limits. Even Citigroup, located comfortably in midtown Manhattan, kept its investment bank and brokerage operations in TriBeCa, just a few blocks north of ground zero.

For all these reasons, Grasso and Pitt agreed it would be a good idea to hold a summit of sorts, assembling his member firms as well as officials from government and representatives from Con Ed and Verizon to assess the damage. Pitt said he would alert the people in the Treasury Department.

Pitt was blown away by the assessment. Now he knew what Bear Stearns CEO James Cayne had meant when he used to tell people that "no one knows his product better than Grasso." For all his foibles, his bad temper and ego, Grasso understood what made the stock exchange work better than anyone in the world.

Grasso had one more request: "Harvey, you got to get up here now; the lunatics are coming out of the woodwork." Pitt knew what he was talking about; given the remarks made by the New York banking commissioner, it would be only a matter of time before the White House stepped up the pressure to open the exchange. Grasso needed political cover.

Pitt volunteered to do whatever he could on his end to run interference. "Dick, you open when you are ready," Pitt said. "I'll be there as soon as possible."

"You're a brother," Grasso replied before hanging up.

Grasso didn't tell Pitt this, but he had another reason to postpone the opening as long as possible, and it wasn't merely to save the stock exchange from embarrassment if trades couldn't be completed. Grasso knew his members better than anyone in the world, and for all his camaraderie with the top players at the biggest firms, he also knew they were ruthless businessmen who would do whatever it took to gain an advantage over a competitor, even one devastated by something like 9/11.

One reason he knew these guys so well was that he wasn't that much different from them. So Grasso assembled a short list in his head: the most ruthless of the firms was, of course, Goldman Sachs, run by a cutthroat investment banker named Henry Paulson, known by friends and enemies alike as "Hank." Grasso had been battling with Paulson for years, defeating Paulson's recent proposal to eliminate many floor trading jobs by installing computerized trading at the exchange. At the time, Goldman also owned the largest chunk of one of the biggest such electronic trading outfits, Archipelago. Knowing the Goldman Sachs chief as well as he did, Grasso knew it was only a matter of time before Goldman began taking advantage of its beaten-down competitors. "These guys will eat their young," Grasso remarked.

Grasso immediately began making plans to hold the meeting some time the next day, Wednesday, September 12, to sort things out. And what better place to meet than at the stock exchange? Even if he couldn't open for trading, Grasso knew the meeting would at the very least assure Washington that the Club was making progress toward reopening. Grasso then began calling the various Wall Street honchos to alert them to the meeting.

His first call was to Cayne. Even under normal conditions, the CEO of Bear Stearns hated to leave his office (he was known to eat breakfast, lunch, and dinner in Bear's dining room). Two of the reasons he had refused Grasso's repeated requests to become a board member were Grasso's penchant for holding too many meetings and his requirement that they all be held downtown.

What would finally bring him on board? Money. Cayne had just made a major investment in a specialist firm, now called Bear Wagner Specialists, run by John Mulheren. Specialist firms perform the most important trading function on the NYSE. As trades are routed to the floor of the exchange, the specialists are supposed to match buyers and sellers whether the markets rise or fall. In exchange parlance, their purpose is to "ensure fair and orderly markets," smoothing out price fluctuations by establishing an opening price for the stocks they control and then a closing price.

Specialists were some of the highest-paid people on Wall Street at the time, earning as much as $5 million a year or even more. The people who run these firms, like Mulheren, make even more money, and Bear's investment in Bear Wagner Specialists was responsible for tens of millions of dollars in revenues for the firm. The exchange actually picks which listed stocks a specialist can trade, so Mulheren told Cayne that one way to protect and grow his investment was to join the board of the exchange and get close to Grasso, who was all-powerful inside the institution. With that Cayne reluctantly agreed.

Cayne was more than reluctant when Grasso called with plans for a meeting down at the exchange. "What, are you kidding?" he exploded. "They're not letting people go downtown." Grasso said he could ensure safe passage, but Cayne had a different idea, namely to hold the meeting up at Bear Stearns's headquarters. It was comfortably out of the fray, located on Park Avenue and Forty-sixth Street, and he had plenty of space. Cayne rarely spoke to reporters, but he did have a room for the media, which he knew Grasso loved to court purely for publicity. Cayne also knew Bear could get some good ink it-self, as the firm open for business when Wall Street was falling apart. It took Grasso only a few seconds to agree as he plotted his next move in what would be the most important week of his career, making everything he did before pale in comparison.

2

THE EARL OF SANDWICH

There are few things more sacred to Dick Grasso than the New York City Police Department. For years, even as he achieved fame and fortune beyond even the highest-paid law enforcement official, Grasso bragged that if it hadn't been for his bad eyesight he would have been an NYPD cop—and that would have been just fine with him. Grasso's cousin was a cop, as were many of his closest friends.

On a warm fall night in 1998, Grasso joined their ranks as he briskly walked up to the podium at New York City police headquarters in lower Manhattan dressed in his customary dark suit, white shirt, and tie, his finely shaved bald head gleaming. He was about to be appointed an honorary police commissioner of New York City, a position that confers no real authority other than that it gives the recipient carte blanche to park anywhere in the city he wants. Even so, the crowd of about a hundred real estate tycoons, political types, and members of the city's police brass stirred in their seats waiting to hear what the star of the New York Stock Exchange had to say.

When Grasso took the podium to accept his award, he chose not to give the speech most of the crowd was expecting. Instead, he spoke about his mother. "My mother always wanted me to be a cop," Grasso said. He added that like all good Italian kids, he had always listened to his mother, and he had applied to be a New York City policeman. But he had failed the eye exam. So he took the next best thing, at least in his world, a job as an $81-a-week clerk at the New York Stock Exchange.

But within a few years, as Grasso put it, he began to move up the corporate ladder, earning far more than $81 a week. "When I finally became a vice president of the exchange," he said, "I couldn't wait to tell my mother." As Grasso retold it, he went back to the old neighborhood in Jackson Heights, Queens. His mom still lived in the same long, narrow "railroad" apartment he had grown up in. Grasso said he wanted to share the news with her in person. The two sat down at the kitchen table, where Grasso broke the good news: "Mom, I just made vice president!" Grasso said, expecting a big hug.

Instead he received an admonition.

"*Stupido!*" Mamma Grasso snapped. "If you'd passed the eye test, you would have made sergeant by now!"

When the wild laughter quieted down, Grasso continued, "Mom passed away a couple of years ago, so she can't be here today, but if she could only see me now!"

The crowd gave Grasso a standing ovation. Grasso would tell the story about his mother's reaction to his success many times during his career, and not just because it was so funny. For Grasso, his mother's sentiments underscored something more significant about his career: no one had given him a chance to make it big on Wall Street, not even his mother, and he had defied them all.

Ask Dick Grasso to describe what it was like growing up, and he says it was like "living in a cocoon." For the first eighteen years of his life, before he went into the army, Grasso's relationships consisted of his immediate family and a handful of buddies from his old neighborhood with whom he remains close even to this day. Jackson Heights, Queens, is one of those places where time seems to stand still. It did so particularly during Grasso's formative years in the 1950s and early 1960s, when it was a solidly Italian and Irish enclave of blue-collar workers, cops, firemen, construction workers, and wiseguys.

Grasso understood class distinctions early on. During his formative years, Jackson Heights still contained vestiges of its upper-middle-class past. So-called lace curtain Irish and second-generation German-American families owned houses off the neighborhood's main drag, Roosevelt Avenue. Grasso, on the other hand, lived in a three-bedroom apartment, known as "railroad rooms" because the rooms were narrow and aligned one after another like rail cars. Immigrants began to pack into these apartments at the turn of the twentieth century. They were one step up from living in a tenement, but a very small step.

There was another thing that made Grasso different: his father had left the family—Dick, his mother, and his sister—when Grasso was only one year old. It was one of the pivotal points in Grasso's life. Even so, Grasso says he was showered with love by an extended family that included his maternal uncle, known around the neighborhood as Uncle Louie, an elevator operator who helped support Grasso's mother and two aunts, who lived in the apartment next door. But money was tight, and the lack of it became a central obsession for his mother, such an obsession that Mamma Grasso spent much of Grasso's childhood complaining about Grasso's deadbeat dad and counting down the days until he could get a steady job like his cousin Buddy and join the police department. Indeed, Grasso's animus toward his father and how he hurt the family financially is palpable to this day. Grasso still talks about the last time he can recall seeing his father. He was fifteen and in Queens County Family Court with his uncle, petitioning a judge to force the old man to make good on his child support payments. He ran into his father in the courthouse elevator. The elder Grasso wouldn't look at his son, which provoked young Dick.

"What this punk needs is a good beating," Grasso loudly told his uncle, who quickly stepped between father and son. The elder Grasso ignored his son, and despite the judge's ruling to start forking over cash to his mother, he ignored the court as well.

Grasso says he doesn't dwell on the difficulties of growing up poor, but he also concedes that during this time he developed a strong sense of resentment about how he had to struggle compared with others. Which might explain Grasso's obsession with money—or, to be more precise, with how to make it. Around the time Grasso turned fifteen, he landed a job at a local pharmacy run by a man named Harry Rosenbaum. Rosenbaum was an early day trader. After hiring Grasso, he immediately taught him how to fill prescriptions so he could spend more time playing the markets.

Before long Grasso was doing more than filling prescriptions; he too began to buy stocks. First, since he was too young to buy them on his own, he bought them under his mother's name. Grasso began copying some of Rosenbaum's research techniques, spending time in the local brokerage office looking at the ticker tape and reading business magazines and *The Wall Street Journal.* Grasso doesn't remember just how much money he made—or lost. One thing is certain, though: it was the start of a lifelong love of the markets.

Grasso may have loved the markets, but he wasn't crazy about school. He attended Newtown High School in Elmhurst, Queens, where he was a middling student who displayed flashes of brilliance, particularly in math, where he scored such high grades that teachers believed he was cheating—an insult that would stick with him his entire life.

Grasso's intellectual gifts aside, he showed little interest in academics. Friends say he skipped classes. In order to graduate, he needed to attend summer school. The root causes of Grasso's problems could be traced to his bad attitude, his lousy family life, and the fact that he had to work after school. Newtown High School in the 1960s, meanwhile, wasn't a very nurturing environment; it had become a hotbed of racial strife (largely between Italians and African-American students), which Grasso knew enough to avoid.

Grasso couldn't avoid boredom with school, which was the real reason behind his less-than-stellar academic record. He loved to schmooze with his friends, a gift that would help him later in life, but at the time it cut into his schoolwork. With little direction from home, Grasso spent much of his time screwing around at the local poolroom, a neighborhood bar named Bud's, or taking the subway to Coney Island. As often as possible, Grasso would convince his buddies to make the trip from Queens to lower Brooklyn, where they would hang out on the beach, ride the famous Cyclone, and just horse around. One afternoon they even decided to pick a fight with a real horse. Grasso and his buddies happened upon a pony ride at the Coney Island amusement park and began taunting the animal. "Be careful, you little bastards, this horse bites!" barked the guy who ran the attraction. As if on cue, the horse bit one of Grasso's friends, Billy Wells, on his hand. Wells was the toughest of the group; he was about five feet tall and five feet wide, a small version of Hulk Hogan. After regaining his composure, Wells hauled off and punched the horse in the mouth, knocking the animal off its feet. The trainer started screaming, "You killed my horse, get the cops!" Grasso and his pals ran for the subway and made their way safely back to Queens.

Grasso graduated from high school with a grade point average just above a C, but because of his high score on the SAT he was accepted by Pace College in Manhattan to major in business administration. Grasso's mother, Jennie, had had enough of her son and his attitude toward school and kept prodding him to get a stable civil service job with a pension like his cousin and become a cop. But Grasso said he was going to school to make his fortune in the stock market. Jennie Grasso said she wasn't holding her breath, and with good reason: Grasso hated college almost as much as he hated high school. After just a semester, Grasso flunked out of Pace (Grasso says he earned an A in accounting but a C or less in everything else). Being out of school meant that Grasso was available for the draft. Working-class kids like Dick Grasso had always been the backbone of the American military, particularly during times of war. Never was this more the case than during the Vietnam War, when college deferments allowed many middle- and upper-class young men to avoid the draft, and the bulk of armed services personnel came from places like Jackson Heights, Queens.

Grasso was shaken when he received the official word he had been drafted. He might have been a lousy student, but he had big dreams. Not long after he received his draft notice, Grasso contacted Pace's dean of academic affairs. His name was Larry Graham, and Grasso asked him for a favor. Grasso, a natural salesman, knew how to sell Graham. He apologized for being such a rotten student, but asked him: Could he have another chance if he made it home alive? Graham appreciated Grasso's attitude, and despite his poor academic record, it was obvious that he was smart enough to be in college. Of course Graham said he believed in second chances. With that, Grasso was off to war.

Grasso's next stop was the military induction station, located on Whitehall Street in lower Manhattan, ironically the same spot where the NYSE's biggest rival, the computerized Nasdaq stock market, would have its New York headquarters. No amount of salesmanship could stop Grasso and his buddies from going into the military. He and two of his best friends, Mickey Kern and Jimmy DiSocio, all got notices to show up at the recruiter's office on the same day. In those days, the military didn't tell you what branch you would be drafted into, and most of the new recruits were praying for any assignment other than the Marines, where the training is the toughest and the assignments almost always involve frontline combat. As the recruits filed in, a smallish Marine recruiting sergeant announced, "This is your lucky day; for the first time since World War II we're drafting Marines!"

DiSocio, who inexplicably thought he'd hit the jackpot, shouted, "I won! I won!" Grasso couldn't believe what he was hearing. "Are you fucking crazy?" he asked his buddy. "You don't want to go into the Marines. Sit down." DiSocio was in fact drafted into the Marines, but Grasso could breathe a sigh of relief: he was a proud member of the U.S. Army.

For the most part, Grasso didn't have to worry about bullets flying past his head. He sat out the next two years of the war stationed at Fort Meade, Maryland, though he did make periodic trips to Vietnam. Grasso never saw combat, but the war had a profound impact on him. The guys he knew who fought and died weren't all that much different from him: poor and working-class kids. The new patriots were the young men with the least to lose, while the rich kids were off studying how to make even more money. The chip on Grasso's shoulder just got bigger.

Fresh from the service, Grasso told his family he was a changed man. He had a new attitude about school and was ready to apply himself. But Grasso soon discovered that the country—and the school—had also changed since he had left. Pace's campus in lower Manhattan was mired in chaos; student protests were almost a daily occurrence. Growing up, Grasso had never been a gung ho patriot—that is, until he saw how college kids wore their anti-Americanism.

Grasso didn't flunk out of school. Instead, after only a year, he planned to drop out on his own. "I just couldn't take it anymore," he said to his friends at the time. "I just didn't fit in." Grasso knew his options were limited. He could apply for another job with the city, possibly in the Sanitation Department. But he couldn't see himself on the back of a garbage truck. Grasso then announced to his mother that he was ready to fulfill her dream for him—that of a steady job with a pension—by joining the New York Police Department.

Grasso has said that he would have been happy being a cop. But that doesn't explain what he did next. Maybe it was because he knew he always had bad eyesight and wouldn't pass the eye exam, or maybe it was because he had a vision about his future and it involved something that his mother and his friends from Jackson Heights could never fathom. But some time after filling out the application for the NYPD, Grasso applied for a job as an entry-level clerk at a Wall Street firm. Such "back office" jobs were filled with working-class outer-borough kids like himself. They were a far cry from the glamour of high finance, but the jobs could be a stepping-stone to something bigger. And Grasso couldn't afford to be picky.

The start of Dick Grasso's Wall Street career can be traced to the late winter of 1968 when he spotted a newspaper ad for a job as a clerk at W. E. Hutton, a midsize brokerage firm started by the same family that later created E. F. Hutton. Grasso got the job but decided not to take it because the employment agency wanted a fee that was the equivalent of two weeks' pay. Billy Wells, the same guy who had punched out the horse, had just gotten out of the army as well and landed a job where he could use his strength: he was a mover with Mayflower Moving Company in Astoria, Queens. "Hey, Richie," he told Grasso one night at Bud's bar, "I just spoke to my foreman, and if you need a job you got one. Meet me in Astoria at seven in the morning and you're in." Grasso said he would.

But he didn't. At twenty-one years of age, Grasso made his next stop the New York Stock Exchange. Located just a few blocks south of Pace College in lower Manhattan, the exchange was formed in the late eighteenth century, when, according to legend, groups of men used to meet under a nearby buttonwood tree to trade Revolutionary War bonds. It wasn't long before the entire street resembled a produce market, but instead of selling fruits and vegetables, these men auctioned bonds and later stocks. It was a highly selective group of men who met to carry out such lucrative business—so selective that they described their business venue as "the Club."

The exchange's dignified marble building commands the corner of Wall and Broad streets. "Time warp" would be too strong a description, but for most of its long history, the exchange had been doing business in much the same way. The businessmen who traded stocks were an odd breed of capitalist: they preached free enterprise and professed a love of markets, but they also created and maintained a monopoly. They agreed to trade only with other members of the exchange and to create rules and regulations for the good of those members, which created a dynamic that would last for generations.

Membership in the Club was, of course, limited to the elite. It was bestowed on a chosen few through the purchase of a "seat." In the beginning, traders would bid on stocks from their assigned seat at the exchange's early headquarters on Wall Street. This practice continued until the late 1800s, when the exchange got rid of the actual seats and traders known as specialists brought together buyers and sellers of stocks that were assigned to them. These shares were auctioned to other members of the Club, known as floor brokers. Unlike specialists, the floor brokers didn't actually take possession of the stocks they traded. They worked for the big Wall Street firms and filled orders for stocks needed by their firm's customers. So-called independent or two-dollar brokers operated much the same way, only these were firms that weren't affiliated with Wall Street. They worked for themselves and got their name because they made money selling stocks for customers and earning a hefty commission, which for years was set at $2.

There were a few rules the specialists had to follow: they couldn't insert themselves between trades when they weren't needed, and they had a "positive obligation" to purchase shares when the markets tanked. But these trade-offs were a small price to pay for the bigger prize—namely, being at the center of all the action and information, which allowed them to profit even when the markets sank.

By the early 1900s, the Club had become a political and social force as well as a place to make money. Presidents consulted their top members before making major economic moves. Politicians running for any major office in New York State were sure to pay a visit to the exchange's headquarters, now a grand edifice with six Corinthian columns on the corner of Wall and Broad streets in lower Manhattan, just across from the headquarters of one of its most powerful members, J. P. Morgan. The building cost an estimated $4 million, and it was known for its extravagance. Separate dining rooms for smokers and nonsmokers, an on-site hospital, miles and miles of cable for an "annunciator board" that would alert brokers when they were needed at their trading post. The building came complete with air conditioning and a thirty-square-foot skylight above its enormous trading floor.

For most of its history, the stock exchange operated by its own set of rules. With membership came the right to make money both legally and illegally. Stock price manipulation was an accepted way of doing business, considered a privilege of those who gained membership to the Club.

The stock market crash of 1929 put the Club's practices under scrutiny. The election of Franklin D. Roosevelt made it a target of regulation. New banking laws forced J. P. Morgan, "the House of

Morgan," to formally separate its commercial bank and its investment house. Fortunes were lost by members of the Club, but things
were about to get worse: Roosevelt created the Securities and Exchange Commission, a new federal agency designed to root out the financial fraud and speculation suspected of being at the heart of the
crash and the Great Depression that followed. His first SEC chief
was Joseph Kennedy, the father of a future president. Joe Kennedy
was himself a stock speculator who had managed to preserve his vast
fortune by pulling his money out of the market before the crash
came.

Despite being a member of the Club with a reputation for cutting
corners, Kennedy took his job seriously. He went after stock manipu-
lators on Wall Street with a vengeance. He registered the exchange's
membership so he could keep a closer eye on the alleged bad guys.
During the 1930s, laws were passed that established formal rules by
which Wall Street and the Club would be governed for years to come;
namely, the Securities Exchange Act of 1934, which forced the exchange to regulate its members, both the floor traders and the big Wall
Street firms as well—all under the watchful eyes of the federal government in Washington. For the first time in its long and storied history,
the Club was answerable to someone. Its leadership finally had a boss,
the chairman of the Securities and Exchange Commission.

The Club barely survived Roosevelt, Kennedy, and the Great Depression. A former NYSE president, Richard Whitney, had spent
three years in jail after being convicted of embezzling money from the
exchange. But the end of the Second World War had brought prosperity back to Wall Street, and for the next twenty-five years, the Club
experienced almost nonstop growth thanks to a burgeoning new middle class that began buying stocks for the first time since before the
crash of 1929.

The spurt of regulation following the Great Depression opened
the Club to its first dose of scrutiny from the outside, but the bull
market that followed the lean years allowed the exchange once again
to embrace practices that made it among the country's most insular

institutions. Large institutional investors, pension funds and mutual funds, became a growing force in the markets and demanded more efficient, automated trading, but they too were ignored, as was a coterie of lawmakers who questioned the fact that so much power and wealth were concentrated in relatively few hands.

The Club did, however, take one major step toward modernity. In 1971, it decided to cease being a "voluntary club" of Wall Street titans and decided to officially incorporate in New York State as a not-for-profit corporation. The reason: to shield its individual members from liability and instead force its opponents to take on the organization's collective might. That, at least, was the thinking. What the brain trust of the exchange didn't realize was that by incorporating in New York State, they had just gained a regulator in addition to the SEC; the state's attorney general could now legally exercise some control over the Club's inner workings, specifically how much it paid its leaders. (More on that later.)

By the time Dick Grasso got to the exchange, the good times were rolling. The seats themselves were long gone from the trading posts, but the 1,366 "seat holders" all held lucrative and powerful positions. Seats were selling at record prices: more than $515,000 each. The Big Board of the late 1960s was now trading stocks in huge numbers—tens of millions exchanged hands each day. The largest companies in America had their shares listed on the exchange, and investors had to pay a commission to the specialists whenever they wanted to buy or sell a stock listed on the stock exchange.

One thing that hadn't changed was the composition of the Club. It still consisted largely of the elite. The seats were owned by a combination of large Wall Street firms, smaller family-run businesses that had traded stock on the exchange for generations, and now a smattering of new-money entrepreneurs who had more recently bought their way in. Even so, it was a difficult network to break into; floor trading jobs were handed down to family members, or through other connections. The leadership of the Club—its chairman, president, and board of directors—was strictly limited to its most influential members.

They were either heads of the big Wall Street firms, known as the "upstairs" firms, or powerful floor traders and specialists, leaders of the "downstairs" firms, so called because their primary job was trading stocks downstairs on the floor of the exchange.

Downstairs is where Grasso thought he could break in. Several friends from the old neighborhood were now working as floor clerks, an entry-level position assisting brokers and specialists. But the floor was hardly a color-blind place. The financier Muriel Siebert became the first woman to own a seat in 1967, but there wasn't an African-American seat holder until 1970. While the floor itself was no longer a purely WASP domain, floor trading positions were increasingly populated by a cross section of Irish and Jewish traders who had fought their way onto Wall Street years earlier—Italian Americans were almost nonexistent. Grasso approached several firms that he had heard had positions open for clerks and was immediately rejected. To this day, Grasso believes he was denied the jobs because of his ethnicity. In a few years, of course, the ethnic makeup would change to the point that Italian Americans became possibly the single largest ethnic group on the floor. But that change wasn't fast enough to get Grasso the job he wanted.

With the floor clerk door closed, Grasso applied for and was offered an entry-level position working directly for the New York Stock Exchange in its listings department. It seemed like a boring job, and it didn't look like a place where one could someday make a lot of money. But at least it came with benefits and paid vacation days. He ran into Wells one night at Bud's bar. "Hey, what the hell happened the other day? You never showed up at Mayflower," Wells asked. Grasso apologized. "I decided to take the train down to the exchange. I got a job as a clerk. I'll see if it works out, but if it doesn't I may come back to Mayflower." Wells said the company was expanding, so the job would probably be there if he needed it.

But that was the last time Grasso would need a job for a very long time as he headed to the listings department of the exchange. For Grasso, the job qualifications were minimal: a high school degree, some aptitude with numbers, and the ability to follow orders. It had something else that appealed to Grasso: he wouldn't have to pay a fee to the employment agency.

Grasso now had a job, but he still had his mother and the police department to deal with. Grasso had been working at the exchange just a few months when he received notice that he was scheduled to take the various tests that would have qualified him to follow in his cousin's footsteps and join the ranks of the NYPD. Just coming out of the army, he was no longer a scrawny kid with a potbelly and flabby arms. He was in good shape and felt reasonably confident that he would pass the physical part of the test and could breeze through any written part of the exam. It was the least difficult part of the test— the eye exam—that he knew would be his downfall.

Grasso had been wearing glasses since he was a kid to correct his 20/40 eyesight, and to prepare for the test, his mom goaded him into consulting a local ophthalmologist who had a reputation for successfully coaching police applicants through the exam. The doctor had a simple trick he said was guaranteed to work; he told Grasso to squint when he began reading the letters of the chart. It would, the doctor said, transform his 20/40 eyesight into perfect 20/20 eyesight. Grasso did as he was told but failed the exam no matter how hard he squinted. Later that night he told his mother she would have to have a son with better eyesight if she wanted a cop in the immediate family.

When people think of the New York Stock Exchange, they think of two things. For the past two centuries, the exchange has been the epicenter of capitalism, and its leaders were the men who ran the nation's biggest investment banks and brokerage firms. These were men of power and prestige, an elite class of men who had graduated from the finest schools. They were men like John Coleman, the legendary chairman of the exchange in the 1940s, whose blessing was sought by nearly every major political figure in New York State until the day he officially retired in the 1970s, and Bernard "Bunny" Lasker, chairman from 1969 through 1971, who played a major role in Richard Nixon's political comeback in the late 1960s. The other image is, of course, the NYSE's famous trading floor, a series of large rooms located on the ground floor of the six-floor building where men wearing smocks over their suits conduct the business of capitalism: finding buyers and sellers of stocks for their customers who trade shares of the nation's and the world's biggest companies.

But there is another side of the exchange that often goes unnoticed, where important "back office" or support functions take place, well out of range of any camera. And that's where Dick Grasso began his career, when he showed up for his first day as an entry-level "listing clerk" on the New York Stock Exchange. In order for stock to be traded, a company must first have its stock "listed."

The listings department is one of the NYSE's largest business units, and for good reason: listings are the lifeblood of the exchange. The process is part functionary and part sales. Companies pay big fees to be listed on the exchange, and they must pass a series of tests before they gain entry. First, people in the listing group must evaluate if the company meets the NYSE's listing requirements; is it big enough to be traded at the gold standard of exchanges? For example, today a company must have $100 million in market value and meet other financial requirements. Listing reps also check if there is enough trading volume in a stock. That's because the NYSE is at bottom a fancy tollbooth; the more a stock trades through its floor brokers and specialists, the more money is generated for the member firms in the form of commissions and fees.

Back in the late 1960s, the listings department took up two floors of the exchange. Although the listing clerks were housed above the trading floor, the area was commonly referred to as "the dungeon." The place was drab, with rows of metal desks. Boxes of company documents were scattered about. There was one window, far in the back, and clerks were expected to work straight through the day without much chatter. Loretta Russo, an eighteen-year-old high school graduate who came to the exchange as a secretary, recalls how sad she was when she went to work for the first time. When she was offered the job, she had images of carpeted floors, men in suits politely asking their secretaries to pull files or pour them a cup of coffee. But the listings department was a hellhole. The men were unshaven, some outright rude. Many were screaming out orders to the secretaries, who worked in makeshift conditions. "I expected a nice desk, just like on television," she said. "But this place was very depressing."

With his long sideburns, full head of black hair combed straight back, and wild sense of humor, Dick Grasso was a welcome relief from the drudgery of the listings department. People who remember Grasso recall a young man who was in constant motion; he loved to tell jokes, recall scenes from his favorite movies, and flirt with the women in the department. Maybe it was his economic situation, or maybe it was the chip on his shoulder, but from the day Grasso started, Russo and just about everyone else noticed that there was something different about him.

In the listings department Grasso began by reading the job manual cover to cover. He sought out and read several books that described the history of the exchange from its beginnings. He read company documents that provided details of stock listings and began to gain a vast knowledge of some of the NYSE's biggest customers.

The more he read, the more he became an expert in just about every major company in America, as well as the arcane rules that govern how those companies trade on the Big Board, and the more he liked the work. For the first time in his life, Grasso had found something that interested him. Part of it was the aura of working for a place that was at the center of the economy. Grasso also finally found something he was good at. His supervisors gave him more and more responsibility; he began dealing directly with the officials of some of the companies that listed their shares on the exchange. Life was as good as it had been in years—so good, in fact, that Grasso quit Pace once and for all. He broke the news to his mother and sister one night after work. His mother scowled at him; in her mind, this "stock exchange thing" was a waste of time. If he wasn't going to be a cop, he should at least go to college. His sister was even more direct. "You better keep this job," is all she said. Grasso said he would.

Throughout the bull market of the 1960s, trades were settled and completed by back-office workers who merely stamped sheets of paper to certify that a buy or sell order had been completed. The paper-based system was bound to fail, and by the end of the decade it did, as heavy trading volume basically overwhelmed the system, creating what was known as the "back-office crisis." Sorting out the billions of dollars' worth of trades was an enormous task, and the exchange was forced to close every Wednesday for about two years through the first six months of 1970 just to get the job done.

The crisis ensnarled more than a hundred Wall Street firms and nearly crippled the entire financial system. Many firms simply stopped processing trades from investors, while others closed shop or merged with those that had better clearing departments.

The crisis was probably the worst systems breakdown in Wall Street history, but for Grasso it was a godsend. It gave him an opportunity to work another eight-hour shift, combing through piles of paper and logging in the appropriate trades, and learn even more about the Club. Grasso's acumen for accounting and numbers helped him understand the bigger picture. Other clerks simply did what they were told. Grasso was fascinated by the technical aspects of how trades were completed and the important role that the stock exchange played in the process.

It wasn't long before Grasso got his first big break, when one of his supervisors asked him to handle a sensitive client matter. South-eastern Public Service, a large utility listed on the exchange, had become the target of the corporate raider Victor Posner. Southeastern's point man defending against the hostile bid was its general counsel, Richard Simmons. Simmons called the exchange to ask for information on the rules involving hostile takeovers and what he could do to put up a defense. He was turned over to Dick Grasso and soon found out.

The late 1960s saw more than its share of hostile takeovers, but it was more than a decade before corporations developed sophisticated legal maneuvers to combat them. That's why the exchange became so important to takeover targets. One way to prevent a hostile takeover was to implement some of the NYSE's in-house rules that could slow down an aggressive buyer. Grasso didn't have a law degree, but he had become an expert at understanding and interpreting those rules. However, he also had to walk a fine line: conflict-of-interest rules prevented Grasso from openly supporting a takeover target.

Grasso managed to split the difference. He didn't openly support Simmons, but he gave Simmons a little insight into Posner's recent activities. As it turned out, he had found evidence that he believed showed that Posner often violated other conflict-of-interest rules, namely those that prevented raiders from holding more than a certain percentage of shares in companies in the same industries. Posner's buyout of Southeastern might well put him over the line once again, Grasso said. Simmons began to investigate and learned that Posner had indeed accumulated a large amount of stock in the utility business. He petitioned the exchange for an accounting of Posner's holdings in utilities.

Ultimately, Posner gained control of Southeastern, but Grasso's deft handling of such a dicey situation spread through the listings department. Some coworkers said he was "made" with upper management; others told Grasso it wouldn't be long before he became Wall Street royalty like Posner and the other corporate raiders who were dominating the markets. Coming from such humble beginnings, Grasso liked the royalty theme. He told his coworkers that despite his Queens background, he was actually an earl, or to be more precise, "the Earl of Sandwich." He explained that in England, when you serve the king honorably for a long period of time, "you become an earl," Grasso said with a smile. "And since I don't come from Nottingham and I bring my sandwich every day for lunch, I should be knighted the Earl of Sandwich."

The Earl was also becoming known around the exchange as "the kid who has a clue." The clue was that Grasso understood what made the New York Stock Exchange one of the greatest institutions in the country, if not the world. It wasn't just the biggest stock market, it was "the greatest stock market," Grasso would tell companies he was dealing with. The floor traders and specialists didn't come to work simply to make money, he would say. They were there to buy shares of a company's stock when there weren't any other buyers around. At times it sounded as though Grasso were quoting from the job manual he had memorized upon taking the position, but over time his natural schmoozing skills took over and it worked. Grasso was slowly becoming the best salesman the stock exchange ever had.

Grasso may initially have been denied a floor job because of his ethnicity, but he soon became part of the team. For Grasso it was the college frat house he had never had. The floor traders were millionaires, but they loved to play practical jokes, something Grasso was more than willing to do. And like Grasso, they were patriots, repulsed by the student protests that erupted just about every day a block or two away from the exchange building in lower Manhattan. Grasso found out how serious the situation had become one hot morning in May 1970, when rumors spread through the exchange that radical student protesters were going to raid the floor and mount their own takeover.

Grasso remembers the excitement on the floor as word spread and traders got ready for a fight. But before a single floor broker could throw a punch, help arrived in the form of a marauding band of construction workers from nearby construction projects who had heard the same rumor and decided to take matters into their own hands. It's unclear if the student protesters' plan to take over the exchange was genuine; but the "Hard Hat Riot" of May 8, 1970, was indeed real. Grasso and his friends watched in awe as burly construction workers carrying pipes, hammers, and wrenches attacked anyone and anything with hair below his ears.

Grasso never gave up on his dream of becoming a floor trader, but many of the top traders still weren't ready to accept him into their ranks. This time, however, it had nothing to do with ethnicity. Plain and simple, Grasso was helping them make money. Listings were, of course, money in the bank for the trading community (the more companies listed, the more they traded through the floor), but the department had a reputation for coasting and not doing enough to bring in new business. Grasso was the exception. Grasso noticed that the guys running the marketing end of the operation had an interesting travel schedule: one would always be paying calls to companies where there was snow, while the other always had a tan and never traveled north of the Mason-Dixon Line. He did a little research and found out why, as he explained to some of his contacts on the floor. "The marketing department consists of two guys," Grasso said, "one guy who takes all the companies in the north because he likes to ski and the other guy who takes all the companies in the south because he hates cold weather and likes to golf."

By now Grasso was married to his high school sweetheart, a neighborhood girl who wanted a husband home at 6:00 P.M., a house in Queens, and a family. But Grasso had found a new family: the NYSE. He regularly worked twelve-hour days. He began traveling to meet companies that were considering listing on the exchange. The more he did, the more he realized just how little corporate America understood about the exchange, so he came up with the idea of bringing floor traders with him on listing calls. He thought it would help humanize the floor and dispel notions that the exchange was nothing more than a club that had a monopoly over stock trading. It was a gamble; many of the traders on the floor couldn't put together a coherent sentence. Most of those who could wanted no part of Grasso's plan, except for one trader named Billy Johnston. Like Grasso, Johnston was in his mid-twenties. Unlike Grasso, he grew up in the business—his father had been a longtime specialist. But Grasso and Johnston hit it off immediately and thus began Grasso's longest standing friendship at the exchange.

The two traveled constantly; they would start in New York on Monday, make a stop in Dallas on Tuesday, swing over to Los Angeles Wednesday, hit San Francisco Thursday, and then take the red-eye home. What made the relationship work was that Johnston had Grasso's sense of humor; both loved to clown around and gossip about exchange politics. The two became so close that Johnston could get away with a little ethnic humor at Grasso's expense. He often referred to him as the "Little Dago." Grasso's response was simply "fuck you," before he began to laugh.

John Coleman was pushing seventy-five in the mid-1970s. He had been head of the exchange in the 1940s and a floor trader for around forty years. Coleman rarely showed up to work these days. His firm, Adler Coleman, was run by his son, but the old man continued to keep close tabs on the stock exchange. It wasn't long before he wanted to meet "the kid" everyone was talking about. Coleman arranged for Grasso to meet him for a stroll on the floor of the exchange. It was something Coleman liked to do when he was in the building. For Grasso, the stroll conferred instant credibility on him both on the floor and throughout the exchange's management ranks. When Coleman was on the floor, the best traders on the exchange practically genuflected in his presence. People he liked he called "judge," and from the minute he met Grasso, he called him "judge."

NYSE chairman Bunny Lasker began calling Grasso "friend," and for the same reason. Lasker took notice of Grasso's efforts. After hearing how he handled the Southeastern matter, Lasker was ready to promote the young clerk. Instead of just clerking, Grasso was elevated to a listing representative and began dealing with real companies. These were essentially the companies that no one else wanted or that didn't fit neatly with an industry group. But it was a promotion for Grasso nonetheless.

Grasso remembers finding himself in the middle of AT&T's various "rights" offerings during this time. These stock offerings allowed existing AT&T shareholders to buy the "right" to purchase other company shares during a secondary offering. Putting together the deal was mind numbing and tedious. But it was great place for a young, ambitious kid like Grasso to learn his craft. Grasso soon handled "rights" issues for dozens of prominent companies. At times Grasso couldn't believe just how far he had come, like the time he found himself surrounded by white-shoe lawyers and accountants inside the office of AT&T's CFO, a spacious affair in midtown Manhattan, putting the finishing touch on one of the largest rights issues the

NYSE had ever done. Jackson Heights, Queens, couldn't have seemed further away.

And it would soon get even further away thanks to someone else. John Phelan was an imposing man. He rarely raised his voice, but when he did, it was like a volcano. People on the floor said he reminded them of General Douglas MacArthur. A former marine and longtime floor trader who had inherited a specialist firm from his father, Phelan had built a small fortune on his own and was now one of the most powerful members of the exchange. He was also the most articulate spokesman for the exchange's place in the American financial system. When critics of the exchange called it a monopoly, Phelan countered that it was a public trust that served the needs of all investors regardless of size. So it was widely believed on the floor that Phelan would someday become chairman because he was already the de facto leader. No one knew the place better, and no one had a broader vision of the exchange's significance.

Phelan also had a dark side. Like most traders, he never showed emotion and rarely gave people any insight into the motives behind his actions. He was also a control freak. He needed to approve just about every major decision, every move. He could also be mean. "He could kill you by looking at you the wrong way," Grasso used to say. Those who crossed him simply disappeared, earning him the nickname "the undertaker" even from his friends. Grasso would later emulate all of these traits.

When Phelan first met Grasso, Phelan was a floor governor and on his way to becoming president, the second most powerful position at the Club, and the two bonded immediately, first over practical jokes. Phelan may have been tough, but he loved to have fun, and Grasso was more than willing to help. Phelan once convinced Grasso to write up a phony press release that called for a moment of silence on the floor to celebrate the Sioux victory at Little Big Horn. It almost worked, and as traders got ready to take a break to commemorate one of the biggest defeats of the U.S. military, Grasso and Phelan started laughing. One trader even showed up in a leather vest and Indian headdress.

Soon Phelan would become Grasso's rabbi, his mentor, and even his tormentor. But no other person did more for Grasso's career. Phelan saw that Grasso had a command of the rules and regulations of the exchange; he knew how to schmooze; and most of all, he knew how to keep the floor fat and happy with new listings.

What Grasso didn't know, Phelan was now prepared to teach him. For years the two were inseparable; Grasso was Phelan's special project. Phelan was the father Grasso never really had. Phelan taught Grasso everything about the exchange, from the necessity of the "central marketplace," a belief that the stock exchange served the function of leveling the playing field between large and small investors, to an appreciation of what the NYSE stood for. In Phelan's view, it was more than a place to transact business; it was a symbol of the United States' economic might.

But filial emotions had little to do with their alliance. At bottom, it was a practical strategy for each man. In Grasso, Phelan saw the perfect weapon for the new competitive environment the exchange faced with the advent of rival markets. Because of Phelan, Grasso saw he could be something more than a listing official.

The 1970s was a difficult time for the markets; stock prices languished for nearly the entire decade. The economy was hammered by stagflation, a lethal combination of high inflation coupled with high unemployment. In 1975, Congress gave the SEC authority to deregulate trading commissions, a move directed at undermining the exchange's position. The specialists and the exchange had maintained their monopoly because investors had nowhere else to go to buy stocks, and the commissions on the floor were fixed at high levels. In May, under pressure from large investors, Congress passed the deregulation of brokerage commissions. Almost overnight, trading commissions tumbled, and with them the specialists' profits. Then the NYSE got some competition of its own. For years, the Club had existed largely on its own terms. The American Stock Exchange and the other regional exchanges could not compete with New York's natural advantage.

But the budding computer revolution was beginning to make inroads into the NYSE's domain, allowing investors to bypass the specialists on the floor and find buyers and sellers electronically, through something called the National Association of Securities Dealers Automated Quotations system, later known as the Nasdaq stock market. The Nasdaq was run by an organization of brokerage firms called the National Association of Securities Dealers. It didn't start off as a market at all, but as a computer screen of stock prices. Traders could avoid the floor of the exchange by looking up stock prices on the Nasdaq screen and then completing the trade over the phone. Many people at the Club didn't take the Nasdaq seriously, but the computer bulletin board immediately found an audience with high-tech companies that didn't want to pay the NYSE's listing fees, and it wasn't long before the Nasdaq computers were able to complete trades as well.

Phelan was one of the first NYSE officials to recognize the damage Nasdaq could do. With Grasso at his side, he began to tour the country, speaking at large gatherings of investment professionals and directly with officials of the listed companies to convince them that the specialist system was worth preserving. Phelan described their mission in grand terms. Specialists were the great equalizer of the market system. Computers could break down, and firms that matched their markets in-house without the transparency that the floor provided were almost always working against the best interests of investors.

Phelan and Grasso began marketing the exchange in ways never seen before. Grasso convinced Phelan that the best way to go after the competition was to take one of the most prominent people at the exchange with him when he made "listing calls," or sales pitches, where Grasso would attempt to convince companies listed on another exchange to come to the big leagues.

One of the first listing calls they made was to Syntex, a company that manufactured birth control pills. It was listed on the American Stock Exchange, which was headed by a man named Arthur Levitt, who had all the pedigree Grasso didn't. His father, New York State comptroller Arthur Levitt, Sr., was one of the country's largest institutional investors; he ran the state's massive pension fund and showered Wall Street trading desks with commissions. Grasso immediately developed a hatred for Levitt as a "lucky sperm kid" and couldn't wait to steal one of Levitt's top companies.

Phelan allowed Grasso to handle the presentation, but it was filled with glitches and hiccups as Grasso's slides unexpectedly melted inside the projector. On the cab ride back to the exchange, Phelan didn't say anything, which Grasso knew meant he was pissed. "Don't worry," he tried to assure his boss, "we'll be all right." Phelan just sat in silence.

But Grasso was confident that he had won the listing. He had handled the melting mishap well and even gotten the board to laugh when he told them he would talk fast before the rest of his presentation self-destructed.

Grasso ultimately got his reward when Syntex went with the NYSE and Phelan gave Grasso a promotion. More followed. Grasso was in his mid-thirties, but he was now a vice president of the listings department and Phelan had become president of the exchange, which essentially gave Phelan carte blanche to run the exchange as he saw fit. Phelan, in turn, gave Grasso carte blanche in the listings department. The first thing he did was change the exchange's marketing plan to have much less to do with golf and skiing and more to do with how to bring in new listing business. With the Nasdaq threat looming, the exchange could no longer afford to ignore initial public offerings and allow companies to "graduate" to the Big Board. IPOs were open game, and so was everything else. Grasso drew up a list of companies to call. There were hundreds, and though Grasso had a small staff, he made every call personally.

Grasso had certainly come a long way since his first days as a listing clerk. His personal life had gone through some changes, too. For one thing, his marriage had ended in divorce. People around the office found out why when they noticed that Grasso had started spending more and more time with his secretary, a pretty, petite woman named Lorraine Pike. Lori had grown up in Sunset Park, Brooklyn, and like Grasso was about as blue-collar as you could get, the daughter of an ironworker. They had something else in common: a love of the stock exchange. A couple of years later they married and had the first of their four children. Before any of the kids could walk, Lori used to brag, "Each first learned to crawl on the floor of the exchange."

Grasso loved the exchange and working for Phelan, and Phelan loved Grasso. In the mid-to-late-1970s, Wall Street was losing money, and seat prices fell to an all-time low of $35,000. But the listings department was booming. Grasso often joked that the best thing about his job was the competition—he really didn't have any. He considered Levitt, the head of the Amex, a rich kid with a pompous attitude, and Nasdaq founder Gordon Macklin a visionary who couldn't find his way to the post office. Companies like American Express and Anheuser-Busch, among the first to list on the electronic market, were easy pickings for Grasso, who turned on the charm about the need to be part of "the world's greatest stock market" and how specialists would always be there to buy their stock. Some weren't so easy. Since around 1934, NYSE listing officials had been making perfunctory calls to the Carnation Company, the manufacturer of a popular brand of evaporated milk, which listed on the Amex. Their best effort consisted of a form letter sent to the company's CFO, who promptly and politely rejected the overture. Grasso did a little research. What amazed him was that whoever had charge of the account had used the same form letter every year going back to 1934.

This time Grasso requested a formal meeting with the company brass to make his case. At the meeting, Grasso extolled the virtues of the exchange and the fact that specialists would reduce the volatility of the company's stock. He then whipped out the first letter ever sent to the company in 1934 to remind them how long the exchange had been trying to get its listing. "Gentlemen, here it is, the first letter we ever sent you," Grasso said, passing it around the room. Then he handed them the first rejection letter written by the company's chief financial officer that same year. "And if you wait another forty-five years, I won't be around here to welcome you to the exchange," he added.

The place erupted in laughter, but the executives still gave Grasso no indication of whether they had bought his sales pitch; that is, until a few days later, when he got a call from Albert Gordon, the chairman of Kidder, Peabody and one of the most powerful people in the Club. Gordon was also a member of the Carnation board. "Oh shit," Grasso muttered as his secretary told him who was on the line, fearing he had come on a little too strong with the Carnation executives. "Good morning, Mr. Gordon, how can I help you?" Grasso asked, his heart racing. "Richard," Gordon answered, "I don't know what you said to those boys, but they were impressed that you went to the trouble of going back forty-five years and researching their company. They called me to say they will list on the exchange in January." Grasso nearly jumped through the ceiling.

So did Phelan. For a time it seemed that Grasso could do almost nothing wrong in Phelan's eyes because he did so much right. He demanded salary increases and he got them—he was now earning more than $40,000 a year. He screamed at subordinates he believed weren't working hard enough, and Phelan brushed it off as just part of the learning curve of a prodigy. More than anything else, Grasso refused to take orders from anyone except Phelan himself. A man named Donald Calvin was technically Grasso's boss, but everything he said to Grasso was ignored. One day Calvin had had enough and told Phelan he wanted Grasso out. "Where are you going?" Phelan asked with his trademark lack of emotion. Calvin was speechless, so Phelan filled in the blanks: "Given the opportunity to lose you or Dick, and given how much Dick is worth to this place, there's no choice." Grasso didn't even know he had been "fired" that day until years later, when Phelan was joking around with his senior staff and told them how he had once saved Grasso's job.

Phelan appeared to be Grasso's ticket to the big time. It was the early 1980s, and Phelan was president of the exchange and the odds-on favorite to become chairman. If and when that happened, Grasso thought, he would be a shoo-in to become president himself. But Grasso was still concerned that he wasn't moving up the management ranks fast enough, and he made his ideas known to Phelan, who simply told Grasso his time would come. Privately, however, Phelan had his doubts, not about Grasso's ability to do the job but about his ability to deal with people. Phelan confided in a few close associates, and those to whom he did said that Phelan would often refer to Grasso's "dark side." Phelan had received reports of Grasso's wild temper with subordinates. Grasso also took a perverse pride in being the only member of Phelan's senior staff who would verbally spar with Phelan, but Phelan thought it was a sign of immaturity.

Grasso's frustration soon boiled over. He made a bold move to get Phelan's attention by quitting and taking a job on the floor with his trading buddy Billy Johnston. For about a week, Grasso was on Johnston's payroll as a trader for Agora Securities and getting used to the new routine. With Johnston there was never a dull moment. Besides the nonstop joking and endless ethnic humor, Grasso noticed that Johnston and his staff would often start boozing it up almost as soon as they got to work. Grasso didn't mind; he was having fun and being tutored in the finer points of floor trading before Phelan finally intervened. "No way am I allowing you to do this," Phelan said. "So stop this nonsense. This is where you belong." When Grasso returned to work, he got the promotion he was looking for: to senior vice president of the exchange. His salary more than doubled, to $85,000 a year. He was in charge of listings, the floor, and nearly all exchange operations except technology. It was almost everything he was looking for.

To make his mark and prove his worth to Phelan, Grasso went on a listings rampage. He targeted the IPO of Microsoft in an attempt to show that the exchange was no longer afraid of initial offerings, as had been its reputation. Grasso didn't get the listing—Microsoft's investment banker was a Goldman Sachs executive named Victor Wright, who was chairman of the Nasdaq trading committee—but the defeat served only to make him redouble his efforts to take another company away from the Nasdaq.

Each year for the previous seven years, Grasso had paid a listing call to Maurice "Hank" Greenberg, the brilliant but volatile chief executive officer of American International Group. Through a series of acquisitions, Greenberg had grown AIG from a small insurance outfit to the world's largest. Grasso's pitch was simple: You're too big to be listed in the minor leagues.

Each time Grasso made an overture, Greenberg would listen for a few minutes before abruptly ending the meeting with a simple "Very good, that's enough."

This time he came back with a different answer: "I'm so sick of hearing from you that I'm ready to do it!" Grasso was ecstatic; Phelan was overjoyed. AIG had the highest market value of any company on the Nasdaq. It was a sweet victory for Grasso.

Despite his success, Grasso continued to feel slighted. He openly complained that Calvin, still technically his boss, was breaking his balls. Meanwhile, Phelan wasn't moving him up the food chain fast enough, he felt, and for a second time he quit; once again Grasso decided to take a job with Johnston, only to be wooed back by Phelan and the promise of a future promotion. Grasso was back snaring listings when he heard a disturbing rumor: exchange chairman William Batten wanted to stay indefinitely. Grasso despised Batten as a lightweight with a great résumé—Batten had been the chairman of J. C. Penney—who left all the heavy lifting to him and Phelan. Grasso approached Phelan, who said he was hearing the same rumblings.

For the third time in about ten years Grasso quit his job at the New York Stock Exchange, and for the third time he came back. Grasso had been working at Henderson Brothers, a specialist firm, for about a week when the news broke: Phelan was the new chairman of the New York Stock Exchange. Although Batten had appeared to have no intention of leaving, the board, Grasso recalls, had other ideas. It was now Phelan's time to officially run the Club. Grasso was elated and asked for his old job back: "I can stay and help you with the listings." Phelan knew he needed help and said the job was still Grasso's.

By 1984, with Phelan firmly in charge of the Club, everything seemed to point to Grasso becoming president of the exchange. In addition to knowing where every body at the exchange was buried, he had gone back to Pace to take a few classes. Phelan sent him to a special Harvard University program for rising business executives. Grasso was so confident he had earned the position that in anticipation he began to lose weight, a lot of weight. Five feet, six inches tall, he weighed close to two hundred pounds. A crash diet cut sixty pounds in a couple of months, but one of the side effects of the rapid loss of weight was an intense aversion to the cold. He could no longer abide cold weather, and he needed the temperature in his office at 90 degrees or higher year round.

Grasso's rapid weight loss did nothing to convince Phelan that he was ready for the job. In Phelan's typical secretive fashion, he assembled his senior staff, including Grasso, in a small room outside his office on the sixth floor of the stock exchange. He handed each of them a list of the candidates to be the next president of the exchange. Grasso's name was on it, as were several others, including the veteran brokerage executive Robert Rittereiser and American Stock Exchange president Robert Birnbaum, Levitt's number two man at that exchange. "So what do you think?" Phelan asked.

It might have been a test—or even an honest attempt to canvass his team for their input. Whatever it was, Grasso's temper would not allow him to abide what he considered an insult. He blurted out, "Anyone but me would be my second choice."

Phelan was stunned by the outburst. But then he laughed. That was when Grasso knew he wouldn't get the job.

Instead, he was appointed executive vice president, a notch above his senior vice president title, and with it, he received a healthy raise to around $200,000 a year. The raise probably kept Grasso from quitting again, because he was crushed. Now Phelan leveled with him. He didn't think that Grasso, all of thirty-eight years of age, was ready—not yet. "You're too young" were Phelan's exact words. What Phelan didn't tell him was that he also had grave concerns about Grasso's management abilities. Grasso had one speed: full speed. He lacked nuance and diplomacy, particularly with the people who reported to him.

Phelan believed Grasso could learn a lot from the guy who did get the job. He was actually on the bottom of the list, but he had all the right experience. Robert Birnbaum was a securities lawyer who had worked at the Securities and Exchange Commission before taking over the day-to-day operations of the Amex. There was much Grasso could learn from this man.

Still, Phelan's pep talk did little to soothe Grasso's anger. The more Grasso thought about being passed over yet again, the more he fumed. Then he sat down with Birnbaum and realized that Phelan was right; this was a guy he could work with and learn from. Birnbaum, as far as Grasso was concerned, was a man without ego. He was well into his sixties and had little desire for the top job. For all his experience on the street, Birnbaum was also a regular guy. He had a gruff New York accent and a plainspoken way. More important, Birnbaum was a friend of Phelan. He was happy in his role and ready to prepare Grasso for the day when he might run the place. All Grasso had to do was relax and enjoy his time.

.   The 1980s were certainly great years to be in the stock market. Trading volume had ramped up dramatically, and the bulls were running wild. In 1982, for the first time the number of shares traded per day passed the 100 million mark—and that was just the start. Spirits at the market ran high, and Phelan knew how to cheer traders on. He chose to end each day's trading by mounting the podium himself to ring the closing bell; in the past, it had been done without much notice. Seat prices were now selling at more than $1 million. As the Dow crept higher with each trading day, each session closed with a sense of accomplishment, even glee. Now when Phelan hit the switch, the bell was greeted with wild applause and, from the large Marine contingent on the floor, a few "ooh-rah"s.

The excitement on the floor didn't mollify the forces of change swirling outside the exchange. Indeed, the pressure grew to update and automate the so-called open outcry system. A major turning point occurred when the London Stock Exchange considered its future course. The LSE, as the exchange was called, was at a crossroads as to whether it should adopt a computerized model for matching buyers and sellers. Phelan traveled to London to make the case for the status quo. He was opposed by the chairman of the Nasdaq, Bernie Madoff. Madoff had built a career out of attacking the NYSE. Phelan argued that a centralized market of buyers and sellers was needed so big brokers could take advantage of investors' positions. The electronic markets like the Nasdaq, where multiple market makers bid on stocks from various locations, exposed trading positions, caused the markets to "fragment," or display different prices for the same shares, and led to greater zigzags in the pricing of stocks.

Madoff said just the opposite: that fair prices are set by multiple players interacting continuously, and investors are smart enough to know how to hide their hands. The New York Stock Exchange, he explained, was a relic; the large investment houses like Fidelity wanted cheap, efficient electronic trading.

In 1986, the London Stock Exchange made it official: it was implementing more computers on its floor, eliminating the face-to-face auction system that had prevailed for most of its history. In Europe it was known as the "Big Bang." Back in New York, major securities firms like Goldman Sachs believed that sending all their orders to the floor was too costly. They began to question the specialist system and whether the exchange should be the preferred monopoly.

That monopoly was maintained by arcane rules that favored the floor. Chief among them was a "best price" rule. It basically meant that unless a trader could find a better price elsewhere, exchange-traded stocks must be traded on the floor. What sounded like a reasonable concession was nothing more than a ruse to force order flow to the floor, critics charged, since a specialist could always step in and top the price of a small part of any block of stock, ignoring the fact that computers could instantly match buyers and sellers in large volume.

Phelan was a second-generation floor trader, a combat veteran of the Korean War, but he was also a politician, and now he had to sell the exchange like one. With that in mind, he went on the road, sometimes by himself, sometimes with Birnbaum, and sometimes with

Grasso, speaking before Congress, investor groups, and any other group he believed would be helpful in reaching his ultimate goal: allowing the exchange to maintain its dominance. He was effectively arguing for a monopoly, but it was a monopoly that if broken would have profound consequences for the capital markets and investors for years to come.

During this time, it was Grasso's main task to make sure the technology at the exchange could meet the challenge. When people at the Nasdaq heard that Phelan had ordered a massive upgrade of the exchange's computer systems, they just rolled their eyes. Not Madoff. He knew Phelan and Grasso well enough to understand what made them tick. They weren't anti-technology, they were just pro-specialist, and they would do whatever it took to preserve the floor—even if that meant installing the latest computer systems to make the auction process as smooth as possible.

And that's exactly what they did. Phelan developed the "DOT" and "Super-DOT" systems, which allowed brokerage firms to streamline trades through a computer that sent orders directly to the specialists, bypassing the floor brokers altogether. Phelan allowed it only for small orders (later the system was upgraded to execute small trades), but it was a recognition that part of the floor's system could be automated. He upgraded the exchange's routing systems so they could process orders in larger volume. Specialists' stations were now equipped with computers and screens showing actively traded stocks. To be sure, the floor was still the floor; trades were matched largely through brokers screaming out their orders, and traders continued to write down their positions on small pieces of paper. In an age where technology was necessary to survive, Phelan and Grasso made sure the floor survived.

On October 16, 1987, Grasso and the entire exchange received the first inkling that something was wrong when the barometer of the exchange's largest stocks, the Dow Jones Industrial Average, fell one hundred points, the first triple-digit loss in the Dow's history. Grasso spent much of that afternoon talking to his buddies on the floor. The consensus was pretty upbeat: the market oversold; prices will rebound Monday.

Then Monday came. By 2:00 P.M. New York time, the Dow had lost 250 points; by 4:00 P.M. it was down by more than 500 points. Phelan called a meeting before the trading day ended. Grasso's head was spinning. The exchange had never traded more than 300 million shares during a single day. On "Black Monday," as it would come to be known, it traded 604 million shares.

Phelan was calm. For the past year he had openly worried about the street's use of program trading, where market bounces would automatically trigger computer programs to send massive buy or sell orders to the exchange. Grasso countered that such programs were good for business because they increased order flow and specialist activity. Phelan worried that they could lead to a market meltdown, and now he was proven right. Even so, he didn't take credit for calling the Great Crash of 1987. By most accounts, he simply set an example for the rest of his staff of how to run the place during a time of crisis.

Initially, all he needed was some basic questions answered: he wanted to know what kind of "brakes" the exchange had to slow down the flood of sell orders prompted by programmed trading.

Minimal, Grasso said.

Phelan came up with a plan to slow down the process. The exchange would suspend the "Super-DOT" system for large orders, which allowed orders to be routed straight from the trading desk to the specialist. All orders would have to be done the old-fashioned way: from trading desk to floor broker to specialist.

For once in its history, the exchange would be applauded for having a system slower than the computers used by the Nasdaq, where prices could plummet faster and traders could simply ignore customers' sell orders from their desks in varied locations. There was a bloodbath on the floor, with traders going crazy trying to meet demands; one specialist firm, Grasso discovered, had lost control of its trading positions—it didn't know what it held long or short as orders flooded its station.

Grasso approached Peter Kellogg, one of the partners at the specialist firm Spear, Leeds & Kellogg, and asked if he would provide some financial backing to the firm. Kellogg said he would, for the good of the exchange.

Grasso now thanked God he had Birnbaum watching his back. Birnbaum knew every major player on Wall Street, and he began fielding the calls from the CEOs of the top Wall Street firms, who were demanding that the exchange close because they couldn't handle the volume of sell orders.

Even as the market recovered on Tuesday morning, both the volume and the selling picked up again. Now the pressure to close became intense. Phelan wouldn't hear of it. He went public with his plan to keep the exchange open, explaining that markets must remain open, even when they're about to crater. That night, Birnbaum and Grasso held a meeting with the top Wall Street firms.

They were in a panic, but Birnbaum wasn't. Grasso recalls one official at a major firm demanding that the exchange close or his firm might implode. Birnbaum then pointed to Grasso. "Let me tell you something, I got a great chief operating officer who makes this place run in good times and bad," he said, explaining that the exchange's processing system was working just fine. "Too bad you don't."

The next day Grasso was in Birnbaum's office when he received a call from Alan "Ace" Greenberg, the CEO of Bear Stearns. Greenberg was one of the most powerful players on Wall Street and one of its best traders, and now he was demanding that the exchange reconsider its position and close because of all the unfinished trades—known as quit trades or QTs—that were gumming up the works at every major firm. Again Birnbaum held tough.

Greenberg exploded. "Do you know how many QTs they have at Merrill Lynch?" he snapped. "As a matter of fact, I do," Birnbaum said, rattling off the number. "I also know," Birnbaum added, "how many QTs you have over at Bear Stearns." Greenberg then changed his tone.

The development of the maturity Phelan believed Grasso needed was now crammed into five days beginning on October 19, 1987.

Grasso watched Birnbaum's poise and control in backroom dealings with the member firms, and he witnessed Phelan become the cool public face of the markets. Aided by his PR chief, Richard Torrenzano, Phelan had been increasing his public profile of late. Torrenzano had convinced him to speak out on the insider trading scandals to help show Middle America that Wall Street wasn't populated by a band of thieves.

Torrenzano believed the crash gave Phelan even more to work with; unlike the Nasdaq, where the market makers simply stopped taking orders, the exchange remained in business. The money Phelan had dumped into technology over the past five years seemed to be paying off.

Phelan agreed with Torrenzano that if he ever needed to put a face on the markets, now was the time, and Phelan delivered in press conferences, one-on-one meetings with reporters, and television interviews. He handled the press calmly, explaining the underlying truth.

Grasso hated the press and did all he could to avoid being interviewed about the crash, but both Birnbaum and Phelan pushed him to begin speaking to the reporters as well. Grasso did it, but only after he saw how Phelan turned tragedy into triumph as the press branded Phelan a near hero for keeping the markets working amid the chaos.

The impact of the stock market crash of 1987 lasted far longer than the week of October 19. Seat prices began a downward drift, falling from $1.15 million to just $250,000. In response to the meltdown, Phelan undertook a massive self-examination of the exchange. First, he made sure Grasso got the job he had coveted for so long—in 1988 he was named president of the exchange as Birnbaum retired. In Phelan's mind, the crash had given Grasso the experience—and maturity—he needed for the next step in his career. The street kid from Queens who had started off as the $81-a-week "Earl of Sandwich" was now the number two man at the New York Stock Exchange and on the verge of becoming the King of the Club. With that distinction would come a king-size salary. Grasso was now earning $1 million a year, at a time when Wall Street was shedding jobs by the thousands. Grasso himself was doing some of that shedding.

The crash affected players across Wall Street as investors fled from the markets. The glory days of the 1980s seemed to be behind them. With the decline in trading volume came a decline in fees. The stock exchange actually lost money in 1990. Phelan ordered cuts—some of the biggest cuts in the exchange's history—to maintain the institution's financial health. Phelan told Grasso he needed to take out 700 people from a workforce of about 2,300. If that didn't seem daunting enough, when Grasso sat down and began looking at where the cuts would come from, he realized he was in a box. He couldn't fire any of the exchange's regulatory personnel, not in the middle of the insider trading scandals that were ablaze on Wall Street.

It was a tough job, but Phelan said he could use buyouts for long-term employees plus attrition to get to his number. That would make the cuts more humane. In the end, Grasso had to fire 120 people; they were the toughest 120 meetings Grasso ever had, but he tried to give out his pink slips personally.

Grasso was less humane to his immediate staff, which meant just about anyone in an executive position. Grasso ruled over them with an iron fist. He seemed to have adopted many of Phelan's bad traits and his control-freak tendencies, but none of his good ones. Grasso was a screamer, and his nasty temper was unleashed in full force not long after he became president.

"Goddamn it, is he on the telephone again?" shouted Dave Komansky, who had just been named to head Merrill Lynch's stock-trading desk. One of Komansky's duties was to decide which market he should send his firm's trades to, and Grasso had been hounding Komansky for months, asking him out for dinner, coffee, drinks, anything to get more business from Merrill, the largest "order flow" provider to the exchange. Grasso had met Komansky years earlier and loved his story because it sounded so much like his own: Komansky had grown up in a small apartment in the Bronx and attended the University of

Miami, but dropped out of school to become a stockbroker at Merrill Lynch's Forest Hills office. He was now one of the rising stars at the fast-growing firm, which was another reason why Grasso was courting him.

There was no law that forced Komansky—or the head of any other Wall Street firm—to send its customers' orders to buy and sell stocks directly to the exchange. Even orders for stocks listed on the Big Board could be filled elsewhere, provided that trades were matched at "best price." Not surprisingly, Grasso always thought the exchange had the best price, and the fact that he convinced people like Komansky of that added to his growing stature on Wall Street. Like any good businessman, Grasso understood that he had leverage over the big firms because the NYSE was also their regulator, and he wasn't bashful about making firms prove that they were giving their customers the best price on trades routed outside the stock exchange. For most Wall Street firms, it was just easier to send their orders to the exchange and stay on Grasso's good side.

Komansky liked being on Grasso's good side for another reason: he and Grasso were fast becoming friends, "brothers," as Grasso would say.

Still, every now and then, Komansky would sit back and consider the following: Grasso was in charge of making sure that the exchange was trading and making markets in 80 percent or more of the orders for stocks listed on the exchange, which meant that nearly every major company in America was trading on the floor, which could mean only one thing: Komansky must not be the only object of Grasso's affection.

And he wasn't. Grasso's Rolodex of connections on Wall Street now surpassed anyone's at the exchange, except possibly Phelan's. Not only did Grasso have a budding relationship with Komansky, he also managed to schmooze his way into a friendship with Komansky's boss, Merrill president and soon-to-be CEO Daniel Tully, as well as a future generation of Wall Street leaders: people like Joseph Grano, then at Merrill but soon to make the jump to Paine-Webber; Richard Fuld, the CEO of Lehman Brothers; Jimmy Cayne, the president and soon-to-be CEO of Bear Stearns; and Sanford Weill, who had been banished from American Express but was now in the very early stages of creating one of the largest financial firms ever and one of the most controversial careers Wall Street had ever seen. With friends like these, Grasso reckoned, it was only a matter of time before he got the ultimate promotion.

That time, it appeared to Grasso, was fast approaching. By early 1990, John Phelan had served as chairman for nearly six years, one of the longest tenures ever. Despite the crash, the Club was now well positioned to continue its dominance as the world's largest stock market. Phelan introduced computerized trading for the first time; he modernized the exchange's systems to withstand another crash. And the brand remained among the most recognizable in the world.

Phelan had done it all. Now he wanted a break.

Grasso had two immediate reactions when Phelan announced he was leaving: shock and a rush of ambition.

His ambition made sense; nearly every major business unit reported to Grasso. No one knew more about how the place worked than he. By giving him so much responsibility, Phelan had signaled that Grasso would be his natural replacement. Grasso took it as an unmistakable sign. For all their knock-down, drag-out fights, Grasso had faith that Phelan would be there when he needed him and use his clout with the board to name him chairman.

Lorraine, his wife, wasn't so certain. She had seen Phelan backdoor her husband before. And Lori Grasso was right about this time as well: Phelan signaled to the board that Grasso shouldn't get the job.

Grasso approached Phelan and asked him the obvious question: Why? Phelan said the matter wasn't as simple as Grasso believed. He had told the board that Grasso was the most talented executive he'd ever met. He had given Grasso rave reviews for his work. But, he told Grasso, he didn't believe it should be his job to pick his own successor. Grasso was crushed again, but Phelan assured him he wasn't out of contention.

A selection committee had been formed, and Grasso's name was on the short list. Grasso went home that night and told Lori what he thought was the good news: Phelan was someone who despised confrontation. That's why he had Grasso do all those firings and why he didn't want to take responsibility for picking his successor.

Ever hopeful of reaching his goal, Grasso thought he still had a legitimate shot.

Lori's response: For all you did for him, you should be on the top of the list—not on the short list.

3

"THE EMPTY SUIT"

"I can't catch a break!" Grasso snapped when he heard that Donald MacNaughton had been appointed to lead the search for Phelan's successor. MacNaughton was one of the most respected businessmen in corporate America, the former CEO of Prudential Insurance and Hospital Corporation of America. He had been a reigning member of the Club for years, having run not just one public company but two.

But Grasso had never gotten close to MacNaughton. In fact, the two had barely exchanged a word in the five years he had been on the board. When they did, Grasso found him to be cold, aloof, and elitist. In short, he was the last guy, Grasso thought, who would give an Italian street kid a break. That became clear when word leaked about the committee's top choice: Richard Jenrette, one of the founding members of Donaldson, Lufkin & Jenrette Securities Corporation. Grasso had nothing against Jenrette, but as soon as the leak started making its way around the office, his blood began to boil.

He wasn't the only one. The floor—now Grasso's power base, not just because of the order flow and listings that pumped profits into the traders' coffers—took the news badly. By the late 1980s, a demographic shift on the floor was obvious: women and African Americans were still rarities, but the anti-Italian bias that had been there when Grasso applied back in the late 1960s was gone. In fact, Italians may have held the majority of trader jobs, and what had really pissed off many traders wasn't just that Grasso was being passed over for the job but the reason he was passed over. Grasso's biggest problem, he recalls being told by a floor trader who had sources on the board, could be summed up in the fact that he was "short, bald, and above all ethnic." The chairmanship, this person quoted MacNaughton as having said, would go to "anyone but that little guinea."

When word of the insult reached Grasso, he decided to quit. News of Grasso's pending resignation spread from the floor to the management suites of the exchange. This time Phelan knew he was serious. The "guinea" reference had put Grasso over the edge. It was one thing for Phelan to say he needed more time to grow and mature; ethnic insults were another thing entirely. When MacNaughton heard about Grasso's plan, he backpedaled and contacted Grasso to ask him to meet over dinner and "discuss his future." Grasso understood enough about the politics of the Club to know this didn't mean he would get the top job. The question facing Grasso was: Should he call the board's bluff and quit? Grasso believed he had waited long enough to run the exchange—more than twenty years. He was earning around $1 million a year, a salary he could quadruple as a specialist. Maybe the time was right to accept Billy Johnston's offer and stay on the floor for good.

But his gut told him something else. He simply loved the exchange. And then the Queens in him kicked in: Why should he give up and give the white shoes the satisfaction of ending his dream?

Grasso agreed to have dinner with MacNaughton—but, he said, it would have to be on his turf, and more specifically, at his private club, named Tiro a Segno, which means in Italian "hit the target," because of a special feature. Tiro's was the oldest Italian-American club in the city, known for its pinkie-ringed clientele, five-star red-sauce dining, and a basement shooting range, which is still open to all members. In short, it was just the type of place, Grasso reckoned, that would make MacNaughton's skin crawl.

To Grasso, MacNaughton seemed uncomfortable from the moment the two sat down. The club was filled with finely dressed men who looked like extras for a Mob movie. MacNaughton wore a conservative gray suit, finely pressed white shirt, and dark tie. As the two ate dinner, they made small talk about the exchange. Phelan's retirement came up several times. Then MacNaughton turned to the subject at hand: Grasso's future. "Look, Dick, you're a great candidate for the job, and you have great potential, but you're very young," he said, according to Grasso's recollection. "I was young once too and was passed over for CEO, but I got there and you're going to be CEO too."

Grasso's natural instinct was to explode at what he took as MacNaughton's phony display of concern, but over the years he had learned a thing or two from Phelan about keeping emotions in check. "You're right," Grasso replied calmly. "I'll be a CEO either here or somewhere else." The two men continued their dinner as if nothing had happened, but something had, and MacNaughton didn't like it.

The next morning, Grasso hadn't had much time to think about his dinner with MacNaughton before the phone rang. "Dick, it's Lasker," the voice said. "Meet me in the luncheon club today around noon." After Phelan, Grasso owed no one more than the guy everyone called Bunny. Lasker had been chairman when Grasso was first hired by the exchange and had immediately seen his promise. Since then, he and Grasso had remained close, and when they met in the lunch club, Lasker didn't waste time letting Grasso know he wasn't crazy about the remark he had made to MacNaughton or his intention to leave the exchange. "If you leave, they win," he said. Lasker made it clear he wasn't speaking just for himself. He was also speaking for Phelan, who now worried that for his faults, the guy who knew the most about the exchange and its inner workings was about to leave.

Grasso thought long and hard about what Lasker was saying. He spoke again with Phelan, who assured him that the job would be his someday; he just needed to be patient. For all the turmoil in their relationship, Grasso's admiration for Phelan was second to none. "If the old man is telling me to stay, then maybe I should stay," he told one confidant. "He's my mentor." But there was another reason: for all Grasso's success, the chip on his shoulder still remained and the chip told him to stay and fight it out. "If I leave, they win," Grasso said, repeating Lasker's advice. "They," of course, meant the blue-bloods like MacNaughton and all the people along the way who had never given him a chance of getting out of the listings department. Grasso didn't want to give them the satisfaction. Anyway, how bad could it be to work for Dick Jenrette?

Not bad, if Jenrette was the guy taking the job. But Jenrette turned down the post to run The Equitable, a large insurance company, offering instead the name of someone else he said was just as qualified, his old partner from DLJ, William Donaldson. On paper, Donaldson looked like the perfect choice. A former U.S. Marine with a tight jaw and broad shoulders, Donaldson cut an impressive profile. He had gone to Yale, graduated from the Harvard Business School, and helped create one of Wall Street's top firms. He had been a personal friend of the president, George H. W. Bush, since their days together in Yale's Skull and Bones society. Under his leadership, DLJ had been the first Wall Street firm to list on the NYSE back in 1969, and Donaldson had strategically maintained his contacts on Wall Street since leaving the business, first to work in the White House under President Richard Nixon and later to create Yale's school of management, where he served as its first dean. When approached by various members of the NYSE board, Donaldson immediately said he was interested. Phelan also made it clear to Grasso that there was a bigger game plan at work; like Jenrette, Donaldson was perfect to appease Grasso's critics and smooth out his rough spots. Grasso, of course, would stay as president and, as a consolation prize, was given the additional title of executive vice chairman. This was apparently enough for Grasso to decide to be part of the new team.

Grasso wasn't sure what to expect from his new boss, but some time after Donaldson's nomination became official, they met for the first time. Grasso was pumped. Later that night he went home to Lori and said Donaldson was the second coming of Robert Birnbaum, someone who was working to help him succeed. Grasso said he was everything his résumé suggested: polished, well bred, and sincere. They had scheduled a dinner meeting in a few days where they would iron out a broader set of responsibilities.

Donaldson set their meeting at a swanky Upper East Side Italian restaurant called Parioli Romanissimo. Unlike in Grasso's Greenwich Village Italian club, there weren't many pinkie rings around here, just Rolexes, investment bankers in expensive dark suits, and doting waiters who knew Donaldson so well they called him "Mr. Donaldson." Grasso had a good feeling going into the meeting that became even better when Donaldson started laying out his vision for the future. For the next four hours, over pasta, veal, and expensive wine, Donaldson treated Grasso like a CEO in waiting. He said Grasso was indispensable to the exchange and that he would help fill in the blank spots in his résumé. Grasso would be able to develop his talent, expand his contacts, and learn what it was like to run a business from a guy who had started one of the biggest on Wall Street. Grasso barely knew Donaldson, except what he read in the newspaper, but his easygoing manner immediately won him over.

One fear Grasso did have going into the meeting was that Donaldson would be a hands-on boss. But instead of limiting Grasso's power, Donaldson wanted to expand it. In fact, Donaldson made it clear to Grasso that he was ready to cede total responsibility of day-to-day operations to the little guy. "You report to me," Donaldson said, according to Grasso's recollection, "and everyone else reports to you." Grasso couldn't believe his ears. In an interview, Donaldson says he didn't use those exact words, but he did agree to give Grasso more responsibility.

That night Grasso went home and was ecstatic; he told Lori that Donaldson was "great" and the arrangement would work out "perfectly." Grasso now had full day-to-day responsibility for not just the moneymaking parts of the Club, but its powerful regulatory function as well. Wall Street's top cop, of course, is the Securities and Exchange Commission, but under the nation's securities laws, the exchange is what's known as a self-regulator, meaning that Grasso was now literally the police chief of the brokerage business and the firms that traded stocks on the floor.

In the wrong hands, such power can be easily misused by a chairman willing to do everything and anything to promote his own agenda because of the conflict of interest inherent in the job where one man serves as a regulator of member firms that also set his salary.

It's unclear if Grasso gave even a second thought to any of this as he weighed his future: with Donaldson off giving speeches, with the vast bureaucracy of the Club in his hands, for all intents and purposes, he was already running the show. All he had to do was wait a little longer and the title would be his as well. In other words, Bill Donaldson didn't stand a chance.

The first major crisis of the Donaldson era occurred not long after the man settled into Phelan's large corner office. As it turned out, the new chairman's personal life was more complicated than anyone had expected. Donaldson had been married for thirty-four years to Manhattan socialite Evan Burger, with whom he had adopted two children.

As far as the outside world was concerned, Mrs. Donaldson was his rock, often seen at her husband's side at New York society events. But Donaldson had had an affair while he was dean of the Yale School of Management with the wife of a U.S. congressman from Connecticut who was employed at the school. To make matters worse, the woman, Jane Morrison, became pregnant and gave birth to a child around the time Donaldson accepted the NYSE job.

Grasso and his head of public relations, Richard Torrenzano, were just getting to know Donaldson when they first heard rumors of a love child. Grasso was still trying to find his footing with Donaldson. Despite finding common ground initially, the two were really polar opposites in almost every way. Donaldson was trim, with a full head of hair; Grasso was portly and bald. Donaldson rarely raised his voice, while Grasso didn't think twice about flying off the handle. Grasso's ambition pushed him to work eighteen-hour days, while Donaldson made it appear as if he preferred to leave the office early.

Torrenzano felt as if he had just survived one of the biggest PR challenges the exchange had ever faced following the 1987 stock market crash, when he had helped craft the strategy that had allowed Phelan to portray the Club as a place of relative stability in a sea of chaos. A Brooklyn boy with a Stanford University education, Torrenzano could mix with the toughest of the Club's floor traders as well as with members of the elite business media who covered the exchange. When it came to Wall Street, Torrenzano was in his element. But then he began having to field calls from several newspapers, including *The Wall Street Journal,* about Donaldson's love child. Suddenly, Torrenzano was dealing with a type of story he had never encountered before.

"He looks like too much of a Boy Scout," Grasso remarked when he first heard the speculation. But Torrenzano did background work and even confronted Donaldson about the matter. It was confirmed: Donaldson, in his late fifties, was the father of a baby boy with a woman who was not his wife.

Donaldson had little clue as to how to kill the story. Torrenzano recalls that his first reaction was to ignore it; later he suggested that Torrenzano might want to begin denying the accounts. Torrenzano knew that neither strategy would work. He knew the love child story was a killer—and he wasn't prepared to go out with a response that required him to believe his own bullshit. Besides, Donaldson wasn't just some nameless government bureaucrat who could stonewall; he was part of the Wall Street elite, with a career that had brought him to the upper reaches of both business and government. His name was on the door of a major Wall Street firm. (Donaldson says he doesn't recall speaking to Torrenzano about the issue, just Grasso.)

Torrenzano believed his best chance of stopping the story would be to embarrass the reporters, particularly those at the *Journal,* into killing it. Over the course of about three days, Torrenzano had several heated conversations with *Journal* reporters and editors, stressing that it was beneath them to write such trash. Whatever Donaldson did, Torrenzano said, it was a consensual relationship between adults that had no bearing on his ability to do his job.

In the end, the *Journal* and the other papers backed off. Torrenzano breathed a sigh of relief, but he resolved not to be put in that position again. Torrenzano had serious doubts about Donaldson from that moment on. He found the new chairman shallow and lacking in the very attributes that had made Phelan a joy to work for. Besides, he knew the love child story would return. It was just too titillating. Within a couple of months, Torrenzano told Grasso he was leaving for a new gig, to head up PR for SmithKline Beecham, a big pharmaceutical company. Grasso asked Torrenzano if there was anything he could do to make him stay. Torrenzano said there wasn't, adding, "The place just ain't the same without Phelan around anymore."

Grasso didn't say so, but he was coming to the same conclusion.

To the public, the Grasso-Donaldson team was known simply as "Mr. Inside and Mr. Outside," and they ran the place like clockwork, or so it seemed. In 1991, Donaldson's first full year in the top job, the exchange rebounded from its loss and posted a profit of close to $12 million. Grasso and Donaldson were the yin and yang of Wall Street. They complemented each other, is what Frank Zarb, then the head of the Smith Barney investment bank, thought. The first time Zarb met Grasso and Donaldson as a team, they had arranged a meeting because his large investment bank was planning to send trading orders to the regional exchanges instead of the NYSE floor. Not knowing either very well, Zarb had his staff give him a briefing: Donaldson, they said, would give Zarb all the business reasons why he was making a mistake, and if that didn't work, Grasso would step in and play the ultimate trump card, gently reminding Zarb that the NYSE was still Smith Barney's primary regulator, which could mean lots of trouble down the road if business were diverted elsewhere. True to form, Donaldson sat down with Grasso and began the conversation, giving Zarb all the positives. Then Grasso turned up the heat. Zarb didn't hear a direct threat, but, as Zarb recalled, Grasso alluded to the NYSE's ability to regulate its member firms and enforce the best price rule. That caught Zarb's attention, enough for him to delay making a decision and continue sending shares to the floor.

Zarb's first meeting with Grasso would be the start of one of the most volatile relationships on Wall Street. At first they couldn't have been friendlier. Grasso did his homework and liked what he saw in Zarb. He was an Italian American from a working-class background who had reached the pinnacle of power in Washington as "Energy Czar" under former president Gerald Ford and then on Wall Street, running one of the street's top investment banks. Zarb was known as someone who didn't cut ethical corners no matter how much money was on the line. In Wall Street lingo, he was a real "Boy Scout."

Zarb, meanwhile, believed in Grasso and began assisting him to convince major Nasdaq listings, including Microsoft, to jump to the exchange. Grasso soon appointed Zarb to one of the Club's most important panels: the "independent" committee that nominates members for the NYSE's board of directors. Zarb and Grasso became frequent dinner partners. During their dinners, Zarb was surprised at Grasso's easygoing manner, given his reputation as a ruthless infighter with an explosive temper. Whether Zarb knew it or not, Grasso's charm offensive had a purpose. At the time, Grasso knew he needed help getting his people on the NYSE board if he wanted to be chairman someday, and it wasn't long before he began handing Zarb and the committee members a list of names of people he said would make good board candidates. It wasn't quite an order to pick from the list, but for the first time, Zarb noticed Grasso's eyes narrow and his voice become direct when talking about the various preferred candidates. In other words, he made it clear he was going to be disappointed, very disappointed, if one of his people was left out. Zarb and the committee got the message.

By the end of 1991, Donaldson was still married, having apparently made up with his wife. He was also settled into his office: the walls and bookshelves contained photos of him with various luminaries from his long years on Wall Street and in the government. There was, of course, one with his fellow old Skull and Bonesman, George H. W. Bush, and several from his Marine days. There was also a giant painting that hung on the wall depicting each piece of Donaldson's life up to his current status as chairman of the exchange.

One afternoon, Grasso was summoned to the sixth floor for a

strategy session. Settling into his chair, he realized the irony in his current position. For all of Donaldson's experience, he seemed unprepared for the job. Phelan had elevated the position of chairman of the Club to the stature of the chairman of the SEC or the chairman of the Federal Reserve. Donaldson, it appeared—at least to Grasso, but also to more and more of the Wall Street elite—was happy to coast. He wanted to enjoy the perks of running the Big Board: the traveling to meet with foreign business leaders, the new listing celebrations, and, of course, the ringing of the opening bell, while Grasso handled the heavy lifting, namely getting companies to list on the exchange and getting firms to send their trade orders to the floor. Indeed, Donaldson told Grasso he was ready to do some worldwide traveling to spread the brand name of the exchange around the globe, where the biggest pool of new listings could be found. He was also ready to do more speeches, not just in New York but also in Washington, D.C., speeches of a public policy nature that would let the competition, namely the Nasdaq, know that the guys in New York were serious players.

Grasso sat stewing with resentment. Now he knew why Donaldson gave him so much responsibility for the exchange's day-to-day operations. Grasso was doing all the work, and Donaldson wanted to take a world tour. Even worse, he didn't show any inclination to leave the chairman's office anytime soon. In fact, Donaldson was looking for a pay raise, at least according to Grasso's recollection. His estimated salary of $2 million paled in comparison to what he could make on the street and the millions more that Phelan was rumored to have made. Donaldson told Grasso he was going to the board to demand more, even as he cut Grasso's salary. Grasso had pulled down more than $1 million under Phelan and now was making around $900,000, he says. All Grasso could think about was that Donaldson had barely been on the job a year, yet he was complaining about his own pay and cutting Grasso's.

Grasso did all he could to keep his temper in check. His favorite movie was *The Godfather: Part II,* and so he knew what it meant to "keep your friends close but your enemies closer." He had just read Machiavelli's *The Prince.* Better than that, he had studied Muhammad Ali's famous knockout of George Foreman in Zaire, known as the "Rumble in the Jungle." Like Ali, he would knock out a bigger, stronger champion by lying low and then picking away at his opponent's weaknesses. And that's exactly what he did. During board meetings, when difficult questions about the exchange would perplex Donaldson, Grasso would jump in and finish his sentences. If Donaldson was attending a luncheon or a dinner, Grasso made sure he was glad-handing floor brokers or treating executives at the top brokerage firms to a spot at his favorite restaurants.

Grasso couldn't always keep his contempt to himself. One afternoon Donaldson asked Grasso to contact executives from the leading specialist firms for a little meet-and-greet in the exchange's dining room. It was too tempting: Donaldson had been on Wall Street for more than thirty years, yet he barely knew a trader on the floor of the place he was supposed to be running. Grasso came up with the perfect way to show how out of touch Donaldson was with the inner workings of the exchange. Before cocktails began, a line of about twelve leading executives from the specialist firms formed to shake hands with the chairman. Grasso stood by his boss's side as Donaldson shook hands in a stiff, robotic fashion. Before the line cleared, Grasso slipped out of place to grab one of the executives. "I'll make you a bet," Grasso said. "Go back over there, and shake his hand again. He won't even recognize you." The executive gave Grasso a quizzical look. Sure enough, Donaldson put out his hand as if the two had just met for the first time. Grasso soon came up with a nickname for his new boss: "the empty suit." Before long, it was all around the exchange.

Despite his anger, Grasso knew he couldn't unseat Donaldson through a series of cheap shots. The more he spoke with friends on Wall Street, the more he realized what he was up against. For all his knowledge of the inner workings of the exchange, for all his skills as a salesman, his support among the floor-trading community and people like Tully and Komansky, Grasso was still regarded by many of the Wall Street elite as an undereducated Italian guy from Queens. Now he needed to change that perception.

• • •

Every institution has its private event where rivals gather to poke fun at one another. Wall Street's hazing ritual is a yearly party held at the St. Regis Hotel in Manhattan for the Kappa Beta Phi fraternity, a night of steaks, wine, cigars, and a "show" that usually includes skits by new inductees, who are expected to dress in drag, sing, or recite poetry (and maybe get pelted with a dinner roll or two).

Kappa Beta Phi gave Grasso a different opportunity. And he jumped at it. In 1993, the list of fellow inductees included Michael Carpenter, the CEO of Kidder, Peabody; the takeover whiz Joseph Perella; Jon Corzine, then a bond trader at Goldman Sachs; a stock trader named Hugh Lowenstein; and James "Jimmy" Cayne, the CEO of Bear Stearns. It was enough to make Grasso salivate at the networking possibilities.

Cayne had come to Wall Street in his early thirties, after a divorce, a career change, and a stint as a professional bridge player. Getting remarried to a former beauty queen gave him all the motivation he needed to give up a bridge career in order to sell stocks and bonds. He started at a small firm, Lebenthal & Company, and later assembled a blue-chip client list that included the Tisch family. He quickly graduated to Bear Stearns, run by the legendary trader Alan "Ace" Greenberg, who shared Cayne's bridge habit.

From almost the moment he arrived at Bear Stearns, former colleagues say Cayne acted as if he wanted to run the place. For years, he drove Greenberg to work. At the same time he was cozying up to his boss, he was making the firm money and pushing competitors out of the way. It wasn't long before Cayne became one of Greenberg's top deputies. Cayne finally got his chance to be number one by assembling support on the firm's management committee and convincing Greenberg that it was time for him to be CEO (Greenberg stayed on for many years as chairman). Cayne's induction into the fraternity made it official to the rest of Wall Street.

For about a week, the group practiced its skit with a professional acting coach. Grasso barely knew Cayne, but during the rehearsals, Grasso and Cayne found plenty to talk about. Soon they were discussing Grasso's frustration with Donaldson. At least Greenberg had built Bear Stearns into a major firm, Cayne thought as he listened to Grasso complain. No one doubted that Greenberg was the best trader on Wall Street. The way Grasso made it seem, Donaldson was one of the laziest CEOs in corporate America.

Cayne sympathized with his new friend's plight as the big show loomed. Cayne took the stage wearing a large brown wig and black stockings and began reading his poem from a series of playing cards. The crowd went wild with catcalls.

Grasso was up next. Like Cayne, Grasso was dressed in drag, in high heels, stockings, and a large blond wig. He was also wearing a pair of huge fake breasts. The crowd burst out laughing when Grasso took center stage. His skit was a takeoff on "White Christmas." In Grasso's version, the song ran "I'm dreaming of a new Wall Street with little Italians everywhere." The crowd erupted into a hail of dinner rolls that rained on his bald head. Afterward, Grasso was greeted by many in the crowd who loved his skit and thought his costume was a hoot. For all the laughs, the message in his skit was real, and the connections he would make that night, the most enduring one being Cayne, would go a long way toward making his dreams come true.

In many ways 1992 was a watershed year. The overhang of the 1987 crash had officially ended, and the markets were finally improving thanks to low interest rates. New listings continued to pour into the exchange as the IPO market revived. That year, the stock exchange threw itself a 200th birthday party. Former Soviet premier Mikhail Gorbachev and former president Ronald Reagan paid a visit. Donaldson made news by touring China and meeting with top economic leaders there. But the most important event was the renewed challenge from one of the NYSE's most potent rivals, the Nasdaq.

The National Association of Securities Dealers, which ran the computerized Nasdaq stock market, was tired of being considered the minor leagues of the stock exchanges. But now it saw an opening, coming to the conclusion that the NYSE under Donaldson was ripe for a fall. The opportunity hit home when Donaldson bobbled a series of hearings on something called "payment for order flow," which involved brokers kicking back money to mutual funds and other large institutional investors. Payment for order flow was one of those inside games that few outside Wall Street understood. It was becoming a hidden tax on the average investor, particularly mutual fund investors and pensioners. The problem was that funds were sending their trades to brokers who wrote them the biggest checks (or in some cases gave them the biggest gifts, such as computer systems, high-speed cable lines, and so on), not to the ones who got the best price for a trade. The extra cost was paid by shareholders because trades were completed not based on the best price but on how much money was paid for order flow.

Prior to one hearing before a congressional committee, Donaldson brought Grasso into his office to give him a refresher course on the subject. Grasso's argument was simple: the system of paying for order flow was corrupt because it warped the traders' priorities. "Listen, this is a breach of your basic responsibility you have to the customer," he said. "You have an obligation to the customer to complete trades at the best price, period. It's pretty simple." Donaldson had that look on his face that Grasso saw every time he ventured into a subject he didn't know; his eyes would narrow, and he would peer at Grasso and repeat what he had just been told. Grasso reminded him to stick with a simple message during the hearing: that payment for order flow screws the small investor.

Donaldson looked confident and assured as the hearings began. He wore a dark suit, and, with his hair perfectly combed, he cut an impressive figure. But as confident as Donaldson looked, he sounded as if he were lost. He must have known he had lost his audience because he began gesticulating with his hands as if he were straining to make his point.

At NASD headquarters on K Street in Washington, D.C., CEO Joseph Hardiman had made the hearing required viewing for his management staff—and they were cheering. On the eleventh floor, a young marketing executive named Patrick Healy was holding court in his office while the hearings played in the background. Donaldson's poor performance encouraged Healy in his belief that they had a shot at taking attention away from the Big Board.

Hardiman, who attended the hearings, was thinking the same thing. The Nasdaq had been created by Gordon Macklin in 1971 as a computerized alternative to the specialist system, and since then it had evolved into a legitimate stock market with traders, known as Nasdaq "market makers," bidding on stocks through their computer terminals. Initially, the Nasdaq was heralded by the press as the future of stock trading; more than a few financial journalists wrote obituaries for the NYSE and the floor, which they believed couldn't compete with the efficiency and speed of computerized trading. But for years, the Nasdaq failed to live up to its advance billing. It boasted lower listing fees and quick, efficient computerized trading of stocks, but companies continued to have their shares listed on the NYSE. The 1987 crash didn't help matters; the NYSE's promise to have a human being ready and able to make markets even when prices fell precipitously proved superior in the crisis. Many market makers simply refused to answer the telephones or to complete trades.

Hardiman had taken control of the NASD in 1987 and had been working hard to improve the system that had failed customers so miserably during the crash. By 1992, the NASD's trading system could handle crash-level selling pressure. Now that Hardiman had fixed the technical problems, he was ready to tackle a bigger problem. Since its inception, the Nasdaq had clearly been the minor leagues, a place for stocks of companies such as American International Group (AIG) to gain market value and meet other financial benchmarks before graduating. Healy remembers the day Hardiman called an off-site meeting. Hardiman's game plan was to create an "us against them" mentality. His marching orders were simple: employees like Healy were to meet with the leading companies that traded on the Nasdaq market and remind them where they had gotten their start, and which exchange had all but ignored them when they were nobodies.

Hardiman didn't stop there. He increased listing fees that were excruciatingly low ($5,000 or less compared to the $500,000 charged by the NYSE) and plowed the money into advertising and promotion. Hardiman opened an office in Silicon Valley, betting on a continued influx of new technology for companies looking to go public. Many of them would fail, many would tread water for years, but those that survived would be part of a new revolution.

Hardiman now had to figure out a way to contain Grasso. He had seen too many companies bolt to the NYSE under pressure from Grasso—and heard the stories about how he had squeezed order flow from the big brokerage houses that were members of the NASD as well as the NYSE. He also knew Grasso had big plans to steal more companies from the Nasdaq; Hardiman ordered his staff to follow Grasso's every move, which meant defending the Nasdaq companies Grasso called the "fearsome foursome": Microsoft, Cisco Systems, Intel, and Dell.

Thanks to Hardiman's outreach, Grasso was now bumping up against a brick wall in his hunt for the big four listings. It appeared that for the first time, a sense of camaraderie spread among the top tier of the Nasdaq listings. Thanks to Hardiman, the Nasdaq stock market was no longer the minor leagues. The companies that listed there considered themselves renegades who had defied expectations and come into their own without the help of the Wall Street establishment but on an upstart stock market that ignored the old money and catered to the emerging entrepreneurial class.

Hardiman began the second phase of his plan, ordering his marketing guru Brian Holland to come up with an advertising campaign that would take the Nasdaq's image to the next level. Hardiman knew what he was up against. He did some market research and found if you asked people to name a stock market, 82 percent of the time they would name the NYSE, 39 percent the rapidly shrinking American Stock Exchange, and only 22 percent the Nasdaq. The advertising blitz would change all that. It was the first time an exchange of any kind had ever advertised.

The Nasdaq's new campaign played on the image that Hardiman wanted. The Nasdaq represented the future. It would be "The Stock Market for the Next 100 Years." For the Club, it was a wake-up call like no other. Grasso recalls sitting in his office when he first saw the ads on television. "What the fuck is this?" he snapped before dialing up Donaldson and alerting him to the move. Then Hardiman upped the ante by doing some negative ads, taking direct aim at the NYSE. These featured testimonials from Microsoft CEO Bill Gates and the chief executives at other Nasdaq companies suggesting that the NYSE was behind the times. "That bastard," Grasso thought. He wanted to respond in kind, but it wasn't that easy: ads like these cost money, big money. To launch a campaign like the one by the NASD might break the bank since the exchange had made only about $40 million in 1992 and not much more in 1993. Raising the floor traders' fees was out of the question, since they were just getting back on their feet after several lean years.

Grasso was in a box, and he knew it. So he called Donaldson and asked him to set up a meeting with Hardiman and issue a not-so-subtle threat: pull back the ads or face the consequences. Hardiman was unfazed. Grasso then laid it on the line to Hardiman: "If you don't stop the ads attacking the exchange, we're going to nuke K Street" with an ad blitz never before seen in Wall Street history. The NASD, Hardiman responded, was just getting started—he would enjoy the competition.

Grasso was seething, and he promised Hardiman a battle to the death. Hardiman said he was ready. Donaldson said virtually nothing, and when Hardiman returned to Washington he relayed Grasso's threat to the staff, as well as Donaldson's relative silence during the meeting. "Get ready for war," Hardiman said.

As it turned out, Grasso's response wasn't exactly the nuclear bomb he had threatened. Whether for the lack of money or imagination, the NYSE's first ad campaign ever seemed to underscore the Club's stodgy image. The exchange was "Not Just a Marketplace, but a Way of Doing Business." When the ads first aired, Hardiman could barely contain his glee; Holland was given carte blanche to ramp up the pressure even more. By the end of 1993, bland, unexciting Joe Hardiman, who could never compete with Grasso head-to-head as a salesman, whose résumé paled compared to that of the great Bill Donaldson, had done something remarkable: he had stopped the outflow of major companies leaving the NASD for the Club. The Nasdaq, which had started at the bottom, had begun leapfrogging the other exchanges in terms of trading volume. Grasso knew the numbers better than anyone.

The executive-suite battles between Grasso and Donaldson and between the Club and the NASD barely seemed to register on the trading floor. By the early 1990s, floor traders were feasting on a return of the good times. Though there had been a crackdown on drinking and drugs at the trading stations, the party raged on in the exchange's luncheon club, in the bathrooms, anywhere traders could get away with it. So many traders at specialist firm LaBranche & Co. were now in a rehab center that traders at the firm simply referred to the center as "Camp LaBranche." Lunch was always a big thing on the floor. Gone were the turkey sandwiches and pizza that had been standard fare during the lean years. Traders and brokers were wolfing down steaks and lobsters at their stations—or sneaking away for an hour to a nearby watering hole, Harry's at the Hanover. The floor always had a frat house flavor, but now that the traders were giddy with profits it got out of control.

Grasso's relationship with the floor had always been a complex one. The big white-shoe firms considered the floor the boondocks of Wall Street, populated by Neanderthals and misfits who had nowhere else to go. But Grasso had long and deep ties to the people at the big floor firms, like Peter Kellogg, the CEO of Spear, Leeds & Kellogg; Billy Johnston, now the senior partner at LaBranche & Co.; Christopher Quick, who ran a specialist operation for the Quick & Reilly discount brokerage; and many others going back to his days as a listing clerk. Longtime floor trader Walter Schubert felt comfortable enough around Grasso that he turned to Grasso for support when he decided to tell his coworkers he was gay. Schubert worried he would be treated like a pariah because of the floor's macho culture. But Grasso told Schubert he would watch his back. "Schubby, this is a historic moment," Grasso said. "It's the first time a dago president of the exchange ever hugged an openly gay member."

But Grasso also viewed the floor as a means to extend his power. The boom on Wall Street handed floor traders power beyond their status in the financial hierarchy. Many of the floor traders and specialists owned seats, and their prices were once again on the rise to Phelan levels, trading above $1 million and making them the de facto owners—very rich owners—of the Club. Grasso had by now made major inroads with executives at the big Wall Street firms, but he knew he couldn't control the most powerful people on Wall Street. He could control the floor, and that's what he did, through assignments to important committees, by directing new listings to the firms in his inner circle, and, increasingly, through intimidation, floor traders say. The exchange was their direct regulator through audits and enforcement actions and Grasso, traders say, began to figure out how to make their lives miserable if he needed to get his way.

By early 1994, Grasso had already assembled his senior staff for what he believed would be Donaldson's inevitable demise and his own ascendancy to the chairmanship of the exchange. Grasso hired a former SEC official named Ed Kwalwasser to be chief of the exchange's regulatory department. Cathy Kinney, who had worked with Grasso for nearly twenty years, was now responsible for the floor; the traders didn't like it, Grasso heard back, because of her "lack of experience." Grasso chalked it up to sexism; the male-dominated floor just didn't want to be taking orders from a woman. Grasso could have switched Kinney with Bob Britz, who was now head of technology, but he decided against it. It's about time the "animals grew up," he said. Anyway all roads were leading to the top, and that was himself.

But Grasso's favorite was a thirty-eight-year-old whiz kid named David Damijan, who headed the NYSE's listings department. For all intents and purposes Damijan was Grasso's number two, but even Grasso would admit that he could just as easily have been number one. Grasso and Damijan had worked together for more than a decade, and during that time they had grown close. Both had grown up working class, and their street-kid personas often boiled over when they disagreed on various issues, with expletives flying and once nearly a fist. But they always found common ground. With Damijan at his side, Grasso was able to snare some of the biggest listings of his life, including stealing AIG from the NASD in 1985. For all these reasons Grasso used to say that if he died a day after he was named chairman, the exchange would be in great hands, led by Damijan.

The Grasso-Damijan team was certainly showing results. They were raking in record new listings, and the share of NYSE stocks that actually traded at the exchange remained steady at over 80 percent. They also had a common enemy in Donaldson, who they believed took credit for these achievements in press releases and interviews with the business press. But Grasso held his tongue, because inside the exchange, there was no mistaking the source of the achievement, including among a growing number of board members who had slowly come to the conclusion that without Grasso, they would be lost. Just how lost became excruciatingly clear after Donaldson briefed the board on his latest trip to South Korea. One of Donaldson's big initiatives was to increase foreign listings, which, to his credit, had grown under his watch. Presumably, that was why he went to Korea. But Donaldson reported back to the board that he had decided to spend two extra days in the country, hanging out at the demilitarized zone to tour the tunnels that had been used during the Korean War some forty years earlier. "I wonder how many listings he got down there," Grasso thought as he listened to Donaldson describe his trip. The board was as silent as Grasso, but later, Grasso discovered that many were thinking the same thing.

When friends and business associates heard some of these stories, they urged Grasso to try to nuke Donaldson immediately. Grasso always came back with his favorite answer: "Remember Zaire!" Grasso hadn't really mellowed since his early days; he'd just gotten smarter. Whether through reading Machiavelli or watching Don Corleone, Grasso had learned that time was on his side. And then there was his favorite heavyweight fight, Ali's defeat of George Foreman in Zaire. Ali had won against tremendous odds, he said, and so would he. A few more punches, and Donaldson wouldn't know what hit him.

Grasso's obsession with taking out Donaldson was put on hold, albeit temporarily, amid tragedy. Damijan, Grasso's right hand, was diagnosed with leukemia, and within seven months he had died. For Grasso, watching a guy he had known since 1979, someone who had become his closest confidant, die so young (he was only thirty-eight) was gut-wrenching. As Damijan got sicker and sicker, Grasso began to spend many afternoons in the hospital at his side, and he came to realize why he liked Damijan so much: he was a younger version of Grasso. Both came from humble backgrounds, both had explosive tempers, and both believed they could run the Club at a moment's notice. They also had something else in common: their disdain for Donaldson. During their frequent conversations, right up until Damijan's last days, they would talk about Donaldson's lack of vision and leadership and how they would run the place when they had a chance.

When Damijan died in the summer of 1993, Grasso declared it an unofficial day of mourning. The funeral service was held in New Canaan, where Damijan lived. Donaldson agreed to buy ads in *The New York Times* and *The Wall Street Journal* commemorating Damijan's years of service at the exchange. During the funeral, Grasso gave a speech mostly about the great times they had over the years, recalling with a smile their travels to California to meet Willie Brown, the powerful speaker of the California Assembly, whom they had convinced to kill legislation that was bad for the exchange, and their dealings with Phelan, who often treated the duo like wayward children. Grasso smiled through most of the speech, but when it was over, he couldn't help but cry.

Damijan had always dreamed of owning a home in the ritzy town of New Canaan. And that's exactly what he had done, buying a beautiful pad for his wife and two daughters in the swanky town that was home to more than its fair share of old-money types and new-money millionaires. There was just one problem: he wasn't a millionaire—far from it. His yearly salary of around $500,000 couldn't begin to pay for his expensive lifestyle, and when he died, Grasso discovered that he was in massive debt, owing more than $1 million on two mortgages and various other bills, which his family couldn't pay. Without help, they would lose their home.

Grasso went to Donaldson with a solution: have the exchange pay off some of the debt. But Donaldson said no, as Grasso recalls the conversation; ads are one thing, but a big payment to the family of an employee was something entirely different. Not as far as Grasso was concerned. If it wasn't for people like Damijan, Grasso believed, there wouldn't be a stock exchange. "If you don't do this, you can run this fucking place without me!" Grasso boomed before storming out of Donaldson's office.

News traveled fast among the upper echelon at the Club, and it wasn't long before Dan Tully heard that Grasso was leaving. By now Tully wasn't just a board member; he was both the CEO of Merrill Lynch and the vice chairman of the exchange. Not long after his conversation with Donaldson, Grasso received an urgent message from his secretary: "Mr. Tully is on the phone." Grasso picked up the receiver and heard Tully's reassuring voice. "Dickey boy, it's your uncle Danny," Tully said. "I want you down here at Vesey Street [the home of Merrill Lynch] to talk this through." Tully said one more thing before hanging up the phone: "You are not going anywhere . . . I'll take care of this thing."

Grasso's meeting with Tully didn't last long, but it didn't have to. Tully said he would personally make sure Damijan's debts were paid (Grasso didn't know if he ultimately convinced Donaldson to put up exchange money or simply paid it out of his own pocket, and he never asked.) And he said something else: now was not the time for Grasso to quit anything; his time to get the big job was rapidly approaching. All he had to do was wait it out and keep doing what he was doing. Grasso said he would and left Tully's office feeling like a new man.

By now, Donaldson's support on the board was rapidly disappearing. A group of executives, many with backgrounds not that much different than Grasso's, were clawing their way from the trading pits and brokerage offices to top management positions. Grano was now the number two at PaineWebber. Komansky was in line to replace Tully as CEO of Merrill. But the most valuable person emerging in Grasso's career was a veteran financier named Kenneth "Ken" Langone.

When Grasso met Langone in the early 1980s, Langone was already a Wall Street legend. In 1981, Grasso listed the company he had cofounded, Home Depot, and since then "Depot," as it was known on the floor, had become one of the biggest companies to trade on the NYSE.

Langone had been working on Wall Street since the early 1960s. He had brought Ross Perot's EDS public later in the decade, and with his investment in Depot, he was now one of the richest men in America. More than that, he was a player at the exchange. He owned two seats, and his partner at Home Depot, Bernard Marcus, was now a NYSE board member. Both viewed Grasso as one of Wall Street's rising stars, especially Langone, who marveled at Grasso's ability as a salesman. Grasso was not just great at getting listings, he was also great at keeping them at the exchange. Langone couldn't get out of his head how Grasso once allowed a company to hold its board meetings at the exchange's own large boardroom. In marketing textbooks it was called "cross promotion," but Langone called it "fucking brilliant."

Unlike Grasso, Donaldson's obsession wasn't the exchange or its competition with the Nasdaq, but something closer to home: his salary. He began to push the board for both a contract extension and a pay raise. Donaldson's move sent shock waves through the Club's leadership ranks. The markets were improving, and so were the various measurements of the exchange's health: listings were up, and exchange-listed stocks continued to trade at the exchange more than 80 percent of the time. Yet the board had become convinced that this had less to do with Donaldson's leadership than with Grasso's hard work.

The knock on Grasso had always been his temperament and stature. The new Grasso, by contrast, was much smoother, at least in public, and much more calculating. The patience Ali had shown in the Foreman fight became Grasso's guiding principle; he knew he couldn't take Donaldson out immediately, but over the past four years, he had built a case, brick by brick, that Donaldson should leave. Donaldson's demise was also self-inflicted: his demands for more money and the impression that he delegated every important task to Grasso played a key role in his ouster. But Grasso's coming into his own also played a part. Grasso now had a presence. He was no longer the wild kid who wanted to rule the world. In board meetings he was self-assured and confident. He stepped up his appearances and found his voice as a public speaker. The exchange's PR staff used to prepare long speeches for Grasso to give about issues affecting the exchange. Grasso now threw them away. "I don't talk about things I don't know," he said. "And when I know something, I don't need notes."

The board's distaste for Donaldson's leadership and his management style was the topic of a memo from Jeffrey Hyman of Hewitt Associates, a compensation consultant who had been working with the exchange. The subject of the memo was an attempt by Donaldson to receive a "materially higher level of compensation" over the objections of several board members. Donaldson was making an estimated $2 million a year, but he believed he should be paid along the lines of Phelan, who had earned close to $6 million, according to people at the exchange.

But the memo didn't stop there. In stark terms, it also described many of Donaldson's shortcomings, which were hidden by his gold-plated résumé: "Some of the scuttlebutt on Donaldson (which I picked up from members of the Compensation Committee) is that he has a tendency to self destruct in his dealings with other people. The perception on The Street is that he lacks political savvy (astonishing given his former governmental status), and that he can trip all over himself trying to bulldoze people into submission. Although I had no first hand experience of these foibles, at least not up until this point in time, Donaldson's lesser attractive [sic] characteristics are beginning to emerge."

Those "lesser attractive characteristics," as Hyman's memo pointed out, had clearly put Donaldson's future with the exchange in jeopardy. "He does not understand the extent of resistance to his requests, nor is he entirely cognizant of just how much each Committee member understands exactly what Donaldson is trying to do, and he does not realize the virulent reaction some Committee members are experiencing." In the memo Hyman said that Donaldson wanted to avoid the NYSE's compensation committee altogether and make his case directly to the committee chairman, Goodyear CEO Stanley Gault. "Personally, I think Donaldson is out of his mind," Hyman continued. "His bullheadedness and lack of process skills may actually turn even more Board members against him. This could make his bid for a contract extension in 1995 untenable."

Bob Zito was among the first people outside the members of the board of directors to know just how little time Donaldson had left. Zito was Donaldson's PR guy, but his heart was with Grasso. He had met Grasso in the mid-1980s, when he came to the exchange to run its PR and marketing department. He had left in 1990 to work as the vice president of PR and marketing for Sony Corp., and now he was back running the Club's PR department. He was reporting directly to Donaldson, but the buzz in and around the exchange was that it was only a matter of time before Zito would be calling Grasso "boss." And that's the way Zito wanted it. The two made an odd couple when they were together. Grasso was short and bald and wore glasses. Zito was tall, with a full head of blond hair spiked on top, and resembled an Italian-American Rod Stewart. But Zito and Grasso shared a vision for the exchange. The brand, they believed, had been wasted under Donaldson, even deteriorated, as the Nasdaq gained credibility.

On Wall Street, the need for a change at the exchange was now becoming obvious. In mid-1994, colleagues on the Street approached Grasso about their desire to get Donaldson out. Grasso told them to keep their powder dry, at least for now. That's because the "Dump Donaldson Movement" was already in high gear. By early 1994, Dan Tully appeared to have convinced most of the board not to extend Donaldson's contract beyond 1995, when it was set to expire, and to make Grasso CEO. The situation was politically dicey; the exchange had a long history of leaders, most of whom had left of their own accord. But even as his support waned, Donaldson seemed intent on staying, and he alerted various members of the board that he wanted a contract extension. At first the board was noncommittal, but that would soon change.

"You're going to get a call from Donaldson; his wife died and he needs help with the obituary," Grasso told Zito one afternoon in mid-1994.

Zito didn't know much about Donaldson's personal life, so Grasso filled him in on some of the details, such as Donaldson's affair with Jane Morrison, and their love child. Zito, meanwhile, did a little research on his own. Donaldson's wife, Evan Burger, had been healthy—that is, until the past week or so, when she had fallen into a coma and died on a Thursday night. Donaldson soon had had her cremated. Less than a week after her death, Donaldson was back at the exchange, Grasso and others recall, attending a dinner that exchange officials had with their wives before board meetings. At one point, Lori Grasso approached Donaldson and asked an obvious question: Are you all right? Are you sure you should be here? Donaldson said he was just fine. In fact, he indicated that he was looking forward to the board meeting.

Lori Grasso was taken aback by Donaldson's upbeat attitude, and she wasn't alone. The rumor mill had turned from nasty to vicious, with scurrilous and obviously false rumors spreading like wildfire, particularly on the floor, where traders wondered how Donaldson could seem so at ease just after a tragedy. Some even asked if Donaldson could be implicated in his wife's death. Why else, these traders said, would he have her body cremated right after she died? When Grasso heard the rumor, he just shrugged it off. "It's bullshit," he told Zito, but "it does give you an indication what people think of him."

The memorial service for Evan Burger Donaldson was held at a fancy church on Fifth Avenue, in Manhattan's Upper East Side. It was an event fitting Mrs. Donaldson's stature within her community of the rich and powerful of Manhattan. About two thousand people attended the elaborate affair. Grasso noticed a line of limos pulling up to the church where women and men dressed to the nines were ushered in for the services. Much of the service went as most memorial services go; it was a solemn day to commemorate the life of some-one who had had many friends and had taken her position in New York society seriously. Grasso had always admired Evan as a smart, nice woman with a charitable heart.

Grasso didn't know much about Donaldson's relationship with his kids, though he had a feeling that it was strained given his affair with Morrison. But if it was strained before Evan's death, it appeared to some in the audience even more strained now, as Donaldson's children went to the podium to speak their minds. Those at the service recalled that Donaldson's daughter gave an emotional speech filled with tears and anger as Donaldson sat mortified. Grasso, like many in the audience, just looked straight ahead. Zito, the former Sony Entertainment flack, was in the back of the church and recalls turn-ing to a colleague and saying: "And I thought I left the entertainment industry."

But the scene got even more bizarre when it was the son's chance to speak. At one point, he spoke about his mother's final hours and how he and his dad had gone to see her. They wanted to ask if there was anything she wanted to say about their final years together. As Grasso and several eyewitnesses recall, the son explained that he told his mother, who was comatose, to "please forgive me and dad for all the trouble" they caused her. He told the audience that his mother couldn't speak at the time, but she did respond by "taking a piss!"

Donaldson's son, Matt, confirms in an interview that he made the statement, but he says that his remarks weren't meant to criticize his father, but to explain "my relationship with my mother." Donald-son's daughter, Kim, says she may have been angry about her mom's death, but her "anger in that speech was not targeted toward my fa-ther." Whatever was said, Zito says he soon received a telephone call from a reporter at *The Wall Street Journal,* who seemed to have some idea of what had transpired at the service and, more important, in Donaldson's private life. Zito remained stoic as the reporter rattled off the sordid details. "You're going with this?" Zito asked. The re-porter said yes, but he first wanted a response from Donaldson. Zito said he would get back to him. "What the fuck do I do?" Zito asked

Grasso. For a guy who knew how to handle any crisis at the exchange, Grasso wanted no part of this one. "You got to talk to Donaldson."

Donaldson, as Zito recalls, suggested that they should deny it all. Zito said that based on everything he knew about the reporter and the facts of the situation, that approach wouldn't work. Zito suggested instead that they make a deal with the paper: they would give it a great story in exchange for killing this one. The best story he could think of, he told Donaldson, was the one that was now making the rounds through the rumor mill of the exchange and had even reached a journalist at *The New York Times:* that Grasso was preparing to succeed Donaldson.

Donaldson didn't react at first. He listened and thought about what Zito was saying. Zito reckoned that Donaldson was still pushing for a contract extension. In other words, by killing the story of his affair and love child, he would be killing his chances of remaining as chairman. "I'll get back to you," Donaldson said.

A few days later, one Saturday night, Zito was home when the phone rang. "It's Bill," Donaldson said. "Make the deal."

Donaldson says he can't remember any such conversation with Zito and he says that he had no intention of extending his contract further than six months after its expiration date in June 1995 regardless of what happened at the funeral. Others dispute that account, saying he wanted to stay at the exchange longer. One thing that can't be disputed is the fact that the *Journal* as well as the *Times* got a story on how he was preparing to hand over power to Grasso. Donaldson got a reprieve from a public airing of his private life and Zito took credit for the deft political gamesmanship. On the board, Donaldson's biggest critics, Tully and Bernard Marcus, the cofounder of Home Depot, were now joined by other board members, all of them growing wary of Donaldson's demands for more money, his work ethic, and now his private life.

Stanley Gault, the head of the compensation committee, was in charge of making it as easy for Donaldson to step down as possible. Gault lived in Ohio, but he came into the city one afternoon and called Donaldson and Grasso for a meeting to discuss the future leadership of the exchange. Grasso had heard through his contacts on the board that the job was all but his—unless, of course, he said something stupid during the meeting. He made sure he was on his best behavior.

As the three sat down, Gault asked Grasso who should run the exchange in the future. This time Grasso didn't threaten to leave the exchange directly. But he did make it clear that he was ready for a bigger role, either at the exchange or somewhere else. "Stanley," he said, "I had a good working relationship with Bill, and if the board doesn't want to continue with Bill, I will be honored to be chairman or work with the person you guys bring in until an orderly transition is complete."

Gault thanked Grasso and Donaldson, but the thought of losing Grasso was apparently too much for the board to handle. In mid-October, Tully proposed the following: make Grasso chairman and CEO. No search committee, no leaking of possible alternatives to see how the choice might be taken by the press and the public. Just put Grasso up for a vote, yea or nay.

The board agreed, and the decision was unanimous. Donaldson went into Grasso's office, congratulated him on his appointment, and said the two of them should ring the closing bell, which they did. Grasso addressed the membership on the floor to wild applause, while Donaldson stood by silently. Donaldson was sent packing, but not without a $3 million retirement package. By the end of 1995, Donaldson had married Jane Morrison and would soon become chairman of the insurance giant Aetna, where, after a mediocre eighteen-month tenure and cashing in a slew of stock options, he would become richer by as much as $150 million, according to estimates.

Stanley Gault and the rest of the board may not have thought Donaldson was worth the money, but they knew Grasso was. Now that he was chairman and Wall Street was booming with IPOs, technology companies, and a rush of new investors coming into the market, they openly worried that the exchange couldn't keep talent from fleeing to better jobs on Wall Street. Gault's solution: make it easier for them to stay. "If the organization is to remain successful," he said, according to the minutes of one board meeting, "we will need to staff the exchange with what the committee has come to call world-class talent. To attract and retain talent, we will be competing directly for people with world-class organizations particularly at the senior management levels."

Gault went on to describe a new compensation plan, put together by an outside consultant, in which top producers at their exchange would be paid based on their performance, graded and paid based on similar positions in outside companies, such as the Wall Street firms Goldman Sachs and Merrill Lynch. Top officials at the exchange would also be able to defer their income into a series of retirement accounts, with guaranteed interest rates much like those of the old corporate pension funds.

The exchange was hardly a major company; it had barely $500 million in revenues, around $40 million in profits, and fewer than 1,500 employees (not counting the floor traders), but Grasso and his team would now be paid like top executives from Wall Street. Grasso would earn $2.16 million in his first year as chairman, a nice raise from the roughly $1 million he had taken home the previous year, but there would be bigger paydays ahead, not to mention various awards and incentives to keep the listings and the order flow coming.

Grasso, meanwhile, was prepared to earn every dime. He reminded people what Phelan had once told him: "You really don't know how great this place is until you're on the outside looking in." In Phelan's mind, competitors come and go, but one of the most enduring brands on Wall Street, in all of corporate America for that matter, was the New York Stock Exchange. It was a brand that had taken two hundred years to build, one that every man and woman on Main Street equated with Wall Street and American finance. Put into the right hands, the brand could withstand any threat. Grasso believed with every fiber of his body that the brand was finally in the right hands, and now he was gearing up for the battle of his life with Hardiman and his computers. "They're not going to know what hit them," he promised his staff, now that he was finally King of the Club.

4

THE LITTLE GUY IN THE DARK SUIT

Dick Grasso's office was on the sixth floor of the exchange. It was about half the size of the one Donaldson and Phelan had occupied, but it was twice as cluttered with photos, plaques, and posters. This "deal memorabilia," assembled from the companies that had listed on the exchange over the years, was Grasso's proof of his own success. Grasso's favorite, however, was a trophy of a different kind. He loved to show off an original photograph of the great boxing referee Arthur Mercante standing over a knocked-down Muhammad Ali. That photograph was Grasso's talisman: he identified with Ali, who had gone on to become the greatest fighter of all time.

Grasso was ready to get up from the canvas himself. He couldn't wait to spread out his trophies in a larger space and, more important, take Donaldson's job. But Donaldson, the "empty suit," in Grasso's words, made it clear he intended to remain as chairman and CEO—and in his office—until the day his contract ended in June 1995. While he was milking the last from his position, Donaldson decided to do some traveling to Latin America and Asia for good measure.

When Donaldson's last night finally arrived, the exchange threw a party—literally. The black-tie affair was held across the street from the exchange's headquarters at Federal Hall to commemorate his chairmanship and officially pass the torch to Grasso. The party was fairly intimate, just one hundred of the most powerful members of the Club, including board members such as Merrill CEO Dan Tully. After the obligatory steak dinner served with expensive wine, there was a program of speakers: Grasso, then Donaldson's former partners Dan Lufkin and Dick Jenrette. Grasso manfully praised Donaldson. Lufkin regaled the crowd with some war stories about the founding of DLJ and how it had been Donaldson's idea to make history by making it the first brokerage firm to go public and list on the stock exchange in 1969.

Then it was Jenrette's turn. Jenrette, whom Grasso wished had taken the chairmanship four years earlier, is considered one of the most decent men on Wall Street. Donaldson called him a "bear" because he was such a lovable guy. He spoke about Donaldson's many achievements: how he had left the firm for a successful career in politics in the 1970s, then had become dean of the newly created Yale School of Management before being named head of the NYSE in 1990. But he ended the speech with a little gallows humor. "Dick," Jenrette said, looking over at Grasso with a smile on his face, "every place Bill has left went down the tubes." DLJ's stock was crushed after he left the firm in the early 1970s, the Republicans had lost the presidency in 1976, and Harvard had become the number one business school after he left Yale. "Good luck," he added to applause and laughter.

Grasso just smiled and said to himself, "You wish." The dinner, meanwhile, dragged on for a few more hours. Grasso thought it would be rude to leave early. But Lori insisted. "Dick, it's ten minutes to midnight, the party's over," she said. "You don't understand," Grasso said, pointing to Donaldson, who was still holding court. "He doesn't think it's over."

At the NASD, however, they knew Donaldson's reign had been over for a long time. "Grasso's been running the place for years," Hardiman, the NASD chairman, told his staff when Donaldson's last days approached. Indeed, Grasso had already begun to lay the groundwork for a massive change in the Club's direction. In early 1995, Grasso told the heads of his business units that they would now be graded on results. The exchange, he believed, had spent far too many years riding on its reputation. Grasso had witnessed the NASD's power grab firsthand while making listing calls. He still could not convince many of the big NASD companies to switch sides.

Grasso wanted that changed immediately. It wasn't long before he set up a stock exchange office in Silicon Valley and began meeting with top technology companies during his frequent trips to the West Coast. Many of the tech CEOs gave him a cool reception. They considered the NYSE an interloper in a world where the Nasdaq both ruled and had given them their start. Some were downright rude. Grasso fumed as executives from Intel all but laughed at his sales pitch that the NYSE and its floor could better serve a tech company's needs. "Who do these guys think they are?" he asked the head of the NYSE West Coast office, Tom Rathjen, before cutting his trip short and returning to New York. He quickly got his frustration under control, however, and continued to woo the outfits no matter how much they laughed at him.

Back at home, things ran more smoothly. Cathy Kinney was now executive vice president in charge of new listings. She was ordered to give Grasso regular updates on potential new targets in the competition. After Damijan's death, Grasso elevated Bob Britz to be the other executive VP in charge of floor activities. Grasso told him he wanted to know every trade that was executed outside the four walls of the exchange. Frank Ashen was now the head of human resources and appointed to the new post of chief ethics officer.

He made Zito the head of marketing in addition to his PR duties and told him to take the gloves off. Zito may have had the toughest job at the exchange aside from Grasso's because, at least in Grasso's mind, if anything had suffered under Donaldson, it was the Club's brand and image. Grasso told Zito to spare no expense—and no amount of gimmicks—to make the necessary repairs. Zito responded with a thirty-page plan of attack. The exchange's ad budget would grow exponentially. The biggest change: the opening and closing bells, which had been perfunctory affairs, would be bigger and grander, a listings draw for CEOs looking for free publicity.

Grasso then needed a front man, someone who could pull off the ceremonies when he was out of town. For that he tapped his old buddy Billy Johnston. Johnston had offered Grasso so many jobs in the past at his specialist firm that Grasso thought he would return the favor. More important, Grasso had seen Johnston in action for years and believed he was not just a good trader and a party animal with a wild sense of humor but also a good salesman. With his thick white beard and easygoing manner, he could handle the inevitable company complaints about floor traders not doing enough to support stock prices, which continued to grow as volume surged through the 1990s. There was also no better guy to watch Grasso's back with the volatile floor trading community than one of their own.

It didn't take long for Johnston to accept the offer. He had spent about thirty years as a specialist, the last seven as one of the top partners running LaBranche & Co., until, that is, Michael LaBranche—"the kid," as he was known by the old-timers—was ready to run the family-owned enterprise himself. By the end of 1995, Mike LaBranche was ready to take charge, and Grasso decided to make Johnston president of the New York Stock Exchange.

Collectively, these were the people who were supposed to mount the toughest competitive battle in the two-hundred-year history of the exchange. Grasso had known them all for a long time and believed they were good at their jobs; but most of all, he believed they were loyal, not just to the exchange but to Grasso personally. It was the perfect combination for Grasso's ultimate goal: to reduce the Nasdaq to rubble as he promoted the exchange and himself as never before.

Grasso's opening salvo came after an unusual request from Zito himself. Zito had a wild idea, so wild he didn't know if even the publicity-hungry Grasso would bite. He wanted to put television reporters on the floor of the exchange, something that had never before been done, not even considered. Reporters were barely allowed in the building, much less on the floor. The reason was simple: the last thing the exchange needed was for the frat house atmosphere to be aired daily in the living rooms of investors around the globe.

But the times were changing. Grasso had already become addicted to a new genre of financial news on television and understood its power to expand the NYSE's brand. Unlike the Nasdaq, a market of anonymous traders at their computers, the NYSE had real buyers and sellers and a wonderful studio like no other in the world: the floor of the New York Stock Exchange.

Zito had contacted two stations, CNN and CNBC, to broach the possibility of live floor reports. Only one showed immediate interest. Jack Reilly, a producer at CNBC, told Zito that he had just hired a reporter, a woman by the name of Maria Bartiromo, a former producer for CNN's business anchor Lou Dobbs, who would be perfect for the assignment. Zito knew Bartiromo to be smart, very good looking, and most of all, ambitious. He recalled the time several years earlier when he had still been the marketing chief at Sony. He had been doing a private screening for the movie *Mo' Money,* starring Damon Wayans. Bartiromo had been hounding him for years to get on Sony's private screening list so she could schmooze with the stars and the broadcast heavyweights who showed up to such events. Zito never returned her calls. Then one night she just showed up, uninvited, and demanded to speak to Zito, who was so impressed by the ballsy move and her Sophia Loren–like features that he made her his guest that night.

Grasso knew there were risks involved in giving CNBC and Bartiromo nearly unfettered access to the floor. Zito, wearing his public relations hat, would have no control over information in the event of another crash. Meanwhile, the floor traders, or "the animals," as Grasso called them, were such an unruly bunch that they made the floor seem worse than the rowdiest locker room. Having someone as hot as Bartiromo down there all day would be a recipe for disaster.

But Grasso's instincts told him to ignore the warnings. Zito was way ahead of his time in predicting Bartiromo's star power, as her career took off almost from the moment she gave her first report from the floor. But Grasso was way ahead at understanding the power of CNBC as a public-relations tool for the exchange that would be putting the stock exchange and Grasso in the living rooms of investors across the globe.

"Do it," Grasso said. "It's great for us. But you're the one who has to sell it to the animals."

Zito just rolled his eyes and said he would.

Despite some resistance, the major players on the floor accepted CNBC and Bartiromo as the cost of doing business against the rejuvenated Nasdaq. By the mid- to late 1990s, CNBC's ratings were surging, and not just because viewers wanted to catch a glimpse of Bartiromo. Small investors were flocking to the markets in droves. Much of it was out of necessity with the end of company pension plans, which forced people to save for retirement through 401(k) and other investment plans. Some of it was the hope of finding the next Microsoft or Intel. Whatever the reason, average Americans had a thirst for financial news, and now they could get it straight from the floor of the New York Stock Exchange. Add to that the images of the frenzy on the floor and the dramatic possibilities of the opening and closing bells, and you had Grasso's vision of how to make the stock exchange the greatest show on Earth.

The market boom was a mixed blessing for the NYSE. Zito's market research showed that CNBC had sent the exchange's brand recognition soaring—a point Grasso drove home during meetings with potential new listings when they questioned just how much the imprimatur of the Club mattered to investors. Certainly, the fact that more people were in the market helped buoy the stocks that listed on the exchange; the Dow Jones Industrial Average, a measurement of the big-company stocks that trade on the NYSE, more than doubled during this time. Brokerage firm profits soared as well.

But there was also action over at the competition—the NASD, which ran the Nasdaq stock market. Hardiman's own marketing effort had worked; internal studies showed that the Nasdaq market's name recognition had soared among small investors. From the time Hardiman first started there in 1987, the market had grown by leaps and bounds, from the sixth largest, according to volume of shares traded, to the second, just behind the New York Stock Exchange.

More than that, the Nasdaq now had greater credibility. Academic studies began cropping up that extolled the speed and efficiency of the Nasdaq computers as opposed to the exchange's floor traders. Large investors started complaining to the exchange about their specialists: Did they really produce the best price for their trades? Even some listed companies began having second thoughts about remaining on the exchange: AIG's chairman, Maurice "Hank" Greenberg, for instance, began to badger Grasso that his specialist wasn't doing a good enough job keeping the price of his stock from falling. Grasso had listed AIG more than ten years earlier, when it was a midsize stock. Since that time it had grown into a colossus. Thanks to Greenberg's management, AIG was now the world's biggest insurer. Grasso told Greenberg that being so big had its consequences; investors tended to flock to smaller companies with greater growth potential.

But Greenberg was not convinced. He had a new theory about listings: smaller companies actually do better on the exchange, and larger ones trade better on the Nasdaq. AIG was too big a stock for the responsibility of setting its price to be left to a bunch of undereducated floor brokers. Grasso hit him with facts and figures about how floor traders prevented wild swings in stock prices, which seemed to appease Greenberg somewhat. But Greenberg kept complaining about how his stock was traded on the floor, and he kept reminding Grasso that maybe it was time to go back to where he had begun.

As 1996 opened, Grasso had yet to celebrate his first year in the top job, and since becoming chairman he had yet to convince a company to jump ship from the Nasdaq and join the Big Board. Grasso felt as if he were in a slump, and he needed something to break out of it. Just one hit, Grasso thought, and he would be back on track.

Grasso went over his game plan again. The companies most likely to jump sides were run by people who knew the value of having their stock traded on the exchange. His staff produced a list of Nasdaq companies whose management the exchange had done some business with. One name stood out: Wayne Huizenga, the billionaire entrepreneur and owner of the Miami Dolphins. Years earlier, Grasso had listed two of Huizenga's companies, including Waste Management.

But there was one that remained, Republic Services, a holding company that bought up solid waste companies and owned a growing nationwide chain of car dealerships.

Grasso scheduled a meeting with Huizenga in Miami. He came prepared with charts and graphs showing how NYSE-listed stocks showed less volatility in their trading patterns. He explained how the exchange was preparing a new marketing push that would better advertise its listed shares. He brought down the specialist in Waste Management to explain how he planned to support the stock, something no market maker with a computer could ever do.

Huizenga told Grasso he was impressed, but Republic was growing just fine on the Nasdaq, which, based on everything he was reading about electronic trading, was the future of the stock markets. Grasso then hit Huizenga with something he knew he couldn't resist: the Brand. The "Big Board" still meant something to investors, particularly the first-timers who were now flocking to the markets. Grasso said that about three times more newspapers carried NYSE stock tables than Nasdaq tables. He had had his staff look at news coverage of the NYSE compared to the Nasdaq. There was no comparison between the two.

"Sounds great," Huizenga said, and a few weeks later, he decided to move. The announcement would be made at Republic's annual board meeting, to be held in a large theater in downtown Miami.

Grasso told friends the meeting reminded him of Woodstock, filled with small investors of every stripe who held shares of Huizenga's various companies. Grasso was seated next to Jimmy Johnson, the coach of the Miami Dolphins. After the meeting, Grasso and Huizenga flew to New York, where Grasso hosted a dinner at Windows on the World at the top of the World Trade Center. "Wayne, you're the best," he said, as the two toasted to their new business relationship. But the night was far from over.

After the dinner, Grasso said he had a little surprise for Huizenga. Stationed in front of the trade center along Church Street were several Waste Management garbage trucks. Grasso, Huizenga, and his staff would be filmed for a promotional video riding in back, all of them dressed in gray jumpsuits worn by Waste Management workers. Grasso had always wanted to know what it felt like hanging on for dear life on the back of a garbage truck. As the caravan of garbage trucks headed south along Church Street, all Grasso could think of was his childhood friend Billy Wells. Wells had worked at a moving company and later became a garbage man, and every time he met with Grasso he bragged that during his twenty years on the job he had "never missed a can."

When Grasso made it to the exchange, he made sure he didn't miss a final opportunity with Huizenga. He quickly took off the garbageman's jumpsuit and replaced it with a uniform from the Florida Panthers hockey team, the NHL franchise that Huizenga owned, complete with a goalie's mask and stick. Grasso gave Huizenga a stick and a puck. Huizenga took a couple of shots at Grasso. "Score!" someone from Huizenga's staff yelled. Grasso didn't mind. He was back in the game.

Grasso began telling people that the best part of the day was getting to the office in the morning; the worst part was leaving. His normal eighteen-hour days were stretched to around-the-clock work at times, given his packed schedule of meetings, which often took him around the globe, particularly when new business was on the line. Things got so bad that Lori began scheduling time for Grasso to meet with his kids. Grasso was perpetually tired. He began taking handfuls of vitamins; every now and then he would steal an hour or so of sleep on his office couch. A large Gray's Papaya hot dog without the bun had become Grasso's diet. Grasso became a devotee of the low-carb, no-bread Atkins diet, and it began showing immediate results. He lost thirty pounds, maybe more. A new workout regimen gave him something that resembled biceps for the first time in years. The glasses went next, thanks to laser surgery.

Grasso also began dressing better. In the past, no one would have confused Grasso with a model from a Brooks Brothers catalogue, but now he never seemed to be out of his finely tailored dark suits, so much so that they earned him a nickname among the floor traders: the Little Guy in the Dark Suit.

Then came the hair. Grasso had been threatening to shave off what remained of his hair for months. "Don't you dare," Lori warned, and Grasso would change the subject. One day, Lori decided to go to their house in the Hamptons to get an early start on the weekend. When she got out there, Grasso called. "Make sure you watch the opening bell," he said. Lori wasn't sure what he was getting at, but then it dawned on her. "You didn't shave your head, did you?" Grasso just laughed and hung up. What Lori didn't know was that Grasso had had a prior engagement with his barber. "Take it off, all of it," Grasso told his barber. "All of it?" his barber asked. "That's right, all of it," Grasso ordered.

The next day Grasso made his way to the opening bell looking like a miniature version of Mr. Clean. At first reporters thought Grasso was sick; several called Zito asking if he recently underwent chemotherapy. Lori thought her husband was ill—mentally ill. But Grasso thought the head shaving was a home run; newspapers across the country picked up the story, as did the financial news networks. The headline in the New York *Daily News* said it all: "Shaved by the Bell: NYSE Chief Shows Up Hairless."

Phelan used to remind his staff that the stock exchange's name was a stronger brand the further you got from Manhattan. Grasso knew there was a certain allure associated with the exchange, which was why CEOs from all over the world loved to ring the opening and closing bells, and Grasso began dangling the opening and closing bells in front of companies like a piece of expensive chocolate. Most couldn't resist. After seeing the performance Grasso put on for Huizenga, officials from Gateway Computer and Anheuser-Busch also decided to switch their listings to the Club.

The battle between Grasso and Hardiman now had all the earmarks of a street fight. Grasso was matching the NASD's $50 million ad budget dollar for dollar, but Hardiman was also matching

Grasso's new listings, with scores of high-tech and Internet companies joining the Nasdaq. Grasso had begun spending more and more of his time overseas attracting foreign listings. Hardiman countered by squeezing the Silicon Valley technology corridor for every tech and dot-com IPO he could find.

Grasso came back with speeches and side comments at conferences that the Nasdaq was rolling the dice with unprofitable startups, the so-called dot-coms, which he labeled "dot bombs." At one conference with Hardiman present, Grasso pointedly assured the crowd that "Public companies need the Nasdaq, except those that can qualify for the New York Stock Exchange." The crowd erupted in laughter, and so did Hardiman. Back in Washington, Nasdaq's marketing ace, Brian Holland, had been cooking up a plan that he believed would send Grasso and the exchange back to the Stone Age.

It was another ad campaign that continued to tout the NASD's Nasdaq stock market as the market of the future and the exchange as a market whose best days were over. Hardiman knew Grasso would cry foul over the negative advertising. But Hardiman reminded his staff that it was necessary to fight the evil empire in New York; its infamous Rule 500, also known as the "Roach Motel Rule," gave the exchange an unfair advantage because once companies list on the exchange, they can't leave. To jump to the Nasdaq, a company must arrange a special vote of its shareholders, who must approve the measure by a two-thirds majority.

Hardiman was so enraged by Rule 500 that he began to call on NYSE listings and say that the NASD would pay the legal fees if they jumped ship and Grasso tried to litigate. So far he had no takers, but he believed they would soon come once they started seeing more of his ad blitz, including another one with Microsoft CEO Bill Gates touting the Nasdaq's expertise over the NYSE.

One of the ironies of the two warring exchanges was that they had virtually the same members, namely the big Wall Street firms that trade stocks for their customers. One of Grasso's best friends on the street was Joe Grano, the number two official at PaineWebber, who was now chairman of the NASD and technically Hardiman's boss.

Grano and Grasso were so close these days that on any given night, the two could be seen spending their evenings laughing and gossiping at the Greenwich Village restaurant Il Mulino. Grasso respected Grano for his business knowledge. He also recognized one other thing about Grano: Grasso knew Grano's heart was with the Big Board and he would give his right arm to be a NYSE board member.

Grasso explained the problem to Grano in a straightforward manner: the negative ads weren't good for the member firms that were part of both markets, he said, and if the ads continued, it would cost all of Wall Street money as both sides slugged it out. That got Grano's attention. Grano relayed Grasso's assessment to Hardiman, who said the negative ads were needed to counter the built-in advantages of the NYSE, such as Rule 500. But Grano didn't want a fight; he wanted peaceful coexistence, and he set up a dinner meeting where Grasso and Hardiman could hammer out their differences.

By now, Holland had grown the NASD marketing unit into a small empire—he was spending big bucks on TV ads and marketing, and had tripled the size of his staff. Grano began questioning the intensity of the marketing plan, forcing the gradual ratcheting down of the ad budget. He explained that while competition between the markets was good, there was room for both. Grano wanted peace.

Hardiman had to alert his troops that they might soon be taking a kindlier approach. When Holland got word that he was being cut back, he couldn't believe his ears. "Joe, what are you talking about?" he demanded, according to an eyewitness. "This is like cornering a rat, and the New York Stock Exchange is a giant rat. You have to go for the jugular!"

Hardiman, along with everyone else in the meeting, cracked up. Hardiman knew Holland was right. But there was nothing he could do as he prepared for his meeting with Grano and Grasso.

Il Mulino is one of those bustling New York restaurants where you can have an argument and no one else can hear you, which was one reason why Grano chose it for the Grasso-Hardiman sitdown. The other reason: it was his favorite place to eat. Grano made sure he had both parties liquored up a bit just to calm the tensions. Grano could see the anger in both men's eyes. "These guys really do hate each other," he thought as they began bickering over the ad war. At one point Grano stepped in with a proposal: ads on both sides must be positive in nature; no cheap shots, no low blows. Grasso said he was on board, Hardiman reluctantly agreed, and the dinner concluded with a toast of limoncello, Grano's favorite after-dinner drink.

Grasso left the meeting with a wide grin on his face as he shook Hardiman's hand and traveled back to his home on Long Island, New York. Hardiman, meanwhile, headed back to Washington to break the news to his staff that they would have to ratchet back their marketing plans a bit, but by no means were they giving up.

Dick Grasso had been chairman of the exchange now for about two years, but his impact seemed much bigger. Pat Healy, the former marketing executive for the NASD, left the organization and started his own firm to cash in on the listings war between Grasso and Hardiman by giving companies advice on which of the warring exchanges would better fit their needs. Healy loved to crunch numbers, and the numbers told an interesting story. Healy called it the "Grasso effect." For years, the NASD had taken for granted the business of listing initial public offerings. Not until 1983 did the Club even accept new companies as listings. But that was now changing as Grasso and his listings staff began courting IPOs as never before. Grasso didn't stop there. With Healy's lobbying help, Grasso snared America Online, where officials were sold the minute Grasso pointed out how a specialist could stabilize the company's stock price, which had been whipsawed by the short selling of traders who were betting it would go lower and those who believed shares were underpriced.

Pat Healy was hardly a household name at the exchange, but he had now become one of Grasso's secret weapons and helped land nearly two dozen switches from the Nasdaq over the next four years.

There was no secret weapon to diminish one of the best selling tools the NASD had over the Club: the assumption that the floor was a rigged system. The argument was that the specialists weren't blind brokers working to make fair and orderly markets in stocks they traded but were busy lining their own pockets at the expense of their clients—the investors and large traders who sent orders to the exchange. Depending on whom you spoke to, the practice of "front running," where traders use information gleaned privately from customers and personally profit from it, was either the work of a few bad apples or a huge problem at the exchange.

Grasso was in the "few bad apples" camp. Even so, he tried to tour the floor at least six times a day when he was in town. His presence and the threat it implied, he believed, might prevent a scandal that could do more damage than any NASD television ad. Whether he was right or not, only time would tell. Meanwhile, it wasn't Grasso who now had to deal with a scandal and its impact on the business, but Hardiman. The Justice Department and the Securities and Exchange Commission, under its chairman Arthur Levitt, had launched a massive investigation into price fixing in the NASD's trading system. For all the NASD's boasting that its Nasdaq system was a technological masterpiece, it wasn't totally devoid of the human element. Nasdaq market makers, the traders who made the system work, used the Nasdaq computer quote system to bid on stocks. The beauty of the system was that it was fast and efficient. Unlike the specialist system, there was complete disclosure of prices. Bids were set by the computer. At least that's how the system was supposed to work. What caught the regulators' eye was a growing body of evidence that the system had been rigged; the market makers were colluding with one another to set stock prices. Investors were being ripped off.

Back in New York, Grasso was delighted. The SEC produced a report critical of the NASD's regulatory structure and demanded a more formal separation between its regulatory unit and the business of running the Nasdaq stock market. But Levitt wanted more, something along the lines of a change at the top. In the end, Hardiman left and was replaced by Frank Zarb.

Grasso had no use for the SEC chief. He still thought of him as a lightweight, the guy who had run the Amex when Grasso had stolen many of its listings. But a Zarb-Levitt combination was different.

Zarb and Levitt went way back. Both had served in government, and, like Levitt, Zarb was a refugee from Sandy Weill's Shearson Lehman brokerage firm. In fact, it was Zarb who had helped Levitt achieve his greatest regulatory victory, cleaning up the scandal-plagued municipal bond market. Zarb had caught a lot of flack from his firm for supporting the cleanup—Smith Barney was one of the big practitioners of what Levitt labeled "pay to play." But he stuck to his guns, which Levitt never forgot.

With this type of background, Levitt thought Zarb was perfect for a job that required a businessman with an ethical compass. Zarb readily accepted. Before making the announcement official, though, he placed a telephone call to Grasso. "Dick, I'm thinking of taking a job as chairman and CEO of the NASD." As Zarb recalls it, the telephone went silent for a brief moment, and when Grasso began to speak, he tried to talk Zarb out of taking the job. Grasso pointed out the uphill battle he would have repairing the market and competing with the exchange. "Frank, in my opinion this isn't the greatest job in the world." Zarb politely thanked Grasso for his advice.

The news of Zarb's appointment startled Grasso; Zarb, after all, had been on the exchange's committee that nominated board members, so he knew how the place worked. Grasso's competitive drive and paranoia shifted into overdrive as he realized, given the relationship between Zarb and Levitt, he would have to fight the Nasdaq with the SEC chief in its corner. "Those bastards have got the system rigged," Grasso told Zito, who couldn't have agreed more.

For now, Grasso didn't fixate on Zarb so much as how he should respond to the Nasdaq's ills—namely, should he directly attack his scandal-plagued chief competitor? The floor sure as hell thought he should. The Nasdaq and its leaders weren't just in competition with the floor; Hardiman had made it clear that part of his mission was to destroy the specialist system once and for all. And it was a mission that Zarb, despite his background of working with Grasso, would have to adopt. Grasso thought long and hard, but in the end, he decided that a direct attack on the Nasdaq, using the market-making scandal as his prop, would be bad for business. The floor was incensed. How could the exchange pass up the chance of a lifetime to put a stake through the heart of the enemy?

Grasso's role as a regulator was always a controversial issue. Big Wall Street firms often complained about the dual nature of the job. But there was always a limit to how much Grasso could bully the brokerage industry with threats of audits and regulatory crackdowns. Goldman, Merrill, and Morgan Stanley could always go above Grasso's head and appeal his decisions to the SEC. But the floor had nowhere to turn. As trading volume ramped up during the late 1990s, Grasso and his market surveillance staff seemed to be everywhere, questioning specialists about their trades. Suspicious trades were deemed "just under guidelines," or JUGs, and once detected they would touch off a regulatory exam that traders referred to as "Justice under Grasso" for its onerous fines and sanctions.

Grasso told people he was just being a tough cop on the beat, but his rep on the floor was that of a bully. "The Little Guy in the Dark Suit" was not necessarily a term of endearment. Rather, it underscored the level of fear and resentment building up against Grasso among some people on the floor. Traders began noticing that floor loyalists received assignments to chair committees that were important in the day-to-day management of the exchange. Grasso's floor buddies found themselves appointed to the exchange's powerful board of directors. More important, they always seemed to have the inside track on new listings, the lifeblood of a specialist. Traders on Grasso's bad side constantly complained that they were the targets of unfair audits designed to find any infraction just to justify a fine and a black mark on the trader's record.

By the mid-1990s, Grasso's regulatory division was indeed a sprawling enterprise. About five hundred people, from low-level clerks to lawyers, worked there. It was the exchange's largest expense item. The unit was led by Ed Kwalwasser, a former top SEC attorney, whose quiet demeanor, at least according to the floor, masked a mean streak, and David Doherty, whom Grasso hired from the CIA to be Kwalwasser's number two.

But the scariest of all was a tall, strapping Irish American named Robert McSweeney. Like Grasso, McSweeney was a lifer at the exchange and an intimidating presence on the floor. In the mid-1990s, McSweeney's obsession seemed to be cracking major cases involving insider trading, when the floor was used as a conduit for potentially illegal activity, and conducting all those annoying audits on floor traders.

As relentless as Grasso's regulators appeared when it came to insider trading and auditing floor brokers over trading infractions, they appeared oblivious to major crimes in their own backyard. Institutional investors such as Fidelity Investments and others continued to complain that they were getting lousy execution on trades; they believed their brokers were improperly inserting themselves in between trades when they weren't needed, something called "interpositioning." Others complained of rampant front running, which was tantamount to insider trading because the specialist used proprietary information he had gathered from a client to trade for his own account and make a profit ahead of the market. A charge of this nature could land the offending party not just out of the exchange but also in jail, and according to many critics, Grasso's regulatory staff did little to curtail it. If he did, Grasso would be indicting the very system he was selling to listing clients and order-flow merchants as the most honest market in the world.

That was the consensus over at Lehman Brothers one afternoon, as several traders met with Billy Johnston and Cathy Kinney to discuss some activity they believed had cost their client, Fidelity Investments, a lot of money. Fidelity had sent order flow through Lehman that was passed on to the floor. The Lehman traders suspected that floor brokers had improperly inserted themselves into trades where they weren't needed, whereas the super-dot system would have automatically connected the buyer and seller without the need for a trader, thus illegally skimming profits in the process.

Johnston and Kinney mostly sat and listened. Then suddenly, according to a person who attended the meeting, Johnston blurted out, "Our guys have got to make some money too." Anyone who knew Johnston knew that he had a warped, politically incorrect sense of humor that had never mellowed with age and his new lofty position at the exchange, so who knows if he was just kidding or not. Still, the Lehman traders were stunned. "Did he just say what I thought he said?" asked one Lehman executive. A bigger question was: Did he mean it?

One thing was certain: Grasso and the exchange were on a roll. In 1996, it signed up a record 275 new company listings; 59 of them were from overseas, also a record. The following year brought similar success. Much of that performance was a function of the booming market, particularly for IPOs. But it was also a function of Grasso, who never seemed to stop working. By now, Grasso had erased any doubt from the heads of the big Wall Street firms or anyplace else that he didn't have the gravitas to lead the exchange. In speeches, he was smooth and confident; his voice developed a raspy quality that suggested a maturity that he hadn't had in the past. Now it wasn't just business leaders but world leaders who couldn't wait to come to the stock exchange to meet him.

Zito believed he could push Grasso's star higher, and with it the fortunes of the New York Stock Exchange. To do that, Zito would make Grasso the centerpiece of the exchange's new marketing strategy. Zito's market research showed that when people were asked what came to mind when they heard about the New York Stock Exchange, Grasso's name was near the top of the list.

Now Zito wanted it at the very top of the list. The exchange, he decided, would blast the world with images of the new New York Stock Exchange, with Grasso leading the charge. For all his stature and success, Phelan had believed the chairmen of the exchange were caretakers, people whose duty was to work for the members and the institution. The old-timers would undoubtedly think that Grasso was overstepping his bounds.

Zito didn't seem to care, and neither did Grasso. They started small: the annual report, once a celebration of the institution, suddenly became a celebration of Grasso, with his photo on nearly every page. Floor events, the opening and closing bells, became more gaudy and sensational, with Grasso acting more like a carnival barker than the chairman of the world's most prestigious stock market. In the late 1980s, Jesse Jackson had come to the exchange to ring the opening bell. He had been roundly booed by the floor. But now that he had launched his Wall Street Project, designed to bring diversity to the financial industry, Grasso welcomed him back with open arms. Jackson began holding his annual gala on the floor of the exchange, with Grasso in attendance making sure he got a few photos with Jackson so they would make the morning newspapers.

The meetings with Jackson also helped Grasso secure his relationship with one of the most powerful men in the securities business, Sandy Weill. The great deal maker had just put together his biggest deal yet, merging his Travelers Group insurance and brokerage empire with the massive bank Citicorp. With such size and scope, Citigroup would become one of the biggest suppliers of order flow in the markets, possibly even rivaling Merrill Lynch. Even before the merger, Grasso had been badgering Weill for years to send all of his trades to the exchange.

Grasso hadn't had much leverage with Weill before. But now he did. The Citigroup merger was technically illegal. A Depression-era banking law, the Glass-Steagall Act, still prevented brokerage firms from merging with banks. It was against this backdrop that Grasso and Weill teamed up to help Jackson start a new effort to increase the number of minorities on Wall Street. Before long, Weill was helping Jackson sell his new book about investing for minorities. He held cocktail parties for Jackson and lent one of his in-house lawyers to the Wall Street Project to make sure things ran smoothly. Grasso's and Weill's names suddenly appeared on Jackson's fund-raising letters sent to Wall Street firms requesting a "minimum financial commitment of $50,000."

Meanwhile, Weill and Grasso's member firms rapidly faced a dead-

line by which they would have to convince Congress to pass new legislation that would effectively kill Glass-Steagall or the Citigroup deal
would die as would a pending wave of brokerage firms merging with
banks. In other words, Weill would have to unwind the largest merger
in financial history and Grasso's member firms would lose big money
in investment-banking fees. The impediment seemed to be a powerful one; Phil Gramm, the head of the Senate Banking Committee,
was having second thoughts about killing the law, despite intense lobbying from Wall Street. That's when Jackson became one of the Club's
most effective lobbyists. He met with Gramm and cut a deal: Jackson
agreed not to oppose another piece of legislation Gramm was pushing, and Gramm agreed to terminate Glass-Steagall once and for all.

Grasso's embrace of the Wall Street Project had many benefits.
His member firms killed a law that they had been trying to nullify for
decades. Grasso was heralded as a defender of "diversity" even though
the exchange still had very few minorities on the floor. More important, he and Weill were now closer than ever, so close that Grasso was
told by a top Citigroup executive that any effort to send trades to
other exchanges was now "dead."

With his growing appetite for public exposure, Grasso was also
glad he had made the deal with CNBC. The opening bell had now become one of the most important money shots on broadcast television
as the bull market continued to roll. The business channel had become so popular that it could be seen in bars and restaurants during
lunch hour because people were so obsessed with their investments.
Grasso monitored the channel constantly, studying camera angles for
ways to get NYSE logos into shots, and even recommending expert
commentators to provide a positive image for the exchange. The network was turning out to be the best ad campaign the Club ever had.

As much as Grasso was using the station and its staff, CNBC was
using Grasso. Maria Bartiromo became a household name thanks to
Grasso's decision to give her a place on the floor. The business channel now had the first crack at interviewing CEOs because they all but
demanded a meeting with "the Money Honey," as Bartiromo was now
being described by the *New York Post*.

And for the most part, "the animals," the traders and specialists Grasso worried would offend their new TV guests, had welcomed CNBC and the omnipresent Bartiromo into their home. But not always. One morning, a frenzied trader pushed his way through the floor to complete his order. Instead of moving out of the way, Bartiromo continued her report. The trader nearly knocked Bartiromo to the floor, and with the cameras rolling he muttered an expletive that made its way onto the air. Grasso was sitting in his office when the incident occurred; he heard the four-letter word and ordered an investigation. The last thing the exchange needed was to be known as a center of boorish behavior or as a place that wasn't safe for Maria Bartiromo. By the time it was over, Grasso's enforcement staff had interviewed seventeen floor traders and Bartiromo herself, who, according to one investigator, calmly recounted the thirty-second episode in great detail. The end result: a fine for the trader and a black mark on his record. But there was a larger issue that Grasso wanted to reinforce: do something to make me or the exchange look bad, or mess with CNBC, and you're in trouble.

Thanks to CNBC and Zito's new marketing plan Grasso's stature was taken to new heights. Now that he was a public figure, Grasso had learned to control his volatile temper, at least in public. To be sure, Grasso was always exceedingly polite to clerks and the exchange's security staff—"average people," as he would say. It was the senior staff who bore the brunt of his wild temper—and behind closed doors that didn't change, no matter how much Grasso watched himself in public view. He was known not just to scream and curse but, according to one person who worked with him, Grasso now liked "to throw things." Cathy Kinney, one of his top lieutenants, remarked after one particularly brutal verbal assault by Grasso that getting screamed at by her boss was like "getting a knife" in her chest. One day Kinney was handling a new listing for a foreign company, but its CEO couldn't make the opening bell. Instead the company's chief financial officer was going to do the honors. Kinney relayed the news to Grasso. "Are you fucking crazy?" he boomed. "I told you we want only CEOs at the opening bell! This is outrageous!" Kinney silently stood in Grasso's office for nearly fifteen minutes as he screamed and cursed, while she tried to recall when Grasso had passed this hard-and-fast rule about having only CEOs at the opening bell. "I got it," she finally said. "It won't happen again." That seemed to appease Grasso, but only momentarily, as Grasso started screaming at her some more.

Richard Simonelli, a NYSE listing official, also knew what it was like to get the full Grasso treatment. One afternoon, after a series of grueling meetings with Grasso, he was getting ready to meet him again. But before he could make it to Grasso's sixth-floor office, he collapsed. "Hey, boss!" an assistant called out. "He's having a heart attack!" Grasso jumped up from his seat and saw Simonelli sprawled on the floor. Simonelli was taken immediately to the hospital, where he stayed for tests and was treated for extreme exhaustion.

"You got to be kidding me!" Grasso bellowed one morning as he peered at his television screen at Michael LaBranche, now the CEO of the specialist firm LaBranche & Co., who was giving an interview for CNBC in front of the Nasdaq headquarters in Times Square. By the late 1990s, LaBranche & Co. controlled and owned more than one hundred seats, making it one of the largest specialist firms on the floor. "The kid" was now one of the most powerful people at the exchange. He was also part of a growing group of traders who believed that for all the money Grasso was helping them make through his new listings, he was also an out-of-control egomaniac who must be stopped. LaBranche considered Grasso a bully, a blowhard, and an interloper with no real historic links to the exchange. He particularly resented how Grasso had taken a two-hundred-year-old public institution with a storied history and turned it into a monument to himself.

Grasso didn't think much of LaBranche either; he compared him to a spoiled brat who didn't know how to run a great business that was started by his grandfather. Grasso says he made LaBranche even richer when he later assisted him in bringing his specialist firm public with an IPO that valued the enterprise $3 billion. But now Grasso was fuming as he watched "the kid" babble about the markets with the massive Nasdaq sign looming in the background. "Get him up here now," Grasso ordered one of his assistants. As LaBranche made his way up to the sixth floor, Grasso made a tape of the interview. When LaBranche sat down, Grasso snapped, "Watch this." Grasso wrote down on a small pad how many times the camera showed the Nasdaq sign during the interview. Grasso was so incensed, he broke three or four pencils in the process; then he handed the pad to LaBranche. "Do you see what I'm saying?" he growled. LaBranche was stunned, not necessarily by what he had done but by how Grasso had treated him.

"There's a reason why the CEO of Coke isn't seen drinking a Pepsi, and there's a reason why I don't ring the Nasdaq's opening bell," Grasso added. LaBranche said he was sorry and left the office with his tail between his legs. But he didn't stop hating Grasso or how Grasso was running the Club.

Criticism from the likes of Mike LaBranche or anyone else was far from Grasso's mind as he rolled out new, ever more outrageous ways to market the exchange. One of the more famous stunts involved Sumner Redstone, the chairman of the giant conglomerate Viacom, which owned Paramount Studios. It was Zito's idea to have Grasso, Redstone, and the actor Kelsey Grammer (at the time Viacom owned CBS, which aired Grammer's show *Frasier*) "slimed" by the Great American Slime Machine, which appears on Viacom's Nickelodeon kids' network. After some wrangling from Redstone's office—he would only do it wearing a yellow raincoat and a hard hat—all three agreed to stand under the contraption and get doused with green slime as the start of trading began.

As outrageous as that stunt was, Grasso now opened the ceremony to people who had no tangible relationship with stocks or corporate America but could generate news coverage, inviting politicians, celebrities, athletes, and supermodels (Grasso made sure Zito continuously booked his favorite, Gisele Bündchen)—anyone who could command media attention—to do the honors.

Animals as well. Gateway Computer was allowed to bring its mascot, a large cow, onto the floor. Grasso walked the floor with a chimpanzee as a favor to a listed company and was captured on film kissing his simian friend on the lips. When AngloGold decided to list on the exchange, Grasso thought it would be fun to leverage the firm's brand image, an African lion, by bringing the big cat to the podium when company officials rang the opening bell. At first company officials thought he was kidding; when Grasso said he wasn't, they explained the dangers. The company does have a trained seven-hundred-pound lion as a mascot, but a lion can be trained only so much. Grasso and the rest of the exchange would be taking a chance with their lives.

Grasso didn't care as he considered the massive publicity the event would generate. Directly under the podium was the specialist station for the firm Benjamin Jacobson. The company's CEO, James Jacobson, noticed Grasso walking with the lion and remarked, "Dick, you're out of your mind!" Grasso shot back, "Don't worry, Jimmy, he only eats Christians." Jacobson, who is Jewish, just shook his head. As Grasso walked the lion onto the podium, the head of AngloGold's South African mineworkers' union, James Motlatsi, quickly moved out of the way, telling Grasso, "I've seen what those animals have done to my people." Grasso just laughed and the big cat promptly sprawled on the floor. As Grasso rang the opening bell, New York City police sharpshooters brought in for the event aimed their rifles at the lion's head. Trading was commenced just as on any other day, with a host of cheers from the floor—only this time, the cheering had a special significance.

Part of Grasso's strategy to win listings from foreign companies was to establish relations with leaders of countries looking to privatize their government-run companies, and Grasso had developed a close relationship with Andrés Pastrana Arango, the president of Colombia. They met in Manhattan at Ronald Perelman's town house to discuss business opportunities over dinner and expensive cigars. Grasso told Pastrana he needed to be more visible in the American business community and offered to bring him to the exchange for a lunch. Pastrana said he would love to do more but he had one problem: a nasty insurgency led by a Marxist guerrilla group named FARC that was killing the local economy. They were led by a Soviet-educated economist named Raúl Reyes, who operated a criminal enterprise, he said, protecting cocaine dealers and kidnapping wealthy South Americans.

When the dinner was over, Grasso told Pastrana to call on him for help anytime. Grasso obviously made an impression on the president. It wasn't long before Pastrana took Grasso at his word. "Richard, I have an idea," he said in a phone call a few weeks later. "I would like you to fly down here and meet with the rebels and negotiate with [Reyes]." Pastrana was trying to open a dialogue with FARC, and he thought that bringing a prominent businessman down to Colombia to explain how the group was ruining the economy might get them to end their uprising. If anyone could make the deal, Pastrana said, it would be Dick Grasso.

"Absolutely, Mr. President," Grasso said, apparently without thinking about what he was being asked to do. "Anything to help."

"I will guarantee your safety," Pastrana added before hanging up the telephone.

It took just a few minutes before Grasso realized that he had agreed to meet and negotiate with a murderer. He telephoned Zito with the news. "You wouldn't believe what I just did," he said, explaining the details and how he wanted the entire matter kept in confidence. No listing ceremony would compare to this stunt. "Are you crazy?" Zito asked, before adding that if Grasso was going, so was he. "No way, you got little kids," Grasso said, ignoring the fact that his youngest was about the same age as Zito's. Over the next couple weeks, not even Grasso's wife knew the exact nature of the trip; she thought he was leaving for a weekend listing trip to Colombia to meet with the president and would be home Sunday night for dinner in the Hamptons.

Grasso left Friday night with his team. He arrived in Bogotá early Saturday for an embassy briefing about the country and its political climate. That's when it finally dawned on him that for all the publicity his trip would generate, he was in one of the most dangerous places in the world. Grasso met with the key officials from Pastrana's government. It was then that they told Grasso for the first time that the meeting wasn't going to be held in Bogotá but in the jungles, the heart of the FARC-controlled territory. It would take about two hours to arrive at their destination; first they would take a small propeller plane to a town named San Vicente, which had recently been overrun by the rebels. They would then take a helicopter to a rebel hideout deep in the jungle. Grasso was accompanied by his security chief, Jim Esposito, who looked at his boss for approval. "We came this far," Grasso said. "We might as well go all the way."

As soon as Grasso and his entourage landed in San Vicente, they were surrounded by about a dozen kids with AK-47 machine guns. Grasso reckoned they weren't more than fourteen years of age. About forty-five minutes later they were deep in the Colombian jungle. The helicopter landed on a makeshift airstrip. Grasso and the others were marched to a small shed, where they met face-to-face with the rebel leader, Raúl Reyes.

Reyes may have led a peasant army but he was highly educated, Grasso was told, a student of Soviet-style economics, which lent a certain air of absurdity to his meeting with one of the biggest capitalists in the world. As it turned out, Reyes was hardly the imposing figure Grasso had heard about. He was a dour man, short and fat with a salt-and-pepper beard. But he was also armed with a pistol at his side, Grasso noticed as he sat down.

Grasso spoke to Reyes through an interpreter. Reyes seemed stiff, so Grasso thought he should break the ice the same way he would with any listing client, by cracking a joke. "Mr. Reyes," Grasso said, "the stock exchange has a rule that says we can't pay more than three dollars in ransom if the chairman is kidnapped." For the first time, Reyes smiled, but this time he responded not in Spanish but in perfect English: "That's okay, we'll just take the minister," he said, pointing to Colombia's economic minister, who had accompanied Grasso to the meeting. The rest of the conversation lasted about an hour. Grasso spoke about how a free-market economy would lift all boats, including the peasant class Reyes was fighting for. Reyes doubted that the business class in the country was willing to give the people their fair share of the spoils. Grasso said that under Pastrana they would have no choice, and he was ready to broker the peace, at the New York Stock Exchange.

"You can even ring the opening bell," Grasso said.

Reyes laughed, and the two promised to stay in touch. When Grasso got back into the helicopter, he said he didn't think Reyes was such a bad guy. Pastrana's economic minister responded, "Try telling that to the business community." Grasso did so that night, explaining that they had a historic opportunity to make peace and he would gladly host the event on the floor of the exchange. The business leaders were polite but they didn't seem too eager to follow Grasso in negotiating with the rebels. Later Grasso found out why: FARC had targeted all of their families for kidnappings.

The next morning as Grasso was preparing to come home, he called Lori, who nearly hit the ceiling. "You were in the Colombian jungle with the rebels!" she screeched, having seen a story about his trip in one of the newspapers. Grasso just laughed, saying he was on his way home.

In the final analysis, Grasso's South American junket didn't do much to calm the tensions between the FARC rebels and the government. In fact, all over Wall Street people were shaking their heads about Grasso's little excursion no matter how many times Grasso said he had made the trip for world peace. Most people believed it was nothing more than one of Grasso's patented publicity stunts, albeit a dangerous one. But Grasso achieved his objective: massive publicity for himself and the exchange. The following Monday, Grasso had a private dinner at Blair House in Washington, D.C., with Egyptian president Hosni Mubarak to talk about bringing Egyptian companies to list on the exchange. Most of the conversation centered on Grasso's now-famous trip. Mubarak sat in bewilderment as Grasso spoke about his meeting with the rebels and how he had risked his life for peace. Grasso said he'd do it again if asked, and no one doubted him.

And with good reason. By the end of 1999, the Grasso brand had become very strong indeed. Grasso was now stealing more companies from the Nasdaq than ever before—about sixty-five that year—and for all the hoopla about electronic trading, Grasso had lost just one company to the Nasdaq since becoming chairman. The NYSE, meanwhile, continued to dominate even in the age of technology. Listed stocks traded on the floor more than 80 percent of the time, and the ultimate measure of success was seat prices, which were now trading at an all-time high of $2.65 million.

Everyone was making money under Grasso. Specialists' salaries soared to at least $2 million a year, while others earned as much as $10 million. Brokers, who bought and sold smaller lots of stocks, now earned around anywhere from $400,000 a year to $1 million, while clerks, who merely serviced the specialists, could earn about $200,000 a year. Grasso wasn't doing so badly either. Grasso's salary, like those of the chairmen before him, was a secret to most of the world. Not even the seat holders, who were the owners of the exchange, knew the salaries of the exchange's chairmen since the Big Board, as a not-for-profit, didn't have to disclose its executives' pay.

But Grasso was certainly paid as if he ran a for-profit company. Like his counterparts in corporate America, Grasso had packed the board with friends and allies who were getting rich as well, thanks to stock options and other payment mechanisms. The exchange wasn't a public company, so it just handed Grasso cash—and lots of it— through huge pay increases that Grasso began to funnel into a series of retirement accounts designed to give him a more than comfortable existence when he left the Club. Since taking over the exchange, Grasso's salary had jumped by leaps and bounds. In 1995, his first year as chairman, he had signed a new contract. He made $2.16 million that year, and by the end of his fifth in 1999, he was earning above $11 million, much of it—all but around $900,000 that year— deferred into those retirement accounts that allowed his savings to grow exponentially.

And the exchange's compensation committee was trying to figure out new ways to give him more. In 1995, he was allowed to take out in cash all the money he had already saved for retirement, more than $6 million, to buy a new home in the upscale Locust Valley section of Long Island. In 1999, the board allowed him to take $23 million out of his retirement account and put it into a NYSE savings account, so, as he later put it, he "could control it more directly."

Grasso was now receiving more money than any chairman had received by a huge margin, even more than the great John Phelan. But the little guy in the dark suit couldn't have cared less. He was living large, at least as large as the institution he had now come to symbolize.

Grasso had certainly grown much since his days working under Phelan. He dressed better, spoke better, and, for the most part, had learned how to keep his temper under control. But Phelan's worry that Grasso had one speed—full speed; in other words, a lack of self-awareness was perhaps as valid now as ever before. Publicity stunts would be tolerated by the rank and file at the exchange as long as Wall Street was making money. But all those big pay days—hammered out privately by the exchange's board of directors and never disclosed to the broader membership—were another matter altogether, as Grasso would eventually find out.

5

SUGAR DADDY

"Champ, take a look at this," Grasso said as he led his famous guest to the corner of his office. Muhammad Ali, once the greatest heavyweight champion in boxing history, was now dealing with the symptoms of Parkinson's disease, which had left him physically weakened—he could now barely talk—but his mind was as sharp as ever. He and Grasso had just finished breakfast in the boardroom while Ali's wife and daughter toured the exchange for the first time. Ali spoke sporadically but gestured with his hands and eyes when Grasso spoke. He laughed at some of Grasso's stories about Wall Street, and after they finished, he found himself in Grasso's office admiring some of Grasso's deal trophies.

Ali dutifully followed Grasso, shuffling his feet, to the corner of Grasso's office where a pair of photographs hung. The first was the famous shot of the champ with his back on the canvas and the referee, Arthur Mercante, giving him the count as Joe Frazier hovered nearby. When Ali saw the framed photograph, his eyes widened as if he recalled the exact moment he had been hit by Frazier's formidable right hand and hit the carpet.

Then Grasso showed Ali the other framed picture, from another famous fight in the annals of the Club. It was from a celebrity fight night months earlier. The picture showed Mercante, now more than twenty years older, raising Grasso's own arm in victory over another boxing champion, Roy Jones, Jr., himself laid out on the carpet. Ali burst out laughing and then suddenly stopped, before pointing to Grasso with his index finger, then pointing to the side of his own head and twirling his finger. The most powerful man on Wall Street, the champ concluded, was crazy.

Ali was at the exchange because he had agreed to ring the opening bell as part of the "Millennium Bell Ringing Series," where the exchange would celebrate people who had a major impact on the history of the twentieth century. Others included the Holocaust survivor Elie Weisel, Bishop Desmond Tutu, Joe Namath, and now Ali. Whether any of this made the markets work more efficiently didn't matter. Ali rang the opening bell to thunderous applause, and then he and Grasso went down to the floor. Grasso had taken other celebrities through the floor, and most of the guys had been too busy making money to notice. Almost from the moment he arrived, Ali was mobbed by traders, shaking his hand, begging for his autograph. Grasso had never seen anything like it before in all his years as chairman.

Ken Langone hadn't seen anything like Grasso, either. Langone was appointed compensation committee chief in 1999. The official "recommendation" came from the prior chairman of the committee, Bernie Marcus, Langone's friend and business partner from Home Depot. But the real push came from Grasso. Langone, as far as Grasso was concerned, was the perfect choice for the job. He owned two seats on the exchange, was the cofounder of one of the exchange's largest companies, Home Depot, and had years of experience as an investment banker. Langone sat on a number of corporate boards, Home Depot and General Electric being two of the biggest. He had a reputation as a demanding board member. But those who met his standards of performance were rewarded handsomely, and Grasso was clearly one of those people.

Langone appreciated Grasso for many of the same reasons Grasso appreciated Langone: they both excelled as outsiders. Langone had grown up in Roslyn, New York, on Long Island, the son of a plumber. He had toiled for years on the periphery of Wall Street at a small investment bank named R. W. Pressprich, moonlighting as a finance professor at New York University. His big break had come in 1968, when he was a thirty-three-year-old stock salesman. He had just received a tip from a friend that one of the nation's richest men, a Texan named Ross Perot, was looking to take his high-flying computer company, Electronic Data Systems, public. EDS was a cash cow thanks to Perot's contract with the state of Texas to process Medicaid and Medicare insurance claims. The deal was one of the most sought-after on Wall Street. Every major Wall Street firm was bidding to be Perot's underwriter, sending teams of bankers down to his headquarters in Dallas to pitch their expertise.

Langone's partners said he didn't have a chance. It was, after all, his first IPO, and he would be cutting his teeth on the deal of the decade. Anyway, how could tiny R. W. Pressprich compete with the likes of Morgan Stanley or Goldman Sachs? But Langone was determined. He contacted a friend, Jack Hight, who ran EDS's Washington office, who agreed to set up a meeting under two conditions. First, Langone could take no more than thirty minutes to make his case and not a minute longer. Langone agreed. Second, Hight knew that Langone wasn't the smoothest operator he ever met on the street. With his gruff New York accent, nearly every other word out of Langone's mouth was an obscenity. Hight made Langone promise he wouldn't curse. Langone knew that would be a more difficult task, but he agreed nonetheless.

Langone arrived at Perot's office in Dallas at 11:00 A.M. sharp. He kept his pitch brief, as promised. Langone is an imposing man, about six feet, three inches tall, with wide shoulders and a crooked nose that resembles that of a prizefighter. The first thing he noticed was how short Perot was, standing only five feet, five inches, with ears that stuck out at right angles from his peanut-sized head.

But he also had a firm handshake, and he looked Langone directly in the eyes. Langone knew nothing scared him. Perot's office was a spacious affair with photos showing Perot with one politician or another adorning its walls. Almost as soon as Langone sat down, Perot explained what each firm had promised as the opening price for the stock and how Wall Street would say and do anything to win this or any deal. Before he was done, Langone looked at his watch. Perot had eaten up twenty-nine minutes of his allotted time. That's when Perot shot Langone his first question of the meeting. "So what do ya think?" he blurted out in his West Texas drawl. "Mr. Perot," replied Langone, "I'm a man of my word, and I have to say good-bye. I gave my word to Jack that I would only take thirty minutes of your time, and I need more than sixty seconds to make my case." But Perot persisted: "Don't give me that, what do you think about what those other guys are offering me?" Langone had just broken the first rule, staying past his thirty-minute curfew, so he decided to break his second rule: "Mr. Perot, that's the biggest pile of shit I ever heard."

Langone gave it to him straight. This was his first IPO, he said, but he knew a lot about Wall Street investment bankers and they would tell you whatever you want to hear. He didn't think the prices being offered were sustainable; he might be able to hit those levels on the opening day of the IPO, but the stock would sink sometime thereafter. Perot couldn't believe what he was hearing; finally a guy from Wall Street who told it straight. Before the day was over, Langone and Perot had spoken for a lot longer than thirty minutes. "So why should I choose you?" Perot finally asked Langone. "Well, it's simple, Mr. Perot," Langone said. "If I screw this up, it's the end for me. But if I do a great job, I'm made."

Perot liked what he heard. A few weeks later, he "made" Langone, giving him the assignment. EDS turned out to be one of the best-selling IPOs in the history of Wall Street and Langone was indeed made—and a millionaire many times over. In the late 1970s, he helped a friend named Bernie Marcus find investors to finance Marcus's lifelong dream: to start a nationwide chain of hardware stores. Langone put $100,000 of his own money into the project and raised the rest. Many people told him he was crazy, but Langone smelled a winner. By the late 1990s, the company, Home Depot, was one of the biggest in the world, worth more than $100 billion. Now he and Marcus were billionaires.

When Langone had met Grasso for the first time during Home Depot's NYSE listing, it wasn't the bullshit sales talk that kept Langone listening to the little guy, but Grasso's knowledge of anything that concerned the New York Stock Exchange. Grasso rattled off statistics and information as no one Langone met before or after him. Grasso had barely attended college, but he spoke with an intelligence and intensity that rivaled even his most polished students. And he delivered.

As head of the compensation committee, Langone would spend long hours going over various measurements of Grasso's performance and the compensation his committee was prepared to dole out. Board members used to joke that during meetings Langone was so engaged that he "never blinked." That much was true. Many board members considered their membership a chore. They often skipped meetings and ignored memos about important NYSE matters, including Grasso's burgeoning pay.

But Langone seemed to know everything there was to know about the components of Grasso's lengthy new contract in 1999 that had locked him in as chairman until 2005, even if no one else did or cared to find out. Langone was now Grasso's "sugar daddy." For 2000, Grasso's salary grew once again, to around $27 million. Langone wanted to pay Grasso like a Wall Street CEO—the same people Grasso was helping to make rich as firms like Bear Stearns, Goldman Sachs, and others now snapped up specialist operations to cash in on the listings and order-flow boom produced by the little guy in the dark suit. But Grasso wasn't just a Wall Street CEO; he was the head of a quasi-governmental institution that regulated the very same people who were paying him all that money. If the size of Grasso's pay ever leaked out, how would that look? Langone didn't care as long as the exchange kept making money for its members. In fact he remarked at the time, "I would pay him more if I could."

And he could, since no one seemed to care. One afternoon, not long after the specialist Chris Quick joined the board, Grasso was speaking about a potential new listing when Quick received an elbow to the ribs from Langone. Langone made a gesture in the direction of another board member, David Komansky, who had succeeded Dan Tully to become the CEO of Merrill Lynch, the nation's largest brokerage firm. Komansky's eyes were shut. He was taking a nap.

"Can you believe it?" Langone quietly asked Quick. "This fucking guy runs Merrill Lynch and he's asleep in the afternoon."

One morning Frank Zarb received a small package. It was from Grasso. In it was a leather case with a photo of a beaming Zarb standing next to the premier of China, Zhu Rongji, with a Nasdaq banner in the background that read: NASDAQ THE WORLD'S LARGEST STOCK MARKET. The package also contained a letter, written in what appeared to be Chinese.

Grasso and Zarb understood the importance of staying as close to the Chinese leadership as possible, given the country's growing economic might. Wall Street investment banks were scouring the country for potential investments. It was only a matter of time before a Chinese company went public, and both Grasso and Zarb wanted the listing. As a result, each went out of his way to embrace these newly minted capitalists despite their thuggish reputation on civil liberties.

Grasso always seemed to get first dibs on the Chinese leadership when they were in town, so when Zhu went to the Nasdaq, his boss, Chinese president Jiang Zemin, visited the Big Board, where Grasso embraced the Communist dictator as if he had just agreed to list a company on the stock exchange. Jiang was one of the first Communists to ring the opening bell (Mikhail Gorbachev was actually the first, in the early 1990s). He waved to the crowd and uttered in halting English, "Good morning, I wish you good trading," before pressing the buzzer to begin trading.

It's unclear if the floor traders were just getting tired of all of Grasso's opening-bell antics or were uncomfortable cheering for an avowed Communist, but as the bell rang, you could hear booing coming from the floor. When Grasso and Billy Johnston gave Jiang a tour of the trading room, they were largely ignored. Grasso, meanwhile, was just happy to get Jiang out of the building alive, because lining Broad Street was an angry crowd protesting China's crackdown in Tibet.

There were no such controversies over at the Nasdaq headquarters in Times Square, just nice photos in the newspapers of Zarb and his guest, the premier, standing in front of the large Nasdaq sign that made Grasso's blood boil. Grasso had become so obsessed with newspaper coverage of his competitor that he studied the shots right down to the smile on Zarb's face. When Zarb smiled, Grasso used to say, he never showed his teeth. Grasso began ribbing Zarb that he must be wearing dentures.

Through Grasso's spies at the Nasdaq, he heard that the photo op hadn't run as smoothly as the press accounts suggested. When Zhu saw the Nasdaq banner, he remarked, "I thought Big Board was the largest?" Zarb explained the difference: bigger companies may list on the New York, but more stock is traded on the Nasdaq.

"What a fucking liar," Grasso said, before coming up with an idea he thought might even up the score.

With the photo he sent to Zarb, Grasso had attached a small note written in fake Chinese, which was sure to spark a call from his good friend. Zarb now had the package and he immediately phoned Grasso. "What the fuck is this! What does this mean?" Grasso barely kept a straight face when he answered, "Well, Frank, I heard about your conversation with the premier . . . anyway, our interpreters here are a little rusty in their Chinese, but I think it means 'He who fails to tell the truth will fail to find his dentures.' "

Zarb didn't need Grasso to explain what he was getting at and uttered a simple "Fuck you" before hanging up the telephone.

By the height of the bull market of the 1990s, the CNBC-Grasso partnership was working better than ever before. Zito came to believe that part of the reason so many CEOs now wanted to list on the exchange was that they became instant business celebrities on the network that aired their opening-bell ceremonies and got to meet the glamorous Maria Bartiromo, who Grasso made sure got first crack at interviewing his new customers.

Zarb thought the same and began demanding equal time on CNBC. He couldn't match the pomp and circumstance of the opening bell, but he could get other concessions from the network. CNBC agreed to start airing Nasdaq market results, first at its offices in lower Manhattan and then from a new Nasdaq market site in Times Square, where stock prices would be displayed on a large, glitzy panel called the "Nasdaq Wall." It wasn't the opening bell, but it was a start.

News of Zarb's actions began to enrage Grasso, who became more determined than ever to wrest Microsoft from the Nasdaq. But snagging Microsoft would take a small miracle because Microsoft's longtime CFO, Mike Brown, served on the Nasdaq market's board of directors. NYSE marketing executives made constant telephone calls to their contacts at the company to see how they could better serve their biggest listing. But Microsoft CEO Bill Gates told Grasso repeatedly that he had no desire to leave the place where he had gotten his start. Greg Maffei, his treasurer and future CFO, was more approachable, and Grasso made sure he called on Maffei anytime he was on the West Coast, but the big boss still resisted.

Then Grasso somehow managed to befriend Gates's father, a prominent Seattle attorney, when William Gates, Sr., toured the floor with his grandchildren. Grasso did the tour personally. At the end of a tour that impressed the kids, Grasso turned to one of Bill Gates's nieces and said, "Tell your uncle, the next time you're in town, for him to take you to the floor of the Nasdaq."

Grasso continued to push. He discovered that Jimmy Cayne had been a close friend of Nathan Mhyrvold, the man credited with developing the Windows operating system, and Grasso sent him an invitation to tour the floor. Mhyrvold agreed, but when Grasso was finished he was hardly impressed. "What's the big deal?" he asked Cayne. Steve Ballmer, then Gates's number two, had a similar reaction. Ballmer seemed to be most impressed with the amount of paper produced by the end of the trading day. He quipped that he thought the process was too "manualized." Gates, he said, was staying put.

Grasso had one more trick up his sleeve. In the mid- to late 1990s, Grasso had become a regular at Rao's, one of the most exclusive restaurants in New York City. The alleged onetime mob hangout is at the corner of Pleasant Avenue and 114th Street in East Harlem, once one of the many "Little Italys" that could be found throughout New York City. Except for Rao's, a small bakery, and a "social club" around the corner, there's little that resembles Italy about East Harlem these days, but that doesn't stop people, many of them rich and famous, from jamming Frankie Pellegrino's restaurant night after night to sample his "kitchen food," including his world-famous meatballs.

Much of Rao's charm isn't the food but the exclusivity. Frankie doesn't take reservations, and he keeps the phone off the hook during business hours. In fact, the only way to get a table at Rao's is to be a regular or to know one. Grasso had become a regular thanks in part to his friendship with Pellegrino, a part-time actor (he appeared as an FBI agent on the HBO series *The Sopranos*) and crooner.

Pellegrino also had become a regular at various events at the exchange, and Grasso would soon have a regular table at Rao's that he shared with Langone and Joe Grano. He had even taken Zarb there for dinner just to show off his clout.

It was this exclusivity that appeared to fascinate Gates and his best friend, fellow billionaire Warren Buffett, and got Grasso thinking about another way to get Gates to jump from the Nasdaq to the NYSE. Grasso had heard through the Rao's grapevine that both men now wanted a table of their own and would pay dearly for it. Grasso believed they wanted a table so badly that Gates might, just might, be willing to change his listing for a permanent seat at New York's most exclusive restaurant. It was a long shot, but Grasso figured his entire career had been a long shot and look how far he'd come.

Grasso approached Pellegrino, who said money wasn't the issue; there were no vacancies available, even for billionaires. They would just have to wait like everyone else. Grasso then asked for the next best thing: a table one night for Buffett, Gates, and their wives. Pellegrino said he would try to fit them in.

Buffett says in an e-mail that he never offered "as much as $1 to buy a table at Rao's or even thought of the possibility." Whatever Buffett said or thought, when Grasso said he had secured a four-seater, Buffett was so thrilled that he agreed to approach Gates about switching his shares to the stock exchange, Grasso recalls.

On the assigned night, security guards armed with submachine guns showed up early to make sure the place was safe for the two richest men in America. Buffett, Gates, and their companions were seated promptly at around 7:00 P.M. Grasso showed up that night too to dine with his friend, private investigator Bo Dietl, who also "owned" a table, and from a distance Grasso kept an eye on his target.

The dinner began with some antipasti, a little salad, and some baked clams, then the pasta and meatballs Frankie had made famous. Then those at the table had a dish of veal or chicken, depending on their preference. Gates and Buffett could have ordered every wine on the Rao's wine list, but instead they drank Diet Pepsi with their meal.

Pellegrino usually ends the night by singing a few of his favorite songs. That night he began with "My Girl," by the Temptations. At one point during the song, he stood beside his billionaire customers, looked them in the eye, and sang, "I don't need no money, fortune, or fame . . ." The crowd caught on and cheered. Buffett and Gates didn't seem to care; they were just happy to be part of the scene.

The next day Grasso says he telephoned Buffett, who thanked him for a wonderful night. Buffett also said he had discussed with Gates Microsoft's switching to the NYSE. Once again, Gates had said he wasn't ready to move. Still, Grasso felt he had made progress; at least he wasn't told to stop trying. In fact, Buffett wanted to know when was the next time he could get a table at Rao's.

News of Microsoft's repeated denials made the people at Nasdaq howl with glee; Zarb began to tell people that Grasso hadn't been able to snare a major Nasdaq listing since he took over. Zarb's contacts out west, the venture capitalists, had confirmed as much. Grasso met with just about every major VC player in the Valley.

Zarb may have spoken too soon. Grasso had been spending a lot of time wooing another big Nasdaq company, the popular online brokerage house E*Trade. For the past couple of years, E*Trade and its controversial CEO, Christos Cotsakos, had been bashing the Wall Street establishment, calling old-line brokerage firms dinosaurs in a world dominated by technology and computers. But Grasso had met with Cotsakos many times, extolling the exchange's value over the Nasdaq. By making the switch, Cotsakos would gain instant credibility with middle America, where the name recognition of the exchange and dinosaurs are appreciated, Grasso said.

Cotsakos weighed his options carefully, until one afternoon when Grasso was giving a speech at Pepperdine University in California to accept an honorary degree from the school, and Cotsakos, who received his PhD in economics there, was in the audience. After the ceremony, Grasso was approached by an elderly woman who had a special request. "I love watching you every morning ringing that bell," she said. "Do you think I could come by and see you do it?"

"Your mother wants to ring the opening bell," Grasso said to Cotsakos as he approached. Then he added, "That won't be a problem if your son lists E*Trade on the exchange."

Three months later, E*Trade listed on the exchange. Cotsakos was on the podium; his mother was supposed to have been there doing the honors, but she was home sick. Grasso broke exchange rules—apparently, you can get smeared with green slime, but you can't carry signs during the ceremony. But Grasso allowed Cotsakos to carry a sign that read I LOVE MOM. Grasso loved her too.

For several years, roughly between 1993 and 1996, a group of brokers working on behalf of a small brokerage firm, Oakford Securities, made $10 million through various illegal trades. They created dummy accounts with the Oakford firm to hide their profits.

When the news of the U.S. attorney's indictments of the Oakford brokers hit in February 1998, the "Oakford Floor Scandal" made national headlines. More than anything, the investigation had exposed the shortcomings of Grasso's regulatory staff. And now the SEC wanted answers from Grasso himself.

"I don't care if the number of people doing things wrong is eight, eighty-eight, or eight hundred eighty-eight," Grasso said to about seven hundred floor traders, clerks, and specialists who packed into the exchange's boardroom for a special membership meeting to discuss the scandal. "Whoever breaks the rules will be out of the building, immediately!"

But the SEC chief, Arthur Levitt, believed that Grasso may have been a ballbreaker with audits on the floor brokers he didn't like, but his enforcement had never taken direct aim at whether there was widespread corruption on the floor, as many large investors believed there was. Grasso had done much to protect the floor over the years, possibly too much, and now he would have to pay the price. The price, of course, was a wide-ranging investigation not just of the floor improprieties but also of Grasso's response to them.

Levitt by now had officially removed himself from the investigation because of his long relationship with Grasso. In his absence, the matter was left to his general counsel, a soft-spoken but tough Columbia Law School professor named Harvey Goldschmid, and Richard Walker, who headed the SEC's enforcement division.

Grasso clearly understood the gravity of the situation. As Grasso recalls, Goldschmid and Walker were brusque and businesslike when discussing the SEC's initial findings against the exchange. After the Oakford scandal broke, the SEC Office of Compliance Inspections and Examinations conducted an internal audit of the exchange's control system. They said it was inexcusable that such troubling evidence of misconduct had gone unnoticed by the exchange's regulatory staff for so long. They wanted a fine, a censure, and they were strongly considering removing the regulation unit from Grasso's control—the same solution handed out to the NASD during its trading scandal.

"You do that and we'll fight you to the end," Grasso countered.

The floor, he said, wasn't the Nasdaq marketplace. The U.S. attorney's office had found no wrongdoing outside a handful of "punks." His regulatory staff should be commended, not penalized, he added. They were helping prosecutors sift through documents and understand complex trades to make their case.

Goldschmid said he would get back to Grasso at some point with his final offer. In the meantime, Grasso decided to add some legal firepower to the exchange's defense team. He brought in superlawyer Marty Lipton, who was the head of the exchange's legal advisory committee, to produce a study of floor-trading practices, and Harvey Pitt, who was possibly the best white-collar attorney in the business, to go up against the SEC.

Pitt had been general counsel to the SEC in the late 1970s before quitting to go into private practice. He had gained some degree of fame for representing Ivan Boesky during the insider trading scandals of the 1980s, cutting a deal for a reduced prison sentence in exchange for Boesky's testimony against the junk bond king Michael Milken, who later went to jail.

Grasso started by telling Pitt that he should do a full investigation and he wanted to hear everything he found. "I'm not hiring you just to defend the exchange," Pitt remembers Grasso saying. "If you see a problem and you find that we did something wrong, tell me how to fix it." Grasso's honesty impressed Pitt; in his many years as a lawyer representing good guys and not-so-good guys, it was the first time a client had actually stated he wanted to be told the unvarnished truth.

Grasso, of course, wasn't the first CEO to order up an in-house investigation. Such inquiries are quite common among companies that find themselves in legal trouble, and almost always they find the wrongdoing confined to people well below the CEO and his immediate staff. The good news was that the investigation followed a similar pattern—the bad stuff was confined to the traders involved with Oakford. But the SEC was unimpressed. Investigators believed that it was the culture of the floor that condoned unethical behavior and the lack of enforcement by the NYSE that allowed it to happen. And they had some good evidence to work with: the traders themselves said their activities were condoned at the highest levels of the exchange.

The SEC appeared determined to use this case to make a statement. If Grasso wanted to avoid an embarrassing sanction by the commission he might have to take the SEC to court.

At a meeting with Pitt and Grasso in Washington, Walker told them the SEC had found some very serious problems, so much so it was prepared to issue fraud charges. There would certainly be a censure and a fine. But that would be the least of Grasso's problems. Like the Nasdaq, Grasso would no longer have control of the exchange's regulatory function.

Then it was Pitt's turn to speak. Do that, he said, and the exchange was ready to go to war. His wide-ranging investigation of floor trader activity had found no systemic abuse. In fact, the investigation had found that the regulatory staff had done everything in its power to prevent abuse over the years. "We're ready to fight," Pitt said.

In the end, the SEC apparently wasn't. Despite Levitt's reputation as a hard-nosed investigator, the reality was far different. Investigations during his tenure had slipped; even worse, wrongdoing on Wall Street involving brokerage fraud and conflicts of interest, allowing firms to promote stocks through research on companies that sent back investment banking business, was running rampant.

Within a few weeks, the SEC came back to the negotiating table with a compromise. The exchange would have to consent to improving its surveillance procedures and do a better job at implementing systems that could catch the bad guys. They wanted Grasso to fire Robert McSweeney, Grasso's enforcement czar with direct oversight of the floor. But Grasso simply moved him to another job. The SEC would issue a civil complaint that slammed the exchange for "fail-[ing] to take appropriate action to police for profit sharing or other performance-based compensation of independent floor brokers."

Grasso managed to lose the battle and win the war. He neither admitted nor denied the charges. Gone was the dreaded censure, and the regulatory department stayed right where Grasso wanted it, under his control. "We are thrilled at the conclusion because we think it strikes the right balance of partnership, and recognition that we could have done a better job in some areas," he told one reporter.

But back at the exchange another scandal was brewing. What had begun as a mere nuisance was now turning into something much uglier. For years Hank Greenberg, the volatile CEO of AIG, had been badgering Grasso and his specialist for better pricing on his stock. Grasso had never met a CEO who wasn't obsessed with his stock price. For a time, Sumner Redstone, the chairman of Viacom, rivaled Greenberg in this department. Like AIG, Grasso had stolen Viacom from a rival exchange. But it wasn't long before he began having second thoughts. Redstone complained incessantly about his specialist until Grasso placed Mel Karmazin, Redstone's number two, on the board of the exchange. The complaints didn't stop, but they began to lose their intensity.

Grasso had no such luck with Greenberg, who gave the word "obsession" new meaning. Greenberg was approaching eighty, but he was like no other eighty-year-old man Grasso had ever known. Greenberg worked out incessantly with weights and a stationary bike that kept him lean and mean. But he scared the hell out of Grasso with his expletive-laced tirades about the pricing of his stock and his threat that he would return to the Nasdaq if the AIG specialist didn't start doing a better job.

Grasso did all he could to appease Greenberg. Greenberg told Grasso he believed AIG had outgrown the exchange; the stock was too big to be handled by some guy on the floor. Only a computer could make the stock trade at a more accurate, loftier level. With that, Grasso began investigating Greenberg's complaints in a more direct way, asking for details about trading positions directly from AIG's specialist on the floor, a man named Todd Christie, just to see if Greenberg's harping had any merit.

News of Greenberg's pressuring Christie, a specialist for Spear, Leeds & Kellogg, soon spread through the floor, particularly as Grasso was spotted more and more over at Christie's station discussing AIG. Grasso was walking a tightrope: if he didn't keep Greenberg happy, he could lose a valuable listing. AIG was one of the biggest stocks in the world, one of the most actively traded on the floor.

But Grasso couldn't just order Christie to create an "unnatural floor" and bid up AIG's stock price. The securities laws were pretty straightforward on this count: the job of the specialist was to keep prices stable, not to satisfy management. If Grasso pushed Christie to bid up shares, he would have violated exchange rules and committed securities fraud. If Christie agreed, both of them could end up in jail.

Whether Grasso crossed the line was an open question at the exchange as Greenberg stepped up his demands. Grasso maintains he never told Christie what to do, other than to "do the right thing." Floor traders, though, say his mere presence on the floor, asking about the pricing of the stock, was problematic.

One morning Greenberg wanted to send a message to Grasso as well. AIG was in negotiations to purchase another insurance company, using its stock as currency, so the last thing Greenberg wanted was a falling stock price that would jeopardize the deal.

Grasso's secretary, SooJee Lee, was often the first to receive Greenberg's calls. Lee wasn't merely a secretary, she was also Grasso's gatekeeper, deciding which calls Grasso needed to answer and which ones he could ignore. There was no ignoring Greenberg, however. Lee received so many calls from the AIG chief, in fact, that she came up with a nickname for the AIG chief: "Mr. Yoo-hoo." Lee was out of the office when she retrieved the latest message. She called one of Grasso's assistants and told her to transcribe the following: "Hank Greenberg is not looking for AIG to go under $76.50 or the deal won't go through."

The deal went through, but the complaints continued. "Mr. Yoo-hoo" was on the telephone again and again, badgering Lee about how Christie priced his stock, demanding information about his trading positions, and generally driving Christie mad. Christie was one of the most prominent traders on the floor and a partner at Spear, Leeds. Langone once described the specialist business as "license to steal," but somehow Christie had figured out a way to lose money with AIG amid the complaints from Greenberg.

Christie e-mailed Lee to tell her he would deliver his long and short positions in AIG to "Mr. Yoo-hoo" by the end of the day, noting that "Mr. Greenberg is a bad man."

"I think he's not happy in general," Lee said. About ten minutes later Christie said, "Neither am I."

Grasso maintains that he constantly reminded Christie not to "do anything stupid" when it came to his dealings with Greenberg, who, for all his complaints, remained at the exchange, probably figuring he had a better chance at getting good pricing for his stock by badgering Grasso and Christie than he would by moving to the Nasdaq. And while Christie couldn't stand being near the old man from AIG, his relationship with Grasso was as strong as ever. Grasso would eventually appoint Christie to his board.

It wasn't bad having Grasso as a friend, unless, of course, the price of his friendship was having Hank Greenberg as a client. Christie kept a photo of Greenberg at his specialist post, right next to a photo of his dog. When Grasso first saw the photo, he couldn't stop laughing, particularly after he heard Christie trying to defuse a particularly nasty call from Greenberg by saying, "Hank, I love you as much as my dog."

In late 1999, a group of major Wall Street chief executives, led by the CEO of Goldman Sachs, Hank Paulson, had taken the first steps toward imposing electronic trading on the New York Stock Exchange. The idea Paulson pushed was called the "CLOB," short for "Central Limit Order Book," and its name sent shivers up Grasso's spine. The CLOB was essentially a computer that served as a clearinghouse for the stocks that Paulson and his growing band of followers on Wall Street believed could be matched without a specialist.

The theory was based on the principle that specialists weren't needed to make markets in the most heavily traded shares. Such stocks traded so frequently that with the help of a computer, buyers and sellers would almost match on their own. Under the plan, one thousand of the Big Board's most heavily traded stocks—in other words, the biggest companies in corporate America—would be filtered through the CLOB so they could be traded electronically. There was just one problem: the vast majority of the specialists' profits and 95 percent of the exchange's volume are derived from the top one thousand stocks traded on the floor.

Paulson is a tall, trim man, with piercing blue eyes that underscore his intensity and ambition. A Christian Scientist from rural Illinois, Paulson attended Dartmouth College and Harvard Business School and worked for a brief time in the Nixon administration. He began his career at Goldman's Chicago office as an investment banker. He thrived in the firm's corporate culture, which stressed, above all, making money. Despite his manicured background, Paulson also proved to be a ruthless infighter.

Grasso's good friend Merrill CEO Dave Komansky once called Paulson a "great banker of dubious repute" for his cutthroat business practices, which included incessant lobbying of clients. Paulson got the top job at Goldman using his sharp elbows when he led a coup d'état against CEO Jon Corzine, convincing the firm's board of directors that change was needed after Corzine botched a plan to take Goldman public. That move made Paulson the CEO.

Grasso held Paulson in particular contempt for two reasons: he just hated Goldman's elite image, which he felt had a cultural bias against people like him, and Goldman's investment in a popular electronic trading network known as Archipelago, which competed with the exchange. Paulson simply told Grasso that Goldman was embracing electronic trading as a necessary step to survive global competition, and the exchange should do so as well. "We don't want to be left behind," he said. Grasso believed he wanted to destroy the floor.

By late 1999 and early 2000, Paulson and Grasso were on a collision course. The exchange passed a rule in 1995 that for the first time allowed the super-dot to actually execute trades; before that it was just a system to deliver shares to the floor. But Grasso limited the execution to 1,100 shares; anything greater must go through a specialist. Paulson pressed his case with the SEC chairman, Arthur Levitt, that Grasso was impeding the advance of technology.

Paulson also found allies in Philip Purcell, the CEO of Morgan Stanley, and, ironically, Komansky, who said he had no choice but to do what was best for the firm and its large customers like Fidelity that were now demanding electronic market making. It was a rare instance of competitors—Morgan Stanley, Goldman, and Merrill—joining forces. Grasso didn't see his situation in such lofty terms. He figured that about 40 percent of his order flow was staging a revolt. He derisively called the trio "the MGM crew." He told anyone who would listen that the plan had nothing to do with making the markets more efficient and everything to do with money and power.

He made the same argument taught to him by Phelan decades earlier: without the floor, without Grasso demanding "best prices" and forcing trading desks to send orders to the exchange, the big firms would simply internalize order flow, matching buyers and sellers on their own and pocketing the difference. Large investors might not care. They're smart and powerful and know when they're getting screwed. But the centralized marketplace leveled the playing field between large investors and the growing number of small investors buying stocks for the first time.

To be sure, Grasso believed in the floor and the efficiency of the specialist system with all his heart and soul, but he wasn't just protecting it for the good of the small investor. He was also protecting his turf and his power. He had recently set up a series of meetings with the brokerage firms' biggest customers—mutual funds and pension funds, the ultimate sources of trading orders that pass through the brokerage firms and onto the floor. Executives at Fidelity Investments in Boston laid into him, accusing Grasso of defending an outdated trading system and ignoring outright fraud among his traders.

Grasso, of course, had heard such complaints from large institutional investors before, so he mostly sat and listened, leaving Boston with his tail between his legs and hoping the storm would pass.

Now that it hadn't, Grasso told the trio that if they wanted the CLOB and electronic trading, they would have to fight for it, and they would be fighting him as well.

Merrill's offices are an imposing sight. They're located in lower Manhattan alongside the Hudson River, in the World Financial Center, a modern facility that houses other Wall Street firms as well as the daily bible of the securities industry, *The Wall Street Journal.* Charles Merrill started the firm nearly a hundred years ago on the premise of "bringing Wall Street to Main Street," and the firm prospered over the next century, becoming the largest brokerage house in the nation.

Komansky had come from that brokerage culture. But both he and the firm had come a long way since the days when it had catered mainly to the little guy. Komansky ran a massive global enterprise with divisions in Europe, Japan and China, throughout Latin America, and in India. The brokerage division was profitable, but Komansky's biggest problem was trying to find investment bankers who could snare more of the high-technology banking deals that seemed to be going with alarming frequency to Morgan Stanley and Goldman.

Grasso was quickly ushered into a special elevator that took him to the executive dining rooms. Grasso was used to getting the star treatment at the NYSE's own dining room, but lunch at Club Merrill was a special event. The room itself was spacious, with a great view of the Hudson River, some of the bedroom communities just across the river in New Jersey, and the Statue of Liberty. White-gloved waiters wearing tuxedos gave the dining hall a regal feeling. Komansky was a tough-talking Bronx native, but he clearly relished the service and the five-star menu, as his bulging waistline demonstrated.

As the meeting began, Komansky settled into his seat in a private room along with Paulson, Purcell, and Grasso. Each engaged in a bit of small talk. Paulson was the first to test the waters. "We believe that electronic trading can coexist with the specialists," he said.

Grasso cut him off. "Gentlemen, you're my biggest customers, so if you want to do it I can't stop you, but let's be honest: if you shut the exchange out of the thousand largest stocks, you might as well shut the door of the exchange to make room for another show off Broadway."

Komansky didn't quite get the joke. "What the fuck are you talking about, 'off Broadway'?" he blurted out.

"Once the NYSE is shut down, it's going to be wild watching you guys start killing each other for order flow and business," Grasso replied with a laugh.

The meeting broke up about an hour later without Grasso budging an inch and with Paulson explaining that he was pushing the effort not to kill the exchange but to make it survive in the future. But whatever Grasso said seemed to have a profound impact on Komansky. Like most Wall Street CEOs, he believed Goldman didn't make any move without figuring out what it meant for its bottom line. Later that day Komansky called Grasso and said, "You know, you're right"—not about the CLOB but about trusting Paulson's motives. Merrill stayed in the MGM crew, but mostly in name only.

The battle over the CLOB moved to Washington, to lawmakers such as Senator Phil Gramm, the powerful head of the Senate Banking Committee, which monitored the SEC and the self-regulatory organizations. Levitt publicly held his cards close to his vest, but Grasso believed that he had now sided with the MGM crew. One afternoon, Jimmy Cayne ran into Purcell and Morgan Stanley's president, John Mack, at Mack's Westchester County country club. They were wooing Levitt with their ideas on market structure in between rounds of golf, and he was listening.

For a time, it looked as though Grasso was losing the battle, but Phil Gramm, himself a PhD in economics, mistrusted the power of Wall Street. Gramm was also a huge fan of the floor of the New York Stock Exchange. He believed the floor was an important symbol of the economy, an exclamation point on the strength of the capitalist system. The trading activity, he said, made his "heart skip a beat."

Well, his heart was still beating, luckily for Grasso. For months, Grasso had his lobbyists making the rounds in Washington explaining how the MGM monopoly would control trading if the new system was enacted. Gramm mostly sat and listened, setting the stage for a special Senate Banking Committee meeting in early 2000, where the CLOB would be discussed and the fate of the floor decided.

But even before the hearing began, it was clear that Grasso had won the day. Gramm gave an opening statement in which he cautioned against radical change and even had some praise for the old specialist system, describing the floor as "hallowed ground." Grasso, Paulson, Levitt, and the rest gave their assessments of the situation, but the committee—and, more significantly, its chairman—had made up its mind.

And Paulson had to adjust his business to meet the new environment. Paulson thought the specialists were an anachronism, but he now directed Goldman to buy one of the biggest specialist firms on the floor, Spear, Leeds & Kellogg, for a whopping $6.5 billion.

For Paulson it was the ultimate hedge. Besides making markets on the floor, Spear has a thriving business clearing stocks on the Chicago Mercantile Exchange. If Grasso maintained his control, Paulson would have control of one of the best specialist firms around. But if he could someday wrest control of the exchange from the little guy, his $6 billion wasn't such a waste.

New listings continued to pour into the exchange, albeit at a slower rate as the 1990s came to a close, from around 200 in 1998 to around 125 in 2000. Order flow, thanks to Grasso's maneuvers with Sandy Weill and the rest of Wall Street, as well as his killing of the CLOB, was as strong as ever. The Dow Jones Industrial Average, the broadest measure of the stock market, now traded above 10,000 for the first time ever, and volume soared to a record of more than 2 billion shares in one day in early 2001.

But much of what Grasso had achieved couldn't be directly measured; at least, that was Langone's rationale for continuing to ramp up Grasso's pay. As compensation committee chief, he was supposed to use a "comparator group" of other CEOs to determine Grasso's compensation. Langone countered that what Grasso accomplished couldn't be compared to corporate America. Grasso was part businessman, part politician, part circus maestro, and part cop on the beat. And how do you measure that great brand that Grasso took to new heights?

Langone himself was a man in perpetual motion. Even as he approached seventy years of age, he worked twelve-hour days, on exchange matters, investments, and his charitable work. But Langone had never seen anyone work like Grasso. The decline in new listings could be easily attributed to a decline in IPOs hitting the market, not to a lack of effort, he said. As Grasso was going toe-to-toe with the Nasdaq, he was also competing with his most powerful member firms over electronic trading and negotiating with the Giuliani administration for tax breaks so the exchange could build a new twenty-one-story building.

Amid all of this, Grasso was planning for the future in another way: he had hired Merrill Lynch to crunch the numbers on what it would take to make the exchange a public company.

The Nasdaq stock market crash in March 2000 signaled the end of the long bull market, but it energized Grasso as never before. It was an affirmation of everything he was saying and believed: that computers and technology weren't the answer to everything. The responsible parties, Grasso said, were high-tech speculators. The crashing Nasdaq had yet to spill over to the big stocks that traded on the exchange, and seat prices stood steady in 2000 at around $2.65 million. If the exchange were to go public, now would be the time. The Nasdaq had already gone public, and its shares now reflected its depressed business prospects. Grasso again turned to his bankers at Merrill about an IPO, and they agreed. The crash would likely spread to the rest of the market. Why not cash out before it was too late?

The exchange could, of course, use the money. IPOs provide currency to expand, and Grasso had grand plans to take over not just one but every one of the big European exchanges: the London Stock Exchange; Euronext, which combined the stock markets of France, Amsterdam, and Brussels; and the Deutsche Bourse in Germany.

Grasso was ready to hit the button and give Merrill the green light for the IPO. That is, until he received a telephone call from Arthur Levitt. The SEC chief was never far behind Grasso, it seemed. He was Grasso's de facto boss, and when he received the NYSE's IPO proposal, he gave it careful consideration. Grasso was now paying the price for dissing Levitt all these years. The SEC chief had no problem with the exchange selling stock. His problem was something else: Levitt didn't think that a for-profit company should be a regulator as well. Levitt told Grasso the SEC wouldn't approve the IPO unless he copied the Nasdaq and spun off his regulatory division.

Grasso exploded, but Levitt stood his ground, and the IPO was called off.

Grasso would later say that he feared he would have to turn over his regulatory staff to the NASD because of Levitt's relationship with Zarb, and he was probably right, because the door would have been open for the elimination of one of the self regulators, and at least in Levitt's mind the most reliable would be Zarb.

Too bad the market that Zarb regulated wasn't as reliable. The Nasdaq crash would eventually seep into the broader markets. IPOs and listings would begin to decline even more than they already had. Grasso's grand plan for a new NYSE building was placed on hold even after negotiations with the Giuliani administration provided the exchange with lucrative tax breaks to make the move.

By the end of 2000 the big companies that trade on the Big Board had their first taste of the bear market that had crushed so many Nasdaq investors for the past year. Through most of 2001, the market would only get worse, and the resentment of the new investing class would grow. There would be hearings and investigations.

If Langone was apprehensive about the markets or the slippage in listings from their heights a few years earlier, or about the fact that the times had changed, he didn't show it when evaluating Grasso's performance to determine his compensation. Langone remained oblivious to this sea of change as his relationship with Grasso appeared to grow closer and closer. To people in Grasso's inner circle, Langone appeared to have replaced Phelan as Grasso's mentor. The two now spoke regularly, almost daily, about exchange business. And that was fine by Langone, who according to his age was in the twilight of his career, but based on his work product—the various boards he sat on, his clout in the Club—was growing in power. In February 2000, when the compensation committee began to deliberate about Grasso's pay, Langone recommended that Grasso receive his biggest paycheck yet: $21.8 million, plus a $5 million bonus he described as "a special bonus," an extra bit of compensation that Langone determined with the compensation committee.

It was the job of Frank Ashen, the head of human resources for the exchange and the Club's chief ethics officer, to explain the various components of Grasso's pay to the board of directors. Most were like Langone; they believed that no amount of money was enough for someone of Grasso's caliber and worth to the exchange. Others just didn't seem to care when Ashen rattled off the facts and figures.

Most, but not all. Charles Bocklet, a floor trader and board member, didn't quite object to Grasso's salary that year but he did make a face when he heard some of the numbers that was obvious enough to catch the attention of Ashen, who quickly reported the incident to Grasso. Bocklet was vice chairman of the exchange, a part-time position that allowed him to continue his job as a floor trader. His office was across the hall from Grasso's on the sixth floor of the exchange, and the two had been friends for years. Bocklet, like most floor traders, viewed Grasso with a mixture of awe and fear, and he suddenly felt his stomach tighten when the little guy dropped by his office one afternoon and asked if he had a problem with his compensation.

When confronted, Bocklet dropped any pretense of opposition. Put on the spot, he immediately began backpedaling, telling Grasso that he had no problem with how much he was earning; in fact, he wanted to know if Grasso was "happy with it." Grasso said he was, and the meeting quickly ended.

Grasso denies that he confronted Bocklet on his compensation, but Bocklet contends that the event did occur. One thing was certain: the Club's good times were coming to an end, and it was beginning to show on the exchange's income statement, something Grasso couldn't keep quiet like his salary. The exchange's profits fell from $75.5 million in 1999 to just over $30 million by the end of 2001. In 1998 more than sixty companies switched over from the Nasdaq; in 2001, around thirty made the move. Grasso increased taxes on the floor to pay for technological and other improvements. Then the exchange introduced something called decimalization, where the difference between how much a stock can be bid for and offered at was narrowed to decimals. The SEC had mandated the move, and the result was devastating for the floor: more orders were matched without the need for a broker to step in and to bring the parties together, cutting floor profits and trader salaries.

One of the benefits of Grasso's decision not to take the Club public was that he wouldn't have to disclose just how much he was being paid as business conditions on the floor deteriorated. Langone expected strict confidentiality during meetings about Grasso's compensation, and most board members, even those like Bocklet, kept whatever concerns they might have had to themselves, at least for the time being.

But what if they hadn't? What would have happened if somehow Grasso's buddies on the floor had caught wind of his salary and retirement package, which now exceeded $100 million?

Bocklet had a simple answer: they would have "hung him."

6

THE SAVIOR

The knock against Grasso was that he was a "star fucker," someone who got off on being around the rich and powerful so he could partake in their celebrity. But it was these very relationships with the rich and powerful that paid off on September 11, 2001, and in the crucial week beyond, when Grasso had to move heaven and earth to get the exchange open again—and reassure the world that American capitalism could still function.

Nine hours after the terrorist attacks, Grasso was physically exhausted and mentally spent. By now he had sent his senior staff home. The entire exchange was evacuated and Grasso ordered his driver to take him uptown for dinner. In the summer, the restaurants on the Upper East Side of Manhattan are normally among the liveliest in the city, but on this summer night, many were closed. The streets were empty; Grasso had never seen the city this way, adding to the growing pit in his stomach about how he was going to pull off what he knew was the greatest challenge in his career. As his driver cruised through the Upper East Side looking for a spot to grab a bite to eat, Grasso noticed that the Italian restaurant Baraonda was still serving, doing a brisk business. He just wanted to eat and head back downtown. At first, the maître d' said the wait would be more than an hour, but he was quickly interrupted by a prominent customer, Salvatore Lombardi, the maître d' from Grasso's favorite spot in the neighborhood, Campagnola, who made sure Grasso got a seat.

Grasso left the restaurant at around 10:30 P.M., completely sober (he didn't even have a glass of wine that night) and very worried. He phoned Lori to tell her he was staying in the city, sleeping on the couch in his office. It was the first time the two had spoken since early in the morning and well after reports surfaced that the exchange itself was a target, a report that sent shivers down Lori's spine as she waited for further news.

Meanwhile, Grasso's driver sped toward the stock exchange. Grasso settled into an uncomfortable sleep on the couch of his office, one that was interrupted by more than a few cold sweats. Grasso didn't know it at the time, but 9/11 was slowly becoming a defining moment in his career. Fewer than twelve hours earlier, Wall Street, as anyone knew it, had been destroyed. Downtown Manhattan was cordoned off as a war zone. Traffic was restricted to essential personnel as the police and fire departments conducted the largest rescue effort in the city's history.

During the first two days after the attacks, Grasso made sure his senior staff was keenly aware of what was expected of them. Kinney was responsible for dealing with the regional exchanges, Britz kept in contact with the member firms, Johnston handled the overflow. Grasso, meanwhile, dealt with top CEOs and the major political players. Amid all of the confusion, Grasso made sure he kept his temper in check and kept speaking to the press. It was one of the many things he had learned from Phelan, who had divided duties among his senior staff during the 1987 stock market crash: it's okay to be a control freak when things are going well, but in times of crisis, let your team do at least some of the work.

Robert Cunningham had worked as a floor trader for twenty years, the last ten as the head broker for Merrill Lynch, which supplied more trading volume to the exchange than any other firm. That made

Cunningham not just a very powerful man at the exchange but also a very important one if the exchange was to reopen anytime soon. Put simply, if Merrill couldn't open, the exchange couldn't either.

Cunningham knew this when he got up at his normal time, 6:00 A.M., on Wednesday, September 12, just like any other day. When he rolled out of bed, his wife pointedly asked him, "Why are you going to work?" To which he replied, "Honey, if the exchange doesn't open, we can't pay the rent." Cunningham was, of course, exaggerating; he, his wife, and their three kids lived comfortably in Ridgewood, New Jersey. Cunningham earned much more than a comfortable living, as did most people who traded on the floor. Still, his wife understood what her husband was up against. The terrorists' attacks were designed to destroy the economy by destroying its foundation—the stock market. By going to work, her husband was playing a small but significant role in making sure that didn't happen.

Things immediately got off to a bizarre start when Cunningham ascended the stairs at the train station on Christopher Street in lower Manhattan, and was confronted by a pair of transvestites engaging in oral sex. He stepped by the couple, walked onto the street, and noticed the putrid smell of the burning rubble. He made his way south toward ground zero. Cops armed with machine guns stood at various checkpoints demanding identification from people trying to get into the financial district. Cunningham had grown up in Woodside, Queens, and one of the cops turned out to be a childhood friend. "Bobby, what the fuck are you doing here?" the cop asked. Cunningham told him he worked for Merrill Lynch and needed to get to the stock exchange. The officer then offered to drive Cunningham to the exchange. But Cunningham refused. "Stay here and do your job, I'll walk."

At the steps of the exchange he was greeted by a security guard. "Mr. Cunningham," the guard said, "the only other person here besides security is Dick Grasso."

"Sounds great," Cunningham said as he made a beeline for the Merrill Lynch trading booth. A few years back, Cunningham had convinced the brass at Merrill Lynch to upgrade the telephone system on the floor to something called "triple redundancy," meaning that the phone system could withstand a complete breakdown in the telecommunications system. The destruction of the lower Manhattan telecommunications grid was so extensive that most firms had no service. But Merrill's phone lines were working, and Cunningham was elated. He called the head trader at Merrill Lynch, Eddie McMahon, who, with the rest of the trading desk, had set up shop in Jersey City. "You see, I told you we needed those extra lines," he said. McMahon just laughed before Cunningham added, "Spread the word, we can trade."

Cunningham spent the rest of the day contacting his brokers and getting ready for the reopening of the exchange, which, as far as he was concerned, could happen immediately. Then he went upstairs to the sixth floor to pay a visit to Grasso. Cunningham wasn't part of Grasso's inner circle of floor traders, but Grasso considered him a friend and welcomed him inside for a quick chat. Grasso had been on the telephone with SEC chairman Harvey Pitt, preparing for the meeting at Bear Stearns that afternoon and discussing how best to reopen the exchange immediately, when Cunningham blurted out, "Mr. Grasso, Merrill Lynch is in the building, and we can open immediately."

Grasso just smiled weakly and said, "Thanks, Bobby," as the phone rang. The two shook hands, and Cunningham left the building with a weird feeling that he had said something wrong.

Bear Stearns, known simply as "the Bear," is one of the most aggressive firms on Wall Street. It's the quintessential Wall Street trading house, where top producers are rewarded handsomely while those who fail to perform are shown the door. Pedigree doesn't really matter at the Bear. An Ivy League degree and a WASPy-sounding last name might get you an interview at Morgan Stanley and Goldman, but at Bear, they're a sign of weakness. The Bear loves competitors, people willing to win every deal and make money on every trade. For more than a generation, the firm had been run by antiestablishment players who fit this mode. Its current leader, CEO James "Jimmy" Cayne, was no different.

Grasso respected Cayne's business judgment—it was no accident, he would say, that Bear Stearns was one of the few firms that hadn't paid for high-priced Internet investment banking talent during the 1990s, only to watch the market crater—but he also understood that Cayne was far from a team player in the Wall Street community. Bear, after all, had been the only firm to refuse to provide money for the bailout of the massive hedge fund Long-Term Capital Management, which threatened to sink the markets in chaos because Wall Street had so much of its money wrapped up in the failing enterprise. Cayne withstood calls from competitors, regulators, even politicians. He nearly got into a shoving match with Merrill CEO Dave Komansky over his intransigence, but he still refused. For Cayne, his rationale was simple: Bear was one of the few firms not to have invested in the hedge fund, so why should he help bail it out? Wall Street is a business, not a charity.

The September 12 meeting was set to begin around midday at Bear's headquarters on Forty-sixth Street and Park Avenue. When Grasso arrived, Cayne was gracious, even though he was opening up his house to his competitors, not to mention the press, which were in an adjoining room waiting to hear when the markets would reopen during a press conference that followed. It wasn't long before it became clear why Cayne was being so accommodating. Bear Stearns's competitors, all representatives of the top securities firms, began filing into the large conference room, many with stern looks on their faces as they realized they would have to hold a meeting not on neutral ground at the NYSE but on Cayne's turf. They knew that Bear would get publicity as being one of the few Wall Street firms open for business following the attacks.

Representing Merrill was the firm's vice chairman, Steve Hammerman. Komansky, a large man with a bad back, had been in constant contact with Grasso, but he was in no shape to travel anywhere, having survived a near brush with death when the towers came crashing down.

Goldman CEO Hank Paulson couldn't make it either, but for a different reason: Grasso heard he was stuck in Japan. After his bruising battle with the Goldman CEO, Grasso had kept his enemy close by asking him to join the board of the stock exchange. Paulson had accepted, but reluctantly and only after telling Grasso he wouldn't be the most attentive board member.

But Komansky and Paulson were the exceptions as the top members of Wall Street's ruling body took their seats in a large conference room, with Grasso sitting at one end of the table and Pitt, the SEC chief, at the other. The list of dignitaries was certainly impressive. Joe Grano, who had been elevated from the number two position at PaineWebber to chairman of the newly combined UBS PaineWebber brokerage firm, attended, as did John Mack, the head of CSFB, and his archenemy, Phil Purcell, the CEO of Morgan Stanley, who had recently ousted Mack in a power struggle for control of Morgan Stanley. Representatives from Citigroup and JPMorgan Chase were in attendance, as was Peter Fisher, the undersecretary of the Treasury; Lawrence Babbio, the vice chairman of Verizon; and Kevin Burke, the chief operating officer of Con Edison, the area's largest utility.

Grasso called the meeting to order, announcing that Pitt would read an opening statement, following a moment of silence. Given his conversation with the New York State superintendent of banking, Grasso knew he needed political cover from those who wanted to open the exchange immediately, and Pitt delivered. The SEC chief simply stated that he was there to help and that there would be no "gotcha" from the commission if they needed more than a week to recover and reopen.

That was music to Grasso's ears and many of those in the room as they began to assess the damage, but not to the White House. Assistant Treasury secretary Peter Fisher relayed a special message to the group that his boss, Treasury secretary Paul O'Neill, wanted Wall Street back in business "as quickly as possible" and the stock exchange opened immediately, as early as Thursday.

Grasso was taken aback; he knew the White House wanted the markets opened soon, but he had thought he would have at least until Friday. He was even more taken aback by the support Fisher received from a few members. Purcell, the CEO of Morgan Stanley, said his firm was ready to open at any time. Hammerman had obviously heard Cunningham's assessment and said Merrill had ample office space in Jersey City and midtown Manhattan. The firm could conceivably open as soon as Thursday, definitely by Friday. Grasso kept silent, but Joe Grano didn't. Grano knew firsthand the nature of the damage and the problems that might arise from opening too soon. "Steve, cut that macho bullshit," Grano said. "Are you really saying Merrill Lynch, with all its problems, can open by Thursday?"

Hammerman excused himself and left the room as the debate continued. Grano received support from Cayne, who simply asked how people were going to work in a war zone. John Mack worried if people were psychologically ready to return to work. Dick Fuld, the head of Lehman Brothers, may have been the most vocal of the group. There was no way Lehman, located across from the trade center, could open, he said. The firm didn't even have office space to trade from. "We don't even know," he added mournfully, "who's alive."

When it was his turn, Grasso said he was relaying a message on behalf of dozens of smaller firms when he brought up the situation of Sandler O'Neill & Partners, which was in desperate need of office space. He brought up the problems faced by Vincent Viola, the head of the New York Mercantile Exchange, the largest futures exchange, who first couldn't get by police checkpoints and when he finally got access, discovered that his phones weren't working. He told the group to consider the following: the cleanup and the logistics of installing electricity and telephone service all would come on top of the fact that bodies were still being pulled from the still-smoldering debris. And he asked the group to consider one last thing: If the exchange opened too soon, if it couldn't handle the huge volume of sell orders that would undoubtedly flood the markets, how would that look?

Hammerman had returned just in time to hear Grasso speak and reported back to the group that Merrill would like to have more time. Without Merrill in the markets, any chance of an early opening was over, given its importance to the markets as the largest order flow provider to the exchange and the firm that dealt with more small investors through its fifteen thousand brokers than any firm on the street. Pitt then spoke up—or, to be more specific, he spoke for Grasso—when he announced that they would shoot to reopen by Friday, if possible. Everyone seemed to be in agreement, and Grasso was relieved, but not as much as Larry Babbio, the president of Verizon, who laid out the scope of the damage: the attacks had destroyed fifteen thousand circuits that supplied nearly 80 percent of both the telephone and data capacity to the NYSE and lower Manhattan. To restore the downtown financial district to anything like it had been, Verizon would have to repair about fourteen thousand of those circuits. It was a monumental task and something that couldn't be done in a day. Officials from Con Ed made a similar announcement, telling the group that the company was bringing huge generators down to lower Manhattan to supply electricity to its customers. Grasso added that his tech staff was working around the clock as well, and he would be coordinating with everyone in the room over the next two days to make sure they did the job right.

By the end of the meeting, Grasso had accomplished two goals. First, he managed to dampen any expectation that the exchange would open in the next twenty-four to forty-eight hours. More important, he got people working together. Purcell and Mack's bitter fallout had been widely chronicled in the press, but after the meeting the two shook hands. Lehman may have been the firm in the most critical state, since it was still looking for space, but that would change as well when Citigroup offered the firm space in one of its buildings.

The meeting had ended on a high note. The firms agreed to do their best not to dump shares when trading began. Grasso said he would shoot to open on Friday; it wasn't a firm commitment but a target date that seemed to appease all sides.

Cayne then volunteered to host a second meeting at Bear's headquarters. Grasso appeared to be on board—that is, until he was pulled aside by Pitt. "Dick, this was great for today but not for tomorrow," he said. Later, the official reason given for the change in venue was a series of bomb scares near Bear's offices in midtown Manhattan. But the real reason was much different. Pitt was blown away by all the Bear Stearns signs that appeared in the media room where the press conference was televised. So the next day, the meeting was held at the offices of Credit Suisse. Cayne, it should be noted, also attended.

Grasso loved the limelight but hated the press, and despite his expertise in marketing and publicity, Zito did little to change his boss's world view of reporters, which at times bordered on paranoia. Whenever *The Wall Street Journal* ran a story he didn't like, for example, Grasso immediately attributed it to a family connection. The Money & Investing editor at the *Journal,* Larry Ingrassia, was a favorite target of Grasso's press paranoia, because he had the same last name as two investment bankers at Goldman Sachs, his enemy. Both were cousins of the *Journal* editor, but their influence at the paper seemed limited.

When asked, Grasso could rattle off a laundry list of examples of how the press manipulated its coverage of the exchange. Whether these examples were grounded in fact or paranoia, one thing is certain: Grasso's distaste for the media, particularly the elite print media, was mostly cultural. Though he had listed both *The New York Times* and *The Wall Street Journal*'s parent, Dow Jones, on the exchange, Grasso felt uncomfortable around the Ivy League–educated reporters and editors who populated most newsrooms. In Grasso's mind, because they couldn't relate to a street kid from Queens making it big, they must be out to get him.

But following the attacks, Grasso made a conscious effort to put his feelings aside and became accessible to reporters as never before. By now, the opening of the exchange had become a massive story, with camera crews and print journalists camped outside the Club on nearly a twenty-four-hour basis. Another thing that Grasso had learned from Phelan during his crisis—the 1987 stock market crash—was how to use the bully pulpit of his office to get his message out. And that message was casting the reopening of the exchange in patriotic terms even if it was, at bottom, a business decision.

In the hours and days that followed the terrorist attacks, Grasso gave speeches, answered reporters' telephone calls, and even tried to develop a more lasting relationship or two where he could speak candidly without being quoted. *The New York Times*'s publisher, Arthur "Pinch" Sulzberger, asked Grasso if a reporter could follow him around as he worked to reopen the exchange. Grasso gave the okay after Sulzberger agreed that the reporter wouldn't take any "cheap shots."

Grasso's critics on the floor would tell you that anything Grasso did, from the floor stunts to the trip to Colombia, he did to promote himself and by extension the exchange. His actions following the 9/11 attacks, they would say, were no exception. But anyone who knows Grasso also knows that patriotism is a big part of his life.

Grasso may have had publicity in mind when he gave these speeches and interviews, but he also spoke from his heart, and in doing so he transformed himself from a CEO into a leader. "Is this not just another one of those moments when America has been challenged, and will rise again?" he told reporters, according to one news account. Grasso opened the exchange's bank account and spent $150,000 on a huge American flag, forty feet high and seventy-two feet wide, which he had draped over the front of the exchange. He called it his "fuck you to bin Laden."

And it was working. Grasso was becoming Wall Street's Giuliani, a voice of calm and reason—and hope. Giuliani and Grasso had rarely spoken since the first days of the attack, communicating for the most part through intermediaries because both were too busy. But as the week wore on, they seemed to be linked. Both had monumental tasks ahead of them: one helping to restore a city and the other to restore the markets—all the complicated trading systems that link thousands of investors, and all the major Wall Street firms, to the NYSE.

Both also understood that recovery would require more than just doing the job well. It would take a narrative, presented every day to a public that wanted reassurance, and both gave as much reassurance as they could muster. In doing so, Giuliani became "America's mayor." Grasso became the public face of Wall Street, by repeating a simple but effective message: the terrorists, he said, would be defeated, and capitalism would survive.

• • •

The meeting at CSFB on Thursday, September 13, had little of the drama of the day before. But it did establish one key fact: that the Friday deadline was out of the question. Grasso; Harvey Pitt; Hardwick Simmons, the CEO of the NASD, who was in the process of replacing Zarb; and Peter Fisher—the same Treasury official who had initially called for an immediate opening—gave a joint news conference announcing that the target date had been moved back. Subject to a successful systems check, the opening would occur on Monday, September 17. Simmons, the former CEO of Prudential Securities, privately told the group that the Nasdaq stock market's situation wasn't all that different from the NYSE's. Nasdaq market makers who traded stocks and matched buyers and sellers could start trading immediately, except for the fact that so many of them worked for the same Wall Street firms that were struggling to find office space and open for business. It was music to Grasso's ears.

Amid the flurry of meetings and phone calls from Con Ed, Verizon, and his member firms, Grasso received a telephone call from Hank Greenberg. Grasso grimaced when he saw the note with Greenberg's name scrawled across it, but even when there was so much to do, Greenberg wasn't someone Grasso could ignore. When Grasso dialed Greenberg back, he was bracing for the worst. Would this be another screaming match about how well his specialists would support the price of AIG shares when the markets opened? As it turned out, Greenberg had a simple request: Could Grasso get Con Ed to give him some generators so he could open the AIG headquarters, located in lower Manhattan, for business? Grasso said he would see what he could do. After the call Grasso remarked, "I can't remember the last time that guy didn't scream at me because of his specialist." Greenberg got his generators.

Friday, September 15, 2001, was a critical day for Grasso. Crews from Verizon and Con Ed were working overtime to restore telephone service and power to lower Manhattan. Grasso was still receiving calls from some member firms whose employees had trouble getting past the checkpoints; one critical call came from the operations chief of

Salomon Smith Barney, the securities unit of Citigroup. Cops were stopping his people dead in their tracks, and he was afraid the firm would have to sit out Monday's opening. Grasso quickly called his friend Richard Sheirer, the head of the mayor's Office of Emergency Management, and arranged for van service and passes that would get the employees through the checkpoints.

On Friday, Grasso was summoned uptown to meet Giuliani and Sheirer at Giuliani's operations center on the Upper West Side of Manhattan, just north of the *Intrepid* aircraft carrier at Pier 86. Before Grasso was to meet the mayor, Sheirer took him to a special center for families of those missing in the attacks. Grasso couldn't believe his eyes as he saw photos of the missing plastered along the walls with telephone numbers of family members hoping against hope that loved ones were somehow trapped under the smoldering rubble and still alive. It was almost too much for Grasso to take, and he was ready to leave when he met a woman who had worked for the exchange for many years. She approached Grasso. She didn't ask for anything. She just grabbed him, hugged him, and began to cry softly, repeating the words "My daughter . . . my daughter." Her daughter had been a secretary at Cantor Fitzgerald, one of the worst hit of the brokerage firms. Grasso just hugged her back, and for the first time all week, he cried as well.

In public Grasso was confident, upbeat, and direct. But at times the pressure took its toll and boiled over in private. Even when Grasso returned to his elegant home in Locust Valley on Long Island, he couldn't forget the putrid smell of burning wires and debris that wafted through lower Manhattan. Grasso had never slept more than six hours a night; now he barely logged four hours of shut-eye.

At the Thursday meeting at CSFB, Grasso made the point that taking the week off made sense not just for business reasons but for psychological reasons as well. "The country needed to take a deep breath," he said. The others agreed, but by the end of the week, whispering about the flaws in the specialist system began to appear in the press with greater frequency. Grasso suspected his enemies at the Nasdaq—not so much Simmons, whom he liked, but Zarb. He thought he had proof one day after a wire service ran a headline that a prominent floor trader believed the exchange could reopen immediately. The veteran specialist Robert Fagenson says he was sandbagged by a reporter, who asked for an assessment from the floor and about the exchange's readiness to get back to business. "We're ready to open," Fagenson said, which, as far as he was concerned, was true. But Grasso nearly hit the ceiling.

"What's wrong with you?" Grasso demanded, making note of the headline. "Are you trying to preempt me?" Fagenson said he wasn't and Grasso just rushed off. It seemed like the first time all week Grasso's temper and ego had really surfaced and Fagenson chalked it up to fatigue. Maybe so, but others said it was the sign that the old Grasso was back, the guy who was obsessed with himself and with maintaining his power. Grasso didn't speak to Fagenson for almost two years after that.

Even so, progress on repairing the communication system was going so well that his tech staff said a Monday opening looked like a layup. Grasso's twin worries, Merrill and Lehman, appeared ready as well, and even Sandler O'Neill, thanks to Grasso's efforts, found office space in midtown Manhattan. By the end of the week, Komansky reported to Grasso that the firm's stock and bond traders were situated in offices across the river in Jersey City, its bankers were at an office in midtown, and its technical staff was completing any additional repairs. In other words, Merrill, the nation's largest brokerage firm, was ready for business.

Lehman CEO Dick Fuld gave Grasso a similar report, having worked out a deal for office space with Citigroup. Grasso was able to report back to Pitt that, barring some unforeseen event, trading at the exchange could start on Monday, only six days after the attacks.

But Grasso wasn't giving Pitt the entire story. He heard from City Hall that One Liberty Plaza was still a problem: the fifty-four-story skyscraper, located just across the street from the trade center, was unsafe. Grasso received word that a final certification of the building's structural safety would take place Sunday. If it failed, the re-opening would have to be delayed indefinitely. Grasso didn't need anyone to tell him what it would mean if the exchange couldn't open. Listed stocks can trade on any exchange that provides the best pricing, and, given the political pressure to reopen Wall Street, much of the NYSE's business would flow to the Nasdaq. Grasso told no one about this worst-case scenario. He just prayed.

Grasso was doing a lot of praying in the final hours leading up to the opening. Pitt called Saturday with an urgent message. Grasso knew it would be bad when Pitt began by asking Grasso "not to shoot the messenger." The White House wanted him in Washington on Sunday to have some photos taken with President Bush before the markets opened. Grasso went nuts; he didn't want to take any chances missing Monday's big event, even if it meant hanging out with the president. "You got to be fucking kidding me," he shot back. "If I'm not here and something happens, I'll be dead."

Pitt said he was just "relaying a message" and urged him to call Treasury secretary Paul O'Neill, who was scheduled to be on the podium himself during the opening-bell ceremonies. Grasso did just that, telling O'Neill he was needed at the exchange. O'Neill agreed, but the insanity continued. Grasso knew the economy was in deep trouble, as were the markets, as his sources on the street told him to brace for a wave of selling even as he put the word out to his member firms "to do their patriotic duty" and support the market as best they could. But Grasso also knew such statements worked, particularly after one anchorwoman, WNBC's Felicia Taylor, remarked that Grasso's statement had been "so powerful and fortifying for everyone here."

Grasso could have used some of the same encouragement himself. By Sunday afternoon, he still hadn't heard back from City Hall about One Liberty Plaza. To break the tension, he went back to his office with Klondike, a bomb-sniffing dog lent by the police department to the exchange. Grasso had broken the monotony of the past couple of days by roughhousing with the big German shepherd and feeding the dog a couple of biscuits. That's what he was doing when Jim Esposito burst into his office.

"Boss," he said, "One Liberty is coming down. You got to get out of here." Grasso and Esposito ran out onto Broad Street. The scene was like something out of a movie, with people running through the streets screaming that the building was about to fall in the direction of the exchange. The two immediately jumped into a waiting SUV and drove down the street, when they received word that it was just a false alarm. In fact, Grasso would soon find out that the building passed inspections.

Grasso slept on the couch in his office again on Sunday night, and after a few restless hours, he woke up with a new set of worries on what was to be the biggest day in his career. For the past week, Grasso had pulled off possibly the greatest feat of any stock exchange chairman ever. During the 1987 crash, Phelan's biggest victory had been to restore confidence in the markets. But at least there was a market. Grasso needed to orchestrate the rebuilding of the very infrastructure that allowed the markets to work, everything from the electricity that flowed through lower Manhattan to the telephone lines that connected the world's largest trading desks to the floor of the exchange, to make sure that Merrill Lynch, Lehman Brothers, and all the smaller firms such as Sandler O'Neill could open for business.

Thanks to his efforts, tens of thousands of people would be coming to work in a war zone. Buildings would have electricity, air-conditioning, and telephone service. Con Ed and Verizon had worked overtime to make sure the wiring was there and the electricity flowed. And even with all of this, Grasso was still uncertain whether the stock exchange could handle the onslaught of sell orders; whether the new wiring could face the test of the massive volume; whether the guys on the floor, many of whom had lost friends and maybe even family in the attacks, could mentally handle what would be the most pressure-filled day of their business career.

One thing that Grasso was certain about was this: he had come too far to screw it up now. The electricity might go out, the trading system might crash, and the markets might falter. Those were all things he couldn't control. But what he knew he could control was the show—9/17 would be the mother of all stock market openings.

Whatever happened afterward would be dwarfed by the spectacle of the celebration. Zito had already come up with a slogan: "Let Freedom Ring." It would be splashed across the exchange's 2001 annual report and run in newspaper advertisements announcing the reopening, and would be followed by a massive ad campaign that would situate the opening in the context of other great moments of American history. One spot even featured soon-to-be-private-citizen Rudy Giuliani speaking about the gravity of the event.

Grasso had already decided that on the podium that morning would be the most eclectic cast of characters ever to have been assembled to mark the start of trading. Wall Street types were out, replaced by what Grasso called the "real heroes of 9/11": firemen, emergency rescue workers, and policemen, as well as the Republican mayor of New York City, Rudy Giuliani, who was fast becoming an American hero, and the Republican governor of the state, George Pataki. President Bush couldn't make it, but some people on his team wouldn't miss the opening for the world: Grasso's friend and former lawyer, Harvey Pitt, and Treasury secretary O'Neill would be there, as well as Bernie Kerik, whom Grasso had credited with being not just a good friend during the most difficult week in his career but an invaluable resource. Kerik's rise through the police department's hierarchy was controversial—after all, he had started as Giuliani's car driver—but during and after 9/11 he earned his stripes. In just a week, Kerik transformed the war zone that was lower Manhattan into a relatively safe work destination for tens of thousands of people.

Although Giuliani and his fire commissioner, Thomas Von Essen, had displayed some signs of indecision over the past week as the death toll mounted—343 firefighters, 23 cops, and 37 Port Authority police died or were believed dead from the attacks, and Von Essen would be blamed for equipping his troops with faulty radios—Kerik never seemed to show signs of strain. At least that was Grasso's assessment. In fact, Grasso was so impressed with Kerik that he simply referred to him as "the rock." As far as Grasso was concerned he deserved to be on the podium as much as anyone else.

But Grasso was sure to spread around the political bounty as well.

U.S. senator Charles Schumer, a Democrat, stood proudly on the stage, as did possibly the most controversial member of the group, the recently elected Senator Hillary Clinton. Despite his liberal leanings, Schumer was beloved by the securities industry, which filled his campaign war chest with huge amounts of money each year and, in return, received protection and a lobbyist in Washington. But Clinton was more of a wild card. Grasso received some backlash from board members when he said he wanted Hillary to have such a high-profile role. Not too long ago, she and Giuliani had been bitter enemies as the mayor weighed whether to challenge her for the U.S. Senate seat.

Grasso reminded anyone who complained about Clinton that the exchange had always been nonpolitical and being nonpolitical had business advantages, for both the street and himself. Grasso had made sure he developed a relationship with Clinton as soon as she was elected, about a year earlier, as the state's junior senator.

Grasso had made contact with her in Washington, and explained how he ran the exchange in an apolitical fashion and that he would love to take her out for dinner the next time she was in New York. Most of his board members recoiled at the thought of having dinner with Clinton, but Grasso knew she was a force to be reckoned with: smart, engaging, and above all ambitious, not that much different from himself. One other thing: Grasso actually liked Clinton, who seemed to like Grasso enough to take him up on his offer to have dinner, at Il Mulino one night weeks before the 9/11 attacks. Grasso told friends it was one of the best dinners he had had in years and that Clinton knew how to throw back a martini.

Even with this star-studded cast, it was clearly Grasso's moment to shine. At one point, Goldman's high-powered CEO, Hank Paulson, asked Grasso if he could join him on the podium, Grasso recalls. "Sorry, only public officials, cops, and firemen are allowed," Grasso said. Paulson simply left the exchange, later blaming his absence on a pressing client matter. Those who know Paulson say it was a slight that he would never forget.

There was a bigger problem for Grasso, at least according to some on Wall Street: Who had anointed him a public official? At least that was the sentiment among many of Grasso's critics on the floor, as they noted the significance of the little guy in the dark suit taking center stage, flanked on all sides by some of the most powerful people in American politics, to ring the opening bell. Chief among them was, of course, Mike LaBranche.

LaBranche was no longer just "the kid." He had quickly become a force on the floor, and an anti-Grasso one at that. For LaBranche, Grasso had done something that others, not even the great Phelan, had dared to do, and that was to try to become bigger than the exchange. The 9/11 ceremony was merely the latest manifestation of the personality cult. On this day, however, LaBranche knew enough to keep his mouth shut, at least for now.

The 9:30 A.M. opening came faster than Grasso had imagined. The floor was packed with traders and assorted Wall Street executives. Langone milled around, talking to friends and telling everyone he knew how he had witnessed Paulson leaving the exchange after he was told he couldn't be on the podium at center stage. Bobby Murphy had come a long way since he had become one of Grasso's closest friends on the floor; he was now the number two executive at LaBranche & Co., which had bought the specialist firm he ran, and a member of the stock exchange board. But he knew Grasso had come a long way too as he witnessed a gaggle of public officials milling around the podium hugging and shaking hands with Grasso.

He also noted some odd additions to the group. In the spirit of cooperation, Grasso had invited his competitors: Sal Sodano, the head of the American Stock Exchange, and Hardwick Simmons, the new chief of the NASD. Simmons and Grasso had grown close during the week, but Sodano was still smarting from his near brush with death and what he believed had been Grasso's initial ambivalence about saving the Amex, particularly in light of all the positive press Grasso was receiving, including an article in *The Wall Street Journal,* which had made Grasso seem like the most charitable man on Wall Street for lending the Amex space after its building was nearly destroyed during the attacks.

Sodano told associates that after he had escaped downtown Manhattan, when the Amex was nearly destroyed, Grasso was in no rush to save his ailing competitor. Grasso may have been distracted with his own problems, but Sodano still chalked it up to Grasso's competitiveness; he had been looking to put the final nail in the coffin of the shrinking Amex for years. But using 9/11 was a petty way of doing the deed. According to Sodano, Grasso lent his traders space only after Zarb, who a few years earlier had completed the NASD's purchase of the Amex, stepped in and pleaded for the extra room on Sodano's behalf.

Floor traders knew it would be a messy day in the markets. Some predicted that stock prices would nose-dive 500 points and then level off later in the afternoon. No one, not even Grasso, could predict with any certainty that the wiring replaced by Verizon could handle the trading frenzy that was about to begin. That was not the only thing that worried Grasso. As the minutes began to tick down to the 9:30 opening, Grasso had yet to prepare a speech. As was his habit, he was ready to improvise, but he wasn't sure how long he should go on. And how would his eclectic cast of characters react to cops and firemen stealing their show?

Grasso put all of that out of his mind as he began the ceremonies with a simple speech about the terrible "crime" that had been committed and what it meant to reopen the exchange—that those who bet against America will lose every time. It was, for all his worries, vintage Grasso. He hit all the right talking points—reopening the exchange wasn't just about stock trading, it was about defeating terrorism, celebrating capitalism and "these wonderful men and women who put their lives on the line to allow us to do what we do," a reference to police and firefighters, both those on the stage and those still searching for survivors at ground zero.

He announced that there would be a two-minute moment of silence for "those whom we have lost, those who are still missing, and, God hope, those still alive." It was, Grasso said, a moment of reflection, focused not on market technicalities, prices, volume, and investor sentiment but on what the markets mean to America, their vital function in the system that produces so much wealth and jobs and goodness, and, of course, what the reopening meant in the war on terrorism.

And just in case anyone had any doubts about whether the country was at war, Grasso invited Rose-Ann Sgrignoli, a Marine Corps major, to sing "God Bless America." The moment of silence might as well have been a moment of Grasso. At one point, Giuliani, standing directly behind the little guy, grabbed his hand. Grasso looked behind, saw it was Rudy, and began to weep. Others on the podium, like Pitt, simply looked over to Grasso, who had his head bowed, seemingly in awe of what he had done. That's when Grasso himself stepped up to the microphone and stated simply, "And now our heroes will ring the opening bell." Grasso watched as four of the city's bravest and finest made their way to the podium. Each would have a turn ringing the bell, but it was one, David Fischer, who stole the show. Grasso knew immediately why Giuliani's office had picked him to be at center stage. Dressed in his blue police uniform, he rolled up his sleeve and flexed his sixteen-inch bicep for the television cameras, paused for a moment, then hit the button to thunderous applause.

Grasso shook some hands and then made a beeline to the floor followed by an entourage that included Schumer, Clinton, Pitt, O'Neill, and New York governor George Pataki. As expected, 9/11 had the obvious impact on the markets, with investors bailing on stocks out of fear that the terrorist attacks would worsen what had been a moderate recession and bear market following the bursting of the Internet bubble a little more than a year earlier. Stock prices sank several hundred points in the first minutes of trading, but there was good news as well: the system was working. Trades were being completed.

The phones worked too; specialists and floor brokers were reaching their customers, and their customers were reaching them. It soon became clear that Grasso had pulled off a near miracle; in spite of the losses, the markets were functioning. On the floor of the exchange with Grasso was Schumer, who at six feet, two inches towered over the NYSE chief. Schumer knew that the best way to attract a camera this day was to be with the little guy. At one point, Schumer turned to a television reporter, Lou Dobbs, and called Grasso "a giant of a man," adding that the NYSE was still the "number one financial market, all because of this man."

Grasso never once strayed from his theme that the opening of the exchange was one way to defeat the criminals and how proud he was of the exchange, "this public-private partnership," as he called it. Praise of Grasso's effort poured in from everywhere. U.S. House speaker Dennis Hastert told CNN, "If it wasn't for Dick Grasso we wouldn't be able to do this today." *The New York Times* called the repairs a "Herculean effort."

Later that afternoon, Grasso traveled uptown to the Nasdaq headquarters in Times Square to show that he was big enough to support his competition during the nation's time of need. The Nasdaq closing bell wasn't the money shot that the NYSE had been able to achieve under Grasso, but Grasso's presence brought increased media attention.

For all the seriousness of the day's events, Grasso still couldn't help himself when he stood at "the Nasdaq Wall," where the fully electronic exchange displays video monitors and its own podium in a studio that holds about twenty people. Before the end of trading, Grasso turned to his favorite friendly enemy, Nasdaq chairman Frank Zarb, and asked a question that he knew would drive Zarb nuts: "By the way, Frank, where are all the people? Where are all the traders?"

Zarb nearly blew his top. "Fuck you" is all he said before smiling at the cameras and hoping his face made the nightly news.

What the politicians didn't know that day were all the little details that Grasso had thought through in order to ensure success. Grasso had spent the past six years making the opening bell the event that it was. The successful opening of the exchange, against the backdrop of patriotism and doubt, was a PR bonanza. Grasso later discovered that 300 million viewers watched the opening on September 17, 2001. For a showman, it doesn't get better than that.

No one knew the guys on the floor—the specialists who match buyers and sellers—better than Grasso. He still called them the animals, and he had counselors stationed on the floor to make sure they had an outlet for their grief and anger. He also ordered five thousand gas masks just in case people were worried about another attack. When the day came to an end, the markets had lost almost seven hundred points, but the exchange had survived. The volume of stocks traded surged to 2.3 billion shares, more than twice what it had been before the attacks, but the technology worked.

During a private moment, Grasso wanted to call Pitt to thank him for all his help. So he used his private emergency line on the floor of the exchange. Pitt was one of a number of public officials Grasso had on direct dial. The secretary on the other end answered the phone by saying simply "The chairman's office," and Grasso said he would like a quick word with the chairman. But it was the wrong chairman. Fed chairman Alan Greenspan's voice came on the other end. For a moment, Grasso was flummoxed, but he quickly regained his composure and thanked the Fed chief for cutting interest rates early in the day. It was, of course, a perfunctory move, widely expected by the markets. But Grasso, ever the salesman, made it sound like a walk-off home run. "It was an incredible contribution," he said.

"Well, thank you so much, Dick," Greenspan responded. The Fed chairman had become an icon not just for his adroit handling of the nation's financial system but also for rarely telegraphing his intentions publicly or even in private. But that didn't stop him from providing a long explanation of why he cut interest rates and what it meant for the economy. Grasso quickly ended the conversation, thanking Greenspan once again, before hanging up and wiping a thin layer of sweat from his forehead.

7

THE LAST HURRAH

Grasso came back to work in early 2002 rested after a few weeks with his family, enjoying the Christmas holiday. When asked to describe his difficult journey to the top of the exchange, Grasso often characterized it as a horse race—one where they "made me run around the track twice." But the old guard on the board who had given him the runaround was long gone, replaced by Grasso's men from Wall Street: Langone, Jimmy Cayne, Dick Fuld, and David Komansky; and his friends from the floor, Bobby Murphy and Chris Quick; as well as a smattering of executives from the companies he had listed over the years, Viacom's Mel Karmazin and Time Warner's Gerald Levin among them.

They were Grasso's people, but in reality everyone wanted to be a Grasso person in 2002. Standing ovations awaited him at his favorite restaurants, Campagnola, Rao's, and Il Mulino. Foreign business leaders begged for a moment of his time when they came to town. Rock stars like Jon Bon Jovi jumped at the chance to ring the opening bell. (Grasso cracked during their meeting that he wanted to play in Bon Jovi's band, but "we have incompatible hairstyles.") The boxing champ Oscar De La Hoya signed a pair of boxing gloves

"To Wall Street's Champ," but Grasso was no longer fighting for acceptance.

With friends like these, it's easy to understand why his name was constantly being floated for a host of government jobs—everything from U.S. Treasury secretary to a possible run for mayor of New York City. Grasso had become so popular that his security staff now considered him a terrorist target, and the board of the exchange no longer allowed him to fly on commercial planes. The exchange would splurge, spending more than $1 million a year for a share of a corporate jet that would take Grasso anywhere at any time. It was worth the money, the board reckoned, to keep a hero safe.

Grasso had been telling people that he felt 2002 was going to be good in another way—the long bear market that had begun with the bursting of the Internet bubble in March 2000 would finally run its course. "I think this market will just take off," he said. All the pieces were in place—the president's tax cuts, low interest rates, and the wave of patriotism that had swept the country in the aftermath of the terrorist attacks all pointed to good things. The Club would benefit as well, he believed. IPOs and new listings had slowed over the past year and a half, but a flood of foreign listings from companies that wanted to show their support for America began appearing on the Big Board.

What didn't figure in his analysis was the return of the scandals. While 9/11 had given the investing public a break from a series of corporate scandals and their coverage in the press, they were back now, and with a vengeance. Enron, a NYSE-listed company, had become the poster child for corporate bad behavior. Grasso knew all the principals well, from the company's chairman, Kenneth Lay, to its CEO, Jeff Skilling, and its CFO, Andrew Fastow. Enron had been among Grasso's most prominent listings—in fact, he had listed the company himself back in the mid-1980s—and he had watched with pride as it grew from a midsize energy outfit to one of the biggest and most profitable companies listed on the exchange.

Enron was now one of the largest frauds listed on the exchange, having escaped scrutiny by the SEC under Arthur Levitt. But Levitt wasn't the only regulator who had fallen down on the job. The same could be said for Grasso's own regulatory staff, who had failed to uncover how its member firms promoted Enron as a viable enterprise through their faulty stock research, which now began to show in the news coverage on what seemed like a daily basis.

Grasso's friend Harvey Pitt was now firmly in control at the SEC. He called a meeting at a New York hotel, renting the room on his own dime, and gave Grasso and his regulatory counterpart at the NASD, Robert Glauber, an ultimatum: clean up your acts or face the consequences. Pitt zeroed in on the conflicts in banking research. Throughout the bubble, analysts had been taking the stocks of companies that were investment banking clients and hyping them in research reports to an alarming degree. Small investors had followed these recommendations as if they were the honest opinions of the analysts. In many cases, they weren't, and now millions of small investors were holding shares of Internet and telecommunications companies that were worthless. Even worse, the regulatory units of the NYSE and the Nasdaq stock market had allowed this practice to grow without raising an eyebrow.

"If you'd only labeled this stuff as marketing material we wouldn't be in the situation we are now," Pitt told the group. He ordered Grasso and Glauber to come up with a plan to deal with the issue.

How seriously either of the men took Pitt is a matter of debate. The "solution" to the research conflict problem wouldn't be on the drawing board for another six months, as Grasso unveiled something more important in his world: a new marketing campaign called "Let Freedom Ring."

Grasso had been looking for a tasteful way to use 9/11 to sell the exchange. He and Zito had done some research, talking to groups representing police and firemen and families of those who died in the attacks about their tolerance for being used as props in an ad war with the NASD. "We're not here to take advantage of your loved ones," Grasso explained. "We want to celebrate their heroism." Grasso and Zito knew they were walking a fine line between exploitation and promotion, and during their visits, they had discovered a huge undercurrent of resentment; family members of the firemen lost in the attacks were still bitter, some at the former mayor, Grasso's friend Rudy Giuliani, but particularly at Giuliani's fire commissioner, Tom Von Essen, for allegedly equipping his troops with faulty radios that had made it impossible to hear the orders to flee the towers.

But these same people who hated Von Essen liked Grasso—at least that's what they said. Grasso's work following 9/11 had made him a hero not just to the financial community but to the families of cops and firemen as well. He had always donated to police charities, but after the attacks he had spared no expense to make life easier for the uniformed service workers: food, clothing, anything they needed for their efforts to clean up downtown was just a telephone call to Grasso away. Whenever he did a television interview, he was sure to thank "the real heroes of 9/11," as he called them. And who could forget that famous opening-bell celebration to commemorate the return of trading after the attacks? Grasso had built up so much goodwill that many of the families wanted him to run for mayor.

Zito was now ready to roll. He had already redesigned the NYSE annual report, usually a tribute to Grasso, to be a tribute to Grasso and a long line of police and firemen who could be seen in just about every photo in the glossy booklet, posing with the little guy. For years Zito had been able to brand the opening bell using celebrities and sports stars as props. Those days were over. It seemed as though not a day had gone by during the end of 2001 and early 2002 when a cop, a firefighter, or some other blue-collar hero of the terrorist attacks wasn't on the podium next to Grasso ringing the bell.

The opening-bell ceremonies were filmed, and each one of these events was carefully choreographed so it could be used in the new television commercials that hit in early 2002, complete with shots of the American flag and patriotic music, and, of course, ending with the four very important letters "NYSE" and the new slogan, "Let Freedom Ring." In typical Grasso fashion, the phrase could be seen everywhere—from new NYSE baseball caps to a plaque outside the NYSE building unveiled at a ceremony that included the other political "heroes" who had emerged following 9/11—Rudy Giuliani, Governor George Pataki, and the recently elected New York City Mayor Michael Bloomberg, who couldn't wait to mug for a shot with Grasso.

The branding edge over the Nasdaq was now bigger than ever. Doing business with the NYSE wasn't just the smart thing to do— it was the patriotic thing to do as well. When some didn't, Grasso showed no restraint in letting the offending parties know the meaning of their actions.

At the beginning of each year, Grasso and his senior staff received their compensation for the previous year. The compensation was set by a committee, headed by Langone, who met in secret, hashed out the details of each executive's pay, and then presented the final numbers to the entire board for approval. That's the way it was supposed to work; the reality was somewhat different. The salaries of co–chief operating officers Bob Britz and Cathy Kinney, as well as Grasso's number two, Billy Johnston, the Club's president, were, for all intents and purposes, set by one person and one person only, Dick Grasso. The board most often approved whatever number he proposed.

For Grasso, having so much say over the pay of his senior staff fit his management style; it instilled the kind of unflinching loyalty he was seeking.

They worked long hours, traveled incessantly to meet Grasso's quotas for listings, particularly those overseas, and put up with Grasso's verbal tirades on a regular basis. But it was worth it. By Grasso's fifth year as chairman, Kinney and Britz were earning multi-million-dollar annual salaries, and in 2001, they each pulled in $4 million in compensation. Ed Kwalwasser, who ran Grasso's regulatory department, earned $1.7 million in 2001 even as rumors of floor trading abuses were beginning to circulate. Billy Johnston pulled in a whopping $6 million in salary and bonus in 2001, his last year at the exchange before becoming a paid "consultant," even though most people on the floor couldn't figure out what he did other than help Grasso with the bell-ringing ceremonies.

One of the more highly paid people at the exchange didn't even hold an executive title: by the end of the decade, Grasso's assistant,

SooJee Lee, had become not just Grasso's main gatekeeper but also a confidante of sorts. Friends and colleagues openly questioned why Grasso had been taking Lee with him to what appeared to be business dinners.

Rumors spread not just about their relationship but about her salary as well. Grasso reminded her detractors that she was more than a secretary, she was his assistant and had a law degree. What he didn't say was that he paid her like a lawyer as well. Lee was on her way to a salary and bonus worth $240,000.

Grasso was officially barred from the compensation committee meetings when his salary was discussed, and things were no different when the committee met in February 2002 to discuss his 2001 compensation. Despite their hard work during 9/11, Grasso and his staff had expected a pay cut. There were several reasons for his pessimism. The markets were lousy, and by the end of 2001, the exchange made just $31 million—a 56 percent decline from the previous year. Maybe the biggest reason why Grasso and his people were prepared for a pay cut was that he and his team appeared to slip in what they considered the most important measure of their job: making sure the stock exchange operated at 100 percent efficiency. During the summer of 2001, a systems glitch forced Grasso to halt trading for an hour or so.

Then there was 9/11. No one expected Langone or the committee to penalize the Grasso team because of the weeklong shutdown that followed the attacks. But nearly every major CEO on Wall Street, from the highly compensated Jimmy Cayne of Bear Stearns to Hank Paulson of Goldman Sachs, took pay cuts for 2001. It wasn't just that the souring markets were squeezing profits and the bonus pools at the firms. Making a lot of money after 9/11 appeared unseemly.

But just the opposite happened. The good news was delivered by Ashen. Grasso was getting a raise, not just for surviving 9/11 but for the effort it had taken to get the exchange back into business and for a rise in new listings from the year before. Grasso was ecstatic, surprised, maybe even a little shocked, but he didn't complain. And why would he? He would receive an additional $5 million "special bonus," bringing his annual pay for 2001 to $30 million, nearly $15 million more than Cayne and $4 million more than the year before, the last year of the bull market.

By and large, Langone and the committee's recommendations had been rubber-stamped by the board. Langone usually came prepared with various metrics, including charts showing Grasso's tremendous contributions to the exchange's bottom line (even if it was shrinking), which no one could really deny. Then there was the manner in which Langone presented the information. He once remarked to one of the compensation consultants that if someone on the board tried to push down his proposed number for Grasso, he would "take a lead pipe to them." Langone says he was kidding and the consultant later said he understood the statement had been made in jest. But the remark clearly underscored Langone's belief that Grasso was worth every dime of the big paychecks he and the committee he chaired handed Grasso each year, and how hard he would fight to get Grasso the money, maybe too hard.

In early 2002, Grasso was richer and more popular than ever, but there was something clearly weighing on his mind. Even as he rolled out his new "Let Freedom Ring" advertising blitz, Grasso decided to tone down the floor antics several notches. The wild stunts to commemorate new listings became more subdued. Grasso's personal temperament changed as well. He seemed more dictatorial and, at times, more irrational.

Though he still kept the same hours and virtually the same travel schedule, where he would fly at least once a month to the West Coast to pay visits to various companies, Grasso complained that he found the job for the first time in years to be more of a job than it ever was in the past. "After 9/11," he told one associate, "the job isn't as much fun." But it wasn't just the tragedy of 9/11 that was weighing Grasso down. The markets never rebounded as he predicted, and Grasso must have heard the howls from the floor when he raised the traders' fees, allegedly to pay for technology upgrades at a time when traders were being killed by shrinking volume and decimalization.

Then there was his salary and, more specifically, all that money he had deferred in his retirement accounts. Grasso's retirement savings had grown by leaps and bounds in recent years, because he had deferred much of his income into all those retirement accounts the exchange had created for its senior executives. When those accounts were created in 1995 by Stanley Gault, it had looked like a no-brainer; they guaranteed a set interest rate, the markets were booming, and executives' pay didn't seem to rub average people the wrong way. Average Americans were, after all, making millions on their own stock investments as well, so why would they care if the leader of the world's greatest stock market made millions from his? But two years into the bear market, there was little doubt that the public's mood had shifted. Wall Street was the home of scandal, the place that had pumped up all those fraudulent stocks with research reports that had called companies like Enron and all those dot-coms strong buys.

Even Grasso was shocked that his deferrals had created a retirement package worth more than $100 million—at least that's what he told Zito one afternoon in early 2002. Zito had decided not to defer his own salary—instinct had told him not to trust long-term layaway plans—but now he wished he had after hearing how it had made Grasso a small fortune. Grasso, meanwhile, was coming to the opposite conclusion as his melancholy about his job began to turn into outright paranoia about whether he would ever get his hands on such a large bundle of cash.

The exchange's board of directors had always been *his* board. They were loyal to him, not just because they knew he could run the place but because he had made many of them a lot of money.

But loyalty on Wall Street is fleeting; it shifts with the public mood or the latest press witch hunt, and overpaid corporate executives were among the most hunted people these days. Grasso had seen it with so many friends, one by one, people like homemaking entrepreneur and NYSE board member Martha Stewart, who had gone from hero to goat almost overnight.

Grasso could remember the day in 1999 so clearly when he listed Martha Stewart Living Omnimedia on the exchange, and he soon had asked Martha Stewart to join his board. Now Stewart was in trouble, mired in an insider trading scandal that became the subject of U.S. congressional hearings.

Grasso had a solution: "Martha, just say you're sorry, you made a mistake, and say you'll give back any profits to charity." But Stewart wouldn't listen. "I didn't do anything wrong," she said, and the bad headlines continued, this time with the U.S. attorney's office launching a criminal investigation into whether Stewart had lied to investigators looking into her trading. Grasso continued to stand behind the embattled homemaker, but privately, every headline made Grasso's stomach churn.

So it was some time in the first half of 2002 that Grasso came to the conclusion that the time was right to figure out a way to get more of his money out of those retirement accounts and into his own pockets. It would be controversial, almost unprecedented in the history of the exchange. Retirement money is intended for retirement, and his contract wasn't up until 2005. Grasso had taken money out of his account in 1995 when he signed a new contract, but that had been just $6 million, and he was using it to buy a house. In 1999, he had merely rolled $29.9 million of his retirement money into an exchange savings account. When he added the money up, Grasso realized he was now sitting on a nest egg of $140 million, a bundle of money that no chairman before him had ever amassed.

All his instincts, the same instincts that had served him so well over the years, were clear: a future board might not be so generous, and if he waited much longer, the fruits of more than thirty years at the exchange might be lost.

Before the spring of 2002, Eliot Spitzer had barely registered on Dick Grasso's radar screen. He had met the New York State attorney general exactly twice. The first time was when Spitzer paid a courtesy call to Grasso just after he was elected AG in 1998, to discuss how the AG's office could better work with the exchange's regulatory staff to bring enforcement cases. The next meeting had come just after 9/11 during the opening of the brokerage firm Sandler O'Neill, which had lost its offices in the trade center.

Since then, however, the climate had changed dramatically, and so had Spitzer. The son of a Manhattan real estate tycoon, Spitzer had gotten off to a rough start as AG, mired in his own scandal as to whether he had lied about money his father had given him for his campaign. His first three years in office had been uneventful, but he was now looking for a case that would remake his image and take his career to the next level. As with Rudy Giuliani before him, Wall Street seemed like the perfect place to start. In mid-2001, his office had launched an investigation into whether the Merrill Lynch analyst Henry Blodget, once the most recognizable technology stock analyst on the street, had hyped his rating on stocks to help Merrill win investment banking business from the same companies.

Blodget had since left Merrill amid the decline of many of his stock picks and doubts about whether they had been objective or merely fueled by a desire to boost his pay to win banking business. The 9/11 attacks had stalled the inquiry by Spitzer's staff, but by the spring of 2002, Spitzer's investigators had resumed their activities and were ready to pounce. The case Spitzer put together was staggering. Blodget, in private e-mails to friends and colleagues, referred to certain stocks as "pieces of shit," "dogs," and "crap." These were the same stocks that received high ratings in his reports, which were distributed to small investors through Merrill's brokerage offices. Indeed, the e-mails from Blodget showed that there was little objectivity in his research—or in the way Merrill itself linked his compensation in his ability to snare investment banking business. Merrill itself was considered the firm with the best compliance department on Wall Street. If this was the best, Spitzer told reporters, the rest of the street couldn't be that much different.

"This guy is a fucking lunatic," Dave Komansky griped about Spitzer as he explained the firm's predicament to Grasso one afternoon not long after Spitzer held a press conference releasing all the Blodget e-mails and demanding that Merrill meet his demands for a settlement or face a possible indictment.

Komansky had just announced that he would cede his job to his second in command, Stan O'Neal. In effect, Komansky would be leaving the firm amid scandal. Grasso just sat and listened as Komansky complained. Getting involved in a regulatory matter, particularly on behalf of a friend like Komansky, was dicey. Komansky was a board member of the exchange, a compensation committee member, no less, who had gladly approved his recent $30 million salary for 2001. In other words, Grasso had to watch his step on this one.

One thing Grasso couldn't deny was Spitzer's heavy-handedness. An indictment of the firm was a possibility that Spitzer had stated publicly, and it would put Merrill out of business, as similar indictments had done to Drexel Burnham Lambert and E. F. Hutton before. Neither Komansky nor his legal staff could tell if Spitzer would really go that far. During settlement negotiations he appeared rigid: at minimum Merrill would have to spin off its analyst unit into a separate part of the firm with its own profit-and-loss statement. Since research made no profits, Merrill would be the only firm on the street without analysts. Without analysts to pump up the stocks of investment banking clients, Merrill would have no clients. Grasso now understood why Komansky used the word "lunatic" to describe Spitzer.

Grasso was already on the hot seat over analysts' conflicts; Pitt now came back to ask what was happening with the new rules he had ordered up months ago, himself blindsided by Spitzer's case and what it meant for the rest of Wall Street. *The Wall Street Journal* had reported that Spitzer wasn't content with settling with Merrill and moving on to the kiddie porn and boiler-room cases that had been standard fare for the state AG. All of Wall Street would be coming under scrutiny in what Spitzer called a global investigation of research practices that pumped up now-worthless stocks to help their firms and themselves make a lot of money but had screwed small investors who followed their advice.

Grasso was sitting in his office one Friday afternoon studying the cover of *BusinessWeek* magazine. The headline said it all: "How Corrupt Is Wall Street?" Grasso winced as he began to thumb through the magazine, studying the package of stories, including one in particular featuring the New York State attorney general announcing his intention to make all of Wall Street pay for its sins during the bubble years. There was a dual message in the stories featuring Spitzer. Spitzer believed the guys in charge of policing Wall Street were nowhere to be found as the financial business preyed upon small investors. Spitzer was a Democrat and one with his eye on a higher office, so his most frequent target was Harvey Pitt, the former Wall Street lawyer now in charge of the SEC, who had already gotten on Spitzer's bad side by putting the AG on notice that he was stepping into federal turf by trying to regulate Merrill.

It didn't matter that Pitt was (a) right and (b) left with a regulatory mess from Arthur Levitt, the last Democrat to hold SEC job. He made such an enticing target since many of his clients from his days as a white-collar attorney were now under scrutiny, and Spitzer never hesitated to let the world know that he believed Pitt was conflicted. Spitzer had equally harsh words for the NASD, which was in charge of monitoring all the dot-com stocks Blodget had hyped that traded on the Nasdaq.

. Like Pitt, the NASD was now fighting Spitzer over turf: Merrill Lynch was a member firm; the stocks Blodget had touted came under its jurisdiction no matter how good a case he had developed. Nonsense, Spitzer said, calling the NASD "a club" that had let its members get away with murder during the past decade, and it was hard to argue with his logic. The way things were going, it wouldn't be long before Spitzer turned his attention to the real club. Grasso suddenly knew what he had to do.

Spitzer was sitting in his office on Broadway in lower Manhattan, preparing for another meeting with his staff about how to deal with the Merrill case, when an assistant interrupted. "A Mr. Dick Grasso is on the telephone."

It had been almost a year since Spitzer and Grasso had last spoken. Spitzer had transformed himself into the nation's leading white-collar law enforcement official by deftly turning the case into a criticism of Wall Street's culture of greed and, most recently, the inability of the Wall Street regulatory apparatus to take appropriate action to protect investors. Grasso marveled at Spitzer's methods. The research scandal had occurred under the nose of Levitt, but nearly every day brought a new attack on Pitt, who had launched his own probe of research but was seen as someone who needed a swift kick from Spitzer to get into the act.

Grasso's conversation with Spitzer didn't last long, but then Grasso believed he knew how to close a deal quickly. Grasso had done his research on the attorney general. For all the good press he was getting standing up for the little guy against the Wall Street giants, Spitzer, Grasso reckoned, was less interested in reform than he was in getting credit for crafting reform—and making a name for himself in the process. But Grasso also knew Spitzer would need an achievement, a large, tangible achievement, to move up the political ladder. And if Spitzer wanted to list reforming Wall Street as an achievement, he needed a guy on the inside, someone who could get the various members of the Club to the bargaining table.

Grasso's strategy was to treat Spitzer like a listing client. There would be no threats or the rude behavior that NASD officials had exhibited when Spitzer first presented his evidence or that Grasso laid on his staff when they didn't do something his way. Grasso would turn on the charm.

So did Spitzer. When he answered the phone, Spitzer couldn't have been nicer, signaling that he was ready to do business. "People are flipping hamburgers" because of Wall Street greed, Spitzer remarked at one point. Grasso agreed but reminded Spitzer that while guilty parties like Blodget should be brought to justice, he should reconsider his actions against Merrill. No firm had ever survived an indictment, and Merrill would most certainly go out of business if hit with one. There would be jobs lost, many of them in the state; market turmoil; and investor losses, all over a couple of e-mails.

Grasso then offered to broker a settlement "without the lawyers in the room." Spitzer signaled he was open to compromise, and Grasso said he was open to helping Spitzer reform Wall Street research any way he could as long as it prevented one of his firms from going down in flames. It was a remarkable concession on Grasso's part: at the time, the entire regulatory apparatus, the SEC and the NASD, had viewed Spitzer with suspicion, as someone trying to make them look bad by encroaching on their turf. Now Grasso was willing to give Spitzer legitimacy if Spitzer was willing to compromise.

He was. In late May, Merrill and Spitzer reached a settlement. Just as Grasso asked, the firm escaped indictment. It didn't have to spin off its research department into a separate unit. The investment banking business would still pay for the researchers' salaries, thus maintaining the same conflict that had caused the problem in the first place. The firm agreed to build a better "Chinese wall" to prevent future Henry Blodgets from misleading small investors. It paid a fine of $100 million, one of the largest in Wall Street history but small potatoes compared to the amount of money it made off its research.

Spitzer, meanwhile, took his victory lap. "The Enforcer," screamed the cover of *Fortune* magazine with a stern portrait of Spitzer adorning it. Spitzer was sure to point out those who had helped and those who had hindered the process of setting things right for the investing public. The SEC and the NASD still didn't get it; they were so obsessed with protecting their turf that they forgot their mandate of making sure the securities markets were safe for small investors.

But with the help of people like Dick Grasso, Spitzer said, he was ready to make Wall Street safe for all. This was, of course, the same Dick Grasso whose friends and "brothers" included the heads of every major firm now awash in scandal and who had just paid him $30 million in salary while he was supposed to be policing research conflicts. But as far as Spitzer was concerned, Dick Grasso was a friend and ally in a crusade that was making Spitzer himself a star and a shoo-in for New York State governor in a couple of years, and that made the little guy beam. Out of respect, Spitzer's staff referred to him as "Mr. Grasso." Out of friendship, Spitzer simply called him "Dick."

For the next nine months, Spitzer and Grasso would make quite a team, something that irked Pitt at times and his competitors at the NASD all the time. It wasn't long before the research probe reached a new stage, moving past Merrill to include new targets, mainly Morgan Stanley and its star analyst, Mary Meeker, as well as Citigroup's Jack Grubman, but Spitzer said he wasn't content to stop there; he wanted a "global settlement," something that would clean up conflicted research once and for all. Publicly, Grasso continued to support Spitzer's broader efforts to bring reform. Privately, he worried that "the lunatic," as Komansky called the crusading AG, was doing more harm than good.

With Spitzer gathering so much media attention, Pitt had no choice but to compete for headlines and launch a massive probe of his own into research practices. The NASD got into the act as well, rushing in with a case of its own against Grubman and Citigroup for hyping shares of Winstar, a once high-flying telecom stock that had funneled millions of dollars of banking business to Citigroup and benefited from Grubman's touts but had since imploded in a sea of red ink.

While the other regulators saw publicity in these tactics, Grasso viewed them with contempt. "They're destroying the markets," he would tell his staff. "They're competing to see who can kill the most business first." The markets were certainly in disarray. Financial stocks, particularly those under investigation, led the losers, but the whole market was being crushed in a wave of suspicion not seen since the 1980s. There was something called headline risk in the stock market. Grasso believed all the elements were in place for a rally—low interest rates, a relatively strong economy—all the elements except one: trust. The average investor believed that Wall Street was a house of cards, and each headline touting a new phase of the probe only solidified that belief.

There was only one solution: to get Pitt and Spitzer to start working with each other rather than competing for headlines. Under the circumstances, forging that deal would make meeting with the Colombian rebels appear easy.

Harvey Pitt detested Spitzer as a showboater, someone who was ready to destroy the credibility of the SEC to win votes. But Pitt hadn't spent so many years as a Wall Street attorney cutting deals for clients not to know when it was time to cut a deal of his own. Pitt had all the attributes of a great SEC chairman: knowledge of the markets and its laws and a get-tough attitude when it counted. But Spitzer had painted him into a corner as a guy who was standing in the way of reform. No matter how many investigations he launched, he couldn't change that perception.

Grasso's solution came straight from his favorite movie, *The Godfather:* he would hold a special summit at his old Italian-American club, Tiro a Segno in Greenwich Village. It would be a gathering of all the regulatory agencies, including the NYSE. The purpose, Grasso told Pitt, was to stop the competition for headlines and work together to produce a global settlement, along the lines of what Spitzer had been advocating but something that the securities industry could live with. The unstated purpose was to give Spitzer his day in the sun, make him an equal in conducting the probe and creating the eventual settlement without indictments or the research department spin-offs many in the business feared. Just a recognition of the wrongs that had been committed so that everyone could move on with life before Wall Street crumbled into New York Harbor.

Pitt ultimately agreed; Spitzer, as it turned out, took far less convincing. He had now gained official recognition as a player, someone to be feared and respected, and as such he began backing away from more severe rhetoric. Grasso no longer heard him say how he might indict this or that firm or sleazy analysts. He no longer spoke about spinning off research departments into separate units.

As Grasso sat at the head of a long table, he explained the seriousness of their work and the good they would accomplish by wrapping up the inquiry in a timely fashion. Glauber and Mary Schapiro, the two top regulators at the NASD, agreed to work with the NYSE and all the parties, as did Pitt and Spitzer. It was a rare moment of solidarity among warring factions.

When the meeting concluded, Grasso's mission had been accomplished. The regulators divided up the street, giving Spitzer first dibs on the biggest cases, namely Morgan Stanley and Citigroup. The NASD would aid Spitzer in investigating Morgan Stanley and Citigroup, because an increasing focus of the probe was a controversial Grubman upgrade of AT&T right before the company picked Citi to handle a lucrative stock underwriting. Grasso's regulatory staff would get other firms, like Goldman. Pitt didn't seem to mind giving Spitzer the lead and agreed to have his enforcement chief, Steve Cutler, work with Spitzer's team, led by Eric Dinallo. Wall Street would have to settle with all of them at once.

The following day, Grasso explained that the meeting would pave the way for a constructive settlement, something that both Wall Street and the regulators could live with. But inside Grasso's little bald head something else was going on. Grasso had been gauging the headlines as much as anyone else. Wall Street was getting killed in the press, but Grasso was still considered Wall Street's 9/11 hero. He believed the stock exchange board was still in his pocket. He knew the SEC chairman was a friend, and Spitzer considered him a political necessity. But would this perfect storm be there in a year? In two years? If there was ever a time for Grasso to start the process of moving his retirement money out of the exchange and into his own pocket, this was it.

Ken Langone's office on the twenty-second floor of the Seagram Building in Manhattan is nondescript. There are no fancy paintings, just a bunch of photos of Langone with CEOs and politicians, including a couple of faded photographs of his parents, both Italian immigrants, and one with him and Grasso. Langone, at six feet, three inches, towered over Grasso in height, but you could tell by the smile on his face that he considered Grasso as big as any Wall Street CEO.

Given Langone's clout and his own immense wealth (he's worth an estimated $3 billion), Langone gets calls from politicians all the time. But this call was different. It was from someone in the White House asking about Grasso—more specifically, explaining to Langone that Grasso's name was on a short list to replace Paul O'Neill as Treasury secretary or Pitt as chairman of the SEC. Langone wasn't sure how much credence to give to the call since Grasso had three years left on his contract. But Grasso's name had been leaked to newspapers, and that's when Langone, for the first time, began to contemplate a Grasso-less exchange.

Grasso was in his office when Langone called and approached the issue directly. "We're worried that you might take one of these jobs in the newspapers," Langone said, pointing out that the time had come to start thinking about an extension of his contract beyond 2005. His preference: a five-year contract that would run until 2010.

Grasso leveled with Langone: he wasn't leaving for the Treasury or the SEC, at least not yet. What the newspapers didn't know was that a White House adviser had already asked if he was interested in doing something different, possibly in Washington, and Grasso had made it clear that he wasn't interested. "Kenny, I got the best job in the world," he said, noting that the only other job he would consider was mayor of New York City.

Grasso then thanked Langone for his concern, but not before using his friend's trepidation to his advantage. Grasso quickly added he didn't want people to think being chairman at the exchange was all he could do. He was fifty-seven, in great health, and at the top of his career. He wanted an extension of maybe a few years, but not out until 2010. Grasso explained to Langone that he would be the longest-serving chairman when his contract expired, and someone on his staff deserved a shot at running the place.

Grasso also said that if he extended his contract, he wanted something from the exchange: the ability to gain more control over his retirement money. The move was best described as a quid pro quo, at least in Langone's mind; the exchange would get to keep what Wall Street viewed as one of the best leaders in the business, and Grasso would get his hands on a heap of his own cash. The move wasn't unprecedented since he took money out of those accounts in 1995 and later in 1999, when he extended his contract the last time. Now he was looking to do the same, only with a larger chunk of cash—more than $120 million.

Langone sat and listened and soon thereafter reported Grasso's stipulations to various members of the compensation committee. Langone wasn't focused on the reason why Grasso wanted the cash;

his bigger concern was that Grasso might leave the exchange even before his contract was up in 2005. With that, his recommendation was to sign him up for as long as possible and give him what he wanted.

While Grasso was contemplating how much money the exchange owed him, America was commemorating the one-year anniversary of 9/11. Much had changed since that tragic day—America was now at war, a global war against terror, and preparing for a possible ground invasion of Iraq. Wall Street's top cop wasn't the SEC but a once little-known Democratic attorney general from New York who had galvanized headlines as no other prosecutor before him except Rudy Giuliani.

But much was the same. The bear market continued to pinch profits on the street. The scandals continued to alienate small investors from the markets as they discovered almost on a daily basis just how much Wall Street sleaze had cost them during the bubble years, and Richard Grasso, the King of the Club, was still a hero in the minds of most Americans. But whereas some people saw sacrifice in Grasso's efforts, others saw Grasso's raging ambition and ego, and nowhere was that sentiment more abundant than on the floor. There were many reasons for his dwindling support among people who owed Grasso so much: the continued bear market, decimalization, and a recent round of floor tax increases. Then there was Grasso's management style, which people like Mike LaBranche believed had morphed from a benevolent dictatorship to a cult of personality. "Who does this guy think he is?" Mike LaBranche asked one associate. "Was he the only guy who sacrificed during 9/11?"

Making the rounds on the floor were some offhand comments Grasso had made about the stock exchange being "his house." Grasso's hero status was now questioned as if it were just another one of his marketing ploys. Others doubted any real accomplishment aside from getting himself more good press. "How many lines of cable did Dick Grasso lay to get the phone lines working after 9/11?" asked another floor trader.

By far the biggest critic was LaBranche, whom Grasso had always viewed with suspicion. LaBranche was a problem, potentially a big one. His company was now the largest independent specialist firm. LaBranche, however, wanted nothing to do with the management of the exchange, refusing to join the NYSE board, where Grasso could keep an eye on him.

As the one-year anniversary of 9/11 came to a close, Grasso didn't pay much attention to Mike LaBranche and all of his floor critics. During the day, he was one of the dignitaries at a memorial held at ground zero who read names of those who had died in the attacks. That night, Grasso was invited to a black-tie event with other dignitaries at the Waldorf, but he chose to skip the event and go to a private party at Chumley's bar in Greenwich Village with firemen from the 24-5 station house, which had lost eleven men in the attacks, including two guys Grasso had called friends. Grasso isn't much of a drinker (except for a few glasses of wine at dinner), but this night he couldn't help but raise more than a few glasses to the fallen heroes, as they reminisced about the good times and of course the not-so-good times.

Jimmy Cayne's distaste for anything to do with the New York Stock Exchange had been smoldering for months. Grasso had offered him a board seat many times, including recently, and Cayne had always replied with the same answer: no way. For Cayne, there was almost nothing worse than leaving his office at Bear Stearns's new headquarters for any meeting, much less one where he would have to sit in the same room with men and women he detested, particularly Langone. He considered Langone a boorish loudmouth and a bully. Langone had his fans among the Wall Street elite because he achieved so much by being himself—iconoclastic and down to earth. But what endeared Langone to some simply rubbed Cayne the wrong way; when Langone spoke in his gruff New York accent, often laced with profanity, Cayne felt a knot tighten in his stomach.

This time it wasn't just Grasso asking, but John Mulheren, who headed Bear Stearns's specialist operation, Bear Wagner Specialists, and was tired of getting screwed at the exchange over business that went to more politically connected specialist firms.

Mulheren had been railing for months that he had lost the chance to be the specialist for Krispy Kreme because a committee made up of senior NYSE officials directed the listing to one of their own, the specialist firm run by board member Charles Bocklet. With Cayne on the board, Mulheren argued, there was no telling how many listings would come their way. "Jimmy, you have to do it," Mulheren said. "We're leaving too much money on the table." With that, Cayne reluctantly agreed.

"I want the same deal you gave that guy from Lazard who went to these fucking meetings once every three years," Cayne told Grasso in alerting him that he had agreed to be on the board. The deal he was referring to was one in which Grasso had allegedly allowed a former board member, Lazard Frères chief Michel David-Weill, to keep his own schedule. Grasso didn't say whether he would give Cayne the same arrangement, but he was ecstatic. He had known Cayne for years and knew he would be an important counterweight to the other board members, like Hank Paulson of Goldman and Phil Purcell of Morgan Stanley, who wouldn't think twice about trading the floor for a computer. Bear was a trading outfit, and Cayne was committed to making sure Bear Wagner made as much money as possible.

Despite his time constraints, Cayne's duties expanded almost overnight. Grasso appointed Cayne to the NYSE's audit committee and saw to it that Cayne found his way onto the compensation committee, which meant spending more time with Langone.

Langone had immersed himself in the intricacies of Grasso's various retirement plans. To board members in need of information about Grasso's pay, Langone appeared to have the answers at his fingertips. Meetings were like State Department briefings; they were long and detailed, often with Langone and Ashen providing tables and charts that described the money Grasso was accumulating in the various accounts, as well as his yearly salary, which had reached double-digit millions while Langone was chief.

Cayne and Langone had been getting along just fine until one meeting in particular. In September 2002, the compensation committee met to discuss what was billed as an urgent matter. The meeting that afternoon was held through a conference call that connected the various members of the comp committee: Mel Karmazin, then the CEO of Viacom; Gerry Levin, the former head of AOL Time Warner; Komansky; the specialist Bobby Murphy; and, of course, Langone, the committee chairman. Hank Paulson, the head of Goldman Sachs, as was his penchant, missed the meeting to take care of important Goldman business. These players were committee veterans. They had been dealing with Grasso's compensation for several years; Paulson had been on the committee since 2001. Cayne was a rookie, as were two other newcomers, Jürgen Schrempp, the CEO of Daimler-Chrysler, and Laurence "Larry" Fink, the CEO of the BlackRock money management firm.

Langone said the purpose of the meeting was to extend Grasso's contract beyond 2005, when it was scheduled to expire, to 2007. That wasn't all. As was Grasso's custom, he wanted to take greater control of the money that had accumulated in his exchange retirement accounts. Greater control, as defined by Grasso, would mean he wanted all the money, somewhere in the neighborhood of $120 million or possibly more, to be put in his exchange savings account as a condition of signing his new contract. Later, Langone would call it a "quid pro quo." There had been rumors, since confirmed, he said, that Grasso was asked to jump ship, possibly to a job in Washington.

Such meetings had usually been mundane affairs; Langone made a proposal about Grasso's salary and the committee approved the measure, sending it to the full board without a second thought. But this time was different. Langone was acting as if the year were 1999, not 2002. He forgot what Wall Street had been going through for the past two years, the scandals, the bear markets. He had no clue how handing so much money to someone, particularly now, would look if it ever leaked to the press, and for all the vows of secrecy board members were forced to take over Grasso's pay, this move was so outrageous that there was no question it would leak. The only question was how fast.

Schrempp was the first to speak up. He was so flummoxed by the number that the other board members couldn't understand his misgivings through his heavy German accent. There was, however, no mistaking what Fink and Cayne had to say. Both had heard about Langone's propensity to lavish huge salaries on CEOs he thought were doing a great job. He was the main architect of Robert Nardelli's lavish employment contract as CEO of Home Depot. But Nardelli ran a public company. Grasso ran the New York Stock Exchange, or in the famous words of John Phelan, a "public trust."

"Kenny, what the fuck is this?" Fink asked as he began to digest the numbers. Fink thought Grasso was one of the most capable men on Wall Street, but was he so capable that he should have been making what appeared to be an average of $20 million a year in recent years? Fink wasn't sure. The rest of the committee remained silent, stunned perhaps, except for Cayne. Despite how much money Grasso had helped Bear Wagner make through his listings and order flow, Cayne had told people he believed Grasso was making a salary along the lines of a highly paid civil servant, somewhere around $250,000 a year, tops, certainly not the Wall Street–sized salary that he saw on paper, and certainly not more than *he* was earning. The $30 million Grasso had made in 2001 surpassed Cayne's salary that year by $15 million.

Unlike Fink, Cayne didn't curse, at least this time, but what he said cut through Langone like a knife. "I got a question," he asked sarcastically. "Where's the decimal point?"

Fink couldn't help but snicker, but Cayne wasn't joking, as Langone clearly understood. Langone assured both Cayne and Fink that the number was just and valid, and above all, it was earned. True, the money had accumulated over a few years, but Grasso had spent more than thirty years at the exchange and had been its best salesman and, by his estimate, its best chairman. During that time, he could have worked anywhere on Wall Street, and his talent and achievement were on a par with anyone's in corporate America.

Unlike some of the people on the board, Grasso didn't run a public company, so he wasn't paid stock options, which had made many top Wall Street executives, such as Cayne, billionaires. These were all compelling arguments, but not compelling enough for either Cayne or Fink. Privately, neither could understand how so much money could have been stashed away without more people knowing.

At one point, Cayne spit out the obvious question: "Are you sure we should be doing this now?" he asked, referring to the corporate scandals and the controversy over executive pay. Above all, Cayne was worried about whether the money had been granted in a legal fashion. He said a compensation consultant should come in and make sure the numbers added up. Langone agreed.

The compensation committee met again in early October, to discuss the matter and review the assessment of the compensation consultant Vedder Price, which had stated that while the numbers were large—Grasso was actually making more money than some of the comparator group CEOs—and while taking money before retirement was rare, there appeared to be nothing illegal about what Grasso wanted to do as long as the board agreed. Not discussed, at least according to board members, was the size of Grasso's compensation in the context of the New York not-for-profit law; the exchange had been incorporated thirty years earlier as a not-for-profit corporation and the law set a broad standard that its executive's compensation must be "reasonable." Most members didn't know the law even existed—or that Grasso's new buddy, the New York AG Eliot Spitzer, was in charge of enforcing it. Nor did they care, as Grasso's performance coupled with the bull market made almost any amount of money seem reasonable for years. Not anymore. In fact, Cayne's main concern was how taking home such a large sum of money would look to the NYSE membership. The 1,366 seat holders, who are technically the owners of the exchange, hadn't had a good year. Thanks to the bear markets, the price of a seat was now about $2 million, down from its high of around $2.7 million.

Cayne felt the knot in his stomach tighten once again. "When this gets out, there's going to be trouble," he muttered. How much trouble, no one knew for sure. At this point so many things were uncertain. Grasso's contract was expiring in 2005, and some board members worried that he might not ask for an extension without the money. Meanwhile, no one really knew how much money Grasso had amassed. All in all, Grasso would be entitled to nearly $200 million in retirement savings, a substantial chunk of it accumulated during the years while Langone ruled the committee, if his contract was extended until 2007. By the end of the meeting, the committee decided to postpone any decision until the new year.

Word of the compensation committee's concerns, particularly those expressed by Cayne and Fink, undoubtedly made it back to Grasso. Cayne himself remarked that Grasso appeared annoyed at him the next time the two met. Grasso, though, knew one thing: if "brothers" like Cayne and Fink were this upset about the money, he stood to lose tens of millions of dollars if he left the decision up to a future board, appointed in the context of Eliot Spitzer and the corporate scandals, which he could trust even less.

8

STAR FUCKER OR SAVIOR?

New York State Republicans could barely muster an attorney general candidate against Eliot Spitzer in 2002, and when they did, Spitzer won in a landslide. He also won a bigger battle for recognition. Spitzer and his staff had now all but concluded that Citigroup's former star analyst, Jack Grubman, would be their next big opportunity.

Grubman made a perfect villain. He was arrogant. He made a ton of money—as much as $20 million a year during the 1990s. He bragged about the conflicted nature of his job: how he snared deals one minute and then posted research the next. But most appealing of all was the evidence of Grubman's possible fraudulent behavior. It was massive—particularly evidence involving AT&T, one of the few stocks Grubman had hated in the telecom world. But in late 1999, Grubman abruptly changed his tune, upgrading AT&T shares just before the company was to select firms to underwrite a massive stock deal. Citigroup won the banking work. It was pretty standard behavior during the boom years, totally ignored by Levitt's SEC and every self-regulatory group, including Grasso's troops.

But Spitzer's investigators believed the evidence they developed took the standard conflicts to a new level. It seems the investment banking deal wasn't the only incentive Grubman had to make the upgrade. Citigroup CEO Sanford Weill, one of the most powerful men on Wall Street, who was leading one of the world's biggest firms, had personally intervened in the ratings decision by giving Grubman a "nudge" to upgrade the shares. Why was Weill so interested in Grubman's AT&T rating? It wasn't just the $45 million in underwriting fees Citigroup received for its share of the deal. AT&T CEO C. Michael Armstrong was on the Citigroup board of directors, and Weill was on the AT&T board. They had a mutually beneficial relationship. In 2000, Armstrong had supported Weill in his successful attempt to oust his co-CEO, John Reed, who shared the job with him after Weill merged his Travelers Group financial company with Reed's Citicorp to form Citigroup.

An e-mail from Grubman to a money manager laid out the enticing details. "Armstrong didn't know what hit him," Grubman said, adding that he later downgraded the stock once the deal had been completed and Sandy had "nuked" Reed. As payback, Grubman crowed, Weill got Grubman's twins into an exclusive Manhattan preschool, the 92nd Street Y. Grubman had been trying for months with no success, but a couple of calls from Weill after the well-timed upgrade, and they were in.

Spitzer's people soon discovered that more than a few calls had been involved. Weill had made a large donation from Citigroup to the school as well. Officials at the preschool readily admitted that the payment was connected to the Grubman kids' admission to a place that Grubman described as having higher admission standards than Harvard. It didn't take long for Spitzer to connect the dots on this one; he now had the mother of all targets in his sights, Sandy Weill.

The securities laws were, of course, pretty clear: Weill could tell Grubman whatever he wanted, as long as he hadn't told him to lie. If evidence was developed that Weill had indeed told Grubman to lie about his upgrade of AT&T, the SEC would be the least of Citigroup's problems. Spitzer could indict Weill himself.

The case presented a multitude of problems, not just for Citigroup but also for Grasso. Citigroup was a huge order-flow provider to the floor, but Grasso heard the firm wanted to send more of it to the regional exchanges or match buyers and sellers in-house. Grasso believed that one way to ensure that Citi's trades kept coming to the exchange was to make Weill a business partner and he now began the process of putting Weill on the exchange's board of directors. Maybe that's why Grasso seemed to ignore the fact that his own regulatory staff had joined an investigation that was looking into someone he was pushing to be a board member.

Even so, Weill was in a state of panic as the headlines continued day after day that Spitzer's probe had begun to focus on Grubman's dubious AT&T upgrade and Weill's actions as well. Grasso could see it in Weill's bulging waistline and then his rapid weight loss as the investigation into the Citigroup boss became front-page news. A newspaper report stated that Weill was on a new diet and fitness regimen. Grasso read that and laughed. "Yeah, Sandy's on a diet, he's on the Spitzer diet. He's shitting his brains out."

It was in the spirit of this rapid weight loss that Weill hired Marty Lipton to work his magic. Lipton's firm, Wachtell, Lipton, Rosen & Katz, was one of the top advisers on mergers and acquisitions, with a formidable white-collar-crime practice headed by Lawrence Pedowitz and John Savarese, two former U.S. attorneys. And, of course, the firm had Lipton, who had friends in very high places.

Lipton and Ken Langone went way back, to their early years on the street; both were trustees of New York University, and they considered themselves to be close friends. Any friend of Langone is usually a friend of Grasso, and Lipton was no different. Grasso had met Lipton some thirty years earlier, when Lipton was a young lawyer handling some exchange-related business. Now Lipton was head of the exchange's legal and advisory committee, one of the most powerful committees on the exchange. Its official purpose was to provide advice and guidance to the board when dealing with critical legal issues. But it also allowed Lipton to act as Grasso's personal adviser on just about any sticky situation he faced. It's the reason why Grasso referred to Lipton simply as "the lawyer."

It's impossible to know if Grasso had given Lipton's multiple roles any thought: not only was the exchange part of an investigation that had one of the NYSE's possible board nominees in its sights, but the exchange's top legal adviser was now the nominee's attorney. Grasso said he never dealt directly with Lipton on any issue involving Weill. Still, Marty Lipton's complicated and varied representations went largely ignored as the investigation continued to roll through the late summer and fall of 2002.

Under Lipton's guidance, Weill's response to questions about the episode was that he had "never told any analyst what he or she had to write." Despite the evidence, Weill's defense seemed to hold. In private, Grasso was already downplaying Weill's culpability. By mid-December, Spitzer had officially made up his mind that the Citigroup chief was to be spared criminal or even civil charges. When Grasso heard the news, he was elated. He began telling people that Spitzer had done the right thing, based purely on the evidence.

Spitzer rarely did anything without weighing the political risks and advantages, and although people have debated for years whether or not he had a good case against Weill, one thing is certain: letting him off the hook was the smart thing to do. Spitzer's larger goal throughout his investigation was to take credit for a "broad reform" of sleazy Wall Street research and tout that reform on the campaign trail. Citigroup had made it pretty clear to all the investigators that if Weill were charged, the largest financial firm on the planet would play no role in a global settlement. With the Weill matter put to rest, Citigroup was now on board, ready to pay a large fine and to agree to reform itself along with the rest of Wall Street.

But the rest of Wall Street wasn't so willing to go along. In late November, a group of firms—Bear Stearns, Lehman Brothers, UBS PaineWebber, and Deutsche Bank chief among them—had banded together to fight being lumped into the doghouse with Citigroup, Merrill Lynch, and Morgan Stanley. The splinter group was led by Cayne, who fumed when he heard how Spitzer, the SEC, and Grasso had arrived at a fine for Bear Stearns's actions as part of the "global settlement." In addition to some structural reforms, higher "Chinese walls," and so on, the firms would have to pay a total of

$1.4 billion in fines, penalties, and other costs. Bear's share in all this: $70 million.

"For what?" Jimmy Cayne howled when he first heard the number. Bear had underwritten only one lousy deal of any significance during the dot-com bubble. Cayne made a few calls to the heads of other midsize firms and discovered he wasn't alone; "the Cayne Mutiny" had begun. Initially, the CEO of Bear Stearns relished the fight, and not just with Spitzer, whom he considered a publicity hound, but with Grasso, whom he called a "star fucker" for all the stunts he had pulled over the years to promote himself. Given Grasso's latest stunt involving his massive pay package, Cayne couldn't believe that Grasso had the balls to be working with Spitzer to take money out of his pocket.

While Cayne had some leverage, given his position on the compensation committee and Grasso's recent attempt to remove his nest egg, he had another card in his favor: there was no way Spitzer could hold a press conference and take credit for a "global settlement" that cleaned up Wall Street research unless he had all of Wall Street on board.

If Cayne was worried about his once close relationship with Grasso, he didn't show it. "Fuck Grasso," he said at the time, "this is extortion." For the first two weeks in December, the telephone lines between Cayne's office and the other recalcitrant CEOs continued to burn, along with them the chances of Spitzer's global settlement happening any time soon.

Grasso saw things differently. Spitzer was looking to "reform" rather than prosecute Wall Street, meaning that no firm would be indicted. The list of targets had narrowed to two individuals, Jack Grubman and Henry Blodget. Wall Street would have to pay some fines and agree to jump through a couple more hoops to satisfy Spitzer's reform agenda, but it was certainly something that all his members could live with.

The Cayne Mutiny now threatened to destroy it all. Spitzer had suddenly become itchy; the negotiations had dragged on for months, and he needed something to show for his work over the course of the year. He set a deadline to come up with an agreement in principle that he could announce to the world. Spitzer knew 2003 was the unofficial start of the governor's race in New York, and Charles Schumer was thinking about leaving the U.S. Senate to run for governor himself. If Spitzer couldn't put together a deal soon, he might as well start thinking about another term as AG. He called on Grasso to help.

Grasso knew that at least for the moment, his own hand with the Bear Stearns CEO was weak, given the delicate salary negotiations and Cayne's general feeling that Grasso's dealings with Spitzer were poison to the securities business. So Grasso decided to talk to Cayne like a friend. Wall Street, Grasso said, had been beaten up enough. The markets had yet to recover from the lows of the bubble, and Spitzer was a wild card; if he indicted a firm, it could mean real trouble.

Cayne wasn't in a bargaining mood—at least not yet. He told Grasso that Bear Stearns wasn't paying a dime before abruptly hanging up the phone. Grasso just smiled as the receiver went dead, and he began dialing the others. Grasso didn't have a great relationship with John Costas, the head of UBS PaineWebber, but he did with Grano, who ran the firm's brokerage unit. After speaking with Grasso, Grano told Costas that in fighting, the firm should be prepared to receive "a proctologist exam." Spitzer, the SEC, the NASD, and even Grasso's troops would be poring over the firm's e-mails looking for any blemish on its record. Grano's message had the intended effect on Costas, who, knowing what had happened to Weill, was looking to avoid the "Spitzer diet" at all costs.

Grasso then called Richard Fuld. Grasso knew Fuld was a friend; the Lehman Brothers CEO had been a stock exchange board member, a compensation committee member, no less. But he was tired of the corporate scandals, which had cost Lehman in recent months. Lehman had been in the news for the better part of the year, not over research improprieties but over news that one of its star brokers, Frank Gruttadauria, had stolen tens of millions of dollars from his clients, right under the nose of the firm's compliance department. The case was being investigated by the NYSE, and Lehman was desperately trying to put the matter to rest. In the conflicted world of Wall Street, having Dick Grasso on your side isn't such a bad thing, particularly when you are being investigated by the NYSE. By the end of the five-minute call, Fuld said he was on board as well.

The Cayne Mutiny now consisted of one person, Cayne himself.

Grasso thought he should pay one last call to his Kappa Beta Phi fraternity brother. Word of Costas jumping ship and Fuld folding had already reached Cayne. "You can't fight these fucking people alone," Cayne muttered as Grasso asked him if he was ready to deal. Cayne said he was, and now it was Grasso's turn to stick it to the card shark. The price tag for a settlement had just risen $10 million, Grasso said, to $80 million so Spitzer could reach his magic $1.4 billion settlement number. "Extortion," Cayne muttered. "Fucking extortion."

Star fucker or savior? That was the question Wall Street was grappling with as the nation's top securities regulators set a December 20 date to announce the "global settlement" of fraudulent research. Sandy Weill clearly needed a savior. Not long after the settlement date was announced, the NASD's enforcement staff was still weighing whether Weill should get the complete pass that Spitzer had envisioned. Citigroup was being charged with civil securities fraud for its and Grubman's research on AT&T. But NASD officials were now considering whether to charge Weill with failure to supervise his top analyst. Grasso heard the news and simply rolled his eyes, but Spitzer knew it was more serious, possibly deal-killing as far as Citigroup was concerned.

This time Grasso couldn't make the call; Glauber and Schapiro would have laughed him out of the park. Spitzer, however, didn't have any such inhibition. Glauber could barely hide his contempt for Spitzer's tactics during the research probe, but Schapiro and Spitzer had begun as enemies and ended as friends. Spitzer knew if he had a shot at quashing the charges against Weill, he should start with a simple but direct call to Schapiro to say that charging Weill would endanger all that they had worked so hard to achieve, namely the reform of Wall Street research. Schapiro thought for a moment, then asked to speak to her staff. When she called Spitzer back, she said the NASD was on board and Weill was in the clear.

Whether Schapiro knew it or not, so was Grasso. With Weill facing no charges, Grasso believed his nomination to the board would be a fait accompli and so would all the Citigroup trading order flow Grasso wanted heading into the exchange. Meanwhile, the fraudulent research that had helped the big brokerage firms rake in billions of dollars in profits over the past decade cost Wall Street only $1.4 billion, half of which was tax deductible! No CEO was charged in the settlement, despite the fact that the practices, as evidenced by Weill's conduct, had been condoned at the highest levels of the street. As expected, only Blodget and Grubman were charged, and both were expelled from the business for life, paying $4 million and $15 million, respectively, for their sins against small investors, though they didn't have to admit to those sins. As part of the deal, neither the firms nor the individuals admitted or denied wrongdoing in conflicts of interest that had cost small investors who relied on the fraudulent research all those losses as they bet on the money-losing stocks. No one seemed to pick up Marty Lipton's connection to both Weill and the stock exchange, which was now ready to give its approval to the final terms of the investigation as part of the global settlement.

Grasso knew he had scored a home run when the final terms were announced, and now he was ready to take his victory lap. Initially, the regulators wanted to hold the press conference announcing the settlement at a neutral location, but Spitzer stepped in and said the best "neutral" location he could think of was the New York Stock Exchange. Spitzer now considered Grasso a "friend" and officials at the NASD were livid, but given Grasso's relationship with Spitzer there was nothing they could do.

Grasso offered one concession: he told each regulatory organization that it could display its banner behind the podium so that when the cameras rolled, viewers would understand that it was a joint effort by the securities industry's top cops. But Grasso had always been a stickler about what he referred to as "brand dilution" with the television media. What Grasso didn't tell his fellow regulators was that the NYSE controlled the camera feeds to the various television stations that carried any event live from its boardroom, and the cameras made sure that when they were shooting the various speeches, including the most important ones delivered by Grasso and Spitzer, it was the NYSE logo that made it into the picture every time.

As he entered his eighth year as CEO of the Club, Grasso believed one of the secrets of his success was that he had learned not just from his mistakes but from the mistakes of those who had gone before him. In reality, though, Grasso was always moving so fast, working so hard, that he never had time to contemplate the meaning of things. His single-minded purpose—to make sure the NYSE remained number one—prevented him from understanding the broader implications of his actions.

It was this same lack of understanding that led him now to put into high gear his decision to make Sandy Weill a member of the New York Stock Exchange's board of directors. According to exchange by-laws, board seats are filled by an independent "nominating" committee. The chairman of the exchange can recommend names of possible board members, but he cannot pass final judgment. Ultimately, board nominees must be approved by the full board, and the membership, the 1,366 seat holders. In reality, however, the process was a rubber-stamp of whatever nominee was presented by the chairman.

For years the process seemed to work without much controversy, primarily because Donaldson followed the example of Phelan and didn't take advantage of the chairman's power. Instead of pushing for securities industry types—the very people who were regulated by the exchange and could fear reprisal if they voted against the chairman—both Phelan and Donaldson tried to make sure more than half of the entire board came from outside the securities industry, mainly CEOs of listed companies who had little if any worry that the exchange's enforcement staff might show up at their door to conduct an audit after a controversial vote.

Under Grasso just the opposite was true. By 2002, thirteen of the twenty-four board members came either from the securities industry or from the floor. In other words, the board of the Club was as Grasso-friendly as he could make it, and he wasn't done yet.

"It's a brilliant move," Langone thought as he sat in his midtown Manhattan office upon hearing that Grasso was ready to nominate Sandy Weill to the board. Grasso may have been friends with Weill's attorney Marty Lipton, and Langone knew the full story about Weill's 92nd Street Y imbroglio. What made Weill's addition so enticing to Langone was the money it represented. Langone had been a seat owner for years, and now being on the compensation committee gave him an insider's view of the exchange's financial statements; Grasso had done well over the past five years, but the exchange itself had taken some lumps from lower specialist profits, a decline in IPOs, and a decline in listings from their bubble-market highs.

Then there was trading order flow, the juice that kept the exchange running. When trades are sent to the exchange, it means more money for the specialists, who in turn pay more to the exchange in the form of taxes and fees. As head of Citigroup, a financial services conglomerate, Weill controlled one of the biggest pools of order flow in the world, and with him on the board most of it would be coming to the exchange.

Now Grasso just had to sell the idea. He quickly spread the word that Robert Devlin, the former CEO of American General Corporation, and chief of the nominating committee, had picked Weill. Board members quietly laughed at that explanation, particularly as rumors spread that Weill's selection was a favor to Lipton. Grasso then laid it out straight: Sandy Weill would be good for the exchange because of the size of Citigroup; the world's biggest financial institution must be represented on the exchange's board of directors.

There was resistance almost from the moment Grasso announced Weill's nomination during a February 2003 board meeting. Larry Fink, Jimmy Cayne, and the rest of the board were blown away when Grasso announced his intentions. To push Weill through quickly, Grasso wanted to give Weill a seat without board debate and put it to an immediate vote of the membership, which was a rubber stamp.

These were, after all, corporate executives used to a little bad press. But what had happened to Weill and Citigroup over the past year was almost unprecedented for any board nominee. Even without taking into account his role in Grubman's fraudulent AT&T rating, Weill led one of the most scandal-plagued firms on Wall Street. Citigroup did business with Enron, WorldCom, and other problematic companies. Making matters worse, Grasso had only one spot open, for a public representative—something that Weill was uniquely unqualified for.

None of this mattered to Grasso as he told the board that "there's only one Sandy Weill" and that his record of achievement on Wall Street was unparalleled. But Carol Bartz, the CEO of Autodesk, a technology company, immediately asked Grasso if he was "sure the timing is right" to bring Weill on board under any conditions. "I think you ought to think about what you're saying when you're telling us there's only one Sandy Weill," she said. Fink agreed, while Goldman CEO Henry Paulson, who had managed to attend this meeting, asked if Grasso could find someone else at the firm without the baggage that Weill brought to the table.

Grasso reminded the board that Weill hadn't been charged in the research investigation. "This is, after all, still America," Grasso said. More than that, the exchange needed Citigroup, he said.

The board sat and listened to Grasso's arguments, but Fink pushed back again—instead of putting Weill to an immediate vote, why not put him on a slate with others? It would also allow some time for the bad smell associated with the Spitzer investigation to wear off before putting Weill on the board. Grasso agreed. To him it was a small concession, and one he thought wouldn't have much of an impact in the end.

There were, of course, those who believed Grasso had yet another triumph under his belt since the exchange would be swimming in Citigroup order flow. But others made a different assessment. Grasso was ready to give another board seat to Joe Grano, an appointment that Grano had long coveted. But Grasso's timing was terrible, as Grano explained one night while they were having dinner at Il Mu-

lino; he took himself out of the running because he was about to retire from UBS and start his own private equity firm.

Grasso thanked him for his candor, Grano recalls, replying,
"That's why I love you," and without missing a beat, he told Grano
he was ready to give an open slot to Weill.

The conversation went downhill from there. "Don't do it, Dick,"
Grano recalls saying. "I like Sandy, but don't you think the timing is
awful?" Grasso then accused Grano of "looking in the rearview mirror." The investigation was over, he said, and Weill hadn't been
touched.

"Dick, you need a rearview mirror," Grano shot back. He argued
that Weill's reputation had been badly damaged, thinking to himself
that the kid from Queens had an ego as big as the borough of Brooklyn if he thought he could pull this off without public outrage.

By the end of the night, the two were arguing, and after a heated
exchange, they left the restaurant nearly at each other's throats.
Grano recalls that they walked around the block for about two hours,
trying to repair their friendship; Grasso told him he "felt terrible"
about thirty times before Grano finally accepted his friend's apology
and called it a night. A few days later, Grasso ordered Zito to prepare
a press release on the Weill "nomination" after the market closed on
Friday afternoon, a time when most reporters are heading home or
just too lazy to start a new assignment.

Zito had his reservations about the move as well. He calmly told
his boss how the press might react, but Grasso said his mind was
made up and with any luck news of the appointment might go unnoticed, buying them some additional time to push Weill through if any
opposition emerged.

Initially, the plan seemed to work. The usual gaggle of wire services wrote straight stories about the appointment, including the exchange's bizarre explanation of how well Weill was qualified to
represent small investors.

There was no mention of Spitzer, Grubman, or Weill's brush with
possible securities fraud. Zito continued to worry that he wasn't out
of the woods just yet.

The next day, *The New York Times* followed suit. "Hey, this is pretty good," Zito said. Grasso agreed. But when Spitzer read the *Times*'s toothless account, he hit the ceiling. Many on Wall Street already thought Spitzer had blinked, not charging Weill because Citigroup was too powerful, particularly in Washington and particularly with people in the Democratic Party whom Spitzer needed to support him for higher office. Weill had certainly created the impression that he was untouchable during that lavish birthday party at Carnegie Hall, inviting nearly every major New York politician, except, as it turned out, Eliot Spitzer, something that Grasso didn't realize but Spitzer did.

Those who knew Spitzer also knew his temper, particularly directed at those who made him look stupid. Now Spitzer looked stupid in *The New York Times* because of Grasso's decision to name Weill as a board member. What steamed Spitzer the most was Zito's explanation that Weill was "qualified" to represent public shareholders on the board because he ran an institution that was considered a bank rather than a securities firm. "You've got to be kidding me!" Spitzer snapped.

Grasso had just discussed the good press about Weill and was ready to complete his Saturday-morning workout when he received a call on his cell phone from Spitzer. Spitzer started with none of the niceties from their previous dealings. "First the birthday party and now this!" Spitzer boomed. "I'm not going to be part of the rehabilitation of Sandy Weill!" Spitzer then asked Grasso if he could reverse his decision. Spitzer was used to politics in smoke-filled rooms; he was, after all, a New York State elected official. But this one took the cake because it made him look bad. Spitzer, after all, must have heard the rumblings that he had given Weill a pass to get the settlement done, and Grasso's move drew attention to it even more.

Spitzer gave Grasso an ultimatum: pull Weill from the list or face the consequences. Grasso said he would see what he could do but reiterated that it would be the board's decision. Spitzer laughed to himself; he knew all roads at the exchange led to Grasso. He said he would call back in the afternoon to hear Grasso's decision.

Grasso held his temper in check, but just barely. It was, after all, Spitzer who had given Weill a clean bill of health, reducing the entire Grubman–92nd Street Y fiasco to a big misunderstanding. What right did he have to come back and tell the exchange that it couldn't do business with an innocent man? When Spitzer called back later that afternoon, Grasso said no decision had been made to remove Weill from consideration—but, he added, the board would still have the final say, and it was quite possible that Weill could be rejected.

Grasso was looking for a face-saving way out of the mess. But he had badly miscalculated. Even before the call, Spitzer and his press office had been contacting reporters about their intention to go to war with Grasso if he didn't reconsider the Weill board seat. It was the first significant split between the two since their relationship had begun nearly a year before, and Spitzer didn't pull any punches. He and his troops reminded reporters about the entire Grubman investigation, Weill's involvement in the Grubman AT&T call, and the fact that the entire investigation, in all its seedy details, should have been fresh in Grasso's mind because the NYSE had been part of the global settlement that had fined Citigroup for the fraudulent AT&T upgrade.

Spitzer made a great case, laying out all that was wrong with Weill becoming a board member, particularly one who was representing the investing public. But he also laid out a great case for why Sandy Weill should no longer be a CEO in the first place. At first Grasso was defiant, telling one newspaper reporter what he had told the board in defending the nomination: "This is America, and this man hasn't been convicted of anything!" Later he continued his mantra that he had very little to do with board selections—the nominations came from a separate committee. It was an absurd statement, at least according to board members questioned on the matter. "Weill was Grasso's choice and Grasso's alone," one board member said with a snicker.

By the end of the weekend, Grasso's defiance turned into apprehension; Spitzer's comments that he was ready to mount a public challenge to thwart the Weill nomination began to appear in various news stories. By late Sunday, the following day, Grasso had made up his mind to pull Weill's name from consideration. Grasso says Weill was disappointed when he gave him the news; now, at seventy years of age, he was about to end his career as a corporate miscreant in the eyes of many people. In order to help Weill save face, Grasso made it seem as though it had been Weill's decision to withdraw, releasing a statement that said that Weill had only "reluctantly" agreed to serve on the board of the exchange and, following the comments from Spitzer, he was withdrawing his name from consideration.

Grasso had hoped for a one-day story, but he got much more, and now he was cringing as he read the various accounts describing the apprehension of some board members over Weill and Spitzer's attack.

Even friends couldn't believe someone as smart as Grasso would do something so foolish. Langone remained loyal, believing that Weill's nomination had been a brilliant business move. Phelan had long since retired from the exchange, and now he barely spoke to Grasso. But if he had offered some advice, he would have once again reminded Grasso that the exchange was as much a "public trust" as it was a business. Its image was as important as its balance sheet.

Spitzer, meanwhile, would once again call Grasso a "friend," but their relationship would never return to its pre-Weill condition. Maybe the biggest blow for Grasso was to his reputation. He was no longer considered the astute political player who had guided the exchange to all those new listings, who had saved his member firms from sustaining massive damage during the research inquiry. Now he was like every other corporate executive: rich, powerful, and vulnerable to error.

Steve Cutler, the SEC enforcement chief, summed it up best after reading some of the stories about the Weill nomination: "Grasso can't take too many more hits like this." Cutler, like many other people in the regulatory community, had been blown away by Grasso's political acumen. Now Grasso seemed like a fatigued long-distance runner at the end of a big race; he had clearly lost a step or two.

9

THE UPRISING BEGINS

The Weill fiasco had overshadowed another fiasco in the making: Grasso's plans to renew his contract and collect his retirement money. The combination of the retirement accounts created by Stanley Gault and the money handed to him by the compensation committee had produced a windfall for Grasso. What had initially been thought to be a nest egg worth around $120 million was actually $139.5 million. The final tally was even larger because hidden inside Grasso's contract proposal was a clause that allowed him to collect another $48 million if he extended his contract to 2007, bringing the total up to almost $190 million.

The exchange had withheld the details of Grasso's pay for years, claiming that as a member organization it was under no authority to publicly release Grasso's salary. But that was before the press began embarking on its crusade to expose overpaid corporate executives.

There were many valid reasons for the press's fixation with executives' compensation. By early 2003, the bear market had abated, but most small investors still hadn't made up all the money they had lost when the market bubble burst two years earlier. Meanwhile, the real incomes of most Americans had been stagnant since the early 1970s, but stretches of prosperity combined with the market bubble of the mid-1990s had made average people feel richer than they actually were. Now that the boom years were over, average Americans went back to feeling average again. Against this backdrop it was hard to defend corporations handing out huge severance packages, golden parachutes, and just plain loads of dough to executives who had done a lousy job for shareholders but were masters at boardroom politics. They selected friends and business associates as board members, who rewarded them with huge salaries regardless of how much (or little) the executives achieved. In other words, stock prices dropped while executive compensation soared.

Grasso may not have known it, but he had set himself up to be the poster child for the scandal. When he first told the compensation committee of his intention, Grasso said he merely wanted to move money from one account to another, an effort, he said, to take more control of his retirement savings. The committee tabled the matter until the new year. Now that the new year was here, Grasso changed his terms: he wanted all the money, delivered to him in a check for $139.5 million, in exchange for a contract extension. When asked, Grasso said he needed the money for "estate planning," but that didn't wash either. Keeping the money in the accounts, given their high interest rates, would have been the best estate-planning decision he could make—unless, of course, he didn't think the money would be there when he retired. And that, in a nutshell, was Grasso's main concern, according to board members he spoke to at the time. The corporate scandals, Eliot Spitzer, and public outrage over a regulator being paid so much money by the people he regulated would prevent him from receiving money that anybody who had seen him work over the past eight years would concede he had earned.

Just how much Grasso wanted the money was evident by the fact that right before the February compensation committee meeting he broke his self-imposed silence with the committee. He told Ashen to tell the compensation committee that his salary that year should decline as he made preparations to remove his massive nest egg.

The committee included Fink, Cayne, Karmazin, Levin, and

Schrempp, plus a "new" addition, Hank Paulson, the CEO of Goldman Sachs. Paulson had been a board member since 1999 and had technically been on the compensation committee since mid-2002. "Technically" is a good way to describe Paulson's status because he had been among the least attentive board members since joining. In fairness to Paulson, he had warned Grasso before joining that he had a full schedule, and Grasso had accepted Paulson's conditions.

Langone was clearly on board with Grasso's new terms. During the meeting, he made Grasso's case the best way he knew how, extolling his various achievements as chairman and explaining what it would mean to the exchange if it lost him. Still, there was some debate and confusion. Fink suggested that Grasso's salary be capped at $6 million to $8 million, given the depressed business conditions on Wall Street. Fink's proposal to drastically scale back Grasso's pay was rebuffed primarily because the exchange had had a better year in 2002 than expected; listings, though still well below their highs in the 1990s, had risen slightly above 2001 levels. Grasso might not have deserved the $30 million he had made in 2001, but he didn't deserve a $24 million salary cut either.

After some back-and-forth, the committee came up with a final number it could agree on: a healthy $12 million. During the meeting, someone remarked that Grasso was making more money than Paulson, to which Paulson remarked, according to one witness, "Yeah, but he had a better year than I did." (Paulson actually made $12.1 million in 2002.)

Now came the heavy lifting involving Grasso's retirement package. Before the discussion began, Paulson said he had to leave to deal with a client matter. As Paulson remained in the dark about one of the most contentious issues affecting the exchange, the rest of the board discovered that Grasso had now abruptly changed the terms of the deal. He wanted all the money, not just moved into his exchange savings account but delivered to him in cash.

Langone laid out the terms again: under the proposal, Grasso's contract would extend to 2007 and he would receive his retirement money, as much as $140 million. The money was Grasso's, Langone said. His biggest selling point: the exchange, Langone said, would actually save money by letting Grasso take the money before retirement because it would no longer be in the accounts earning the high rates of interest that the NYSE had been paying.

Maybe so, but Cayne and Fink were flummoxed. Cayne, for one, wasn't quite sure how much money was due to Grasso. After the discussion, he came away with the impression that Grasso's package had somehow been reduced to $80 million. He was, of course, wrong. But he had other concerns, as did Fink.

Both said they weren't sure if the money could be legally removed—whether it was "vested"—and they doubted Langone's assessment that the move would save money. In the end Fink and Cayne pushed for more time and more analysis. The other board members agreed.

As much as Langone believed the money was Grasso's fair and square, he did something he wasn't accustomed to doing when it came to Grasso's compensation: he compromised. The committee would send its $12 million salary recommendation to the full board. Approval for the retirement package would have to wait until the next committee meeting in April. For a change everyone was in agreement.

Grasso took the news well enough, though Cayne kept remarking that whenever he ran into the little guy, he seemed to give Cayne a look as if he held the Bear Stearns CEO responsible for depriving him of money he had earned. Meanwhile, a series of events began to underscore just how reckless Grasso's desire to take all the money immediately had become. The Sandy Weill board fiasco became huge news in the financial world, shining an uncomfortable light on Grasso's leadership and judgment. Harvey Pitt would be ousted as SEC chief after a series of political missteps that allowed Democrats in Washington to make him a scapegoat for the corporate scandals, and Grasso was deprived of a key friend and ally.

News of Pitt's replacement sent shivers up Grasso's spine as word leaked that his old nemesis Frank Zarb, the former NASD chief, was up for the job. Zarb says he didn't want the appointment, but he let it leak that he was interested, not because he was but because he knew it would drive Grasso crazy, which it did. Grasso quickly began making calls to various public officials, demanding that Zarb remove himself from any discussion involving the exchange because of his allegiance to the NASD.

Zarb laughed when he heard Grasso's response, but Grasso was hardly laughing when he heard who was likely to get the job instead of Zarb: the "empty suit" himself, Bill Donaldson.

Donaldson had been doing some investment work after a few lack-luster years at Aetna that had allowed him to make an estimated $150 million through stock options, and now he was ready to return to the limelight. At least Donaldson was a fan of the stock exchange, Grasso reckoned, when he heard that the rumblings were for real. What Grasso didn't know was that even after all these years Donaldson wasn't a fan of Grasso. Grasso was now demonstrating why Phelan had had so many misgivings about his becoming chairman years earlier. As the April compensation committee meeting approached, Grasso didn't seem to understand that the world had changed since his glory years of the 1990s. Nor did he seem to give a second thought to the absurdity of a regulator being paid so much in cash from the people he regulated. Neither did Langone. With multiple studies completed on the pay package, Langone believed the time was right to finish selling the measure to the compensation committee, before sending it to the board for full approval. That task was left to Frank Ashen, the head of Grasso's human resources department. Ashen had worked at the exchange for about two decades, much of it in the human resources area, though he had also been given the additional assignment as the exchange's chief ethics officer. But like most people who made it inside Grasso's inner circle, Ashen proved himself to be someone Grasso could trust, so much so that Ashen was now one of the highest-paid people at the exchange, earning around $2 million a year.

Hank Paulson's office was located at Goldman Sachs's headquarters on Broad Street, just a few blocks southeast of the stock exchange, where Grasso held court. But the two cultures couldn't have been more different. On any given day, you could see burly specialists huddling outside the exchange on Broad Street clad in their blue and green smocks, smoking cigarettes and loudly discussing stocks as if they were on the trading floor. The only thing you would find outside Goldman is a long line of black limos waiting for the next elegantly dressed banker to jump in and be driven off.

Once a refuge for Jews who couldn't find employment on Wall Street, Goldman had morphed over the years into the whitest of white-shoe Wall Street firms. Paulson's crowning as CEO marked the high point of the WASP ascendancy.

Paulson, the former Illinois farm boy, Nixon administration aide, and longtime Goldman investment banker had made many enemies inside the firm because of his ambition and relentless drive to get the top job. But he was now regarded as one of the best CEOs on Wall Street because under his leadership Goldman had solidified its place as the elite of Wall Street, cranking out profits above and beyond its competitors.

With the goal of extending Goldman's reach further, Paulson lusted for control of the NYSE. It began with his plan to implement more electronic trading and reduce the floor to irrelevance. This proved to be a bitter defeat at the hands of Grasso and was the likely cause of Goldman's purchase of Spear, Leeds & Kellogg, one of the largest floor trading operations in the business. Still, Paulson never gave up his ultimate goal of making the world safe for electronic trading, particularly when it concerned the NYSE. Goldman had been the major investor in the new electronic trading platform named Archipelago, which top officials at Goldman believed would make a perfect fit at the technology-challenged NYSE if it weren't for Grasso's opposition.

The first time a detailed explanation of Grasso's retirement package and his intention to cash it in immediately entered Paulson's mind was in March 2003 when Ashen paid him a visit to discuss a proposal to extend Grasso's contract. But it was the last thing Paulson had wanted to deal with. Goldman may have been making loads of money under Paulson but it was also in transition; Paulson had assumed control in 1999, when the bankers were bringing in big bucks through technology offerings and the traders were losing money on their Long-Term Capital Management trades. Now it was Paulson's turn in the hot seat. The balance sheet was once again flush with trading profits, and the firm's head trader, Lloyd Blankfein, was itching for Paulson's job. Paulson was now doing what he did best: politicking with Goldman's board and helping to secure his future as the traders demanded a bigger role in the firm.

As Ashen presented the details of Grasso's compensation, Paulson was blown away. The money accumulated in the account had been earned over the past five years, when Grasso had deferred nearly all of his bonus and salary into various retirement plans. In 1999, when he re-upped, Grasso had moved about $30 million from a retirement account to his stock exchange savings account, which allowed him to invest money in a series of Vanguard mutual funds. That money, in addition to the other money he had deferred and the interest he had accumulated, added up to roughly $140 million. As Ashen put it, "This is Grasso's money."

Paulson is known for his intensity, and upon hearing what Grasso wanted to do with his retirement money, not to mention how much he had accumulated, he was about as intense as ever. He would later tell people that after hearing the exact details of the compensation, he "gasped at the numbers" though, as Ashen recalled the meeting, he remained calm, as if not to give away his true feelings.

Paulson's mind shifted into overdrive; he might have missed most of the compensation committee meetings, but he immediately realized that the problem stemmed not just from Grasso's huge salary—which had grown by leaps and bounds under Langone—but also the generous terms of the retirement account that had sent Grasso's savings into the stratosphere in just a few years. Paulson ran a big Wall Street firm, so he understood just how much Wall Street fat cats were hated by the general public, given Enron, WorldCom, and the scandals made public by Eliot Spitzer. In other words, Grasso might have earned every dime he was paid, but he was also looking to cash out a fortune just when the public had soured on overpaid execs.

Like Cayne and Fink, Paulson was initially concerned with how Grasso's decision would look to the rest of the world—"the optics" of taking so much money before retirement. In other words, it might be legal for Grasso to take the money in order to keep him at the NYSE a few more years, but it looked like shit. Again, Ashen said the money was Grasso's and all the consultants agreed. The only thing left was the approval of the compensation committee and then the full board and Grasso stays at the exchange until 2007.

Ashen left the office thinking that Paulson had no major complaints—that was the beauty of all those years Paulson had spent deal making. It made Paulson among the best poker players on the street. But after Ashen had left his office, Paulson called Goldman's general counsel to see if he could contact Grasso and Langone directly about the matter. His general counsel said he could.

Paulson had now become more engaged in NYSE business than ever before in his career. Cayne met with Ashen as well and didn't hide his emotions. "If the money is his, he can have it," Cayne snapped. "But Grasso is making a big mistake, and when this gets out it's going to blow up like a volcano!"

Paulson agreed and now began telling associates on Wall Street that Grasso's taking the money would destroy not just his career but possibly the exchange itself now that the business press had made executives' pay a crusade.

At one point he asked Langone if it would be possible to keep certain details of Grasso's retirement package from the entire board. His big worry: that the embarrassing details of the pay package would be leaked once they got outside the compensation committee, which had been sworn to secrecy by Langone. Paulson would be known not just as an enabler of an overpaid executive but as a guy who cared so little about his fiduciary duty that he hadn't shown up to the meetings when the compensation was discussed.

Langone turned to the guy who he believed always had the right answer: Marty Lipton, head of the exchange's legal advisory committee, who told him emphatically the entire board needed to know everything. Langone and Grasso believed Paulson was just being an asshole, voicing concern over something when it was too late and trying to protect his own skin. Whatever his motives, Paulson was right on at least one count: the "optics" of Grasso's taking the money were lousy to just about everyone except Langone and the little guy himself. And it wouldn't be long before Grasso and Langone discovered that Paulson might be an asshole, but he was a very prescient asshole.

As the April board date approached, the compensation committee received word that Grasso's money grab was being delayed, at least for the time being. The official reason the committee members heard from the sixth floor of the exchange: Grasso and Langone wanted to let the controversy over the failed Weill nomination die down before embarking on another battle.

But that didn't stop the issue from causing major indigestion behind the scenes. One Saturday afternoon in late March, Chris Quick, the CEO of Fleet Specialists, took a needed break from the insanity of the Club to attend his daughter's squash game at the exclusive Groton prep school in Massachusetts. But it wasn't long before he found himself right in the middle of exchange business and at odds with the all-powerful man who ran the place.

Like many of the second- and third-generation floor traders at the Club, Quick had been born into his job and, to a large extent, his wealth. Quick & Reilly had been cofounded by his father, Leslie Quick, Jr., and it had soon become one of the biggest discount brokerage operations in the country. In the late 1970s, Les Quick bought a small specialist firm and appointed his son, Chris, to run it, and in a few years it was one of the biggest specialist firms on the floor.

The Quick family had just sold the entire operation to Fleet Bank for $1.6 billion, and traders on the floor began referring to Chris as "Richie Rich" after the comic book character who was blessed with family wealth. In many ways, Quick and Grasso couldn't be more different, but over the years, they had grown close, bonding over a mutually beneficial relationship that had begun with Grasso's belief that he could trust Quick to be one of his allies on the floor, and with

Quick's desire to have friends in high places. In 2001, Grasso appointed Quick to the board of the stock exchange. Unlike Paulson, Quick attended all of the meetings, particularly the ones where Grasso's pay was discussed. Though he never told his good friend he was making too much money, by early 2003, Quick was starting to feel that the board had made a colossal mistake giving so many perks to the man at the top.

Because Quick wasn't on the compensation committee, he didn't have direct knowledge of the size of Grasso's entire retirement package, which remained a secret among the compensation committee members until they decided to take it to the board. But, as he recalls, he had several casual conversations with a member of the committee, the floor trader Robert Murphy, who gave Quick some indication of the retirement package's size and scope, and he was blown away.

That said, Quick had kept mum about the money—that is, until an afternoon in late March while attending the squash game. He was approached by a senior Goldman Sachs executive named Robert Steel. Steel knew Quick's connections with Grasso and asked him about a rumor that was circulating through the halls of Goldman Sachs that Grasso was making millions, certainly millions more than anyone thought a regulator should.

"So how much money is Grasso making?" Steel asked. Quick was caught in a bind: board business, particularly compensation of NYSE executives, is supposed to be off-limits to outsiders. But Steel wasn't an ordinary outsider. Shares of Goldman Sachs trade on the NYSE. Quick's firm was the specialist for Goldman's stock and that made Steel, the head of Goldman's equities division, a client. "A lot more than you think," Quick blurted out. In fact, he added, "They're paying Grasso like a rock star."

Quick says he didn't provide actual numbers to Steel. When Steel prodded him for specifics, Quick says he shot back, "Why don't you ask Paulson? He's on the comp committee." And that's apparently what Steel did.

On Monday morning, Chris Quick was looking forward to an uneventful start to his week until he received an urgent message from his secretary that Hank Paulson wanted to meet with him immediately at his office on Broad Street to discuss NYSE business. As Quick walked briskly down Broad Street past the exchange, he wasn't sure what to expect; by now the conversation with Steel had receded from his memory. Paulson was all smiles as Quick sat down, and they began to speak about the trading in Goldman's stock. Suddenly, the conversation turned to Grasso's compensation, or, to be more precise, how much Quick as a board member knew about its size and scope.

"Hank, it's a lot of money," Quick recalls saying. Paulson then asked if details about Grasso's salary were "out there" among the floor traders he socialized with. Quick was circumspect in his answer; Paulson might be a client, but the last thing Quick needed was to get on the wrong side of Grasso. For all he knew, Paulson was setting Quick up as the possible leaker of the information Grasso wanted to keep secret.

"It could be out there," Quick said, thinking it was odd being grilled about Grasso's pay by a compensation committee member. By the end of the conversation, Quick noted an odd look on Paulson's face, as if he were hiding a bigger agenda.

After his meeting with Quick, Paulson relayed their conversation to Grasso. It was, Paulson said, a breach of board confidentiality, what Quick had told both him and Steel, who wasn't even a board member. If Quick was blabbing to him, who knows how many people he had told?

Grasso was livid; Paulson said he should be. Paulson told Grasso he was personally offended that a board member would so blatantly break board rules and said he gave Quick a lecture on the "confidentiality" of board items. Grasso said he would do the same.

Sometime later, when Quick was back at the exchange, his worst fears seemed confirmed when he received a request from Grasso to meet him in the chairman's sixth-floor office. Quick could immediately see the anger in Grasso's eyes—the "Grasso stare" was in full force. Paulson had fingered Quick as the leak of Grasso's compensation, first to Steel and then to himself.

"What is this charade you pulled at Goldman Sachs?" Grasso demanded, adding, "If you have a problem with my compensation, you should come to talk to me directly." Quick told Grasso he had no problem with his compensation and had had no choice but to talk to Paulson and Steel about it; Goldman was a client, and Steel had put him on the spot. When he received a call from Paulson, he couldn't ignore the request. He was, after all, Goldman's specialist.

Grasso was perplexed. What do you mean, Steel asked you? Paulson said you just gave up the information Grasso said. Quick said he had only told Steel what he knew, but only after Steel had asked. As for his talk with Paulson, it had hardly been adversarial; Paulson had slipped in a question about Grasso's compensation as one of about a half-dozen items. He had seemed more focused on how many people knew about Grasso's compensation.

Quick left Grasso's office believing he was now on Grasso's shit list. Grasso, meanwhile, didn't know what to make of what had just gone down. Why would Steel and Paulson care about how many people knew about his pay package and whether a floor person like Quick had been speaking out of turn? These questions were all dancing through Grasso's head, but one thing was certain: with Paulson now intensely focused on his pay package, he had bigger problems on his hands than Chris Quick's big mouth.

Grasso and Paulson would have several more conversations in the days and weeks ahead, none of them good as far as Grasso was concerned. After the meetings with Ashen, the compensation committee seemed largely in agreement that Grasso should get access to his money immediately as a condition for his contract extension—that is, except for Paulson, who, despite Ashen's initial assurances that he was on board, was now clearly having second thoughts, at least according to the conversations he was having with Grasso.

Grasso had appointed Paulson to the board of the exchange not just because Goldman owned a large specialist firm, Spear, Leeds & Kellogg, but Goldman, being a major trading firm, sent order flow to the floor. Also, Grasso wanted Paulson where he could keep tabs on him; ever since the CLOB debate, which had nearly allowed Paulson to replace the floor with a computer, Grasso knew he needed to keep this enemy as close as possible. Now Grasso began speaking to Paulson about his compensation as if Paulson were someone he could trust. During one meeting, Paulson told Grasso that he believed it would look bad if Grasso took the money before his contract was ended and that he should consider a compromise; instead of taking all the money all at once, he should roll it into his savings account, just as he had in 1999, and delay any decision until the controversy over executives' pay died down.

Grasso listened to Paulson's advice, but he also knew time wasn't on his side, as he revealed some of the real reasons why he wanted all the money as soon as possible. At least according to Paulson's recollection of the events, it had very little to do with the "estate planning" that would be Grasso's mantra as the details of his salary became public. Grasso's main concern was more visceral, namely whether a future board would be so consumed with the furor over executive pay that it might not give him money he had rightfully earned.

Paulson wasn't sure what to say. When Grasso asked him when the issue of overpaid executives might "blow over," Paulson said he didn't know. Later, when Grasso asked Paulson if he thought he had a "valid claim" to the money, again Paulson sidestepped the question. Grasso had signed a contract that had allowed him to become very rich, and "a contract is a contract," Paulson said. But once again he referred to the "bad optics" involved in the decision to take the money immediately.

Paulson's nonanswers caught Grasso off guard. What was he getting at with the "contract is a contract" remark? After all, the debate they were having had nothing to do with his contract; it was whether the board should approve his taking his retirement money as a condition of extending his contract. There was another strange comment; Paulson asked at one point if Grasso had sought legal advice. It was an odd statement since he wasn't stealing the money. He could withdraw the money from the account only with board approval. But it made Grasso think: there was something else going on inside Paulson's head besides "optics."

• • •

Grasso didn't discuss the matter with a lawyer, but soon events would force his hand. On May 8, 2003, *The Wall Street Journal* ran a story that for the first time attempted to estimate the size of Grasso's pay. The *Journal* didn't have all the numbers right—in fact, it lowballed both his annual salary at $10 million and his retirement package at between $80 million and $100 million. One problem was that for all the disclosure Langone had provided over the years, confusion continued to reign among the committee members over the exact size of the retirement package: Cayne, for one, still believed that Grasso had agreed to take only around $80 million out of the system; others believed it was as much as $100 million.

But even the lowball account of Grasso's salary and pay package created a firestorm of negative publicity. Grasso had sensed as much in the days preceding publication of the article. Grasso believed the story had been leaked; Quick was an initial suspect, but he denied having ever talked to the reporters. In fact, Quick blamed Paulson as the leaker.

Before the story broke, Grasso and Zito plotted strategy. For a guy who was supposed to be so media savvy, Grasso was caught flat-footed when the *Journal* pressed for answers. He offered nothing to soften the blow. Neither Grasso nor Langone would comment on his salary. "Tell them they're on their own" was Grasso's order to Zito. But Grasso knew that if he wanted a balanced story, someone should at the very least tout his achievements. At nearly the last minute, that someone turned out to be Dave Komansky, the retiring CEO of Merrill Lynch, who was also retiring from the board of the stock exchange. Grasso trusted Komansky as much as anyone on Wall Street; he was maybe the last honest guy on Wall Street. The problem was that Komansky was no media spinmeister; his last years at Merrill Lynch had been among the most controversial in recent decades in large part because he didn't understand the media, and it was evident in the way he answered questions regarding Grasso's pay.

Komansky kept to the script by refusing to comment on the exact numbers of Grasso's pay or compensation package or provide many details about how the process of determining Grasso's compensation worked. Rather, he was there to show that Grasso was worth every dime of whatever salary he was earning. He spoke about his contributions to the exchange, his long years of service.

Unwittingly, Komansky did something else: he gave credibility to the larger story that Grasso was pulling down a salary that was way out of line with that of any regulator, explaining that the size of Grasso's pay package "seems startling" because Grasso had deferred large chunks of his annual salary into retirement accounts. Those chunks were so large because Grasso was paid like a CEO. "Conceptually, there was always a strong feeling as long as I was on the compensation committee that Grasso be paid comparable to a CEO on the street," read his quote.

Komansky all but said that the $10 million salary was a lowball estimate since Wall Street CEOs had regularly been earning $20 million or more a year before the markets crashed. At least, that's how many reporters took the news, immediately comparing Grasso's "$10 million salary" to the paychecks of the SEC chairman or the Federal Reserve chief, which barely cracked $170,000 a year. Given all the new listings Grasso had brought in, $10 million or even the $30 million he made in 2001 might seem completely reasonable. But in refusing to address the story head-on, the exchange allowed Grasso's critics to define it.

Number crunchers came out of the woodwork, gleefully pointing out that $10 million a year was a lot of money for an institution whose profits had declined in recent years. But the core of their argument was the obvious conflict of interest involved in Grasso being paid so much by the very people he regulated.

Grasso didn't help matters by continuing to remain silent, and while he did so, at least in public, his critics went on the offensive. Paulson began to openly discuss the issue with fellow board members. Grasso's growing list of critics on the floor, the loudest being Michael LaBranche, began to link recent NYSE floor taxes and fee increases with the high salary that Grasso was collecting, all while the floor was trading stocks in decimals eating into profits even more. "Now we know why Dick kept raising fees," LaBranche told one floor trader.

It didn't take Grasso long to hear from his buddies on the floor that LaBranche was on the attack, telling larger and larger audiences that Grasso had sold his brethren out. Who ever heard of the chairman of the stock exchange making $10 million? LaBranche asked.

Up on the sixth floor, Grasso now reckoned that it wasn't Quick but LaBranche who had been the ultimate leak of the story to the *Journal,* because compensation committee member Bobby Murphy was technically LaBranche's number two. Murphy at one point tried to intervene, to get his boss to stop attacking Grasso, but even he was powerless to convince LaBranche to end the assault. For years LaBranche had hated Grasso, and now that he smelled blood he was going to stop at nothing until he got Grasso out, including forcing Murphy out of the firm a few months later for supporting Grasso. For once Grasso wasn't sure what to do.

"Those bastards," Grasso muttered as he read the *Journal*'s story that morning as his driver chauffered him from his home in Locust Valley to the exchange's private jet waiting to take him to Washington, D.C. For Grasso, the only thing worse than the story's headline— GRASSO: THE NYSE'S $10 MILLION MAN—or the illustration, an unflattering photo, was its timing. The *Journal* story came out while Grasso was in Washington, scheduled to speak before the Senate Banking Committee about the research settlement he and Spitzer had put together less than a year before. That morning Grasso found it hard to concentrate on his testimony; he believed the *Journal* had delayed the timing of the story to coincide with the hearing to give it maximum impact, and he wasn't far off. Though the timing was coincidental, the impact was just as Grasso had imagined: massive.

Just before the hearings began, Grasso sat at a long table with his fellow panel members, Eliot Spitzer; Bob Glauber, the head of the NASD; and his old nemesis, Bill Donaldson, who was now officially the SEC chairman. Grasso had made sure he said nice things about Donaldson when he was appointed to replace Harvey Pitt, dodging questions about their difficult relationship by extolling Donaldson's selection as an "outstanding choice" because of his knowledge of the markets.

But in reality, Grasso's insides were busting as he looked down the table toward Donaldson, who flashed Grasso that phony half smile Grasso so detested. Grasso believed he had worked long enough with Donaldson to know what was going on in his mind: jealousy of all the money Grasso had been making and a desire for revenge now that he was Grasso's boss. Grasso believed that Donaldson was just waiting for the right time to make his move.

Donaldson kept silent, at least for now, but Spitzer didn't. Grasso's photo was plastered above the fold next to the *Journal*'s story on the cover of its Money & Investing section. As Grasso sat down before the meeting, next to Spitzer, the *Journal* was on the table staring both of them in the face. Grasso made it seem as if he didn't notice, but not Spitzer, who turned to Grasso and snapped, "Nice picture."

If the reporters seemed bored by the substance of the hearings, that changed the moment they ended. Grasso was surrounded by reporters asking him for a comment on the *Journal* story. Grasso explained that he had nothing to do with setting his compensation. "It was the board's decision, not mine," he said, adding that the reporters should speak to the board if they wanted answers about how much he was earning. It was an effective short-term dodge, as the reporters went back to their offices, working the phones and trying to confirm the *Journal*'s account. But the way things were going, Grasso would have to come up with a better excuse if he wanted the matter to die.

By the spring of 2003, Marty Lipton was more enmeshed in exchange business than ever before. At Donaldson's request, the exchange had to develop a new set of corporate governance rules much like the "high standards" it had asked its listed companies to adopt. The task of overseeing the creation of those rules fell, in part, to Lipton, who helped a NYSE committee adopt rules that included the addition of non–Wall Street types to the compensation committee, something that had been cited as a conflict of interest even before Grasso's pay package had become huge news.

Grasso had good reason to lean on Lipton as much as possible. He was one of the best attorneys on Wall Street; Lipton's power at the exchange could not be underestimated. It escaped the press largely because he wasn't under contract; there was no formal arrangement between Lipton, his firm, and the exchange. But when there was trouble, Grasso didn't think twice about giving Lipton a call, and that's exactly what he did after the *Journal* story appeared.

Just after the *Journal* story came out, Lipton did a little investigating of his own, speaking to people, including Langone, about the pay package. Lipton seemed less concerned about the size of the package than how it had been arrived at. He told Grasso that taking the money was completely legal—"undoubtedly enforceable," meaning that Grasso was entitled to the cash if the payments "were properly authorized by the board."

By the early summer of 2003, it was clear that Grasso's clout with the traders and specialists had begun to slip. Officials from the "upstairs" firms and the heads of the top Wall Street firms were still reeling over the public spectacle over Sandy Weill, and now there was the controversy over how much Grasso was being paid. Meanwhile, the floor was growing restless. The last time the exchange had faced a controversy over an executive's pay had been in 1991, during the last bear market, when reports surfaced that the great John Phelan had left the exchange with a retirement package worth $10 million. Back then it had been up to Grasso, as president of the exchange, to defend his mentor, telling *The Wall Street Journal* that "whatever he got was pursuant to a formula that applies to all employees in the exchange benefit programs."

Now there was no one to defend Grasso because there was nothing in his pay package that applied to all employees. After speaking with Lipton, he promptly relayed the lawyer's words of wisdom to Ashen and, more important, to Paulson, who seemed, at least for the moment, satisfied with the result. Still, each day seemed to bring a new revelation about his pay. One day it was the *New York Post* reporting that the *Journal*'s numbers were low; Grasso had made at least $15 million in a year. The *Journal* soon reported that his annual salary was as high as $20 million. Langone was livid, calling the leakers "cowards." But the leaks kept happening, and Grasso remained silent.

Grasso had another set of worries on his hands. For years, Grasso had ignored rumors that his cherished specialists were ripping off their customers through various trading schemes. But in late 2002 his regulatory division uncovered a series of suspicious trades that seemed to confirm his worst nightmare: a large number of specialists had engaged in a series of improper, possibly illegal trades.

Grasso was furious—and he let the specialists know it. Grasso's main objective now was to keep the matter quiet until he could get a handle on what exactly had taken place. But as the months passed and the discontent on the floor grew, it wasn't long before word leaked to *The Wall Street Journal,* which ran a front-page story on how the exchange was investigating many of the largest specialist firms for a trading abuse known as front running.

As the *Journal* prepared its story, Grasso could barely contain his anger. In his mind, the *Journal*'s coverage of the trading problems was off base, overblown—and factually incorrect. At least that was the message he wanted conveyed to the rest of the world.

Shortly after the *Journal* story appeared, Grasso assembled several key members of his staff to figure out how to deal with the story. Attending were Grasso, Zito, and Ed Kwalwasser, his head of regulation. Typically, investigations by the NYSE are done in private and officials are held to a high standard of confidentiality. But Grasso decided that now might be the time to break with tradition.

Grasso wanted an assessment of what the investigation had uncovered. Was it as serious as the *Journal* suggested? Was it front running, which is a form of insider trading, or some lesser evil?

Kwalwasser, according to a person with knowledge of the meeting, couldn't have been more emphatic. Based on everything he knew about the probe, his staff was looking at specialists jumping between trades and improperly taking commissions they weren't entitled to, a practice called "interpositioning." This was a less serious issue than front running, where traders benefit from their inside information on certain stocks at the expense of their clients.

Kwalwasser's assessment was the green light Grasso was looking for. The next day, Grasso issued a statement to set the record
straight. The allegations involved interpositioning, not front running, it said. "This investigation," the statement added, "has generated erroneous reporting and speculation in the media, led by the
Wall Street Journal."

It's impossible to know what exactly was going on in Grasso's
mind with such a frontal assault on corporate America's newspaper
of record, but the statement only added to the firestorm. The *Journal*
ran a story about how its original account was now being questioned,
but most of the media quickly came to the conclusion that the upshot
of the story was right. After all, the exchange had just censured and
fined Fleet Specialists for trading violations, and the firm's lead
trader, David Finnerty, who made markets in General Electric Company, had been barred from the floor of the exchange. Large investors
claimed that no matter how Grasso spun his investigation, the allegations proved what they had complained about for years and what
Grasso had long ignored: that the specialist system was outdated and
corrupt.

Still, Grasso felt like himself again: instead of getting kicked in
the ass, he was kicking back. He was cochair of a gala for the National
Italian American Foundation that honored his good friend the mercantile exchange chairman, Vinny Viola, and his not so good friend
Amex chief Sal Sodano as great Italian-American financial leaders. As
he strutted around the spacious ballroom of the Regent Wall Street
hotel, two blocks away from the exchange, Grasso was all smiles, telling people that the *Journal* had gotten what it deserved, and much of
the audience, made up of Grasso friends like Joe Grano, various Wall
Street types, and even the private investigator Bo Dietl, agreed.

The accolades seemed to be pouring in from everywhere that
night, as friends and colleagues kissed his ring before he was to give
his speech announcing the honorees. Grasso was introduced by
CNBC's Maria Bartiromo, who referred to Grasso as her "mentor"
and "friend." Grasso was beaming as he walked to the podium to a
standing ovation and gave a speech that was vintage Grasso: no cue

cards, speaking purely from his heart about important Italian Americans, who, like himself, had done great things.

A couple of blocks west at the *Journal*'s headquarters in the World Financial Center, there were no celebrations, just anger and bitterness. The *Journal*'s editorial page ran a piece headlined LITTLE BIG BOARD accusing Grasso of "maintaining a monopoly that has opened the exchange to charges that its middlemen profit at the expense of stock buyers and sellers." On the news side, Paul Steiger, the *Journal*'s managing editor, openly wondered why Grasso, if he had a problem with the paper's reporting, hadn't come to him first.

Grasso and Steiger did eventually sit down and talk, but the damage had already been done. Not long after the meeting, Steiger ran into Paul Critchlow, the veteran public relations executive at Merrill Lynch. After discussing some Wall Street business, the conversation turned to Grasso and his attack on the *Journal*. Critchlow just sat and listened as Steiger began complaining about Grasso's statement. He was genuinely angered by it, so angered that he blurted out, "I take this one personally," according to Critchlow's recollection. That's when Critchlow knew Grasso was in trouble.

And he was. A scandal of this magnitude could make the games played by the Oakford boys several years earlier look like a walk in the park, reigniting calls for Grasso to shed his responsibilities as a regulator.

Grasso was suffering from the downside of loyalty; he spent so much time surrounding himself with people he could trust that he forgot he also needed smart people who could get a job done in times of crisis, and he was now facing the greatest crisis of his career.

Kwalwasser, his head of regulation, says he was merely looking to correct inaccurate reporting when he helped Grasso put out the statement about the specialist probe. But its impact was far different: his boss essentially downplayed a serious regulatory problem after speaking with his regulatory chief. Billy Johnston, the old specialist who had been brought to the exchange by Grasso for his contacts among the traders, was now retired but serving as a consultant to Grasso. But it became excruciatingly clear through the spring and summer of

2003 that he had no clue how to handle the uprising led by LaBranche and the unrest on the floor.

Langone was a great entrepreneur who took his job as board member and compensation committee chairman so seriously that he missed only one NYSE board meeting in six years of service. But Langone knew nothing about the politics of perception. Langone and Grasso say they rarely socialized, but the general perception was that the two were joined at the hip, with multiple conflicts of interest that enriched both sides.

The *New York Post*, an aggressive city tabloid, began chronicling Grasso's travails with blaring headlines and a daily "Grass-O-Meter" that gauged his chances for survival between safe and toast.

While other newspapers covered the pay scandal and Grasso's deteriorating position in a serious manner, the *Post* added comic relief to the story (unless, of course, you were Grasso). At one point, looking for a clever way to show the close ties between Grasso and Langone, the *Post* ran a photo of a mother and baby in bed. In place of the mother's face was a picture of Langone; the baby's face was Grasso's. The composite showed a wide-eyed Grasso cuddling with his mentor, with both men in bloomers. When business editor John Elson first saw the illustration, he couldn't contain his laughter. The photo composite soon became the talk of Wall Street, even if the accompanying story merely stated the obvious.

The joke wasn't lost on either Grasso or his friends. Komansky called the photo "pornographic." Bo Dietl, the famous former New York City cop and private investigator, blew up the *Post*'s photo manipulation into a large poster and to add insult to injury took it down to Rao's one night to show it off. By now, having heard from nearly all his friends about the salacious nature of the photo, Grasso was fuming.

Grasso had often referred to the *New York Post* as "a comic book," but it was a remark that understated the paper's influence, particularly in New York media circles. With its wild headlines, snappy writing, and timely reporting, particularly in covering city hall, business, sports, and celebrity news, the *Post* was a must-read among a wide spectrum of people. Indeed, it boasted a readership on a par with that of *The New York Times:* upscale and highly educated. The photo of Langone in bed with Grasso was anything but upscale, but it resonated because for the most part it was true as it related to the various conflicts in their relationship: Langone not only helped Grasso get a board seat on Home Depot, but he headed the compensation committee that paid Grasso all that money, while Grasso regulated Langone's investment firm, Invemed Associates. For this reason, Grasso knew he had to at some point attempt to get the *Post* to soften its coverage as the paper began to make Grasso's pay controversy its own little crusade.

People at the exchange had been complaining for months to *Post* editors about the paper's coverage. A few days after the *Post* ran the infamous Langone-Grasso bed scene, Grasso himself asked its publisher, Rupert Murdoch, for a meeting. Murdoch and Grasso were acquaintances since News Corporation, the holding company for Murdoch's media empire, which includes the *Post* and Fox cable news, was listed on the exchange. The meeting was held in Murdoch's offices. Seated with Murdoch were Col Allan, the *Post*'s editor; Roger Ailes, who runs Murdoch's highly profitable cable television network, Fox News; and the various editors responsible for the Grasso coverage.

Grasso started the meeting by telling Murdoch that the NYSE had plenty of cash on hand and he was looking for possible investments. Maybe the *Post* was available, he said, because he was thinking of starting a "fish-wrapping business." Everyone, including Murdoch, had a good chuckle, but it was a lame bit of humor as the *Post* editors privately seethed. For the next hour or so, Murdoch listened to Grasso's gripes about the *Post*'s coverage. But when the meeting was over, Allan was stunned. "Who does he think he is?" he asked angrily when Grasso left the room. It wasn't long before the *Post* reporters were given the green light to continue their reporting.

With that performance, Grasso pissed off not just people at the *Post*, which continued its parade of negative stories, as did the *Journal*

and the rest of the press. It underscored one of Grasso's key weaknesses: he was a genius at generating publicity, but he didn't have a
clue about public relations. While the leakers were reaching out to reporters to bash Grasso, the little guy was attacking the reporters, who
now had a double incentive to screw him. And they did: the *Journal*
kept its coverage focused on the pay scandal and the specialist inquiry. The *Post*, meanwhile, continued its special brand of journal-
ism, proving once again that Grasso's media strategy had backfired.
Grasso's friends were perplexed. Owner Rupert Murdoch is one of the
nation's leading conservatives. Why would he be on the executive-pay
witch hunt like *The New York Times*? Grasso explained it this way:
Murdoch just wants to sell newspapers, and his reporters have free
rein to write anything "as long as it's not about him." The reality was
somewhat different: Grasso had allowed himself to become too great a
story to pass up.

As the summer of 2003 dragged on, there was nothing fictional
about Grasso's troubles. The specialist investigation was not exactly
the jaywalking violation that Grasso had hoped for. Now the Securities and Exchange Commission's Office of Compliance Inspections
and Examinations began looking into the matter. This unit of the
SEC, also known as OCIE, was in charge of conducting regular examinations of Wall Street firms and the self-regulatory organizations,
which made it Grasso's de facto regulator. It was run by a career SEC
official named Lori Richards, who despite her soft-spoken demeanor
was one of the toughest investigators at the commission. Inside the
SEC, many staffers came to the conclusion that the floor of the stock
exchange was a free-for-all of sleazy dealing and that the specialists
would do anything to make a few extra bucks, even if it involved
stealing from the customers. Now, with Grasso weakened and debili-
tated, he was ripe for a full-scale inquiry. Richards hadn't needed
much convincing that she should revisit specialist trading when a
new senior official at OCIE, John McCarthy, had informed her that
he believed the infractions were much more serious than people at the
exchange were letting on.

McCarthy was the former head of compliance for Knight Trading, an upstart trading firm that itself had once been under a regulatory cloud, and he understood the details of trading as well as anyone. When he began looking at various trading patterns, he found something interesting: many of the orders that wound up on the floor were filled in ten seconds or less. But when he looked at various trades, it appeared that some took longer than others. He began to see many instances where trades took as long as thirty seconds to complete.

In McCarthy's mind, that lapse in time was significant because it meant that traders weren't matching orders quickly and instead were looking for opportunities to involve themselves in trades where they weren't needed. If true, it would mark a huge turning point in the investigation, moving it away from violations of exchange rules and into the criminal realm, where people are indicted and, if convicted, they go to jail.

Grasso may initially have downplayed the specialist probe, but now his regulatory staff addressed the issue with guns blazing. The exchange began demanding e-mails from the major specialists under scrutiny. Conspiracy theories swept through the floor. Michael LaBranche, who had strained relations with Grasso to begin with, believed he was being set up; his big fear, according to people at his specialist firm LaBranche & Co., was that Grasso would use e-mails of a personal nature, much like the way Spitzer had pilloried Grubman and Weill with the 92nd Street Y e-mails, to force LaBranche out and put in his place the longtime Grasso loyalist Bobby Murphy.

What those e-mails discussed, no one knew for sure, but people inside LaBranche speculated that they involved embarrassing details of the private lives of top executives at the company. LaBranche then did something unusual, almost unprecedented, telling the exchange that it couldn't have any e-mail of a personal nature. LaBranche in an interview says the e-mails contained nothing more than "mundane and personal information about my employees' daily lives." LaBranche added he believed Grasso was up to his old tricks: using his regulatory arm to squeeze an enemy into submission so he could find out who was leaking his compensation to the press. He might not have been far off; traders at his firm noticed that Grasso's surveillance unit seemed to question more of their trades just after LaBranche denied the e-mail access.

Grasso, for his part, denied that LaBranche was being singled out. After all, since Spitzer's investigation, e-mails had become a standard investigatory tool among Wall Street regulators, and Grasso says he took no personal interest in the probe; it was handled by his regulatory staff. But Grasso's argument hit a brick wall on the floor as the NYSE sought a court order to compel LaBranche to turn over the documents. All those years of specialists complaining that Grasso used his regulators to get his way had now come back to haunt the little guy. LaBranche might have been guilty as hell, but the general feeling on the floor was that he was being set up by a cop with a reputation for brutality.

Richard Grasso: When asked to describe his difficult journey to the top of the exchange, Grasso often characterized it as a horse race—one in which they "made me run around the track twice" before he took over as King of the Club. *© 2007 The Associated Press. All Rights Reserved.*

Grasso became known for his wild stunts to bring publicity to the New York Stock Exchange. Here he is on the podium of the exchange with the mascot for mining company AngloGold, a real African lion. *© 2007 The Associated Press. All Rights Reserved.*

Grasso's mentor, NYSE chairman John Phelan (FAR LEFT), sits with NYSE president Robert Birnbaum (THIRD FROM LEFT), NYSE spokesman Richard Torrenzano (SECOND FROM LEFT), and Grasso himself (FAR RIGHT) as they brief the press during the 1987 stock market crash. *Photo courtesy of Richard Torrenzano.*

Referred to by Grasso as the "empty suit," William Donaldson succeeded Phelan as NYSE chairman. Grasso bristled under his leadership and successfully convinced the exchange board that the job should be his. © *Bachrach.*

The legendary trading floor of the New York Stock Exchange, one of the most powerful symbols of American finance. Here it is at its height, with around 2,000 traders and other personnel matching buyers and sellers of stock in the world's biggest companies.

Onetime Grasso associate Frank Zarb became his bitter enemy when he took over the rival Nasdaq stock market as CEO and chairman of the National Association of Securities Dealers. *© 2007 The Associated Press. All Rights Reserved.*

The front of the Club: NYSE headquarters is a grand edifice with six Corinthian columns on the corner of Wall and Broad streets in lower Manhattan. Here it is after the 9/11 terrorist attacks with Grasso's self-described "fuck you to bin Laden," a forty-feet-high, seventy-two-feet-wide American flag draped across its front.

Grasso's PR man and marketing maestro, Bob Zito (CENTER), was more instrumental in building the NYSE brand during the Grasso years than anyone except Grasso himself. Pictured here standing on the floor with Grasso (LEFT) and actor and soon-to-be California governor Arnold Schwarzenegger. *Photo courtesy of Mel Nudelman.*

Zito helped market the exchange by turning the opening bell into one of the greatest money shots on television by bringing celebrities to the exchange, even as Grasso's career imploded in scandal. Here he gives actress Sarah Jessica Parker a tour of the floor. *Photo courtesy of Mel Nudelman.*

Maurice "Hank" Greenberg, the brilliant but volatile CEO of insurance giant AIG, was a thorn in Grasso's side nearly from the moment that Grasso listed the company on the exchange. *Photo courtesy of Maurice R. Greenberg.*

Michael LaBranche: Known as "the kid" on the floor of the exchange because he inherited his family's specialist business, LaBranche believed Grasso was turning the NYSE into his personal fiefdom and later joined Paulson in helping to push Grasso out. The move was costly, however: Grasso's departure allowed the new leadership to offer investors electronic trading, which decimated the floor and LaBranche's own business as well. © *Salzano Studio.*

Henry "Hank" Paulson (RIGHT): Grasso called him "the snake," but the cunning CEO of Goldman Sachs and future secretary of the Treasury had battled Grasso for years over control of the exchange and later orchestrated Grasso's ouster. Pictured with John Thain (LEFT). © *2007 The Associated Press. All Rights Reserved.*

Grasso on the podium on September 17, 2001. The scene of Grasso's greatest triumph: the reopening of the exchange following the 9/11 terrorist attacks.

Rudy Giuliani: one of the few people to remain friends with Grasso after his career imploded in scandal. Like Grasso, Giuliani became a hero after the 9/11 attacks. *Photo courtesy of the Rudy Giuliani Presidential Committee, Inc.*

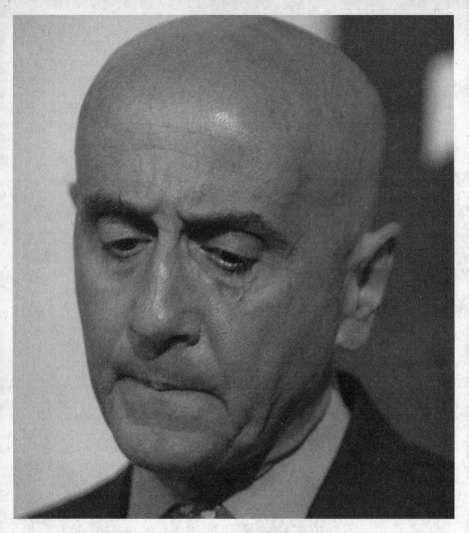

Grasso during his last days as King of the Club, defiant to the end. After the board voted for his ouster during a conference call, he remarked, "These guys would have never had the guts to assassinate me to my face." *© 2007 The Associated Press. All Rights Reserved.*

Kenneth "Ken" Langone: Known for his sharp wit and even sharper temper, Langone, cofounder of Home Depot, became Grasso's biggest supporter on Wall Street and on the NYSE board. As head of the compensation committee, he paved the way for some of Grasso's biggest paydays. *Photo courtesy of Ken Langone.*

Wall Street lawyer and Grasso friend Harvey Pitt became SEC chief just after the stock market bubble popped and jousted with Spitzer when the corporate scandals became front-page news. He was forced to resign after a series of political missteps. *Photo courtesy of Harvey Pitt.*

Once Grasso's competitor as head of the American Stock Exchange, Arthur Levitt, Jr., became Grasso's boss as SEC chief during the 1990s, and he confronted Grasso over floor-trading abuses. *© 2007 The Associated Press. All Rights Reserved.*

Wall Street's onetime regulator and nemesis, Eliot Spitzer, was befriended by Grasso during one of Spitzer's first investigations. Grasso played a key role in Spitzer's first major victory against Wall Street, a $1.4 billion settlement over fraudulent research practices, but then antagonized Spitzer by attempting to put Sandy Weill on the NYSE board. Their relationship soon turned into outright war. *© 2007 The Associated Press. All Rights Reserved.*

The former CEO of Citigroup, Sanford I. "Sandy" Weill, is one of the most powerful and controversial men in Wall Street history. Against the advice of top Wall Street executives, Grasso attempted to install Weill as a NYSE board member just after Citigroup and Weill were ensnarled in a wide-ranging probe by New York attorney general Eliot Spitzer. Grasso was forced to withdraw Weill's nomination following an angry protest from Spitzer. *© 2007 The Associated Press. All Rights Reserved.*

Laurence "Larry" Fink, the powerful head of the BlackRock money management firm and onetime Grasso ally, blew the whistle on Grasso's pay package and ultimately voted in favor of his ouster. *Photo courtesy of Larry Fink.*

James "Jimmy" Cayne, the street-smart CEO of Bear Stearns, is one of Wall Street's most highly paid executives, with a net worth once estimated at above $1 billion. But Cayne was shocked to learn the massive size of Grasso's pay package after telling people he had been under the impression Grasso was paid the salary of a civil servant rather than that of a Wall Street CEO. *Courtesy of Bear Stearns.*

Martin "Marty" Lipton: Known simply as "the lawyer" for his legal expertise to Wall Street heavyweights during times of crisis, Marty Lipton became a key Grasso adviser during his final days as NYSE chairman. *© Christian Steiner.*

The former comptroller of New York State and sole trustee of the state's massive pension fund, H. Carl McCall was tapped by Grasso to be head of the compensation committee to quell the controversy over Grasso's pay. But McCall's selection backfired and Grasso was forced to leave the exchange a poster boy for excessive executive compensation. *© 2007 The Associated Press. All Rights Reserved.*

After Grasso was ousted, John Reed took over as temporary chairman of the stock exchange, agreeing to work for a "symbolic $1," and then launched a major investigation into Grasso's pay package.
© 2007 The Associated Press. All Rights Reserved.

John Thain: Named CEO of the Club after Grasso's ouster, he quickly launched the biggest transformation in the NYSE's history by bringing electronic trading to the exchange, a move that doomed the floor traders who had ruled the exchange for generations.
Photo courtesy of the New York Stock Exchange.

On many days of late, the exchange floor looks like a ghost town. John Thain's implementation of electronic trading through the Club's purchase of Archipelago decimated the floor. With Grasso gone, the traders had lost their protector. © *2007 The Associated Press. All Rights Reserved.*

10

ONE BAD DAY

As it turned out, Mike LaBranche wasn't Grasso's only enemy on the floor, which was now in open revolt. Zito noticed an ethnic split among the traders. Italians and Jews favored Grasso, while almost everyone else opposed him, lining up behind their leader, LaBranche. Grasso dispatched his buddy Bobby Murphy to try one last time to tame his boss. Murphy asked LaBranche to meet him outside the exchange where they could talk in private. LaBranche agreed. Murphy met LaBranche on Broad Street. He began the conversation by conceding that Grasso had made many mistakes over the years, but, he asked, for all his faults, isn't he good for our business? Isn't he good for the floor? Then he asked LaBranche another important question: "Will life be that great after Dick?" LaBranche, without emotion, simply answered, "Things couldn't be any worse."

They were, at least for Grasso. This time the attacks now came from Washington—from Donaldson, no less—who now wanted the NYSE and the NASD to adopt the same rules they were asking their listed companies to adopt, which included better disclosure of CEOs' and executives' compensation. Donaldson made sure to direct his order to both the NASD and the NYSE, but Grasso and everyone else at the exchange believed they were Donaldson's principal targets.

To comply with Donaldson's order, Grasso set up a committee, headed by board members Leon Panetta, the former Clinton chief of staff, and H. Carl McCall, the former New York State comptroller. Both had impeccable résumés and were respected in both the public and private sectors. Grasso decided to roll out the reforms at a press conference with Panetta and McCall at his side as he attempted to put the best face on an increasingly dangerous situation, as least as far as his chairmanship was concerned.

The reforms mandated by Donaldson did more to damage Grasso than anything Mike LaBranche could say or do on the floor. For all its coverage in the press, the final decision on whether to allow Grasso to take his pay package had been put off again once it became clear that Donaldson was going to ask for new rules, which now called for no securities industry types on the compensation committee. That meant Langone was gone, as were Cayne and Murphy. Even more scary for Grasso: for the first time in exchange history, his pay as well as that of his senior staff would be revealed, some time next year, but revealed nonetheless, while Grasso's bigger plan, to take his retirement money immediately, would be decided in part by strangers.

With McCall and Panetta at his side, Grasso proudly announced that the changes were "a very powerful first step" toward making the exchange an exemplar of corporate governance. But it also had the effect of magnifying Grasso's problems and the perception that his chairmanship was nothing more than one giant conflict of interest.

For Ken Langone the pay controversy was an embarrassing moment in an otherwise flawless career in business, where he had been accused of almost nothing other than having a big mouth. Now he read his name in the paper almost daily, and it wasn't just about Grasso's compensation. In the spring of 2003, the NASD was investigating Langone's brokerage firm, Invemed, for allegedly charging its customers inflated commissions on some stock sales in exchange for giving them access to hot IPOs. It was similar to the accusations swirling around the former CSFB banker Frank Quattrone: if a customer wanted a hot tech IPO during the bubble, one that would soar the minute it was free to trade, he or she had to buy other stocks at inflated commissions. Quattrone was later cleared of all charges and Langone believed the practice was perfectly legal, nothing more than an arrangement between sophisticated parties where both sides win.

But the NASD considered the practice something close to a bribe, and during the spring of 2003 its investigation turned into an ultimatum for Langone as he sat in his office in midtown Manhattan and received a call from his attorneys. The NASD, they said, was giving him twenty minutes to start settlement discussions or get ready for Invemed to get blasted with rule violations. Langone was defiant. Tell them to "save their twenty minutes," he said, adding that he had done nothing wrong and was ready to expend resources to fight the charges to the bitter end.

At sixty-nine years of age, he was no longer obsessed with money; Langone's obsession was his reputation, which until the Grasso pay scandal had been largely blemish-free. Before the end of the day, news of the civil case hit the wires, and the battle was on. "If other people want to roll over and admit they did something, if they did something, good for them," Langone told *The Wall Street Journal.* "We deny any or all wrongdoing. We did not engage in profit sharing or any other conduct in violation of NASD rules."

Grasso had now become political fodder for a powerful contingent of state officials, many of them liberal Democrats who had influence over billions of dollars of public pension funds, where they were invested and, most important for Wall Street, including which firms would earn the right to invest them. The most vocal of these were, in fact, the most powerful: Alan Hevesi, the New York State comptroller, who was the "sole trustee" of New York's massive state pension fund, estimated as having $150 billion in assets; and the California treasurer, Phil Angelides, who was a board member of the granddaddy of all public pension funds, the $200 billion California state fund, known as CalPERS.

Being in New York, Grasso knew Hevesi's rep as a politician who used his position to squeeze campaign contributions out of firms that wanted business from the fund. "This is the guy who thinks I'm a crook," Grasso said. Angelides, based on press accounts, wasn't much better as far as Grasso was concerned. But somehow, the irony of the attacks by Hevesi and Angelides was lost in the obsessive nature of the Grasso coverage that was intent on painting him as an enemy and all those who opposed him as white knights coming to the rescue of the investing public.

The attacks by the state officials started to hit home. Grasso didn't trust Paulson's judgment on most issues, but Grasso did on this issue, as Paulson warned him that the street could ignore these guys for only so long. They were major clients of just about every Wall Street member of the board, and they were customers of the exchange. They could direct trading order flow away from the exchange at a moment's notice, and that would be disastrous.

Grasso thought he had a solution in Langone's abrupt departure from the compensation committee. Langone was Grasso's main defender and a lightning rod, particularly now that the NASD had filed its case. So the loss of Langone presented an opportunity for Grasso. He was, in effect, looking for someone who could put the best possible face on a bad situation, someone who could appease the press and the Alan Hevesis of the world and allow him to get his money, all at the same time. This should also be someone who could save his job, as it became increasingly clear that his board, whatever loyalties they once had to Grasso, would turn on him in a minute if the controversy didn't come to an end.

For over ten years, H. Carl McCall had been the New York State comptroller, occupying the office now held by Hevesi until he ran for governor of New York State in 2002, losing to George Pataki. He's tall and well dressed, usually in a dark, finely tailored suit. He looks far younger than his age of sixty-seven and was one of the highest-ranking African-American leaders in New York State, and one of the country's most powerful investors in his position as "sole trustee" of the state's massive public employees' pension fund.

McCall had been a NYSE board member since 1999. In fact, it had been Grasso's idea to make him a board member in the first place, thinking that someone who controlled that much public wealth should be represented on the NYSE board.

McCall, by all accounts, had jumped at the opportunity when Grasso offered him the job, and it's easy to see why. McCall had been out of politics for a couple of years, and now he would be thrust into the limelight. Grasso believed he had hit a home run: a liberal politician who was supposed to be good with numbers and ethically clean. "Let Hevesi attack McCall," Grasso thought as he explained that the nominating committee had just approved McCall for compensation chief following his recommendation.

But a closer look at McCall's background suggested it wasn't as squeaky clean as Grasso believed. He had been attacked in newspapers for much the same thing Hevesi had been attacked for, using the state pension fund to drum up campaign contributions. Meanwhile, there was nothing in McCall's background that suggested he was good with numbers. In actuality, the state comptroller has very little to do with the investment decisions of the fund; most of them are made by a professional staff. It didn't take long for people like Paulson to notice that McCall appeared out of his depth when it came to the details of Grasso's very detailed contract. At one point, Paulson described him as being not "financially sophisticated."

If McCall did one thing right, it was that he began asking various board members and others what they thought about the package and whether Grasso had received the money in a proper manner. In early June he spoke to Ashen and the exchange's compensation consultant, who walked him through the convoluted series of accounts that made up Grasso's retirement savings.

One of his first conversations as a board member was with Langone. Langone told McCall to start over if he felt uncomfortable with what Grasso was doing. Langone reiterated his start-from-scratch statement during the first compensation committee meeting McCall chaired in June 2003. But according to McCall, Langone also said that the comp committee had been unified on one very important aspect of the entire mess: to keep Grasso at the exchange as long as possible.

For McCall the conversation with Langone, with all its contradictions, should have been a wake-up call that he had been thrust into an impossible situation. Most of the compensation committee members McCall spoke to said they were fully aware of the details of Grasso's pay, but among the various board members, the details were more sketchy. The way Langone worked, the compensation committee did the heavy lifting, deliberating the fine points of Grasso's pay, from his yearly salary to how the various accounts made up his retirement package. But some people on the board didn't even know that Grasso was looking to take the money out. Even Ashen, the man assigned to keep the board informed about Grasso's compensation and contract extension, at one point seemed confused. In several documents he wrote that Grasso was still looking to roll all the money into his savings plan and invest it as he had in 1999.

On July 14, the newly constituted compensation committee, led by McCall, included Gerald Levin; Mel Karmazin; Larry Fink, and now Herbert Allison, a former Merrill Lynch president running the teachers' retirement system known as TIAA-CREF. The new committee picked up where the old, allegedly conflicted committee under Langone had left off. They approved Grasso's massive pay, sending the measure to the full board. For all the hoopla about conflicts of interest and Langone's heavy-handedness, the vote was unanimous.

But a debate had started elsewhere. The final measure was to be presented at an August 7 board meeting. Under the plan, Grasso would get his money, $139.5 million, and the exchange would get Grasso for four more years until 2007. But as Ashen and McCall began making the rounds to explain the measure to the various board members, the opposition became louder and louder, as did the various contradictions that made the issue even more difficult to deal with. There was little doubt that the various retirement accounts had been voted on and approved by the entire board, but recently picked board members such as Madeleine Albright joined JPMorgan Chase CEO William Harrison; Phil Purcell, the CEO of Morgan Stanley; and of course Hank Paulson in questioning Grasso's decision to take the money. Langone believed that this was nothing more than the voice of the weak: board members who either were too stupid to pay attention during meetings, or were folding from the negative press over Grasso's pay, or, like Paulson, were so inattentive to detail that they now found themselves in a pickle.

Grasso and Langone certainly had their supporters as the August 7 board meeting approached. Mel Karmazin argued that if Grasso had gone to work on Wall Street he would have been receiving stock options. Given Grasso's skills as a salesman, he might have earned even more money than the $140 million. And what would have happened if he had taken those job offers to be a floor trader? Many of the guys who ran those operations were worth far more than $140 million.

All of those arguments may have been true, but they ignored the reality of the situation: that taking the money, exposing the exchange to further turmoil and abuse, wouldn't be good for either the institution or Grasso himself. That was the argument made by board member William Summers just days before the August 7 board meeting. Summers is one of those rich, successful people on Wall Street who hold prominent positions and almost never make the press, and he likes it that way. The chairman of a midsize brokerage firm, the Cleveland-based McDonald & Co., Summers had known Grasso for some twenty years, mostly because he had served as chairman of the competing Nasdaq stock market, and he marveled at how Grasso seemed to win nearly every battle.

Summers grew up in Cleveland and worked his way up from an intern at McDonald's bond desk to become its CEO in 1995. He engineered the firm's sale to KeyCorp in 1998 and now, at the age of fifty-five, was heading for retirement. One afternoon, Summers received a call from an intermediary, who said he was nominated to be on the board of the NYSE. A few days later, Grasso interviewed him, and the appointment was made official.

Grasso would later say he had appointed Summers to his board precisely because he was both honest and loyal, traits that are hard to find on Wall Street. When Summers heard that Grasso was about to become $140 million richer by extending his contract, he was stunned. Like most of the board members, Summers voted for Grasso's yearly salary, but until recently he had had no idea that the accounts created back in 1995 by Stanley Gault would take a couple good years of salary and turn them into a fortune. More than that, it just looked bad, given everything he was reading about executive pay in the press. Summers lived up to his reputation and minced no words, telling Grasso, "Now is not the time to do this." Grasso thanked him for his time and hung up the phone, choosing to ignore a guy he had brought to the board because of his honesty.

It wasn't long before the list of naysayers grew to include one of the most respected men ever to serve on the NYSE board of directors. Leon Panetta was no longer an NYSE board member having completed his last task before leaving the exchange, the corporate governance reforms mandated by the SEC, but he was still following the pay controversy closely. Panetta and Summers stayed in contact, having developed a friendship while working on various exchange projects, and both agreed that Grasso needed to be talked out of taking the money. Like Summers, Panetta admired Grasso for all the reasons that had led the board to hand him all those huge paychecks in the first place.

Panetta may not have been a Wall Street expert, but he knew politics as well as anyone. Summers had briefed Panetta on the situation in the hope of talking Grasso out of making the biggest mistake of his career, and possibly his life. Panetta did just that, contacting Grasso at his office and telling him in no uncertain terms that he was about to go down in flames if he took the money. Again Grasso just sat and listened, thanking Panetta for his advice but not indicating which way he would ultimately decide.

Panetta then called the one person he knew could talk some sense into Grasso, and that was Langone. Panetta says he told Langone that the situation at hand had nothing to do with merit, it was all about politics, and Grasso was making a politically stupid move, as was Langone. "Kenny, you're probably one of the best business minds in the country, but you have a tin ear when it comes to politics," Panetta said. Langone responded with a laugh, Panetta says, admitting that the "last thing I am is a politician." (In an interview, Langone said Panetta never gave him such a warning.)

By all accounts Langone never wavered from his position that Grasso should take the money, and it's easy to see why. By refusing the money, Grasso would have been making a statement about Langone as much as himself. Langone always believed Grasso was worth every dime, and if Grasso turned around and gave the money back, he would be saying that Langone had somehow screwed up, that his role as compensation committee chairman had been compromised.

But Grasso wasn't as blindly loyal to Langone as it seemed to Panetta, whose advice, as well as the advice of Summers, Albright, Harrison, and even Paulson, was now having a profound impact on Grasso's thinking. As loyal as Grasso was to Langone, the little guy was now wavering about taking the money.

Again he turned to Marty Lipton for advice. Grasso had already asked Lipton if taking the money would be legal; now he asked again, though in a slightly different way: Was it reasonable? Meaning, did he think the amount of money was so outlandish that it defied rational expectations of what someone in his position should be paid? Again Lipton made it clear that based on everything he knew, the money passed the smell test.

For Langone and Lipton, the decision was easy; from a purely legal standpoint, Grasso's attempt to cash out his retirement package violated no laws. But the situation had now become a political issue, and on that score Langone and Lipton showed a tin ear. On Wall Street money is the ultimate barometer of success, but if Grasso loved his job and wanted to salvage his reputation, he might have to deny himself the trophy. For all the bad ink he received, the press and the public still had no idea that he was trying to convince the board to hand him a $140 million check as a condition of his contract extension.

Grasso made his decision in private, though he contacted both Lipton and Langone and gave them a heads-up: he was not going to take the money, at least not now. Both said he was crazy, but Grasso said he thought he was doing the right thing. Lipton summed up Grasso's decision in an e-mail to a colleague: "There was concern on the b/d [board] and Dick decided to shelve it."

Grasso telephoned McCall just two days before the August 7 board meeting and told him he wasn't going forward with the plan, either to take the money or to extend the contract. "You have me for two years," Grasso indicated. He made no promises about the future, though he indicated he had no plans to leave the exchange.

McCall breathed a sigh of relief and said he would tell the compensation committee members before the meeting. Grasso, it appeared, had finally come to his senses.

In the days that followed, Grasso called a floor directors board meeting and told them he wasn't going ahead. He called Paulson and told him the same: considering all the controversy, he didn't think it was time to extend the contract and take the money.

Gerald Levin was one of the board members who believed Grasso was making a mistake if he *didn't* take the money. Levin had been on the compensation committee for the past three years, but unlike Paulson he had attended most of the meetings, had been involved in every vote, and believed he knew as much as anyone about the size of Grasso's pay and the reason it had grown so large. In his view Grasso was worth not just every dime but every penny, and the money had been awarded with full disclosure to the board.

In the moments before the full board meeting, Levin was to attend a special compensation committee meeting to discuss Grasso's contract at the exchange. He had a few minutes to kill, so he decided to pay Grasso a visit. Grasso repeated to Levin why he had decided to reverse course, based on the opposition of so many board members. In Grasso's view, it wasn't worth the risk to his chairmanship. But Levin said it was; there was little downside to taking the money now. Everyone knew he had made a lot of money; it would be a matter of time before the rest leaked. He should take the money and have the board make a statement in support, and everyone should move on with their lives. Grasso simply told Levin that the decision at this point wasn't his; it was up to the board. By the time the conversation ended, another compensation committee member, Larry Fink, the head of BlackRock, came by and echoed Levin's comments.

Grasso hadn't survived at the exchange for so long without understanding the convoluted nature of boardroom politics, but the politics of his current situation left him bewildered. During his glory years he had walked the floor about six times a day; now he was rarely seen, as the uprising led by LaBranche continued to gather converts. But Grasso decided the time was right to pay a visit to the floor to meet one guy he knew was on his side; Grasso had long since forgiven Chris Quick for his comments to the Goldman people, believing that he had been set up by Paulson, who would use the information for his own benefit when the time was right. Now he needed Quick's assessment of the situation: Should he take the money or not? If he did, how would the floor react?

Quick likened Grasso's situation to death by a thousand cuts; it was long, slow, and excruciating for everyone involved. He needed closure, and so did the exchange, something that could end the fuss once and for all. Quick was emphatic: get that money out of those accounts now!

The compensation committee agreed with Quick's assessment. It met for about thirty minutes. McCall opened by stating he was under the impression that the matter was now off the table, but Levin and Fink said it was back on. At one point Schrempp chimed in that he had had his in-house legal counsel look at the issue. He said it passed legal muster and he was comfortable with joining those who wanted Grasso to take the money ASAP. The rest agreed: Grasso would get the money, and they would extend Grasso's contract until 2007. McCall told Ashen to bring Grasso in.

When Grasso entered the room, he told the committee that he was ready to postpone any decision until his contract expired in 2005. "I'm not going anywhere," Grasso said. But if they wanted him to extend his contract, then he wanted his money. McCall put it bluntly: the committee wanted to go forward and put the measure to the full board at the meeting scheduled for later that morning. The money would be his.

To hear it from the compensation committee members, the meeting was a pretty mundane affair once Grasso agreed to do whatever they said. Mundane but confusing. Some members clearly knew the fine points of Grasso's new employment agreement; others, just as clearly, did not. In it were provisions that entitled Grasso not just to the $140 million but to an additional $48 million in what was described as "prior earned awards not yet vested and not yet accrued" when his contract was up in 2007. Though the matter wasn't formally discussed, people like Fink understood that Grasso would receive more money. McCall would later say he did as well, but according to people who were at the meeting, McCall seemed clueless about the extra money as the committee unanimously approved the measure and moved it to the full board. Grasso's pay package had suddenly risen to close to $190 million.

Later that morning, the full board met to discuss Grasso's pay package. Things went badly almost from the start, when McCall told Ashen to get out of his seat and leave the room. McCall later explained his decision as a way to remove bias from the process; in speaking with board members, McCall discovered that many considered Ashen too much of an advocate or a salesman for Grasso's compensation. Even so, aside from Langone, no one knew the convoluted nature of Grasso's contract and retirement package better than Ashen, certainly not a rookie compensation committee chairman who would need as much backup as he could get. Confused, Ashen asked McCall if he was sure he wanted him to leave. McCall indicated with a sweeping gesture of his hand that he wanted him out. The move was so startling that Karmazin asked McCall to bring back Ashen into the room. Again McCall demurred. Ashen had even drawn up a cheat sheet of sorts outlining how much money Grasso would receive, including the $48 million in additional payments when he left the exchange in 2007. McCall admits he never read it.

If McCall thought he could handle the situation solo, he was badly mistaken. As soon as the meeting began, it spun out of control. Even if the comp committee was united about Grasso taking the money, McCall had misread the sentiment of the larger board. Purcell, Harrison, and Albright emphasized the negative public reaction that would take place when the whole sordid mess came out. Grasso's supporters mounted their own counteroffensive. Karmazin, Levin, Fink, and Langone pointed out that it would be foolish to postpone the inevitable. It was Grasso's money. No one had been fooled. The board had voted on his salary. The accounts had been created in good faith. Levin stated that the delay would weaken their already weakened chairman. The details of his pay package had already leaked. "We need to control our own destiny," Karmazin said. Board members began to point fingers about who had been the leaker of all the stories about Grasso's pay. Fink believed McCall was a possibility, though he didn't know for sure.

The only thing it seemed board members could agree on was that McCall was clearly out of his depth. He couldn't answer key questions from board members, and other compensation committee members had to help him out. People started talking out of turn. Schrempp appeared so confused he began speaking in his native tongue, German. "Jurgen, I can't understand you, speak English!" Quick snapped. Langone had earlier asked Zito to provide him with the objective evidence of Grasso's accomplishments, and during the meeting he rattled them off: in 2002, a down year for the markets, Grasso had snared 152 new listings and 43 from the Nasdaq, a 39 percent increase from the year before. The exchange had more than $1 billion in assets on its balance sheet.

Even Cayne chimed in. The Bear Stearns CEO hated board meetings so much he rarely said a word, but at one point he thought he had heard that by giving Grasso the money now, the exchange would save several million dollars because the NYSE would no longer be paying interest on his savings. "Let me get this straight," he said. "This is the guy's money, and we actually save money by giving it to him now?" He added, "In my mind this is a no-brainer."

The arguments from the pro-Grasso side began to shift the tide; after all, where would the exchange be if it didn't have Grasso? What would happen if he left in a year and a half, when his contract was up? By now the tone of the full board was shifting: maybe it was better to give Grasso his money and get the matter behind them. Abright, Harrison, and Purcell agreed as well, albeit reluctantly. Everyone did—that is, everyone except Paulson, who was on a bird-watching trip in the jungles of Brazil.

The board was now ready to vote. Harrison and Albright attempted to get their votes modified to reflect their initial disagreement but were convinced by others that that would make a bad situation worse. Despite his initial misgivings, Summers was now on board as well, swayed by the argument that the best way to deal with the controversy was to give Grasso the money he earned and release the details to the public. It was unanimous; Grasso would get his money.

McCall relayed the news to Grasso, who took it as a vote of confidence, telling the board that he would follow their edict. But their confidence was a mile wide and an inch deep. Bill Harrison remained concerned, so concerned that after the meeting he told Grasso that he still wasn't sure if he could survive the public relations fallout. Under the new disclosure rule, the exchange could wait until the following year to make the package public, but McCall had decided to do it sooner, to end the controversy once and for all. There was another problem that neither McCall nor Harrison nor Grasso nor anyone else on the board seemed to fully understand—the additional $48 million due Grasso in 2007. McCall had never brought it up, according to board members. McCall would later say that even if he didn't mention the exact number it was his belief that board members knew Grasso was due additional money as part of his new contract. To this day, the vast majority of board members say they believed they were voting on a $140 million package that, when all was said and done, had just grown to $190 million in the space of a few hours.

A few days later, when he returned from his bird-watching trip, Paulson called Grasso, asking for an explanation about his change of heart over the $140 million. Paulson was angry—at least, that was the impression Grasso got from the tone of the conversation. "You promised me that the matter was tabled!" Paulson shouted. Grasso said he had had no choice in the matter. The compensation committee had forced the issue, and the board had voted unanimously to move forward. Somewhere during the conversation, Paulson's anger waned and he began to think about damage control, namely, how the exchange would release the details of the pay package to the public. His advice was simple: issue a press release as close to Labor Day, as close to the end of August, as possible. It was the slowest news week of the year. As Grasso remembers it, Paulson suggested that most of the journalists covering the story would be in the Hamptons sipping drinks, not in New York monitoring the newswires. Grasso agreed: the announcement of his contract and extension and the details of his pay package would be released on August 27.

Afterward, Paulson told people on Wall Street he would never have left for his bird-watching trip if the Grasso matter had been on the agenda, and if he had been at the meeting he would have done his best to prevent Grasso from taking the money. But that runs counter to at least one version of events leading up to the now-infamous board vote. According to Levin, Paulson knew on the morning of August 7 that the board was ready to vote on the pay package. Not only that, Levin says in documents that he remembers a phone call he had from Paulson about the vote and that he believes Paulson said he was "supportive" of Grasso's new contract and the allotment of the money by the board.

The reality, as most people on the board understood, was that as bad as they would look allowing Grasso to take the money, one person would look even worse, and that person was Grasso himself. All of these factors were being weighed by Paulson, one of the most calculating minds on Wall Street, in the weeks leading up to the August 27 release date. Paulson had by now moved beyond his initial embarrassment about not showing up to meetings where Grasso's pay package was approved, and began looking toward the future, namely, what would the exchange look like if Grasso imploded, and how might Goldman Sachs benefit?

During the weeks that preceded D-day for Grasso's contract extension, the exchange and the little guy received a welcome respite from the intense pounding they had been taking in the media. Of course there were stories here and there about the trading investigation, an update or two about Grasso's pay. For the most part, Grasso and the exchange managed to keep a lid on just how dangerous both issues had become, but the controversy was taking its toll. One of Grasso's kids had to sit through a class lecture on overpaid executives that focused on her father. Grasso exploded when he heard about the incident, but Lori counseled the children not to pay attention to people who didn't know what they were talking about.

At the exchange, Grasso had a well-earned reputation of being both charming and nasty with his staff, screaming at them one minute and then playing practical jokes with them the next. As the summer of 2003 wore on, gone were the practical jokes as his staff faced more and more of the screaming. One reason was listings, or the lack of them. Grasso and his staff had been so preoccupied by the pay scandal and how to deal with it that they had had no time to deal with business issues.

Then there was the specialist probe. The press had been largely silent so far on the latest development: by mid- to late summer, the SEC had asked the exchange's enforcement staff to broaden its investigation into new ways in which specialists and floor traders could screw their customers.

The new probe focused not just on interpositioning, or jumping between orders, but also trading ahead of customers' orders. The SEC's heightened interest in the specialist probe brought back another debate at the SEC. Now top officials at the SEC were openly debating whether the NYSE and its adherence to floor trading was behind the times, inhibiting capital formation and creating costly barriers for investors.

Still, with the relative lack of press coverage, the board's support of Grasso seemed to strengthen. "I'm there for you," Fink said at one point. Paulson, Albright, and Harrison seemed to back away from their earlier concerns. For a time, Grasso felt energized. He went back to handling exchange business, searching for new listings, putting in his obligatory calls to Microsoft in the hope that one day the tech giant would jump from the Nasdaq, and marketing the exchange to the world as his troops prepared his defense. His bit part in the popular HBO series *Sex and the City,* in which he rang the opening bell with the character played by actress Sarah Jessica Parker, brought back memories of the old Grasso. He began telling people he believed the worst was over. But like many predictions Grasso was making these days, this one would turn out to be wrong.

Marty Lipton had been vacationing in Italy on August 7, the day the board met to extend Grasso's contract. He was now back at home and fully engaged in helping Grasso and his team prepare for the big announcement. Lipton had been asked by Grasso to provide a legal opinion on the contract and its most controversial provision, allowing Grasso to recoup the $140 million, and since that time, almost no detail about the package had escaped his scrutiny. Lipton also knew that Grasso was due additional money under the new contract even though that fact had slipped by many members of the board and apparently the attention of McCall during their last meeting.

Lipton knew one other thing: the stock exchange may have been the center of capitalism, but it was a nonprofit corporation. What Lipton knew, at least according to Grasso, was that the status created an interesting legal quandary. Under the state's not-for-profit law, the compensation of top executives must be "reasonable and commensurate with duties performed." The law is enforced by the state's attorney general, Eliot Spitzer. One of the first things Lipton focused on when reviewing Grasso's contract was whether it was "reasonable," and he believed at least from a legal standpoint, given all the debate by the compensation committee, the votes of the board, and Langone's insistence that he had disclosed everything, that Grasso passed with flying colors.

Lipton took his task seriously. He questioned Langone and others about the process that had produced Grasso's massive yearly salaries and what disclosures had been made to board members to make sure they knew how much money was building up in Grasso's accounts. He looked at Grasso's work product—namely, the objective measures of his job performance: listings, order flow, and the amount of money

Grasso had made for his member firms. If anyone was worth the money, Lipton opined, it was Grasso.

Now it was his job to help Grasso pass a different test. In the days and weeks that followed, Lipton began consulting the NYSE in a number of areas, including how the exchange should handle the pay issue from a public relations standpoint. With Lipton's increased involvement, Zito knew he was on the hot seat. For years Zito and Grasso had maintained an unusually close relationship, primarily because Grasso didn't look at Zito as a mere flack. He was an adviser and marketing genius, and he was also a friend. Now the flack was getting some flack himself. Grasso let him know that the board, and mainly Langone, wasn't happy with the uniformly negative press coverage. An outside PR firm, Ketchum Communications, would be hired to assist in the PR efforts. Lipton would now be consulted as well.

The addition of Lipton rankled Zito. Lipton might be a great lawyer—around the exchange Grasso simply referred to him as "the lawyer." But Zito believed Lipton and his firm had too many business relationships with people who weren't necessarily Grasso's friends—namely Harrison, Purcell, and of course Paulson—to be trusted. In fact, Lipton didn't even officially consider the exchange and Grasso as clients; any advice given was in an unpaid capacity. But the firms of some of his board members were clients for corporate legal work and in M&A deals, and if Lipton ultimately had to pick sides, Zito asked his boss, why would he pick Grasso over one of his paying customers?

Grasso brushed Zito's advice aside and continued dealing with Lipton. As close as Grasso was with his PR chief, he kept his own counsel on many issues, including the one Zito had been blamed for doing a lousy job explaining to the press: his retirement package. Zito, as it turned out, had little understanding of the recent machinations of the board and what they meant in terms of Grasso's retirement account.

Now that Grasso's retirement money was to be released, Zito was brought into the inner circle. Ashen gave him his first real briefing, and it nearly blew Zito away. For years Grasso had told Zito to defer his own hefty income—by now he earned more than $1 million a year—into the lucrative exchange retirement accounts. As Ashen explained the various retirement plans, Zito learned why his boss was so high on deferring all those big paychecks. Zito was shocked when he heard how much the money had grown to over the years—$140 million. He had been all but certain that the amount was closer to the $80 million to $100 million that the *Journal* had reported in May. As he sat and listened to Ashen, Zito's stomach began to churn. "If Langone thinks I'm doing a bad job now, what will he think when this comes out?" he wondered.

Zito wasn't the only person in Grasso's inner circle who would soon find out as the release date neared. Disclosures were made to Grasso's two chief lieutenants, Cathy Kinney and Bob Britz. Grasso even broke the news to SooJee Lee, his secretary and gatekeeper, as an advance warning of the coming media firestorm if Paulson's ruse of releasing the figure close to Labor Day didn't have its intended effect.

Grasso signed his new contract on August 27, 2003. Zito faxed a draft press release announcing his contract extension through 2007 to his home in the Hamptons. McCall and Ashen also reviewed the release. The plan was for Grasso to be out of town when the announcement was made; the less he said, the greater the chance that the issue would finally die.

In order to focus the media on the least salacious elements, Zito prepared a series of questions and answers, focused on the reasons why Grasso deserved the money. Before giving Zito the go-ahead, Grasso made a few minor edits to the document and then made a couple of important telephone calls to people he knew he needed in his corner.

One call was to New York attorney general Eliot Spitzer. The next was to SEC chief Donaldson. As SEC chief, Donaldson was Grasso's de facto boss. Under the system of self-regulation, the exchanges provide frontline regulation of the securities industry, and the SEC jumps in on the big issues. Watching the exchanges was of course the SEC, and there was no bigger issue in the financial world at this point than Grasso's pay package.

Donaldson answered Grasso's call immediately, though Grasso probably wished he hadn't because the tension was palpable. Grasso did all he could to keep his anger under control as he explained that his contract had been extended to 2007 and would, for the first time, detail his pay and the enormous check he would be cashing once the deal was finalized: $139.5 million. Donaldson didn't allow his jealousy or anger to boil over. He didn't need to. He told Grasso that he was concerned about how the PR fallout might affect the exchange. He told Grasso that he might want to wait for a better time to take the money, whenever that might be. Grasso said he couldn't; his board wanted the controversy to be over as soon as possible. Before hanging up, Donaldson gave Grasso some advice: "Don't do it." Grasso simply said the choice wasn't his.

Paulson's advice to issue the release as close to Labor Day as possible had little impact on the press coverage either in tone or in volume. There were some bright spots; friends and admirers called and said he was worth every dime. The board seemed to be on his side, at least for the moment, as well as Spitzer, who returned his call from a few days earlier. Under the not-for-profit law, the attorney general was supposed to regulate Grasso's salary, but Spitzer didn't suggest anything was wrong. "Glad to have you around a few more years," Spitzer said.

Others did. Zito and McCall handled calls from reporters, and Lipton monitored the newspapers. Despite all the leaks about Grasso's pay, the full picture of how much he had accumulated had never been public—that is, until now. The *New York Post* seemed to sum up the media's opinion the best, with a blaring headline, GRASSO'S JACKPOT. Other media outlets weren't far behind. Reading the coverage, Lipton asked Zito, "What's your assessment?" and then issued his own: "I think W.S.J. and N.Y.T. as expected. FT and Lex not so good," referring to the *Financial Times* and its popular "Lex" column.

Grasso's pay package had now reached a new stage. Before, it had been a controversy, but with full disclosure it had become a full-fledged scandal. Grasso, it was revealed, had made the bulk of his money in a relatively short period of time: all the bells and whistles in the retirement accounts had multiplied the hefty paychecks granted by Langone's committee by tens of millions of dollars. The links between Grasso and Langone were revealed: the Home Depot connection of Grasso serving on the board of the company Langone had created and whispers about their late nights at Rao's.

"The $140 million pay package," as Grasso's money was termed on Wall Street, was universally derided in the press and by corporate governance experts as the work of an out-of-control board and a man who had too much power over the people signing his paycheck.

Grasso couldn't escape the attacks. He got tired of reading about himself in the papers or seeing a weekend stroll in the Hamptons featured in the *Post* with an embarrassing headline, so he stopped reading newspapers and got much of his news from television. But the television reporters weren't much better.

Grasso and his pay package made great TV, which even his friends at CNBC couldn't pass up. By now Maria Bartiromo was no longer just "the Money Honey"; she was a star who had used the opportunity Grasso had given her eight years ago to become possibly the most famous business reporter in the nation. For months she largely ignored the exploding controversy that had engulfed her "friend" and "mentor." No longer. "If you are retiring in 2007 and you just do a new contract up until 2007, why would you want to take the lump sum now?" she asked during one broadcast in mid-September 2003. "I mean, if it's retirement, then it is retirement."

When Grasso saw Bartiromo's performance, he felt betrayed. "She threw me under the bus," he said in disgust. From then on, Grasso rarely called Bartiromo by her first name. She was known sarcastically as "the beauty," and it wasn't because Grasso thought she was beautiful.

Grasso now spent much of his time trying to keep his job and less and less time doing it. Business continued to suffer. With his pay package consuming the news pages and CNBC, he had become the enemy even inside "his house." The same guy who had snared all those listings for the exchange during the past thirty-five years was now the guy who responsible for losing listings to the Nasdaq. Morale was so low that Kinney, the listings department chief, decided to hold a staff meeting. Kinney said the exchange was like a big "family," but even families have secrets. She said she had been as "surprised" as anyone by the money Grasso was receiving but that she hadn't known about the compensation until now because the salaries at the senior level were confidential.

And it was a good thing they were confidential, because in 2002, she and Britz had earned $3.6 million each, when the salaries of many nonexecutive staffers had declined along with the exchange's profits.

Pat Healy was no longer Grasso's secret weapon in directing listings to the exchange, but he still considered himself a supporter. Healy was now the director of marketing for Bear Wagner Specialists.

With Grasso entangled in scandal, Healy's business was in deep trouble, and the firm's CEO John Mulheren wasn't happy. Mulheren had remained a Grasso loyalist because he knew Grasso helped the floor stay in business. With him gone, specialist investigation or not, Paulson would finally have his way and computers would replace the floor. In other words, they were all toast. Mulheren tried to convince the floor of this simple logic, though it became more difficult with each passing headline. Healy tried another tactic among his floor buddies.

Healy knew what it was like to be paid on commission; it was his job to get his big institutional investors to trade listed shares through his firm's floor trading operations. Healy argued that if you added up all the new listings, all those $500,000 annual listing fees, and, more important, the trading profits of the specialists and brokers on the floor that were a result of all those listings, Grasso was nothing short of a "bargain."

If Mulheren can make more than $20 million a year, Healy asked, why couldn't Grasso make $30 million?

As news spread about the $140 million pay package, Grasso's fortunes declined even more. James Rothenberg, a lawyer working for

Bear Wagner, wasn't surprised just by the size of the payment but by the fact that the exchange had approved them in the first place. Rothenberg had worked for the exchange early in his career and was well aware of its not-for-profit status and the state law that said executives at nonprofits must be paid a "reasonable" salary.

Many board members later said they didn't even know the law existed, but Rothenberg quickly found a citation to show his boss, Bear Wagner's chief legal officer, William Dailey. "Bill, you know I think Dick's compensation is a problem." Dailey studied the document as well; he too had been in the exchange's legal department and knew about the law, but like most people was unaware of how much money Grasso was earning. "You know, I think you're right," Dailey said.

A couple of days later, on September 2, Grasso received two checks totaling $139,486,000. It should have been a day of celebration, but Grasso was hit with another broadside. Donaldson sent a nasty letter to McCall asking for a detailed analysis of the process that had produced Grasso's windfall. Donaldson hadn't been kidding when he told Grasso that he shouldn't take the money—now he was launching a probe into Grasso's pay. "In my view," he wrote, "the approval of Mr. Grasso's pay package raises serious questions regarding the effectiveness of the NYSE's current governance structure." Making matters worse, Donaldson wanted to know everything, not just the process that had produced the payment but a detailed explanation and supporting documents, which meant that the exchange would now have to make public the additional but yet to be fully disclosed $48 million in payments due to Grasso when his contract was finished.

The explanation from McCall for not disclosing the $48 million was simple: it wasn't part of the deal. He had a point. Grasso wouldn't get the $48 million immediately, just the $140 million he was seeking as a condition of his contract extension. The additional money would be collected in 2007, when his contract ended. Still, this explanation missed the larger point. While the compensation committee, and maybe many board members, believed Grasso was worth the money, almost no one else did.

McCall must have had an ominous feeling the minute he realized that he had to tell the entire board that Grasso was due more dough. McCall had made many mistakes since taking over the comp committee post. He admitted that he had failed to read Grasso's entire contract (he later said he reviewed the pertinent parts with counsel). He had thrown Ashen out of the last board meeting and had not read his summary of Grasso's contract.

But failing to include the $48 million in the initial disclosures may have been the worst mistake of all. With Donaldson's demand looming, Grasso and McCall called a board meeting for September 9 to discuss the matter. Lipton began preparing a response to Donaldson that most certainly would include an explanation of the $48 million, and McCall began to think about how to break the news. At one point McCall approached Grasso, raising the issue of whether he should simply forgo the payment. But Grasso had already talked to Lipton, who had told him not to do it. The money was rightfully his. Lipton, Grasso said, thought it would be "idiotic" to forgo the money. Lipton offered his two cents as to how to present the $48 million in an e-mail to Ashen. "Ken Langone told me that all of RAG's [Richard A. Grasso's] compensation was determined by the comp committee on its own initiative after advice from consultants and extensive discussion of the value of the contribution made by RAG, that RAG never suggested his compensation or asked for anything, and that the compensation was recommended by the comp committee to the board, and that several times the board increased the recommended compensation." Lipton then added, "I hope that we can convey this without looking defensive and I will continue to seek a way."

If Lipton thought this explanation would work with the entire board, he was badly mistaken. In the days leading up to the meeting the telephone lines between the Wall Street executive suites were jammed, as the CEOs of Wall Street's biggest firms passed around news of the new chunk of money Grasso was to receive.

Fink had read Grasso's employment agreement, so he knew he was entitled to additional money, and when he heard that it was as much as $48 million it made no difference to him: given all Grasso had done, he was worth the money, Fink concluded.

But others weren't so sure. McCall suggested that he too was just finding out about the money as well, several board members later recalled. "Can you believe it, there's another $48 million," McCall told JPMorgan Chase CEO William Harrison, tracking him down on a golf course to break the news. Harrison was shocked. McCall made a similar statement to Madeleine Albright, she later recalled. "I can't believe I have to tell you this, but [the $140 million] is not all the money Grasso is owed," McCall said, according to Albright. (McCall later said he didn't recall that conversation.)

Even though Jimmy Cayne was on the compensation committee, he had no idea Grasso was getting the extra $48 million—that is, until he heard from Fink. His response: "Wow!" Cayne later said, "They treated this like it was Monopoly money." Grasso began hearing from board members as well. The floor trader and board member Robert Fagenson was shell-shocked when he found out about the money following an offhand remark from Grasso. He then shared the information with fellow board member and floor trader James Duryea, who was also surprised.

Not surprising was Paulson's reaction. As news of the payment spread, Paulson worked the telephones overtime, spreading the anti-Grasso message, and he soon found an unlikely ally. Hank Paulson and Mike LaBranche were hardly friends. The "upstairs" Wall Street firms and the "downstairs" floor traders and specialists had been at war ever since Paulson had tried to kill the floor with an electronic system, and LaBranche held Goldman in particular contempt for the firm's general attitude that the floor was populated by the Neanderthals of the financial world.

It was Grasso who had maintained an uneasy peace between both sides over the years by befriending people both in the brokerage industry and on the floor and using the threat of regulation on anyone else. Now the upstairs and the downstairs, through Paulson and LaBranche, were united as never before as word of Grasso's extra money spread across Wall Street.

LaBranche found no lack of support in his ditch-Grasso effort among the traders, who had once been evenly divided pro and con.

Like LaBranche, Paulson now had a following. Aside from Madeleine Albright, Bill Harrison and a number of CEOs switched sides, albeit unofficially. The CSFB chief, John Mack, the former Morgan Stanley president, and Phil Purcell, the current CEO, had gone back to hating each other after a brief rapprochement during the 9/11 rebuilding effort. But they found common ground in Grasso's pay package and their belief that sooner or later, Grasso might have to go.

"Hey, Jimmy!" called Cayne's secretary through an opening in the glass partition that separated her and the other secretaries from her boss and his noxious cigars. "It's Paulson on line one."

Cayne swiveled in his chair to face the Manhattan skyline, placed his cigar in an ashtray, and picked up the phone. "What's up?" he asked.

"Grasso," Paulson said. His concern was simple: Grasso's survival wasn't worth the survival of the stock exchange. He was making it difficult for the exchange to win new listings and hurting the franchise. According to Cayne's recollection, Paulson said there was only one solution: Grasso must go. Cayne just listened. He didn't hold Paulson in contempt the way Grasso did, but he didn't trust him either. He had seen how rough Goldman played when competing for deals; he heard his traders complain about the way the firm used its clout to control the market. Cayne despised Goldman Sachs so much that in Bear's office he often referred to the firm as "Goldman Sucks."

In Cayne's mind Paulson had an angle. If Grasso was out, what would he gain and how much money would it mean for Goldman? For all his faults, Grasso had made Bear Stearns a lot of money through his leadership of the exchange. He was someone you could trust, certainly more than Hank Paulson.

"A contract is a contract," Cayne told Paulson, indicating that he wanted no part of a dump-Grasso effort. Cayne hung up thinking that the upcoming board meeting would be a doozy. "High drama," he said to himself as he went back to smoking his cigar.

The September 9, 2003, board meeting to discuss the "additional forty-eight" was held mostly over the telephone. McCall opened by discussing how the money had come as a surprise to many board members, and several chimed in, demanding an explanation. Lipton told the board he had reviewed Grasso's contract and the money was legally his. The board debated the future of Grasso's retirement package in private; Grasso and Lipton were now off the call. Meanwhile, Grasso debated his own future. The choice in his mind was simple: given all the negative press about his pay package, given the feeling among board members that they had voted for a contract without knowledge of the $48 million, Grasso came to the conclusion that if he wanted to survive he would have to give up the money.

He spoke to Lipton, who again urged him not to do it. For weeks, friends had advised Grasso to give up part of his pay package to charity. Grasso resisted. The money was his, so why should he give back a dime? But Grasso felt he had no choice with the $48 million if he wanted to save his job or at least be able to leave the job when his contract was up in 2007 without the taint of scandal following him for the rest of his life. As the board debated the issue, Grasso broke in. He told them that based on the statements several board members had made, he would give up the $48 million, no questions asked. He wasn't admitting wrongdoing; in fact, he still believed that while some members hadn't known about the money, others had, and those who hadn't should have. But he was giving up the money for the good of the exchange, and his own good as well.

Paulson was ecstatic. "This is wonderful, you're a statesman." Fink, ever the optimist, told Grasso, "Hang tough and it will soon be all over." After the meeting, Grasso received a call from Madeleine Albright. Grasso had selected her to give gravitas to the board, someone who didn't think like a Wall Street guy. But what he received instead was the worst of both worlds: a board member he couldn't trust and who he believed hadn't a clue about what she was doing. The call only solidified Grasso's opinion of the former secretary of state.

Grasso didn't trust Albright, so he took notes on the conversation. According to the notes, Albright said she believed Grasso showed real leadership skills, but she then added, "I know this will sound sleazy, but you are going to be with us at least four more years and we will find a way to get you the money back."

Grasso said thanks, hung up the phone, put the pad in a safe place, and immediately called Joe Grano to tell him what had just gone down. "You wouldn't believe what Albright just said to me," Grasso said. After hearing Grasso's tale, Grano replied, "You can't make this shit up." (Albright both denied the conversation and in a later deposition said she had no recollection of it.)

Grasso believed he had just saved his job by giving up $48 million and was in high spirits. But others believed time was running out on his chairmanship. He ran into Chris Quick, who as a board member had listened to the meeting over the telephone. "Do you know what I just did?" Grasso boasted. "I just left $48 million on the table."

"Well," Quick replied ominously, "you gave up $48 million but you are still going to get crucified." Grasso could barely keep his temper in check. Quick later said he could see "those little veins he's got running down the side of his little bald head" that were beginning to "pulsate" before Grasso stormed off. Quick feared he was back on Grasso's bad side even if he knew he was right.

The exchange had now completed its response to Donaldson's letter asking for a complete accounting of Grasso's pay. Grasso decided to release it all to the press, including his decision to forgo the $48 million, before it was leaked and he looked even worse.

But things couldn't get any worse for Grasso. During a press conference he was asked what he had to say to the board, which had agreed to hand him not just the $140 million but another $48 million. Grasso acted as if he had never had to answer a tough question. He said that he had had nothing to do with his compensation and had had no contact with the board that approved it, adding, "Some will say, 'You waived $48 million' in payments. I'd like to say, 'Look what I've achieved and how I've been blessed by this board and the compensation committee.'"

Grasso certainly could have used some divine intervention, as the explanation fell flat. For a guy who had once understood how to hit all the right buttons with the media, Grasso had clearly lost his touch.

His "blessed" statement became the butt of jokes in newsrooms across the city. Much of the reporting reflected the widely held view among journalists that Grasso's statements did little more than give the story legs. *The Wall Street Journal* wrote how the additional $48 million was a "source of tension" with the board that could undermine his chairmanship. Langone continued to support Grasso and said the people who hadn't known just hadn't done their jobs as board members. "I knew about it," he said. "They can speak for themselves." McCall said the board was still behind Grasso, but the reaction elsewhere was uniformly negative. DITCH THE LOOT screamed the *Post*'s headline. Corporate governance cops opened a new offensive by denouncing the process that had led to Grasso's pay package—particularly the various conflicts of interest that had led a board of Wall Street executives to hand one of its regulators so much money.

Meanwhile, the floor was going bonkers. LaBranche used the news to drum up the anti-Grasso sentiment on the floor, which was now spreading like wildfire. "This is outrageous," he said as the news of Grasso's pay seemed to overshadow even the markets for the floor.

Grasso used to say that if the elites at Goldman or Morgan Stanley tried to force him out, he would lead a peasant uprising, turning to his people on the floor for help. But even Grasso realized that whatever support he once had among "his people" was evaporating.

For Grasso, these were among his darkest days as chairman. Zito noticed the difference—the fight had been taken out of him. The multiple telephone calls to various friends to lobby for support had become secondary. Grasso began to sit in his office, staring at the four walls, the visible reminders of his accomplishments: the deal plaques and the photos with CEOs and all those celebrities, not to mention his greatest marketing feats, the Wall Street boxing tournament and his trip to Colombia to speak to the rebels at the request of the country's president. It seemed like a lifetime ago that Grasso had been a hero. Now he was just another scandal-tarred Wall Street guy who made too much money and abused his power.

With the walls closing in around him, Grasso turned to the one man who he believed would know what to do. Grasso rarely spoke to

Phelan these days. Langone and Phelan didn't get along. Langone had made it known that he believed Phelan had sold out Grasso early in his career by choosing Donaldson as chairman. People who know Phelan say he believed Langone was a loudmouth and a bad influence on Grasso: if anyone didn't understand the "public trust" nature of the exchange, it was Langone.

Grasso traveled to Phelan's home on Long Island and met him in the backyard, where the two could speak in private. Grasso didn't waste time getting to the point. "Should I resign?" he asked. "Never resign," Phelan shot back. "Let them fire you first." Then Phelan made one more statement about the Club that haunts Grasso to this day. Referring to Grasso's cherished specialists, who had now lined up against him, Phelan added, "They always eat their own."

The remarks were vintage Phelan, who always kept his true feelings to himself. What Grasso didn't know was that Phelan had been fielding calls from some of his opponents as well, including LaBranche. The two had met for lunch at the University Club in Manhattan to discuss what might have been the biggest scandal in the exchange's long history. Grasso, LaBranche remarked, seemed to be hanging tough, but the exchange was getting killed in the press, and with investors. *L'affaire de Grasso,* as the pay scandal was known among the Wall Street elite, was the best advertisement for the Nasdaq ever created. "What do you think we should do?" LaBranche recalls asking the wise old man. Phelan didn't add fuel to the anti-Grasso fire, but his statement suggested to LaBranche that he was close to giving his approval for replacing the dictator.

"I don't know," he answered. "But it looks like he's dead."

Before they finished lunch, Phelan made one other remark that provides some insight into just how badly Grasso had bungled the situation. When Phelan was chairman, his board hadn't been packed with so many brokerage industry executives. It had helped insulate Phelan against charges of cronyism, even when he walked out of the exchange with a then-staggering $10 million. With so many Wall Street types on the board, it fueled the notion that no matter how hard he worked over the years, Grasso had somehow rigged the system. On that score, Phelan couldn't help himself. "Grasso," he told LaBranche, "shouldn't have had all those people from the brokerage industry on the board."

Back at the exchange, nothing could stop the juggernaut that had assembled against Grasso. Langone had been working the telephone, explaining how much Grasso had done for the exchange and that the money was his. Grasso made his calls as well. He knew the floor was in near rebellion, but he continued to talk to the three floor representatives on the board, Chris Quick, Bob Fagenson, and James Duryea, and they were still behind him. The same went for people like Cayne, Karmazin, and Levin. With a little help he could convince those he considered the fence straddlers, people like Purcell and Mack, to stay on his side.

But Grasso had overlooked the one guy he had vowed never to turn his back on. Not long after the September 9 board meeting, Paulson made his most aggressive move yet, pressing board members that for the good of the exchange, they should vote Grasso out. Grasso heard through the grapevine that Paulson had a partner in his crime, Bill Harrison, the CEO of JPMorgan. To Grasso the combination of WASPs like Paulson and Harrison lining up against him had the earmarks of ethnic cleansing of the exchange: "They think I should be selling fruit on Mott Street," he said about the two. But the opposition to Grasso was by now no longer ethnically based. Grasso knew that the minute he heard from BlackRock's Larry Fink, a Jew from Los Angeles and a longtime friend. Fink told Grasso what Paulson was up to; he also told Grasso that his position might be changing as well. He was behind him 100 percent until the day he became a liability, and he said that day might soon be approaching.

The week after the September 9, 2003, meeting was one of the longest in Grasso's career. It wasn't lost on him that the irony of the predicament was its timing. Just about two years earlier, he had achieved his greatest triumph, opening the exchange after the 9/11 attacks and being heralded as a hero. Now he was considered no different from a corporate crook, the most prominent symbol of excess since Michael Milken.

As Paulson continued to dial for votes, he reminded fellow board members that the public pension funds in their opposition to Grasso could redirect order flow elsewhere and hurt the exchange in its competition with the Nasdaq.

But there was more to Paulson's calculations. Grasso's belief in the floor was rooted in the philosophy that all investors, large or small, should be treated equally. The floor was the great equalizer; by brokerage firms being forced to send all their trades there, small investors get the same pricing and treatment as large ones.

Goldman might have owned a specialist firm, but its big clients were not small investors—they were the large mutual fund companies such as Fidelity and other large institutional investors, which had for years attacked the specialist system as a needless tax. Paulson knew how to make these players happy, and it went beyond getting rid of Grasso. It would be to transform the exchange to fit their image of how Goldman believed an exchange should work and introduce electronic trading. Paulson even had the platform to transform the exchange into a new and improved version of Nasdaq at his fingertips: the firm's investment in Archipelago.

Paulson, of course, didn't make these points to the various CEOs he had been dialing to get them to join him in his effort to unseat Grasso. In those conversations, he was looking out for the good of the NYSE. But it was around this time, when a damage control expert named Tim Metz, a former reporter for *The Wall Street Journal* who had written about the 1987 crash and how the specialists had saved the day while the Nasdaq computers crashed, sent Paulson an interesting e-mail pitch to work as a damage control consultant for the exchange.

"I'm convinced that what we are seeing, masked as a corporate governance dispute over pay," Metz wrote, "is actually a battle for much higher stakes than Dick's future at the Exchange. It is a battle about whether institutional investors can break the Exchange or at least ride roughshod over it—over the Exchange and its board, and indeed over the equity markets from now on. It's about whether a human-based auction market really is obsolete in America today." Metz continued, "With Dick out of the way and the board intimidated, it's a good chance the NYSE's opponents can sell that proposition. But anyone who knows just how the Exchange specialists, with Dick's leadership and planning, saved the market in 1986–1987, also knows how terribly wrong-headed that argument is. And while the pension fund folks howling for Dick's scalp richly deserve what they would get if they undermine the NYSE's power to deal with the next Black Monday, America doesn't."

Metz didn't get the assignment, and Paulson later said he didn't remember the e-mail; his inbox was flooded by hundreds of others, many of them, he said, "that had just the opposite view coming to me."

And coming to the other board members as well, as one by one the leaders of the top Wall Street firms who had for so long considered Grasso their friend and ally began to desert him. By late in the week, Paulson had assembled an impressive list of dump-Grasso votes: Morgan Stanley CEO Phil Purcell, CSFB chief John Mack, Bill Harrison, Madeleine Albright, and a slew of others. Fink, once one of Grasso's biggest supporters, had finally made up his mind that Grasso was hurting the exchange, and he joined as well. This sentiment made its way into the press in a September 15, 2003, *Wall Street Journal* article headlined SEVERAL NYSE DIRECTORS CONSIDER REMOVING GRASSO TO STEM PAY FLAP, suggesting that Grasso's days were indeed numbered.

The article was prescient but also inaccurate on one important level. There were more than "several" directors now looking for Grasso's head; it was a majority of the board. McCall understood how the political winds were blowing. McCall, of course, didn't explicitly call for Grasso's head; that would be too obvious, too unseemly. He was merely quoted in the *Journal* parroting Paulson's line, that the pay controversy was a "distraction" that prevented Grasso and the exchange from fulfilling its mission. "In any situation, if this kind of issue continues to be such a distraction that the board, Dick and the exchange can't focus on their primary mission, that's a problem," he said. "And I hope it doesn't come to that."

But it had, and McCall had now jumped sides, as he sat down with Paulson for breakfast at Goldman's headquarters, just blocks from the exchange, telling him that he didn't think Grasso could survive and he was now fully on board for his ouster.

On September 17, 2003—two years following Grasso's fabled reopening of the New York Stock Exchange just six days after the terrorist attacks—Grasso was seated behind his large oak desk, the same one used by his mentor, Phelan, and his archenemy, Donaldson, weighing his options. A week earlier, he had traveled to Washington to poll key politicians on how they felt about him staying the course. Their sentiments were best summed up by Barney Frank, a ranking member of the House Banking Committee. The liberal Democrat from Boston was no patsy for big business—and, given his brand of left-wing politics, would seem a natural critic. But like many of his colleagues, he had been wooed by Grasso over the years with campaign contributions and, of course, the best photo op on Wall Street, the ringing of the closing bell just a few weeks earlier, when the calls for Grasso's resignation began to grow. "I don't give a shit how much money you make," Frank said.

Others did, however. Angelides and Hevesi were back, joined by another good-governance cop: North Carolina treasurer Richard Moore. Senior players in Washington began getting into the act as well. Senator Joe Lieberman said he had to go, as did others.

Grasso continued to look for ways to survive. Langone was doing double duty, calling in every favor he had. He was looking for a few stand-up guys, as he put it. But reality for Langone and Grasso began to set in with a single telephone call from Larry Fink. Fink understood the importance of people like Angelides as well as anyone on Wall Street. Grasso was his friend, but the stock exchange couldn't survive with a symbol of greed at its helm. Fink had just spoken to Paulson, who had been making another round of calls, repeating his belief that Grasso would have to leave for the good of the exchange.

This time Fink agreed. At 1:00 P.M., he called Grasso and told him to "take control" of the situation. In other words, resign.

Fink's call hit Grasso particularly hard. Grasso was hardly surprised when Zito told him he was all but certain that Paulson was the source of all those leaks to the *Journal* about his pay package. But Fink was one of the few large investors who believed the exchange was necessary to thwart the influence of big trading firms like Goldman. Fink now told Grasso that the tide had turned against him—and he was part of that tide. "I said I'd support you until you being here was hurting the exchange," Fink said. The call was in many ways a watershed moment in Grasso's thirty-five-year career. When Fink finished, Grasso didn't reply other than to say he would set up the "phone call" for an emergency meeting that would decide his fate.

Grasso began to mentally calculate the number of sure votes against him and those who were still in his corner. The day before Grasso had been confident that he had the votes necessary to hold on. Now everything Grasso was hearing—from the floor, from his connections at the big Wall Street firms—suggested otherwise, as did what he just heard from Lipton.

"How's it going, boss?" Zito asked as he walked into Grasso's office. "Ya know," Grasso said. "I think you were right about the lawyer." Zito was stunned, so much so that he was wasn't sure what Grasso had meant. He soon found out: Lipton had told Grasso that he too believed that Grasso should think about resigning. Zito wanted to say "Told you so," but he didn't.

Bill Summers made it a point not to miss NYSE board meetings, and when possible, to travel to the exchange in New York so he could be there in person. It just so happened that on September 17, 2006, Summers was in town. Like most of Grasso's supporters, Summers had watched Grasso's chairmanship unravel with a sense of horror and disbelief: horror because even though he thought it looked bad for Grasso to take the money, he still believed Grasso was worth every dime of what they were paying him; disbelief because he couldn't believe how Wall Street could so quickly abandon one of its own.

Summers didn't even know an emergency meeting was being called when he ordered his driver to go downtown so he could see how Grasso was doing. When he received word that Grasso had called the meeting, he was stunned. The full board had just extended Grasso's contract. Member after member had congratulated the little guy for his leadership over the years and his decision to give up the $48 million. Hank Paulson's words were still echoing in Summers's mind: "This is wonderful, you're a statesman."

When Summers arrived, Grasso pulled him aside and laid out the details: The meeting was scheduled for 4:15 P.M. and it could end his chairmanship. Because most members were out of town, they would be dialing a secure toll-free number so the meeting could be conducted through a conference call. Grasso said Summers could go into a private office for the call. That's when it hit Summers: Grasso was resigning.

"Dick, don't resign," Summers said, adding that the board members would eventually come to their senses once all the facts were laid out before them. Grasso looked him straight in the eyes and said in a low voice, "It may not be of my choosing."

And it wasn't. In many ways, the meeting was nothing more than a formality, as most members had already made up their minds. If Grasso had any thoughts that he could pull out a last-minute victory, they were dashed when he noticed that Summers was the only person to show up at his office that day. Even his good friends representing the floor, the board members Chris Quick and Bob Fagenson and the ex–board member Bobby Murphy, didn't show up as the votes were being counted. Instead, they parked themselves across the street at Quick's office, where they didn't have to watch in person as Grasso went down in flames.

As the meeting began, Lipton was present, as was Grasso and his senior staff: Britz, Kinney, and Ashen. Unlike the others, they'd had the misfortune of having to watch their boss, a man who to them was all-powerful, self-destruct on a daily basis—and it wasn't easy. Grasso had worked with them for a combined half-century or more. He had been a tough, sometimes ruthless boss, but he paid them more than anyone could imagine. They were all millionaires because of Grasso, and it was unclear if they would remain millionaires when he was gone.

Grasso apologized for calling the meeting on such short notice, but "the events of the past twenty-four hours" made it necessary to do so, he said. He read a statement. It was brief but carefully worded; in it he discussed how after thirty-five years at the exchange, he would step down *if* that's what the board wanted. "I want to say that I have tried to analyze this situation from as many perspectives as I can objectively, and while I say this with the deepest reluctance . . . it seems to me, is that I should submit my resignation . . . *if you wish me to do so* for the benefit of the NYSE and to help preserve what we have tried together to preserve over the past 35 years . . . I look forward to supporting the board and the NYSE in bringing about a smooth transition to a successor management team. I believe this course is in the best interest of both the NYSE and myself."

To most of the board, Grasso had resigned, yet he had never once said that he had resigned—only that he agreed to resign, something that Cayne picked up immediately. "He wants us to fire him," Cayne thought as Grasso hung up the phone, and the board went into executive session to make whatever it was that Grasso had agreed to official.

"Let me make sure I understand what's going on," Summers said with a distinct edge to his voice. "We're asking Dick to resign after we told him he was doing a great job and paid him too much money?" Summers suggested that the board should merely renegotiate the contract, find some compromise to keep Grasso at the exchange. Carol Bartz, the CEO of Autodesk, made a similar comment. "Maybe we should be fired," she said. "We gave him the money."

At one point Cayne said what he had been saying throughout the entire bizarre upending of Grasso's career: "A contract is a contract." Cayne had another, more fundamental reason to keep Grasso around: he knew that Grasso made the specialists like Cayne's Bear Wagner a lot of money. But the majority opinion may have been best summed up by the board member Larry Sonsini, the high-powered Silicon Valley lawyer whom Grasso had named to the board to give the exchange access to technology deals: "This situation has gotten out of hand and it's bigger than Dick."

McCall, who was nominally leading the meeting, asked for a tally of votes for and against, but the star was really Paulson, the master-mind of Goldman Sachs and now of the demise of Dick Grasso. Paulson had been brilliant in recent weeks. He didn't know Mike LaBranche, but he knew that once the floor abandoned Grasso, he was home free because the upstairs firms would quickly abandon someone they had never really considered one of their own.

He was right—or mostly right—but exactly how right didn't matter anymore. Only Cayne, Summers, Carol Bartz, Mel Karmazin, Chris Quick, Bob Fagenson, and of course Langone supported Grasso. Everyone else, thirteen in total, from Fink to Mack to Purcell, McCall, Madeleine Albright, Bill Harrison, and one of his floor-trader buddies, James Duryea, had joined the Paulson bandwagon and voted to throw Grasso out.

Grasso was in his office with Zito when he received the news from McCall: the board had voted thirteen to seven to "accept your resignation." Grasso obviously knew his contract better than the board did; if he resigned, he would be out a significant amount of money, namely the $48 million he had agreed to give up as a condition of extending his new contract. But if he was fired, all bets were off. "Carl," Grasso said, "I want to be clear, I'm not resigning. But if you're asking me to resign, that's another story."

There was a pause in the conversation; McCall appeared unsure what to say next. Paulson broke the silence. "Dick, we just want you to know how much we appreciate all your years of service," Grasso recalls him saying. Fink immediately thought, "We screwed up here." It had been Fink's intention never to fire Grasso but to accept his resignation. The difference was subtle but an important one to Fink. Firing Grasso would mean that he had done something wrong. "We did not vote on that," Fink said, adding that the exchange should go back into executive session to sort the matter out.

McCall regained his composure and jumped in. "I don't think we need to," he said, adding, "Dick, we are then asking you to resign."

Grasso responded, "Good," and then went on with his own speech about how it was a pleasure to have served at the exchange for so long before offering to stay on until a successor was found. McCall said that wasn't necessary; he should plan on leaving the exchange immediately. But before hanging up the phone, McCall asked to speak to Zito. He said he needed him to write up a press release announcing whatever it was they were doing to his now ex-boss. "Sorry I got to do this," Zito said, and quickly walked to his office to prepare the official announcement. Even before Zito finished writing the announcement, it was leaked to the *Journal* and was being reported on CNBC. "That fucking Paulson," Zito muttered to himself. McCall, meanwhile, wasn't about to argue about whether Grasso had resigned or was fired, he was simply relieved that Grasso was out the door, or close enough to the door to bring the whole controversy to an end. The press release, quoting McCall, was equally noncommittal: "Dick offered to submit his resignation if the board requested, and the board did so and accepted that resignation."

That night, as Grasso left the exchange for the last time in his life, he didn't shed a tear, at least not one that anybody saw. First he called Lori. Grasso's wife had endured a lot during their marriage; his long days at work, the late-night dinners, and most recently, having her husband go from hero to corporate villain almost overnight. Now she was relieved that the entire spectacle was over and she could have her husband back again. "Get a bottle of champagne and tell the kids we're going to celebrate thirty-five great years and one bad day," he said. Lori said she couldn't wait.

"Use the back entrance, boss," Zito said to warn him to avoid the waiting media frenzy now taking place outside the front of the exchange. As the two walked down a long hallway, neither said a word. Zito was close to despair. When Grasso got to the door, he turned to Zito, and the two embraced. "I love you, man," Zito said, now visibly upset and crying. Grasso, still not crying, said, "I love you too."

CNBC had been tipped off that Grasso might leave through the back and filmed his exit. Again Grasso remained stoic as he walked with his jacket draped across his shoulder and got into a waiting car. The drive home seemed odd to him as he peered out the window, looking at the marble facade of the exchange. He was too shocked to be shaken, but for the first time, he clearly understood what Phelan had meant when he said, "They eat their own." Grasso's response now was a little different. "This is the last time I'll ever come near this place," he said to himself as his driver sped away to Long Island.

Later Grasso would say that one of his biggest mistakes was doing the entire last board meeting by phone instead of having the board members come down to meet Grasso in person before they stuck the knife in. "These guys would have never had the guts to assassinate me to my face," he remarked. Grasso, of course, would never know whether the board had the guts to fire him to his face as the directors dialed into the "secure" line to finish what they started: finding a replacement for Grasso until a permanent chairman could be named.

Cayne jumped in again. "I didn't hear him say he resigned . . . this guy thinks he's fired!" Having been a CEO for so long, Cayne clearly knew the difference. He told the board that Grasso had been "constructively terminated" before the end of his contract and that "we could have big problems" if Grasso wanted that $48 million he had agreed to forgo as part of the deal to extend his contract. Cayne believed that Grasso could recoup not just the $48 million if it was proven that he had been unfairly axed but triple damages if he was successful in court. Most of the board sat and listened but didn't give Cayne's theory too much credence. Grasso was a beaten man. Did he have it in him to sue the exchange after all of this? But Cayne knew Grasso pretty well, and he knew Grasso wouldn't give up easily.

The conversation soon turned to the matter of finding an interim chairman. It was interesting to note that none of Grasso's team, from Kinney to Britz to even Johnston, now in retirement, were serious contenders. Fink's name came up, but he demurred. Paulson couldn't do it because he had been so public in his opposition to Grasso. No one else really wanted the job, so it fell once again to McCall.

The public reaction to Grasso's ouster was fast and furious. The corporate governance cops, politicians like Hevesi and Angelides, cheered. President Bush remarked privately that Grasso was "a good man," but he added with a chuckle that he was sure that they could find someone to do the same job for half as much money. That was about the sentiment of the rest of Wall Street and beyond.

Former New York City mayor and Grasso's friend, Rudy Giuliani told CNBC that Grasso's firing was almost unprecedented since "it's one of the few times someone has been removed for doing a good job." Spitzer, for his part, was silent, though he did place a call to Grasso not long after his firing that Grasso never returned. It seemed that the implications of a Grasso-less exchange finally began to seep into the consciousness of the floor. Many floor people began to worry that Grasso and Langone's long-held conspiracy theory, that Paulson wanted to push Grasso out to kill their jobs and turn the exchange into a computer, might actually come true.

11

WITH FRIENDS LIKE THESE . . .

Dick Grasso, who had spent much of his adult life promoting and defending Wall Street, now felt like one of its victims. It was, after all, the street that had turned on him, while keeping his $48 million and making him a pariah.

Grasso's predecessors left to become senior statesman of the financial world; Phelan was an influential board member at Merrill Lynch, Donaldson was the SEC chief. But Grasso was an untouchable: he left the Home Depot board, effective 2004, and was offered only two other appointments, one from a technology outfit called Novellus, and the other from Knight Securities. Grasso turned both down, sparing friends who ran these firms the embarrassment of being associated with a controversial and overpaid executive.

With Grasso gone and McCall filling in, the exchange needed to find someone quickly to restore credibility to the institution. Fink led the search committee. At the top of his list was a man named John Reed, the former co-CEO of Citigroup. Like Grasso, Reed knew what it was like to be banished, Wall Street style. He was pushed out of Citigroup by Sandy Weill after pulling off one of the biggest mergers of all time, combining the bank he ran for decades, Citicorp, with

Weill's Travelers Group. Reed thought he had a guarantee from Weill that the two would run the new company together, and leave together. That didn't happen, as Weill forced Reed out in early 2000.

Since then, Reed and his second wife, the former Cynthia McCarthy, whom he met when she was a married stewardess on Citi's corporate jet, had moved to a small resort village on the coast of France and hadn't been heard from again, until now.

Fink alerted Paulson of his decision and the Goldman Sachs chief was delighted. Reed was a perfect choice, Paulson said. He had a stellar reputation and not a blemish on his regulatory record. During the 1990s, he had saved Citicorp from near collapse. But what Paulson also saw in Reed was a fellow traveler in the world of technology. Reed had been one of the first to embrace technology in the banking industry with his push for ATMs. He was the type of person, Paulson believed, who could usher in a new era of technology at the stock exchange as well. Paulson volunteered to contact Reed and make it official.

Reed immediately said he was on board to serve as temporary chairman and CEO until the exchange could find a permanent replacement. He would work for what he called a "symbolic $1" in compensation. Reed's selection passed with flying colors as he was heralded by the press as a savior; a "lion" of Wall Street, as the *Journal* put it. When Grasso heard the news of Reed's selection, he was overjoyed as well. "He's great," Grasso remarked. "He hates Wall Street," thinking maybe Reed hated Wall Street enough to give him his $48 million. Langone agreed.

About a month after taking over at the exchange, Reed was still classified as "interim" chairman, but now he was clearly looking to undo just about everything the last chairman had done during his eight years in office. Indeed, his announcement that he would work for a "symbolic $1" a year was the opening salvo in his bigger war. Grasso's regulatory chief, Ed Kwalwasser, would eventually be out, replaced by Richard Ketchum, the former head of regulation at the NASD and a top investigator for the SEC. Unlike Kwalwasser,

Ketchum would not report to the chairman; his boss would be the board, where the chairman's influence over the exchange's regulatory functions was less direct. The board was a target for reform as well. Reed shrank it from twenty members to no more than twelve. Because of the obvious conflicts of interest, no longer could securities industry executives serve as board members. They would be ushered onto something called the executive committee, an advisory council of sorts that had no real power but would meet periodically with the chairman and a soon-to-be-appointed separate CEO to make recommendations as to how the place should be run.

People who had worked for Grasso found the changes daunting. Just weeks after Grasso was out the door, there was barely a visible sign of him at the exchange. Several specialists led by LaBranche lobbied to replace Grasso's plaque commemorating the 9/11 heroes with a new one minus Grasso's name on it, and found an open ear with the exchange's new management. Even worse were the fates of the Grasso loyalists at the exchange. Zito and Ashen felt the chill immediately. Within weeks of Reed's appointments, Ashen announced that he was ready to retire. Zito knew it was only a matter of time before he would be gone as well.

At one point Reed called Zito into his office and asked his opinion about how to repair the exchange's image. "Do all you can do to end this as soon as possible," Zito said, referring to the controversy surrounding Grasso's pay package. Already there were rumblings that the fight over Grasso's compensation would take a new turn. His old boss now wanted the $48 million he had given up; Grasso was now telling people he had given up the money only to keep his job, and because he had been fired he was thinking about suing the exchange to get the money. "If this controversy continues, it will kill the brand," Zito added.

Reed just sat and listened. He asked a few questions and seemed receptive to Zito's point of view. But in fact the opposite was true: in the coming days Reed would take a course of action that left even people like Paulson wondering if he was now engaged in overkill. It was one thing to remove all of Grasso's photos from the walls of the exchange or to continue to deny the tradition granted all past chairmen: a hand-painted portrait in the Club's boardroom. Now Reed was looking for a legal remedy to deal with Grasso's salary. He hired a former federal prosecutor, Daniel Webb, to investigate the circumstances behind Grasso's compensation. Reed described it this way in a letter to board members: "I felt the need to start an internal investigation in part because we had to know and understand what happened, and in part, to avoid having others tell us what happened."

But the reality was much more profound and, for Grasso, more dangerous than he ever realized. Reed may have hated Wall Street, but he believed Grasso was as greedy as any Wall Street CEO; at least that's what he told Fink. Reed said that just after the Citicorp-Travelers merger he too had been making a Grasso-sized salary and had a retirement account that would have exploded if he hadn't had the good sense to revamp his account so he could take less money out of the firm. Grasso, he said, should have done the same.

But there was something else: not only was Grasso greedy, but Reed was now suggesting that Grasso's pay package might be illegal despite the fact that Grasso had had Lipton review the matter at Paulson's request. In one particularly nasty move, Reed denied Ashen about $6 million in retirement benefits that were due to him. That came just as Ashen was informed by the Webb people that he was likely to be a key witness in any case against Grasso. To Ashen the tactic was hardball at its worst: Reed was squeezing him to be a witness.

The Webb investigation soon became the talk of Wall Street. His investigators assured participants that whatever they said would be held confidential; the report itself would not be released to the public. All of the information would be used for one reason and one reason only: to determine what legal action, if any, should be taken against Grasso or those responsible for paying him so much money over the years. Grasso suddenly realized just how wrong his initial assessment of Reed had been.

For the next three months, just about anybody who served in any position of power at the exchange received a call from Webb and his people. McCall appeared so worried about what the investigation might turn up about his role in the Grasso pay fiasco that he taped his own interview with the investigators. Bear CEO Jimmy Cayne told investigators that when he had first seen Grasso's retirement package, he hadn't thought it was a real number. Basically, he couldn't believe that someone who ran what was essentially a utility was paid like someone who ran a major corporation. But Cayne also conceded that Grasso was the best NYSE chairman he had ever seen, someone who knew his product better than anyone ever. "If he left," Cayne told one of Webb's deputies, Robert Michels, "it's good night, Irene."

"What does that mean?" Michels shot back. "That means the exchange as we know it is finished, it's through," Cayne shot back. Grasso was simply the most talented guy in the business, and, given the competitive pressures from the Nasdaq, Cayne didn't know of a single other person who could keep the place alive. Michels also took mental note of just how critical Cayne was of his fellow board members. He was obviously building his case around the notion that Grasso had packed his board with people he thought he could manipulate, or, in the case of Langone, someone he knew was willing to lavish on him a salary beyond all comprehension.

When the interview was over, Michels remarked, "So there aren't many people you do respect on the board?" Cayne shot back, "That's right." Well, Michels said, tell me who you think is smart. Cayne rattled off three names: Mel Karmazin, the former Viacom CEO; Larry Fink, who ran the money management firm BlackRock; and Hank Paulson, who, he said, might be the smartest of them all.

Paulson himself may have offered the most convoluted explanation of his role in the pay controversy. He clearly understood his weak spot, having missed all those meetings where votes had been cast in favor of Grasso's massive salary. Having ignored all the correspondence about Grasso's pay would not be viewed positively if Reed decided to sue the board for malfeasance. Paulson tried to impress upon the Webb people that he had been "very, very active at the end," when it had mattered the most. He told Webb that when he had seen the total package he had "gasped at the numbers," and then began asking a lot of questions. He said he couldn't believe Grasso's pay had actually increased in 2001, "in a year that people were jumping off buildings." Maybe the biggest revelation from Paulson was a conversation he recounted having with Grasso when he had first heard about his wanting to take out his retirement money. He said that Grasso had asked him if he thought he had a "valid claim."

Paulson said that Grasso had openly worried whether a future board would award him the money because of the spotlight being shined on executive compensation and had asked Paulson when he thought the matter would "blow over." Grasso had never let on his true reason for wanting to take the money. Through Paulson, Grasso had now offered a more plausible explanation, one that could help Reed prove that even Grasso didn't think he deserved all the cash.

But Paulson was far from the perfect witness. Paulson said that he believed Grasso deserved his $12 million salary for 2002 because as CEO Grasso had been "off-the-charts good at his job." Paulson had much lower marks for Grasso as the chairman of the board, the part of the job that had more to do with corporate governance and image than running the place like a business. That's where Grasso had earned a C or a D, Paulson said.

By the time it was all over, Webb's people had interviewed just about everyone who knew anything about Grasso's compensation, except for one very key player. They decided not to interview "the lawyer," Marty Lipton, and began putting together their report without information from one of the most important parties in the case. Their reasoning may be best explained by a confidential memo Webb himself wrote in late October that described a conversation he says he had with the man himself. According to the memo, Webb had a "telephone conversation" with Lipton, who had told him that "he does not feel it would be appropriate for him to give a formal interview in connection with our internal investigation" because, he said, "he has almost no information about Grasso's compensation issues."

The memo continued, "He [Lipton] told me, Number 1, that prior to the compensation being awarded and voted on by the board in August that he knew nothing about it and read about it in the newspaper. So he knows nothing about it at all." According to the memo, Lipton told Webb that "at no time did he provide any legal advice or was in any way counsel to Grasso in connection with any compensation issues, and he understood Grasso had his own lawyer, and that he—Marty Lipton—had nothing to do with representing Grasso and gave him no advice whatsoever." Webb, according to the memo, simply accepted Lipton's explanation. Because he didn't have subpoena power, Webb wrote, there was little he could do to push the issue. Lipton's account, Webb said, received some support from Richard Bernard, Grasso's general counsel, who was still at the exchange.

At Citi, Reed had always been an enigma, largely because he rarely spoke to the press, though when he did, he had the reputation of saying things he should have kept to himself. Such was the case in late December when Reed gave an exclusive interview to *The New York Times*. Though the Webb investigation had yet to be officially completed, he told the reporter, "If you read this report and if you were trained in law, you would say that there is information in that report that would support potential legal action." Reed, of course, wasn't a lawyer, but he went on to say that the report's contents were "embarrassing," and then, in a direct attack on Grasso, he passed along this message: "If I were him, I'd call me up and say, 'John, let's talk,' " adding that Grasso might then agree to "write a check for $150 million." Reed seemed to forget that Grasso had received $139.5 million and had already signed two checks, one to New York State and another to the federal government, totaling $69 million for taxes. In fact, Reed publicly stated that the report could be used for litigation, not just against Grasso but also possibly against Langone, the alleged architect of the biggest paychecks Grasso had received.

Before the article appeared, Grasso exhibited signs of depression. Friends noticed his downcast mood during lunches and dinners. He grew a beard and allowed his head to go unshaven. He told people that he had just gone from "who's who to who's that?" Grasso's friend John Mulheren, the head of Bear Wagner, died unexpectedly of a heart attack. Grasso attended the funeral, where he saw many of his old colleagues, like Jimmy Cayne, for the first time since his "execution," as he called it. Grasso came to understand what most people who find themselves banished from Wall Street learn rather quickly: that you have few real friends because most last only until the end of the last deal. And Grasso was in no condition for deal making.

There were, however, some pleasant surprises that helped sustain Grasso during the initial dark days and weeks after his ouster. Komansky, Grano, and of course Langone made sure they called him nearly once a day. Sumner Redstone, the chairman of Viacom, called as well. Redstone was one of those CEOs, who often complained about the performance of his specialist, in this case Grasso's nemesis, Mike LaBranche. "I told you he was no good," Redstone said of LaBranche. Grasso agreed. Another caller was unexpected. Senator Hillary Clinton, now contemplating a run for president, simply asked Grasso how he was doing and if there was anything she could do to help.

Of course there wasn't, but Grasso was grateful for the gesture, he said, before some of the old Grasso humor reappeared. "You know, Senator, being out of this nonpartisan job does free me to be part of the Clinton '08 campaign," he said. The senator burst out laughing. "Dick, you can always be on my team." Grasso said thanks, and for a brief moment, he felt like his old self again.

Something else would jolt Grasso back to reality. One thing that Grasso had never done was back down from a fight, and Reed's interview with the *Times* seemed to be the wake-up call he needed.

One afternoon, shortly after the Reed interview appeared, Grasso told Langone he had a surprise for Reed: not only was he going to sue the exchange for his $48 million, he was going to sue Reed as well. Reed's statements to the *Times* were in violation of the nondisparagement clause in his contract, Grasso said. As far as Langone was concerned, Grasso's new attitude was music to his ears. Langone had never given up the way Grasso seemed to have in the weeks after his ouster. Langone was still fighting the NASD (his firm would later be cleared of the charges filed against it) and still fighting anyone who thought he had overpaid Grasso, and now he was ready to join Grasso in fighting Reed. He recalled having recently read that Reed's tough stance about Grasso's pay had its roots in his deeply held "Presbyterian values." Langone could barely control his temper. "Tell that fucking Reed his affair with the stewardess offends my Roman Catholic values!" The war had begun.

Chris Quick was no longer on the board of the exchange, so he wasn't privy to all the gossip that usually gets passed around the sixth-floor executive offices. But he still spent much of his time on the floor, which had its own rumor mill. Quick had never given much credence to the conspiracy theory bandied about by Grasso and his supporters that the exchange was being transformed into a wholly owned subsidiary of Goldman Sachs—that is, until mid-December, when the exchange announced an important management change: John Thain, Paulson's number two at Goldman Sachs, would become the new CEO of the New York Stock Exchange. Thain was selected by a search committee led once again by Larry Fink, and on paper, he seemed like a real find. He was young, just forty-seven; he was rich, having earned close to $300 million during his years at Goldman, so he didn't need to take the job for the money; and above all, he was available.

A lean, intense man with wire-rimmed glasses who had spent his entire career at Goldman, Thain had survived and at times thrived in Goldman's snake pit culture by shifting his loyalties depending on the direction of the political wind. He had begun as a protégé of Jon Corzine, who had quickly moved Thain through the management ranks. Thain was to be Corzine's right hand when the decision was made for Goldman to transform itself from a partnership to a public company in 1998. Goldman was suffering from the collapse of the hedge fund Long-Term Capital Management, and that's when Hank Paulson made his move and staged a coup. Thain quickly forgot his allegiance to his mentor and found a new one. Before long, Corzine was out, Paulson was in as CEO, and Thain was named copresident and, at least on paper, Paulson's heir apparent.

In early 2003, a new regime was in the making at Goldman, led by a commodities trader named Lloyd Blankfein. Being the architects of Corzine's execution, Paulson understood the rules of the road at Goldman, as did Thain, who knew his prospects at Goldman were now limited. Anyway, being the CEO of the world's largest stock market didn't seem like such a bad gig considering the alternative, which was being forced out once the next coup took place. And for Paulson, who was hanging on to power by his fingertips, having an ally at the exchange certainly had its benefits.

Paulson immediately sought to quell any speculation that he had played a role in Thain's getting his new job. He told one newspaper that when Thain had alerted him that he was taking the position, he had thought he was crazy and told him not to do it.

Thain's appointment seemed to coincide with the return to the exchange of Duncan Niederauer, the Goldman markets expert whose life's mission was to end the specialist system. Niederauer was no stranger to the exchange and no stranger to controversy among the floor traders. Like Paulson, he was an advocate of dumping the floor for computerized trading. He was most infamous for a statement he had made to Cathy Kinney that explained his hatred for the floor and his preference for electronic execution: "I don't want five guys named Vinny executing my trades." After Kinney passed along the comment to Grasso, he responded with a famous line from the movie *Animal House:* "Niedermeyer—dead!" And with that comment, Grasso had banned him from the exchange.

Now he was back. Quick witnessed Niederauer himself spending more and more time in the executive suites. If the floor needed any more evidence its days were numbered, the return of Niederauer was it.

Mike LaBranche, who had said the situation at the exchange couldn't get any worse than it was under Grasso, learned just how wrong he was: shares of LaBranche & Co. were tanking amid jitters over the future of the specialist system and the continued government investigation over trading practices that targeted every firm, including his own. Thain did little to calm the floor's nerves. In meetings with the floor traders and specialists, he dropped any pretense of a bright future, simply reminding anyone who would listen that the Grasso-less exchange would be more Darwinian than ever before. One meeting stood out. Thain was describing his vision for the future, his belief that specialists could survive if they embraced technology. One trader who also owned a seat shot back that he believed Thain was looking to kill the floor. "If you believe that, you should sell your seat now and do something else," Thain replied. The trader said he might just do that. Another shot back, "I don't own a seat, what will happen to me?"

Growing increasingly testy, Thain didn't mince words: "You can walk out the door and get a job at McDonald's."

The next day, the floor traders were in an uproar. It became clear that ousting Grasso, for all his faults, had been the worst trade of their careers. Not only were their jobs in jeopardy, but seat prices plummeted below their Grasso-era high of around $2.65 million to about $1.5 million. Still, one trader displayed a little gallows humor by passing out $200 worth of McDonald's hamburgers to his fellow traders as they discussed Thain's remark and their increasingly uncertain future.

Grasso's future was equally uncertain. Newspapers continued to pump out unflattering profiles about his legacy. Maybe the most damning press revelation during this time involved his old pal Hank Greenberg. Todd Christie, the AIG specialist, mysteriously quit his job in March 2003. Now that Christie had become one of the specialists being scrutinized by the government for improper trading, his own dealings and his dealings with Grasso suddenly came under the government's microscope. A key piece of evidence: an entry from Grasso's phone log recording the angry call from Greenberg demanding that the shares of AIG trade above a certain price.

If it didn't, the message suggested, AIG's purchase of another insurer would be jeopardized. The evidence didn't end there; Spear, Leeds had apparently lost money trading in shares of AIG. Investigators at the U.S. attorney's office even questioned SooJee Lee about Greenberg's frequent complaints, how they had been handled inside the exchange, and how Grasso had responded.

It wasn't long before Grasso received a subpoena to testify in the specialist case. Meanwhile, he was gearing up for his own fight with the stock exchange, and as his legal problems multiplied, Grasso needed a lawyer who could fight, and fight hard. Once again, he turned to Marty Lipton for advice. He drew up a short list of possibilities, including David Boise, Alan Dershowitz, and Brendan Sullivan.

Grasso called Harvey Pitt for a second opinion. "If you want to fight," Pitt said, "Sullivan is your man. There's no better litigator in the country."

On one level, Sullivan was an odd choice for someone like Grasso, who cared so much for his public image and how the press shaped it. Despite earning fame for publicly defending Oliver North during the Iran-Contra hearings, Sullivan rarely speaks to the press and advises his clients to follow his lead. When the two met, Grasso explained the process involved in his pay package: how it had been approved by the entire board and how the compensation committee had recommended that he take the money even after he decided not to. And most of all, he spoke about how old friends had turned their backs on him when the public outcry, not the facts on the table, had made him a villain. He spoke about Todd Christie and the pressure CEOs like Greenberg put on the exchange to jazz up the price of their stock. Grasso said he had relayed the messages to Christie, always telling him to do the right thing.

Sullivan said he had several concerns, chief among them Christie. He was worried that Christie might turn evidence against Grasso. His brother was the U.S. attorney for the District of New Jersey, a possible New Jersey gubernatorial candidate. If it looked as if he were going to be indicted, Sullivan feared he would cut a deal. Grasso needed to cut off contact with the former Spear, Leeds trader no matter how close they had been in the past. And one other thing— Sullivan said he had an ironclad rule for clients involved in such open-ended probes: Grasso was ordered to take the fifth on any question of substance if and when he was deposed by the SEC, the Justice Department, or any other investigator looking at alleged floor trading abuses.

Grasso reluctantly agreed, but then he addressed one of his concerns: the fact that Sullivan had no use for the press. Grasso had spent the past year getting his brains beat out, and to him it meant all the sense in the world to come out publicly and fight to get his reputation back. "At some point I have to do something" with the media, such as a long interview or a television spot, he said. Sullivan reluctantly agreed as long as he maintained a low profile. The lower, the better, he said. Sullivan assured Grasso that if he let him do his job, there was no doubt that he would win.

12

ENTER THE ENFORCER

But win against whom? That became the central question facing Grasso and Sullivan in early 2004, after Reed was presented with Webb's final report on the Grasso pay package. The "Webb Report" was a blistering attack on the process that had led to Grasso receiving his $140 million pay package. McCall was described as inept and the board as feckless in its service of the ultimate owners of the exchange, the 1,366 seat holders. The rest of the board wasn't treated much better. But the 130-page tome was most critical of Grasso, whom it accused of running an organization rife with conflicts, selecting board members who had an interest in paying him handsomely because they represented entities that he had regulated. In the end, the board had shelled out an amount of money to Grasso that the report said was far from reasonable.

Reed and the exchange may have had a civil case against Grasso, but bringing one would have been time consuming. Webb came up with a different scenario that would put enormous pressure on Grasso to come to the negotiating table. The law firm Proskauer Rose had drawn up Grasso's new contract, and one of the Proskauer attorneys, Ian Levin, had asked Frank Ashen to make sure Grasso and the exchange received a "reasonableness opinion." Ashen said the contract had been reviewed by Wachtell, Lipton and Vedder Price, a law firm and compensation consultant. Levin was concerned that the $140 million payout could be attacked for not comporting with the provisions in New York State law dealing with the compensation of executives working for nonprofits, which must be "reasonable" and "commensurate with duties performed."

The guy who was in charge of enforcing that law, New York attorney general Eliot Spitzer, had remained relatively quiet about the Grasso pay controversy. In Grasso's mind, Spitzer was and always would be a friend. But that was about to change. Spitzer was now in campaign mode, gearing up for a New York State gubernatorial run in 2005.

In early January 2004, Reed sat down with Spitzer. Reed and Spitzer offer somewhat different accounts about the exact nature of the conversation. According to Spitzer, Reed told him that the Webb Report made a compelling case that Grasso's pay package violated the not-for-profit law and that the AG must file a case against Grasso. Reed maintains he spoke with Spitzer only as a courtesy to show him its findings. He also gave the Webb Report to the exchange's primary regulatory agency, the SEC, and then left it to both regulators to decide if they wanted to pursue a case against Grasso.

One thing is certain: after reading the Webb Report, Spitzer couldn't wait to launch a new crusade. Spitzer had elevated his stature by carefully choosing targets that could generate the maximum amount of publicity for him, and this one, he knew, would take his stature to new heights.

By the late winter or early spring of 2004, *l'affaire de Grasso* had quietly faded from the front pages, but the rumor mill surrounding Spitzer's interest was working overtime. Grasso still couldn't bring himself to believe that Eliot Spitzer was about to turn on him, but he didn't take any chances either. He and Sullivan continued to map out a strategy for if and when Spitzer filed a case. Grasso told Sullivan that it was unlikely, in his view. Grasso himself never gave much thought to the New York not-for-profit law; he left that to his attorneys and Marty Lipton, who he says gave him every indication his pay met the test. Meanwhile, he recounted the conversations the two had had when Grasso had still been in office and the controversy had been making huge headlines. "Why didn't he do anything after the first story in the *Journal*?" Grasso asked, referring to the article in May 2003 that had first outlined his pay. "Why did he congratulate me when I signed the new contract?" It didn't make sense, at least according to Grasso. Marty Lipton, the best lawyer in corporate America, had given the pay package a clean bill of health. Moreover, Grasso believed that if Spitzer charged him, he would also have to charge the people who had given him the money: the board of the New York Stock Exchange and, more important, its last compensation committee chief, Spitzer's fellow Democrat. Carl McCall was one of the highest-ranking African-American leaders in the state and someone he needed in his corner for his political future.

If Spitzer took any of this into account as his investigators combed Wall Street for information, it didn't show. The investigation had all the earmarks of one of Spitzer's earlier crusades against the likes of Henry Blodget or Jack Grubman, and the questions raised by his investigators seemed to underscore the same level of outrage. Spitzer's people were accompanied by officials from the SEC, which gave an extra level of seriousness to the proceedings, but according to the Wall Street executives who sat through the depositions, there was no mistake who was leading the charge.

To justify his moral outrage at his former friend, Spitzer began telling anyone who would ask that the case was compelling because it underscored one of the biggest issues of the day, executive compensation and how Wall Streeters got rich while small investors got screwed when the stock market bubble burst. Moreover, Grasso had let him down and "lied" to him about something of importance. He wouldn't say what that lie entailed, and it didn't matter. In Grasso, Spitzer saw a wounded animal, a target that was so beaten down that with a little pressure he would beg for a settlement where he could keep some of his money, and fade from existence, allowing Spitzer to take his stature to new heights, as the one prosecutor who clamped down on overpaid executives.

Grasso had heard through friends that Spitzer was now offering an olive branch, looking to settle the matter before it got really ugly. Grasso was a fighter, but he was also a negotiator, and if Spitzer was ready to deal, he was ready to listen. Word leaked to the press that he was interested in Grasso giving back around $50 million. But when Spitzer approached Dave Komansky with "a deal," his number was much higher: $125 million. Komansky didn't even have to approach Grasso to tell Spitzer that Grasso wasn't interested.

Leading the investigation for Spitzer was a little-known litigator named Avi Schick, who headed Spitzer's nonprofit investigations. Schick was a large man with a thick Brooklyn accent and an even thicker beard. He didn't have the polish of others in Spitzer's office, and he certainly wasn't a known quantity on Wall Street. His biggest cases didn't even involve nonprofits but instead religious discrimination and voter fraud, and he had done some work on the nationwide tobacco settlement when he started in the AG's office in 1999. He hadn't even been involved in the closest thing to a precedent the state had in enforcing its nonprofit law involving excessive compensation. In 1997 the state had sued the head of another New York not-for-profit, Adelphi University's former president, Peter Diamandopoulos, to refund a chunk of his pay, which had risen to around $500,000 despite the school's faulty finances.

But Schick took on the assignment like an old pro. He began aggressively taking depositions. Jimmy Cayne bitterly complained that Schick reneged on a promise that the deposition would last a little more than an hour after he found himself being grilled for eight long hours. At one point, Cayne was so disturbed by Schick's interrogation—he asked Cayne the same question six different ways—that Cayne stopped what he was saying, turned to his lawyers, and asked, "What the fuck is wrong with this guy?" Cayne's attorneys stepped in to rescue their boss from a confrontation with the attorney general's point man on the investigation, and Schick ended the deposition.

Inside Spitzer's office, there were those who wanted their boss to focus on other, more important targets that affected small investors more directly, since under state law, any money Spitzer received would be sent back to the exchange itself. None of it would repay shareholders screwed during the bubble years. The state wouldn't even be compensated for the expenses associated with the investigation. Spitzer and Schick, however, believed the case had merits. As far as both were concerned, either Grasso would bend or he would face the consequences: further public humiliation and the real possibility of losing all his retirement money. In Grasso, Schick saw a man obsessed with wealth and, more problematic, the trappings of wealth. On the other hand, Schick believed his work was a noble calling: an Orthodox Jew from Brooklyn, he and his wife helped run a charity children's clothing store started by his grandmother.

Meanwhile, Schick was impressing Spitzer with the evidence he gathered to support his notion that Grasso had used the exchange as his personal piggy bank. In Schick's view there was no personal expense that was too large or too small for Grasso to bill to the exchange. Frank Ashen was the exchange's chief ethics officer, but Ashen gave Grasso carte blanche to spend at will, according to Schick. There was the use of private jets, the endless restaurant bills picked up by the exchange. Schick also discovered receipts for hundreds of dollars for pretzels (Grasso loved to eat pretzels on the job) and flowers that had been sent to Langone and his wife right after the two and their spouses had held a meatball-tasting contest at Grasso's home in the Hamptons. With all of this, Spitzer continued to believe that Grasso would fold. "Ninety percent of all settlements are made on the courthouse steps," he said at the time. But Grasso by now was no longer depressed; he was just angry at the exchange, at Reed, and now at Spitzer for turning his back on a friend. When Grasso read the quote, he just laughed and said, "I guess I'm in that ten percent." Grasso thought he held the ultimate trump card in McCall. "If he charges me, he has to charge McCall," was Grasso's mantra. Another trump card was Charles Schumer, who continued to make noises that he was interested in challenging Spitzer in his candidacy for governor.

Schumer would have posed big problems for Spitzer; he was a rank-ing member of the Senate Banking Committee and would be well funded. More than that, he hated Spitzer, and he had connections to others who hated Spitzer, namely the big financial institutions that had been the AG's targets over the years.

At one point, Grasso ran into Schumer, who told him to keep fighting the AG. Spitzer, he said, "has feet of clay."

With Grasso holding out, Spitzer turned up the heat even more. As far as the Spitzer people were concerned, Grasso couldn't have used the exchange as his personal credit card without an enabler, and that's where Langone came in. In Langone, Schick saw the evil ge-nius behind what he viewed as the Grasso pay scandal. He was a guy with decades of compensation experience behind him and a keen un-derstanding of boardroom politics.

A key discovery for Schick was a worksheet prepared by Frank Ashen but presented by Langone to the compensation committee, which he believed didn't accurately explain Grasso's receipt of $18 million in his retirement package and may have duped them into granting Grasso the money. It was part of the plan known as the CAP, or Capital Appreciation Plan. For three years, there had been no sep-arate column in any worksheet presented to the board to explain the size of the plan, just a footnote at the bottom of the document that Schick believed was misleading because it looked as though the money were included in Grasso's overall retirement package and wasn't an addition to it.

By late April, Spitzer had all but decided he wasn't going to charge his friend McCall and the larger board of directors, except for Langone. He would later tell the press that he was differentiating be-tween the deceivers and the deceived. A bigger reason may have been Carl McCall's political ties. The clout of the former compensation committee chief loomed larger every day Schumer said he was still in the governor's race. In Spitzer's world, McCall was untouchable.

Like Grasso, Spitzer believed Langone made an enticing target. He was loud and brash. Langone's other board work showed the same predisposition to overpay CEOs, but now he was dealing with a nonprofit, where the rules were different. As Langone came under pressure, Grasso started to think seriously about settling, basically giving himself up for Langone. But Langone would have none of it. He relished the idea of going to trial to clear his name. "If you settle, Dick, I'll never speak to you again," he said.

In early May, Spitzer and Sullivan held a private meeting to discuss the case. Sullivan wanted to talk Spitzer out of bringing charges. Despite Spitzer's boast that he wanted to settle the case, he never directly approached Sullivan or his people with a number, and this meeting was no exception.

Sullivan may be tough in the courtroom, but he can be exceedingly polite in private, and during their meeting, he calmly provided Grasso's side of the story. The crux of his argument: The exchange isn't a run-of-the-mill not-for-profit. Its status is more like that of the NFL than the United Way. It wasn't a charity, and the board hadn't wanted to pay Grasso as though he were heading a charity.

The meeting lasted for several hours. When Sullivan called Grasso, he gave him the Cliffs Notes version of the sit-down. Spitzer had been gracious, he said, explaining that the AG had told him he didn't really want the case; it had been all but forced upon him by John Reed and the exchange, which had jammed the Webb Report down his throat and forced him to enforce the not-for-profit law. Sullivan believed that Spitzer was ready to bring charges unless Grasso was willing to pay back a chunk of money—a big chunk of money—and settle. With Langone's warning running through his mind, Grasso waited for about two seconds before saying that he had gone through too much over the past years to turn back now. Sullivan told him to be prepared for war. Grasso said he was as ready as ever.

Grasso had remained silent for months, not uttering a public comment since his last days as chairman nearly year before. Sullivan wanted to keep it that way, but Grasso was now ready to fight back publicly. Grasso gave his first major interview as a civilian to *Newsweek* magazine. In it, he laid out his defense: that he had done nothing but accept money given to him, and he was ready to go to war with anyone, whether it was John Reed at the exchange or Eliot

Spitzer in the attorney general's office, who wanted to take away compensation he believed was rightfully his.

For Grasso, finally getting his side of the story into print was a liberating experience. The interview took place across the street from the exchange on the steps of Federal Hall, where Grasso posed for a series of photos. It was the first time Grasso had returned to lower Manhattan or anywhere near the exchange since his firing. It didn't take long before he was spotted, first by a homeless woman who hung out near the exchange and whom Grasso used to hand a few bucks to on occasion. "Hang in there, Dick, I know you didn't do anything wrong," she told Grasso as he pulled some money from his wallet. Grasso then said hello to a couple of cops who recognized him and several traders on their way to work.

Over the previous three years, Eliot Spitzer had developed a "playbook" or set of rules that he followed to gain maximum exposure for his various investigations. The first page of the playbook is the press conference, where Spitzer unveils his charges, wild e-mails, and, of course, his determination to bring the bad guys to justice. The second, and maybe most important, chapter is where Spitzer plays hardball. Press leaks, offhand comments about indictments and charges of fraud, even when there aren't any, designed to put maximum pressure on the target, are all part of the Spitzer playbook. Spitzer's people were now getting as nasty as ever, telling reporters that Grasso had been spending time at Rao's not just with business associates but with his secretary SooJee Lee, where something other than business had been discussed. They provided no evidence other than suspicion that the two had had an extramarital affair ("everyone knows Grasso was boning SooJee," one senior advisor to Spitzer told this reporter during an interview), nor did they say what any of this had to do with the New York not-for-profit law or executive compensation. As far as Spitzer was concerned, it didn't matter, if it brought Grasso to the negotiating table with his checkbook in hand.

Grasso heard what Spitzer's people were saying about him and Lee and brushed it off as "sleaze" that would have no bearing on what he might do. (In several interviews, Grasso has vehemently denied anything more than a working relationship with Lee; Lee's attorney has declined to comment.) But then he woke up to a bizarre series of stories that couldn't be easily ignored. It began with some leaks about the case, how the board might not be named in any suit, and one scenario that had Spitzer considering bringing criminal charges against Grasso. Grasso checked with his attorneys about the story, and they said the best thing he could do would be to stop reading the papers for the next couple of days until Spitzer made his move. Then the news hit: *USA Today* and *The Wall Street Journal* reported that Ashen had now become a witness for Spitzer, agreeing to give back money and admit some wrongdoing. More important, he was now ready to testify against Grasso. When Ashen's attorney Bruce Yannett saw the headline, he threw the paper down in disgust. The story had distorted the true nature of Ashen's settlement; he had admitted to next to nothing other than making mistakes in preparing the material given to Langone about Grasso's compensation. In his deal with Spitzer, Ashen had been careful not to attack anyone, much less Langone or Grasso. Would he cooperate? Of course, but he wasn't cooperating against anyone, just telling what he considered the truth.

Yannett quickly figured out why Spitzer had apparently leaked it in the way he did: for all his bluster as the toughest cop Wall Street had ever seen, Spitzer wanted a scalp. The Ashen leak was his last-ditch attempt to get Grasso to the bargaining table by hyping the odds against him. Like most of Spitzer's attempts to get Grasso and Langone to fold, it didn't work.

Spitzer filed his case against Grasso and Langone on Monday, May 24, issuing a press release entitled "Former NYSE Chief Sued over Excessive Pay Package." As leaked, Langone was the only board member charged. The AG told reporters he had tried to settle this case but both Grasso and Langone had refused. Now that he was forced to go forward, he was looking for Grasso to repay most of his enormous compensation award to the NYSE and Langone to return $18 million, the amount of money that he had "deceived" the board into approving without proper disclosure.

Spitzer didn't end there. While Grasso had been earning all this money, he was ignoring his duties as a regulator, Spitzer suggested. He drew a connection between Grasso and Pitt, the former SEC chairman. The AG said his crack investigators had come up with a memo, written by Pitt, detailing what they viewed as some lame attempt by the SEC to clean up research that Grasso had ignored while small investors got burned. Grasso, Spitzer said, "did nothing" when his boss, the SEC chairman, called him to action on an important investor issue. To top it all off, he cited the testimony of one board member who had ultimately voted for Grasso's compensation, saying, "Thank God I escaped that one. This man was also our regulator, and I'm a member of the New York Stock Exchange . . . and when he's . . . your supervisor and regulator you have to be careful."

For all Spitzer's rhetoric during the press conference and the overheated language of the civil filing, the specific charges against Grasso were pretty narrow: he had simply made too much money and Spitzer was demanding that Grasso return around $100 million of it to the exchange. There had been no fraud on Grasso's part, which is why the SEC, after initially teaming with Spitzer in the probe, had decided to drop the case. The best evidence Spitzer had was a mountain of conflicts of interest: Grasso's appointing friends in the securities industry, people he regulated, to the board.

There was, of course, a memo that Spitzer's people dug up from Harvey Pitt about his plan to clean up research that Grasso had allegedly ignored. But the investigators hadn't done their homework. If anything, Grasso wasn't the only culprit to largely ignore Pitt's call for reform. Both the NYSE and the NASD did eventually follow Pitt's edict, though late in the process.

The charges against Langone, at least on paper, seemed even less compelling. The cornerstone of any financial fraud case is a purposeful withholding of information to decision makers, i.e., investors or board members. The case against Langone seemed to hang on something far less onerous, because the evidence wasn't there. Spitzer couldn't find a smoking gun that had Langone and Grasso cutting a deal to mislead the board.

Spitzer, of course, was a savvy enough prosecutor to understand how to manipulate both the English language and the law. So instead of fraud, he accused Langone of "deception" on an $18 million piece of Grasso's pay. At bottom, it was a critique of just how well Langone had communicated the various details of the pay package to the board. His evidence: the document in which $18 million of Grasso's pay could be seen by board members only if they read the footnote, coupled with Spitzer's assertion that the way the footnote read was misleading: the $18 million could be on top of the money or part of the overall package.

Langone had been well prepared by his lawyers that the charges were coming, but seeing them on paper made his stomach turn. He had spent forty-five years on Wall Street mostly without a blemish other than the general belief that on the boards he served on he lavished CEOs with a lot of money. Now he was being singled out as the mastermind of one of the biggest scandals on Wall Street. His first call was to Grasso as both of them watched Spitzer announce his case on CNBC. "Can you believe this shit?" Langone said. "It's crazy," Grasso countered. Before hanging up, Langone repeated what he had told Grasso several weeks earlier. "Dick, if you settle, our friendship is over."

"Don't worry," Grasso said, "I'm not settling with anyone."

Despite the intense press coverage and the sordid details about Grasso's conflicts of interest, many legal experts believed Spitzer's case faced several significant hurdles, both political and legal. By not charging McCall, Spitzer left himself open to charges of political favoritism. By giving most of the board a free pass, Spitzer signaled to directors across corporate America that it was OK to ignore their fiduciary responsibilities. Maybe the biggest problem with the case was the lack of witnesses to the alleged crime. Compensation consultant Mercer Human Resources, which did work for the exchange, and more important, Frank Ashen, agreed to testify as part of deals with Spitzer, but Ashen was hardly adversarial to either Grasso or Langone, as his deposition would later show. Former board member Charles Bocklet would say in a deposition that Grasso briefly confronted him years earlier when he questioned part of his pay package.

Dale Bernstein, Ashen's number two, said that she was kept out of meetings involving Grasso's compensation because she raised concerns about its size. But that's about it. At bottom, most of the board liked Grasso, including Paulson, who constantly referred to him as something close to a superstar when it came to how he had run the exchange. Schick was hard pressed to find a board member to admit that Langone had misled or manipulated the numbers. When Sullivan and Langone's attorney Gary Naftalis saw the signed statement Ashen had given, they were thrilled: if this was the best Spitzer could do, his case had real problems.

Spitzer and his staff reminded reporters that his case against Grasso was fairly straightforward: the office wasn't charging fraud, it wasn't charging deceit, just that his pay package was "unreasonable." It was, they said, something they would win at trial because the public hated overpaid executives. In addition to Langone and Grasso, Spitzer also named the New York Stock Exchange, the nonprofit entity that he was trying to help, as a defendant in the suit. Spitzer never really explained why the exchange was named in the lawsuit, other than to say that new management had taken steps to clean the place up and that the filing against the Club was somewhat perfunctory because the old management (read: Grasso) had failed to enforce the not-for-profit law.

It didn't take Grasso long to figure out another possible reason. Under his contract, Grasso's legal fees were to be covered in large part by the exchange insurance policy. But who would pick up the exchange's legal costs when Grasso countersued his old place of employment and its new management for the additional $48 million and for those comments Reed made to the *New York Times*? No one, Grasso realized, having signed the policy with AIG several years ago—unless, of course, the exchange was sued by Spitzer as well. Grasso reckoned that Spitzer and the NYSE had cut a deal that had saved the exchange tens of millions of dollars in legal expenses depending on how long the case went on. "And they accuse *me* of conflicts of interest," he said with a laugh.

13

THE GOLDMAN SACHS EXCHANGE

John Thain was meeting with his top brass at the NYSE, including Cathy Kinney, Bob Britz, and his new CFO, Amy Butte, when Spitzer's face suddenly appeared on the television screen in the office to announce the Grasso case. The group had spent the past hour discussing a new compensation plan for exchange executives, and the irony of the situation wasn't lost on anyone sitting in the room.

Except for a few snickers when Spitzer took a particularly nasty dig at either Grasso or Langone, Thain just sat and listened, though Butte noticed an odd look on the faces of Kinney and Britz. Initially, the feeling around the exchange had been that as former top Grasso officials they would be asked to leave. But Thain had kept them around because he needed people who knew how the place worked. Now they were watching the latest twist in their old boss's messy exit from the exchange.

Maybe they felt sorry for Grasso, Butte thought for a moment. Maybe they're just happy to have escaped Spitzer's wrath and still have a job. Neither had called Grasso since his departure, so maybe they felt some guilt. Butte couldn't tell and really didn't care. She was more concerned with what was going on inside the head of her new boss.

Like Thain, Butte was a devotee of electronic trading; she had once written a report that attacked the specialist system and had had Grasso steaming. She also knew Thain wanted the Grasso case to go away so he could move forward with his grand redesign of the stock exchange. It was something he had tried to make clear to Reed when he was hired but Reed had chosen to ignore: Grasso's plan to fight back, aided by the almost unlimited resources of Langone, could keep the story in the headlines for a year, possibly more, a time Thain believed could be better spent bringing the Club into the twenty-first century.

Back in Locust Valley, Grasso was putting into place the plan that would turn up the heat not just on Thain but on Reed, Paulson, and every Wall Street executive who had ever sat on the board for the New York Stock Exchange. Grasso was having Sullivan's staff put the final touches on a suit against Reed for defamation because of his statements to *The New York Times,* and a separate action against the exchange, which continued to withhold the $48 million in additional benefits Grasso believed he was entitled to under his contract. To top it off, Grasso had no plans to keep the dough—he would give it away to charity, he said, "to the sons and daughters of police and firemen."

As he was plotting and scheming, Grasso was feeling pretty good. He hired a PR man and began to hold off-the-record meetings with reporters. He and Langone both laid out their cases in strongly worded columns on the *Wall Street Journal* editorial page, which became ground zero of the Grasso defense in the coming months. The onslaught had one immediate effect: the exchange postponed its decision to remove the now-infamous Grasso plaque, which remained outside the building even as this book went to press.

Grasso felt he was merely setting the record straight, but Langone's attacks soon turned nasty and personal. Spitzer hadn't just brought a lousy case; his whole career was a series of lousy cases. He was a publicity hound, a spoiled rich kid who had bought his way into office and broken the law by lying about how Daddy had funded his campaign.

It wasn't long before Spitzer began hearing Langone's backlash from his friends and associates who dined with Langone, and it made his blood boil. By late summer, Spitzer was certainly feeling the pressure. When one reporter asked him to defend his decision not to charge McCall, he exploded, attacking the question as stupid.

Langone decided to turn up the heat against Spitzer another notch. He hired his own PR guy, and suddenly a spate of stories began to appear not just in *The Wall Street Journal* but in conservative magazines and other news outlets that described the evils of Eliot Spitzer. It was the first bad press Spitzer had received in years, and he wasn't happy.

Former GE CEO Jack Welch knew Langone well—he had appointed him to the GE board—and he knew Spitzer mostly by reputation. Welch was in Boston to attend the Democratic National Convention when he ran into Spitzer. The former GE chairman barely said hello before Spitzer connected the two and launched into a verbal tirade against Langone. Spitzer got right into Welch's face to make his point; Welch could see the anger in his eyes as he vowed "to put a spike through Langone's heart."

Welch, a tough Irishman from Salem, Massachusetts, isn't intimidated easily, but Spitzer's anger nearly blew him away. Spitzer was, after all, the attorney general of New York State, and even as a private citizen Welch didn't need such a nasty or powerful man as an enemy. Welch told just a few close friends of the incident, including Langone, who seemed to enjoy the attention. "Bring it on, baby," Langone said when he heard Welch's account, "bring it on."

Being in full battle mode, Langone didn't need much convincing to sit down with *Fortune* magazine for an interview about a potential cover story on the Grasso pay controversy. Langone believed he had the magazine on his side; he said at the time that he had been guaranteed by people inside the magazine that the article was going to be more than fair and it would allow him to elaborate on the problems in

Spitzer's case. Langone told Grasso that he should do the interview as well. If there was one person whom Grasso had listened to over the years, it was Langone, and he wasn't about to stop now—that is, until he heard from his press adviser, Eric Starkman.

Starkman didn't share Langone's enthusiasm for *Fortune*'s coverage of executive compensation—it almost always came out against the executive. If he cooperated, Starkman assured Grasso, there would be an unflattering cover story. If Grasso didn't cooperate, Starkman said, the story would turn out to be just another hatchet job in the back of the magazine.

Grasso alerted Langone to what Starkman had said, and Langone weighed in once again, telling him that he had been given every assurance that he should do the interview and that the story would be good for Grasso. Grasso decided to split the difference: Starkman would help the reporter with key facts, directing him to talk with friends who could provide color about his life and times at the exchange. But Grasso wouldn't give an interview. Langone was steamed, but Grasso felt that he was making the wise choice.

It's impossible to know what exactly was going through Langone's mind when he sat down for the *Fortune* interview, but the end result was nothing like he had planned. The story line fell about as close to Starkman's prediction as it could get. Entitled "Fall of the House of Grasso," the article painted Grasso as an egomaniacal czar of the stock exchange who had rigged the system by appointing friends to the board. In that sense, the story didn't really present much news, though it added some juicy details about Grasso's management style (one unforgettable anecdote involved Grasso losing his temper with a subordinate who fainted from the stress). Just as Starkman predicted, the story didn't make the cover of the magazine.

But what gave the story legs were the comments made by Langone. In short, he was unplugged and uncensored. Langone must have forgotten he was speaking to a reporter from a major publication because some of the language he used seemed to come straight from the streets. "They got the wrong fucking guy," he was quoted as saying, a direct attack on Spitzer. As for his friends on the street, all those directors who thought he hadn't done the right thing as chairman of the comp committee, he issued this warning: "I'm nuts, I'm rich, and boy, do I love a fight. I'm going to make them shit in their pants. When I get through with these fucking captains of industry, they're going to wish they were in a Cuisinart—at high speed." Langone referred to the anti-Grasso board as "pet rocks" who had barely been awake during most meetings. "You know why they didn't care about what was going on at the exchange?" he asked the reporter. "They had to go back to their offices so they could rip off their customers!"

Langone's tirade took special aim at Paulson and Bill Harrison of JPMorgan Chase, the two people most responsible for Grasso's demise. Langone suggested they had other motives, namely to push through electronic trading and kill the specialists, as part of a Goldman takeover of the Club. The *Fortune* writer, Peter Elkind, didn't buy that argument, calling it a "conspiracy theory" and quoting a Goldman spokesman as saying, "On the scale of silly suggestions, this scores a perfect ten." What Elkind did buy was Langone's overheated rhetoric, quoting Langone as saying that "Paulson is the guy that's going to have not only egg, but shit all over his face." Langone then called Harrison "the fucking genius that gave Enron all the money." (JPMorgan had been one of Enron's top bankers.) Then he issued a not-so-subtle warning to his good friend Grasso, just in case he had any thoughts about settling: "If Grasso gives back a fucking nickel, I'll never talk to him again."

Langone might have thought he was presenting himself as an honest man looking to fight to save his reputation, but his comments came across as boorish and crude. Langone maintains that Elkind misled him to believe that he would not quote his use of profanities during the interview; Elkind says "there were no assurances whatsoever." Even so, Langone sat on the board of General Electric, one of the most respected companies in the world. When company insiders read some of his remarks, they couldn't believe that someone of his stature would tell a reporter that the head of Goldman Sachs was going to have "shit all over his face." Langone left the GE board a few months later.

The remarks underscored the central flaw in Langone's personality: he has no clue about public perception. His record on that front was pretty clear: He had favored Grasso appointing Weill to the board. He had then favored all the big paychecks heading Grasso's way and never once flinched from his support of Grasso's taking the money. Langone had made Grasso a millionaire many times over, but it had also cost Grasso his job and, more important, his reputation.

Back at Spitzer's office, Langone's comments sparked a wave of laughter (those were pretty funny statements, one aide said at the time) and fear, namely that a lunatic billionaire was now gunning for their boss. For the past two years, Spitzer had scared the daylights out of the nation's business community and, in doing so, created himself a national reputation as the toughest white-collar law enforcement official in the country. For all its crudeness, Langone's basic message struck home. Langone had been pointing out that if he and Grasso gave back money, it wouldn't go to the state taxpayers who were subsidizing Spitzer's case, because under law the money would have to go back to the exchange—all those millionaire seat holders, the owners of the NYSE. This argument started gaining traction even among Spitzer's loyalists. A longtime New York Democrat, Meyer "Sandy" Frucher, attended one of Spitzer's fund-raisers and told him that he was crazy to use state taxpayer money for the case. He should figure out a way to give the money to charity.

Spitzer listened and gave no indication of what he would do because there was nothing he could do. The law was clear: if he won, Grasso's money would go back to the Club. Spitzer's actions suggested that he was feeling the heat. At one point he wanted to put a spike in Langone's heart in private, but when he came face-to-face with the blustering billionaire, he took a different approach. The impromptu meeting occurred at the Alfred E. Smith Dinner in New York City. Named after the great New Deal governor of New York State, the dinner is actually an annual fund-raiser run by the Catholic Archdiocese that features top politicians and businessmen from around the country. After one of the speeches, Spitzer, clad in a black tux, spotted Langone and approached him with a smile on his face.

"Mr. Attorney General, what can I do for you?" Langone asked sarcastically. "You know, we have mutual friends who say that in another life we could be friends," Spitzer said with a smile.

"Not likely!" Langone snapped, before turning his back and walking away.

In late 2004, Thain's plan to reconfigure the exchange was beginning to take shape, and the conspiracy theorists seemed to have called it right. Goldman might have owned one of the biggest floor brokers, Spear, Leeds & Kellogg, but the company's long-range plan had never wavered. Electronic trading was the future of market making at the Club, and the clients that mattered the most weren't those issuers who listed on the exchange and wanted their floor trader to even out the ups and downs of the market, but the large institutional investors, such as Fidelity Investments, that wanted their orders sent through a computer and no longer trusted human beings to get the job done.

Thain moved slowly and methodically in making what might have been the largest structural change in the exchange's history. First he let the government's case against the specialists gain momentum, showing the investing public just how corrupt the system had been. Prosecutors now targeted as many as twenty top traders, including David Finnerty, the specialist in GE stock and one of the most prominent floor traders at the exchange.

He then had his staff study whether they should buy an electronic trading platform or build one from scratch. Butte sold Thain on the idea that there was no better way to immediately integrate electronic trading at the exchange than through the purchase of an existing system, and Archipelago was better than anything she could find. Archipelago had something else going for it: the imprimatur of Goldman Sachs, a brand that Thain trusted. She was right.

The plan Thain now envisioned would be controversial. It would signal the coming end of the specialist system. Thain would say there would be a role for the specialists, through something called a hybrid network of trading stocks, when the computer couldn't provide the best price. But Thain wasn't worrying too much about the floor, or anything else for that matter, and it showed. He had no problem allowing Goldman to serve as the banker on the deal, despite his connections to the firm and Goldman's huge ownership stake in Archipelago. He also had no problem making Archipelago's founder, Gerry Putnam, the same guy who had commissioned a song mocking the floor traders as moronic crooks, one of his top officials if that was what it took to get the deal done.

There would be opposition, and Thain couldn't just enact the deal by fiat; he needed approval for such a radical change from a "supermajority," or two thirds, of the 1,366 seat holders, and many of the seats were still owned by present-day traders. Their investment had taken a beating in recent years; seats were now selling at around $1 million, a far cry from the Grasso-era high of close to $3 million during the height of the bull market. The guys on the floor would call it bribery, but the idea was simple: to convert seat ownership into stock that was worth around $2 million for each seat owned and allow the seat holders to cash out by owning shares in the world's greatest brand. The New York Stock Exchange would become a public company.

By February, Goldman was formally engaged as the deal's investment banker. Thain's staff was put on notice to keep the negotiations secret. Thain did the same. At a meeting with floor traders who owned seats in February 2005, Thain was asked to comment on rumors that he had something up his sleeve, a big deal to do what Grasso had weighed doing for so long and take the exchange public.

The trader who asked the question was named Richard Wey. He owned a seat in his wife's name and was thinking about selling it— unless, of course, he could cash out through a stock deal that had been rumored for years under Grasso but was now considered a real possibility given the management change. Thain, according to Wey and other people in the room, couldn't have been clearer. "It takes an awful lot to go public," Thain said. "It's not going to happen anytime soon."

The next day, Wey sold his seat for $1.5 million after telling family and friends he thought Thain was a straight shooter. But Wey, a veteran floor trader, had learned to survive on the floor by conducting himself by a simple code: your word is your bond. He had obviously never dealt with someone at Goldman Sachs.

In the spring of 2005, there was a noticeable lull in the Spitzer-Grasso-Langone war, but things were heating up elsewhere. Schumer had announced that he wasn't going to run for governor of New York State, giving Spitzer clear sailing to the governor's mansion in Albany. John Reed had finally decided to step down as interim chairman of the exchange, handing the job of chairman to the former head of State Street Bank, Marshall Carter. The Wall Street executives who once considered Reed a perfect replacement for Grasso were thrilled that he was going, now blaming Reed for the fact that they wasted countless hours giving depositions in the Grasso case. Prosecutors, meanwhile, announced the indictments of fifteen specialists, including Finnerty. But Grasso breathed a sigh of relief when he noticed that Todd Christie wasn't named in the indictment. He called Sullivan and gave him the news, but his attorney wasn't as sanguine. Christie was charged with civil violations by the SEC. The government, from what he gathered, was still investigating the entire issue, including the trading in AIG stock. He told Grasso to be prepared for the possibility that Christie had turned informant, given evidence against Grasso in exchange for leniency. Grasso couldn't believe what he was hearing.

It wasn't long before Spitzer's case against Grasso had been assigned to a state Supreme Court judge, a longtime Democrat named Charles Ramos, who was elected to the court in 1993 and now was looking for his next move. He needed a gubernatorial appointment for a promotion to a higher level in the state court system, and with Spitzer looking more and more unbeatable for the state's highest office, Ramos had every incentive to craft his rulings to favor the governor-in-waiting.

If that was troubling, the rest of Ramos's résumé was downright scary, at least as far as Grasso was concerned. His legal career was largely undistinguished—except for one ruling that strongly suggested that he had little use for highly compensated executives. He had been assigned to New York's portion of the tobacco litigation case and promptly slashed how much the state's assigned lawyers should be paid out of the $25 billion settlement award. Ramos said the $625 million in legal fees might not be reasonable—not much different from the standard Spitzer was now using against Grasso. Ironically, Ramos's ruling had put him at odds with Spitzer, whose office supported the level of attorney fees granted and won on appeal.

Given the judge's past rulings, Spitzer's office was not complaining when Ramos was assigned the Grasso case (in New York State judges are selected randomly unless they have some prior experience in the area being litigated). Even better for Spitzer was a series of letters a headhunter had written on behalf of Ramos a couple of years back. One was to Grasso when he was CEO of the exchange that had asked Grasso to consider Ramos for a board seat. Grasso had said no. When John Reed took over, Ramos came calling once again, only this time touting his experience in executive compensation matters, going as far as to cite his decision to cut the legal fees in the tobacco case. Reed said no as well, and Ramos was back on the bench, assigned to hear one of the most controversial cases in Wall Street history.

Grasso and his attorneys weighed the obvious: whether to try to get rid of Ramos immediately. Ramos himself seemed to have some inkling that Grasso might ask him to step down when he met with his lawyers to discuss the case. At that point, Ramos disclosed his first letter to Grasso but not the more important one to Reed, which cited his executive compensation experience. Grasso, meanwhile, had already done a little homework on Ramos: he wasn't considered a legal heavyweight; Gerson Zweifach, Sullivan's number two, discovered that many of his decisions had been reversed and that the appellate courts had removed him from some of his cases.

Still, Ramos had a reputation for being the most independent and unpredictable judge in the state court system and in Grasso's mind, unpredictable and independent were good qualities for any judge. Ramos only strengthened his hand with Grasso one afternoon when he met with Grasso and his legal team. He told Grasso that he considered him a hero for the work he had done during and after 9/11. As

Grasso remembered the conversation, Ramos said that if Grasso lost and had to write a check, Ramos was going to make sure that none of the money went back to "those millionaires" at the exchange. Grasso remembers Ramos telling him something else: that he would be willing to step down if his attorneys thought his conflicts were too much to bear. Grasso and his attorneys came to the conclusion that this was a guy they could work with. Anyway, the alternative might have been worse. (Ramos, through a spokesman, declined to comment, citing the ongoing litigation at the time of publication.)

Ramos immediately threw Grasso a bone, granting a long-standing request by the Grasso legal team to release the once-confidential Webb Report. For Grasso the move was dicey; he knew the report was critical of him and his leadership. But he also knew it was critical of the board's actions as well, thus underscoring the central weakness in Spitzer's case: that he wasn't charging most of the board, including McCall.

As expected, the initial press for Grasso wasn't great; most of the media focused on the amount of money paid to Grasso and the conflicts of interest between the board and its chairman. But the release of the Webb Report had also led to release of Webb's interview notes, which seemed to put a different spin on the controversy. Far from fearing Grasso, many of the board members had looked at their duties at the exchange with ambivalence and let Grasso run the show because he knew what he was doing.

The Wall Street Journal editorial page detailed some of the findings in the Webb interview notes, showing how the board had been either in favor of Grasso taking the money or too complacent to care about Grasso's salary. These stories came down hardest on Spitzer for giving his friend McCall a free pass and ignoring evidence that seemed to buttress Langone's case that he had misled no one, and that senior Wall Street executives, including Paulson, said that they had dumped Grasso for one reason: the controversy over his pay package, not because he did a bad job. Langone was ecstatic; he had all but forgotten the miscue of the *Fortune* interview and now was looking to widen his attack on Spitzer. His press aides said he might take out ads attacking Spitzer during his run for governor, and he was looking to endorse and fund a primary challenge to Spitzer in the person of Tom Suozzi, the Nassau County executive.

"Tom, meet Dick Grasso," Langone said as he introduced Suozzi to the little guy at his own spacious home in Sands Point, New York. Langone's "home" is less than a home than a mansion, complete with a massive wine cellar and a huge underground garage. From his backyard, you can see the New York City skyline, and that's where Langone had Suozzi seated next to Grasso as he laid out his plan to make sure Spitzer didn't get a free run at the governor's mansion of New York. Langone, of course, was a Republican, and a very rich one at that, while Suozzi was a Democrat, the son of one of the most prominent lawyers on Long Island. But Langone believed Suozzi could make a race out of the Democratic primary. Despite his low name recognition, Suozzi had done a great job as Nassau County executive, bringing the county back from near insolvency. Langone had also seen Suozzi in action taking on Nassau County's Republican machine, which was run by former U.S. senator Alfonse D'Amato, and believed he was tough enough to do battle with someone of Spitzer's political skill set. Langone was willing to take a chance on Suozzi. It was the same feeling he had had about Grasso not too long before.

Grasso just sat and listened as Langone laid out his plan to raise money and fund a Suozzi candidacy. Suozzi himself didn't make any promises, but he seemed to accept Langone's contention that Spitzer could be attacked because he'd been bad for business in the state. The Wall Street cases had done nothing more than serve as a tool for publicity for Spitzer without doing much for state taxpayers. He had all but ignored cases such as state Medicaid fraud, which costs taxpayers real money, to focus on silly prosecutions like his own.

When the meeting was over, Langone was ecstatic, but Grasso was distracted. Langone didn't know it, but Grasso had told his PR aide, Starkman, who was planning a major new press offensive, to stop what he was doing, effectively terminating Starkman's service. Grasso had given no work-related reason; he merely said he wanted to be out of the press immediately. It seemed like an odd move for someone who was fighting to clear his name. But Grasso signaled that the last thing he wanted to do was continue to go on the offensive against the exchange or Spitzer, for that matter. The change of heart was baffling for Starkman, and Grasso has never really offered a viable explanation for his abrupt about-face, but he did have one additional worry that might have pushed him to take this lower profile.

It was around this time that Grasso received another subpoena from the SEC, which was continuing its investigation of floor trading activities. It was now clear that while Grasso might not have been the specific target of the probe, his actions regarding AIG and Todd Christie had certainly caught the attention of SEC investigators and even the Justice Department. Sullivan, of course, took credit for having seen the writing on the wall with regard to AIG and Christie, and he reminded Grasso of what had to be done: Grasso couldn't answer a single question. He would simply take the Fifth Amendment. The last thing he needed was Grasso pulling a Martha Stewart and getting nailed for perjury for saying something different from Christie or any of a number of traders who had given testimony to the feds. Grasso resisted at first. "What, are you crazy? I'll look guilty," he said. Sullivan said he didn't care how he looked; it was his job to protect him from going to jail. When the big day came around, Grasso took Sullivan's advice when questioned about his interactions with floor traders like Christie and took the Fifth 168 times.

As Langone schemed, Grasso stewed in his Long Island home, thinking about lost opportunities and worrying about what was in store for him in the future. Whatever was about to happen to him couldn't be as bad as what was happening to the floor, which slowly but surely was disappearing. The reason was obvious: so many traders had left the business over the past year that the place had started to resemble a ghost town. It had begun with the brokers—firms like Merrill that sent orders to the exchange had cut their staff, who were usually stationed at booths surrounding the perimeter of the floor. But the cutbacks had now spread to the specialist firms and the smaller $2 broker outfits, which were in a state of permanent downsizing.

They offered many reasons for the cutbacks. Many experienced traders didn't want to risk going to jail, given the government's jihad against the exchange, and decimalization had made trading less lucrative as well. But the number one reason was the direction they believed the exchange had taken in the post-Grasso era: electronic trading was a fait accompli. They were just waiting to see how far Thain would go in implementing the system and eliminating their way of life.

The black cloud of uncertainty hung over the exchange for most of 2005. Mike LaBranche sensed it as well. When the specialist indictments were handed down, he went on the offensive, once again blaming Grasso for starting the whole mess with his initial investigation of his firm. Others argued that Grasso had conveniently looked the other way during the trading abuses because part of his enormous pay package was based on the volume of trades. LaBranche's attacks continued to carry weight on the floor, though less and less as it became increasingly clear among the traders that, warts and all, Grasso had been the only thing standing between them and extinction.

On April 20, 2005, just days after the specialists' indictments became public and less than two months after Rick Wey sold his seat, Thain and the new leadership announced their own indictment of the floor trading community. The stock exchange, Thain said, planned to merge with an electronic trading company, Archipelago, in a deal that initially valued the largest stock market in the world, one of the greatest brands in corporate America, at $3.5 billion. The deal would be one of the seminal events in the exchange's 215-year history. Gone would be the stock exchange's not-for-profit status and much of its infrastructure on the floor. The traders who survived would be the ones who embraced technology. If the Archipelago computer couldn't match a trade, the specialists, aided by their own computers, a "hybrid trading model," would do so. For the 1,366 seat holders, the changes meant money in their pockets—about $2 million per seat. The exchange was now joining the ranks of Nasdaq and the Chicago Mercantile Exchange and would become a public company, with its stock traded on the Big Board through the symbol NYX.

Not only would the exchange get the necessary capital to hunt for acquisitions—an expansion in Europe with the London exchange or the pan-European exchange known as Euronext was a possibility. Everyone seemed to benefit, except the floor. Thain tried to reassure the floor community that he wasn't selling them out, but his manners were so wooden and scripted that many on the floor began calling him "I, Robot." They renamed the exchange the "Goldman Sachs Exchange" and yearned for the days of the little guy in the dark suit.

The floor was in a state of shock. Paulson, just as Grasso and Langone had predicted, had taken over the stock exchange or, at the very least, achieved something very close to a takeover. Key Goldman staffers were now running the Club, and its bankers had brokered a deal that benefited the firm, given Goldman's ownership stake in the electronic trading company. Goldman's ECN unit, Archipelago, was now an integral part of the New York Stock Exchange.

Meanwhile, no one on the floor, not even LaBranche, could clearly articulate how or what this "hybrid" trading system would look like, or how much floor trading manpower it would need. Grasso could have taken perverse glee in watching the guys who had betrayed him the most become obsolete when the details of Goldman's involvement became obvious. But as he sat home and watched the story unfold on CNBC and in the newspapers, Grasso came as close to crying as he had at any time since his troubles had begun. He was powerless to stop a way of life he had tried to protect from being flushed down the drain. "This is a very sad day" was all he could say.

When news of the pending Archipelago merger was announced, Langone was sitting in his midtown Manhattan office and like Grasso was watching the initial details being spelled out on CNBC. Langone had been around Wall Street long enough to know that the first impression of any deal coming from the press is usually banker spin. Langone wanted the unspun version, so he called the man who knew the inside of the NYSE better than anyone else to give him the real story. "Dick, what's the building worth?" he snapped. Grasso estimated the value of the land at around $1 billion, but that was just a rough estimate. It could be worth much more. Langone then hit him with a more important question: "What do you think the brand is worth?" The man who had made the NYSE the most recognizable trademark in corporate America took a deep breath. "More than they say it is" was all he replied.

By the end of the conversation, Langone had come to the conclusion that he could offer the seat holders a better deal. The one on the table, he said, reeked of conflicts. How could it be trusted, Langone asked, since Goldman had brought the deal to the exchange in the first place? Meanwhile, the ultimate payoff wouldn't go to the seat holders of the exchange but to Goldman, which had just unloaded its ECN unit onto the exchange. The firm would receive tens of millions of dollars when Thain, its former president, signed the documents allowing it to monetize its investment in Archipelago.

"Now I know why he wanted you out of there so badly," Langone said. Before Grasso could say anything, Langone cut into the conversation once again. "I bet I can offer them a better deal," he said, "them" meaning the seat holders. Langone calculated the figures in his head. The floor could be eliminated, he said. "I don't buy any of this hybrid crap," he told Grasso. He believed the place had enough technology that with a modest investment it could create its own computerized trading system without the need to buy Archipelago. Langone said he would discuss his idea with his friend the prominent hedge fund manager Stanley Druckenmiller, who could get the right people to begin crunching the numbers on how best to launch a hostile takeover of the New York Stock Exchange.

Grasso wished Langone good luck and thought, "I want nothing to do with this."

Langone's bid for the exchange may have been a long shot, but he was successful in scaring the daylights out of Thain, who knew as good as his deal looked on paper, he now would have to sell it even harder.

Many of the top Wall Street executives viewed Goldman's growing role in the management of the exchange with a mixture of skepticism and trepidation. Now that Goldman had sold its investment in Archipelago, widely viewed as Goldman's ECN unit, to the exchange, using Goldman's investment bankers no less, the street was in an uproar. Merrill CEO Stan O'Neal immediately voiced his concerns to the exchange leadership, reminding them how Merrill brought more order flow to the exchange than any other firm. Why should Merrill continue to send so much order flow to the exchange if it was simply lining the pockets of one of its top competitors? Jimmy Cayne of Bear Stearns, another large order-flow provider, didn't complain to Thain directly, but when Langone called him and asked if he would listen to an alternative plan for the exchange, he said he was all ears.

John Mack, who was no longer in charge at CSFB but was now a chairman at the giant hedge fund Pequot Capital, was at a board meeting in Beijing, China, when he received what was said to be an urgent telephone call. He thought it was a family matter, but when he heard Langone's voice he was shocked, even more shocked when Langone blurted out his intention to take over the stock exchange and name Mack chairman to rescue the place from Goldman. Mack was intrigued; he said he was returning the next day and they should speak.

Mack's involvement in Langone's long shot demonstrated two things: Langone's continued clout in corporate America and the hatred so many leaders on Wall Street had for Goldman and its tactics. But the more Mack thought about a hostile takeover of the exchange, the more insane the idea seemed. Langone, after all, was the same guy who vowed to smear shit on Hank Paulson's face.

Thain got wind of the meeting and telephoned Mack, asking, "So you want my job?" Mack told Thain that the problem was that people on the street believed Goldman was stealing the exchange; he had to better describe the benefits of the deal to the street, and to the seat holders, or Langone would make a run at it.

Mack was right to have second thoughts about Langone's takeover plot. When the news broke the next day, the *New York Post* called it "Langone's Lulu," and the feisty tabloid wasn't far off the mark. Langone's effort was indeed a long shot, and one fueled by revenge: Langone was getting back at the exchange for getting rid of Grasso and at all those who doubted Paulson's desire to make the exchange a subsidiary of Goldman Sachs. But Thain knew the situation was serious; for all the long-shot predictions, Langone managed to gather enough interest in the deal to call a meeting at Druckenmiller's headquarters.

Langone's pitch to about a dozen executives and representatives of Wall Street's top firms was simple. Goldman's presence in the deal was troubling, but more than that, the exchange was being sold for a song. Many of the people in the room were seat holders, and Langone said if this deal went down they would be leaving money on the table. He asked for money from each member to defray the costs of examining an alternative proposal. Then he turned to Mack. "I'm a lightning rod for controversy," Langone said. "John, you continue." Mack nearly fell off his chair; he didn't mind working as a go-between to broker a peace or to study the idea, but the last thing he wanted to do was to lead Langone's lulu.

Mack told the group that he believed they needed more information from the exchange, and with that Thain managed to buy himself some time. Others agreed. As much as Cayne hated Goldman, he also hated the fact that Langone was now asking him for money. Cayne told Langone that Bear Stearns wouldn't chip in a penny until he saw a deal on the table. Discontent began to spread to other Wall Street executives as they heard more about what Langone was proposing.

By the end of the day, Thain knew that he had a tough sales job ahead but one that he would probably win. It would be even easier if he could somehow end the pissing match between the exchange and Grasso. When that was over, maybe Langone would leave him alone. Thain soon turned to the only guy he believed had the credibility to broker a deal with Langone and bring Grasso to the bargaining table: Larry Fink. Grasso still harbored a deep resentment toward Fink for voting for his ouster, but Langone and Fink remained fairly close. They could be seen dining together in the afternoon at San Pietro or at night at Campagnola discussing business.

One afternoon, Fink approached Langone with an idea he said had come straight from Thain: if Grasso were willing to pay $25 million, Thain would be willing to use his influence to convince Spitzer to drop the case. Grasso had already hinted that he would be willing to accept a deal to the CNBC reporter Scott Cohn, only to back down after a brutal tongue-lashing from Langone. But this deal would be good for both sides, Fink said. The $25 million payment was a mere fraction of the amount of money Grasso had earned, and it would allow everyone to save face.

Langone nearly blew his top. Not only was he never going to settle, but why should Grasso? He hadn't done anything wrong.

Later that afternoon, Langone informed Grasso of what Fink had said and then reminded Grasso of the repercussions if he accepted the offer. "Dick, you settle this case, and I'll never speak to you again." Grasso told him that he was ready to fight until the end, even if his heart wasn't in it.

The reason was obvious: for months, Spitzer's investigators, as well as lawyers for Grasso and Langone, had taken depositions from board members and Grasso's former associates. Altogether, the investigation included 1,454 hours of depositions, in addition to the 200 hours Spitzer and the SEC put into the case before filing the charges against Grasso and Langone. Spitzer was certainly being exhaustive; his lead investigator, Avi Schick, had flown to ten different cities across the nation and to London to depose former board members. Attorneys involved in the case estimated that Spitzer had requested and reviewed more than 1 million pages of documents; going through those documents would be like reading the novel *War and Peace* seven hundred times.

Grasso had received reports about the outcome of the depositions; he had personally showed up at others, including Paulson's, Reed's, and McCall's. While there were those like Komansky, Levin, Karmazin, and Langone who supported Grasso, others showed why the case could not be cast in black or white. Jimmy Cayne, who had voted to keep Grasso, told investigators he had done a great job as chairman but said that he had been blown away when he first saw the size of the pay package. Meanwhile, Schick was clearly searching for dirt; he pointedly asked Grasso's old secretary SooJee Lee about her personal relationship with Grasso, specifically whether she had ever been with Grasso alone in his apartment without his family present. Her answer was a simple "no."

In early March 2006, it would be Grasso's turn. Grasso spent more time giving depositions—nine grueling days—than any other witness except Frank Ashen, who spent thirteen days on the hot seat. Now it was clear why Grasso no longer relished this fight. He was hit with every question imaginable, from his dealings with board members to his knowledge of his pay package to his spending habits. Grasso took the Fifth Amendment when he was questioned by the SEC about his dealings with floor brokers and Todd Christie, but Sullivan gave Grasso the green light to answer the same questions posed by Spitzer's investigators since he believed the SEC investigation into Grasso had concluded.

Grasso answered the questions so matter-of-factly that it was hard to determine what his lawyers were worried about. Schick then launched a new offensive into his personal life. This time it involved Grasso's relationship with a woman named Karen Ross, the sister of someone Grasso described as his "best friend growing up." Ross had sent Grasso some seemingly provocative e-mails that made Schick believe that she and Grasso were more than just childhood friends, that they had a sexual affair, according to Grasso's attorneys and others involved in the case (Schick declined to comment about this and other questions concerning his investigation). Adding to Schick's suspicion about their relationship were documents that Spitzer's investigators discovered showing that Grasso had paid part of the college tuition of Ross's daughter.

At one point during his deposition, Schick asked Grasso point-blank whether Ross's daughter was related to him "in any way"—in other words, whether she was a love child. Grasso's attorney exploded: "I just don't think it's an appropriate subject of examination. It has nothing to do with the case. And it's private information!" Schick asked again. This time, Grasso looked at his attorney, who nodded that he should answer. Grasso then flashed Schick that famous Grasso death stare and answered, "No."

Grasso was exhausted but happy that he had survived the ordeal, only to find himself in another messy public relations spat when Ramos granted a request by Schick to have Grasso's deposition with the SEC—all 168 Fifth Amendment pleas—released to the public. The reaction could best be described by the *New York Post* headline: GRASSO PASS-O—HE TOOK THE FIFTH 168 TIMES WITH SEC. Ramos had by now seemed to give up any pretense of impartiality as Spitzer seemed destined for the governor's mansion, and he had one more zinger for Grasso. In effect, Ramos became judge, jury, and, as far as Grasso was concerned, executioner, ruling from his bench in a summary judgment that Grasso must repay around $100 million without even a trial by jury. Spitzer claimed that the ruling was a victory for the small investor, but many legal experts questioned whether the ruling would stand; after years of depositions, motions, and briefs, Ramos had given Grasso all the legal rights of a detainee at Guantanamo Bay.

Grasso was almost too shell-shocked to say anything, other than he would appeal, which he did, and try to get the judge thrown off the case, which he should have done from the beginning.

By mid-2007, much had changed on Wall Street since Grasso's troubles had begun nearly four years earlier. Many of the floor traders rounded up in the government's probe beat back criminal charges, though they still faced SEC actions that made it difficult for them to get a job on Wall Street. (A judge threw out Finnerty's conviction, saying that the feds failed to prove their case.) Hank Paulson was out at Goldman; the traders, led by Lloyd Blankfein, had finally taken over, and Paulson was now the U.S. Treasury secretary.

Grasso himself received a rare jolt of good news. The state's appellate court threw out the vast majority of the charges Spitzer leveled against him, leaving a much narrower and, some say, more difficult case for the new New York State attorney general, Andrew Cuomo. At the time of publication of this book, the appellate division had yet to rule on whether Grasso should be given a new trial and whether a judge or a jury should preside. Ramos's role was undefined as well.

Spitzer was now the governor of New York State, having been elected to office by one of the widest margins in modern history, gathering around 70 percent of the vote. He vowed to do to New York State what he had done to Wall Street and steamroll the special interest groups that had made the state one of the most highly taxed and dysfunctional in the nation. But after a few short months, it became clear that Spitzer without a subpoena is far less scary than Spitzer with one. Much of his reform agenda had been thwarted, and with it, his once sky-high approval ratings.

Spitzer, however, was far from humbled when I spoke with him in mid-July 2007 about Grasso and Langone, and his controversial case against them. "There's a very, very simple reason why we brought this case," Spitzer reminded me. "He [Grasso] was paid more than it was appropriate, the stock exchange didn't have the proper procedures in place when the payments were made, and we had a responsibility to bring the case when we were given the Webb Report." Spitzer grew testy during our interview, particularly when I questioned his decision not to charge the board of the NYSE or his political ally, Carl McCall, the compensation committee chairman when Grasso's massive pay package was approved. Unlike Langone, who Spitzer still maintains misled the board into approving the money, the actions of people like McCall were mere mistakes that weren't "actionable" under the state law, Spitzer says.

Spitzer also has no second thoughts about the actions of his lead investigator in the case, Avi Schick. Spitzer obviously likes Schick's abilities. He recently nominated Schick for a top economic-development job in his administration and continues to commend Schick's performance during the case. "We won the case on summary judgment," he told me several times. But I asked Spitzer whether he supported some of Schick's tactics during his investigation, namely spending taxpayer money examining Grasso's relationship with his secretary, SooJee Lee, or whether Grasso had subsidized the college education of a young woman who Schick thought might have been Grasso's love child. "Avi Schick did a complete investigation" is all Spitzer would say. "The issues raised generated many leads and Avi pursued them."

As for the New York Stock Exchange, Thain beat back Langone's lulu and completed the Archipelago deal. Investors initially embraced Thain's the new business model for the Club, with its emphasis on electronic trading, by bidding up shares to astronomical levels. The floor, however, isn't celebrating. Langone had once predicted that the floor traders would be "shining shoes in Florida" were it not for Grasso, and now they knew what he meant. Duncan Niederauer—the same guy who said he didn't want "five guys named Vinny" executing his trades while he was a top markets expert at Goldman—was named by Thain to be the exchange's president and his presumptive heir apparent. The computers were doing so much work that the place looked like a ghost town. Many floor trading firms have closed up shop, while specialist firms like LaBranche weighed leaving the floor altogether. Thain was such a hated figure on the floor that when he went down there he was at times accompanied by security.

"The irony is that the seat holders have done well, but the floor hasn't," said Mike LaBranche as he weighed his role in what was the single most significant factor in the demise of the floor—the fall of Dick Grasso. It certainly isn't lost on LaBranche and many floor traders who lined up against Grasso that they expedited the disastrous turn of events that followed his ouster: the Goldman takeover of the exchange and the advance of computerized trading. LaBranche owned about forty seats; based on how NYSE stock is trading, each seat was worth $8 million, or a total of $320 million by his estimates.

But LaBranche isn't celebrating; his business is losing money, the market value of his company is down around 90 percent from its height during the Grasso years, and he has done what would have been the unthinkable just a few years ago: He's weighing whether to leave the floor by putting his specialist business up for sale. Still, LaBranche maintains he had little choice at the time but to push Grasso out. "Even at the end Grasso thought he had it all under control and he didn't," LaBranche said. "There were no easy answers. This was a tragedy."

Grasso would agree that the events of the past four years could make a great tragedy with him as the lead character. For his part, Grasso says he "would like to forget about my final days at the New

York Stock Exchange altogether," but he knows he can't; for better or worse he will always be linked to the institution, which he came to symbolize. "Sometimes I can't believe that I've been on the beach almost four years now," Grasso says, with a hint of amazement. What's more amazing is that Grasso, the man in constant motion, barely moves much anymore. He concedes that since his last days as King of the Club, he hasn't done much more than hang out around the house with his family, watch CNBC, and put in a few hours of work at Joe Grano's private equity firm. He still dines at Campagnola, has lunch at San Pietro, and frequently speaks to floor traders who give him regular updates on their dismal state of affairs. He's also still in touch with friends like Langone, Grano, Dave Komansky, and former police commissioner Bernard Kerik, who developed an even closer bond with Grasso following Kerik's own brush with scandal that forced him to withdraw his acceptance of the nomination for Secretary of Homeland Security and may yet land him in jail. Grasso also says he has seen the movie *Borat* a half-dozen times.

Like Spitzer, Grasso doesn't seem humbled by the experience. As the stock exchange under John Thain evolves into a global brand with its purchase of Euronext and possibly other exchanges, Grasso says he can take pride seeing the brand he built grow into an international powerhouse. And he has a point. For all the controversy surrounding his pay package, for all the abuse heaped on him by Spitzer and his minions, Grasso's mark on the New York Stock Exchange is indelible. He played a hand in the listing of nearly every major company listed there today; he grew the brand like no one before him and led the exchange through one of its deepest crises following 9/11. John Thain knows firsthand just how good Grasso was at his job; during the Grasso years, Nasdaq-listed firms couldn't wait to make the switch to the exchange. These days, companies rarely make the switch. In fact, just the opposite is true, with several large NYSE companies leaving the Big Board for the exchange that was once considered the minor leagues.

For these reasons, and many more, Grasso maintains that he earned every dime of his pay package—something more and more people on Wall Street now agree with given the recent disclosures of how much money other less successful executives are earning. "The notion that these guys didn't know what they were doing when they were voting to give me the money is a joke," he says. He holds particular contempt for his immediate successor, John Reed, even more so than Eliot Spitzer, who used Grasso as a prop for his successful gubernatorial campaign. "If Reed didn't go to Spitzer in the first place I wouldn't be in the position I am today." Four years after Grasso left the exchange, many on Wall Street also agree with Grasso's assessment of Reed as the case against him continues and their own roles in the scandal are being dissected by lawyers for the state as well as Grasso's own legal team.

Despite all that he has gone through, and all that he might lose if the case against him isn't overturned, Grasso says he's optimistic about his future. He can't wait to get the Spitzer case behind him, he says, so he could do what he truly loves—work. And he bets there will be a place for him somewhere on Wall Street even if he's considered, perhaps unfairly by some, as one of the most enduring symbols of corporate greed. "I'll do something," he says. "Remember, I have the best Rolodex in corporate America."

EPILOGUE

For a guy like Dick Grasso, someone used to perpetual motion, the wait must have been horrific. By the spring and summer of 2008, it had been almost two years since Judge Ramos ordered him to return nearly all the money he left the exchange with—almost $140 million—an amount of money Grasso once said "would force me into bankruptcy." It had been a year since the appellate division of the state courts rendered Ramos's decision moot by throwing out four of the six claims Spitzer brought against him and freezing the rest, pending the outcome of various claims and counter claims that needed to work their way through the court system.

While Grasso waited, Wall Street burned, though it had nothing to do with Grasso's pay package.

The financial system was now collapsing in a story that made all the hoopla over Grasso's salary appear trivial. The "subprime crisis" didn't just eclipse Grasso, it eclipsed just about every major scandal to hit the Street in years. The biggest Wall Street firms, and many of the same executives who decried Grasso's greed, had been forced to write down more than $150 billion in losses because they rolled the dice on a bit of financial alchemy known as "structured finance" that now threatened not just job security among top executives on Wall Street, but also the nation's economy.

What allowed Merrill Lynch, Citigroup, Bear Stearns, Morgan Stanley, and other big players to crank out record earnings, and pay their CEOs $40 million, $50 million, even $60 million a year, wasn't sound financial management, but gambling, and in late 2006, their luck ran out when the nation's housing market—the very underpinning of the American economy and the Wall Street profit machine—began to implode.

For years the big firms made billions of dollars in profits by underwriting securities packed with so-called subprime home loans sold to people who couldn't qualify for regular credit. The magic of Wall Street is when you match a Harvard MBA with a computer program: You can get an answer for everything. The answer for allowing banks to continue to lend money to people who couldn't afford homes was "structured finance," where rocket-scientists on the street created bonds that were nothing more than a bunch of subprime loans of various levels of credit quality. They were able to achieve a "triple-A" rating, the highest rating from the likes of Moody's Investors, Standard & Poor's, and Fitch, because the risk was spread out among different types of loans; not all would go belly-up at once, according to the computer models.

But many did, beginning in late 2006, and as the housing market began to falter so did Wall Street. Just as the nation's biggest firms were telling the world how Jimmy Cayne of Bear and Stan O'Neal at Merrill deserved salaries that surpassed Grasso's by millions of dollars, Wall Street began sliding into a deep recession that it would take years to reverse. It began slowly. First the big firms could no longer sell those "structured" securities to investors who became increasingly skeptical that the housing market would continue to go up. So Wall Street kept warehousing the bonds—known variously as CDOs, CMOs, and several other acronyms—on their balance sheets, waiting for the market and their luck to turn.

They rationalized their new "investments" this way: The bonds were rated triple-A—the highest assessment. But the housing market never recovered—it got worse, a lot worse. The rating agencies, who were shown to be incompetent when Enron failed and during a half dozen other financial crises in recent history, were not just incompetent in determining the quality of CDOs and other mortgage bonds, they were possibly corrupt as well. Rating those risky and complex securities was a lucrative business, so lucrative that the raters looked away from the risk and pretended that housing prices would never go down, and that a subprime loan of $400,000 to some government worker who earns $35,000 a year was a worthy investment. In just a few months, the big Wall Street firms were hemorrhaging more money than they had in anyone's memory.

The "subprime" crisis caused financial panic in the markets—the stocks of the big firms began to tank, the economy began to falter because banks were no longer selling mortgages—and in the executive suites themselves as CEO after CEO lost his jobs. Jimmy Cayne, the Bear Stearns honcho who was smart enough to see Grasso's mistakes, couldn't see his own. His glib comment when he saw Grasso's huge pay package—"Where's the decimal point?"—had become Wall Street lore, as were his bare knuckles management style and growing arrogance in the way he ran Bear. Instead of tending to the growing crisis at Bear as two of its hedge funds began to implode, touching off the subprime panic that was sweeping the street, Cayne was playing golf and his favorite card game, bridge.

"Pigs always lose," he once said about Grasso and his decision to take his money before his retirement.

But it was Cayne who was losing now. As the crisis grew, Cayne began panicking as well, looking desperately for bank lines of credit, trying to sell risky subprime bonds on Bear's books. But it was too late. In early 2006 Cayne was a billionaire, but by the Spring of 2007 he watched his net worth decline by the day, sometimes by the minute, as analysts worried about Bear's balance sheet and its holdings of CDOs that couldn't be priced or sold. Not only couldn't firms like Bear make money underwriting CDOs, the ones they had on their balance sheets couldn't be sold. The firms were being squeezed on both ends: lower profits and huge losses.

Grasso understood how quickly Wall Street "eats its own," in the famous words of his mentor, John Phelan. Now it was Cayne's turn to be eaten. Cayne took Grasso's place at the top of the list of Wall Street bad guys and became a symbol for the greed of the era. In the spring, summer, and fall of 2007, not a day went by, it seemed, that Cayne wasn't held out for ridicule by friend and foe alike, but not Grasso.

Cayne may not have liked Grasso's pay package, but in the end, he voted to keep Grasso as CEO back in 2003. For that Grasso would always consider Cayne a "friend," he told more than a few people. "He was loyal," Grasso said. Maybe even more important to Grasso was that in Cayne's demise, he saw his own: A man who achieved so much during a long career—Cayne had taken over Bear in the early 1990s trading at $20 a share and grew the stock to above $170—was being crucified for the Wall Street equivalent of what Grasso considered "one bad day." Like Grasso, no matter how hard Cayne tried to redeem himself during the spring and summer of 2007, he came out on the losing end. Frustration set in; Cayne privately conceded that what was happening on Wall Street and to Bear Stearns and to his career was "Armageddon," as the losses at Bear mounted and analysts began to question Bear's ability to survive amid the smoldering sub-prime crisis. "I've got my future at stake here, my kids' future, and my grandkids' future," he fumed at one point. "If I'm going down, I'm going down like a samurai!"

But like Grasso, there would be no honorable corporate death for Jimmy Cayne. His health began to fail him. A urinary track infection turned almost deadly, with poison spreading through his body. He was rushed to the hospital and nearly died. When he recovered, Cayne needed more cash to prop up Bear's depleted balance sheet stung by subprime losses and an even greater loss of confidence among investors. After obtaining an agreement to receive a chunk of cash from a Chinese bank, he turned to a billionaire commodities speculator for financial help, but that move only heightened the sense of desperation that pervaded the firm. A near uprising swept through Bear Stearns after Cayne fired his No. 2, Bear co-president Warren Spector, the man who oversaw the now defunct subprime hedge funds and the entire bond business, including the firm's underwriting and balance sheet exposure to the mortgage market. For many years, Spector was a money machine inside Bear, thanks to his knowledge of structured finance, but he had bet big and lost. Cayne needed a fall guy to show investors that he was taking action by holding those accountable for the desperate shape of the firm.

Not even Spector could argue that the screwup occurred under his own watch. But to the rank-and-file Bear Stearns executives, Cayne should have fired himself as well. "We're being run by a seventy-three-year-old CEO who is busy playing golf half the time," one executive told me. At Cayne's country club he was accused of cheating at golf, reported CNBC. *The Wall Street Journal* wrote that he liked to smoke pot. The guy who always seemed to come out ahead now seemed perplexed not just by his personal vilification, but with the firm's rapid demise. Analysts who once praised Bear's business model now only recommended the stock for its takeover value, and they blamed Cayne for his inability to restore confidence in the firm.

By early 2008, Cayne, like Grasso, was out as CEO of the only place he ever wanted to work for. A further indignity would follow.

The mess created at Bear would not subside with Cayne's departure. By March 2008, traders began making their bets: The CDOs on the firm's books were still difficult to price. The market that made Bear rich over the past decade never came back. Short sellers began to pounce—betting that the firm would implode in a sea of red ink. Then came the hammer in the form of an old-fashioned bank run: Hedge funds who lent the firm money began pulling their funding, protecting it, many would tell Bear officials, until they received some "clarity" about Bear's financial situation.

That clarity would come when, in a span of five days, Bear fell into insolvency. An emergency bailout, led by the Federal Reserve, was arranged in a deal in which JPMorgan would bid $2 a share for Bear, which traded at about $170 a share a little more than a year earlier. Later JP Morgan's CEO, Jamie Dimon, upped his bid to $10, but the disaster was complete. Thousands of layoffs would ensue; Bear executives who had been paid in Bear stock and encouraged to hold onto their shares saw their net worth dissipate over night.

Jimmy Cayne was now "non-executive chairman," having handed over the CEO job to investment banking chief Alan Schwartz. But when the crisis hit, Cayne was out of town, playing at a bridge tournament.

For much of the past two decades, Grasso was the Wall Street point man when trouble hit. During the federal government's bailout of the giant hedge fund Long-Term Capital Management, Grasso was at the table, advocating for his member firms, which could have lost billions of dollars without the rescue plan. After 9/11, Grasso orchestrated one of the biggest rebuilding efforts Wall Street has ever seen. When Spitzer put Wall Street in his crosshairs, Grasso made peace with the enforcer, softening the blow in terms of fines and regulation.

But as the subprime crisis continued to roil the markets and the big financial firms, Grasso was a mere spectator. Cayne wasn't the only CEO to lose his job. Grasso's friend, Angelo Mozilo, was considered one of the most successful CEOs of his generation given the performance of Countrywide Financial, the mortgage company that revolutionized the subprime mortgage and used securitization to become one of the biggest lenders in the market.

But the company, like Bear, became a symbol of the times. Mozilo was soon sitting with Cayne in the hall of shame, having to sell Countrywide, a firm he built almost from scratch, for a bargain basement price to Bank of America, and retiring from corporate life amid growing calls for some sort of regulatory response to Countrywide's lending practices. Many argued that Mozilo himself should face legal scrutiny as well.

Grasso called what was happening to Mozilo and his reputation "a shame." He had other words for the lack of leadership on Wall Street, which changed much in the five years since his ouster. In the past, there was a "financial family," as former Merrill CEO Dave Komansky once said about the street where firms took care of each other. No longer.

Each firm, in their attempt to match the outsized profits of the high-flying Goldman Sachs, had begun to take on Goldman's ruthless corporate culture. The firms no longer considered themselves part of the financial community. Grasso saw it in the feckless way the new leader of Wall Street, the former Goldman CEO and current treasury secretary Hank Paulson handled the Bear Stearns fiasco. Grasso loved calling Paulson "the snake" because of the way he led the charge to remove him as CEO of the exchange.

His opinion of Paulson was solidified when he saw how Paulson worked to "bail out" Bear Stearns. When the crisis first started, Paulson told Jimmy Cayne that Bear was lucky to have him as CEO and the government would do what it could to help the firm survive. But when JPMorgan's CEO Jamie Dimon bid $2 a share for Bear, the Treasury Department all but ordered the firm that it had no choice but to accept the offer and that it couldn't look elsewhere for a competing bid.

When Grasso heard of Paulson's move, he shook his head in disgust, believing that if he were on scene, things would have been handled differently "There is no Wall Street," he said. "They're now all out for themselves."

Dick Grasso used to refer to Merrill's CEO Stan O'Neal as "Stanley," and it wasn't a term of affection. O'Neal was one of the thirteen board members who voted to oust Grasso. But more than that, O'Neal ousted Komansky as CEO of Merrill, forcing Komansky out faster than he wanted or, in Grasso's estimation, deserved, given his long years of service to the firm and the decency in which he approached a job that attracts its share of ruthless, power-hungry individuals.

In the minds of Grasso, people inside Merrill, and people on Wall Street, O'Neal was about as ruthless as they come. When O'Neal took over at the top of Merrill, he demanded change. Longtime managers were fired and demoted. He replaced them with loyalists who followed his every whim. Independent board members, even those who supported him as CEO, were fired as well. More than anything, he demanded profits—big profits—just like Goldman Sachs. Those who didn't produce were out.

O'Neal ridiculed Merrill's corporate culture, known as "Mother Merrill" because it protected and promoted is own, as overly paternalistic and a throwback to a less competitive era. When O'Neal joined the NYSE board in 2003, he was also known to have ridiculed Grasso as a throwback—someone who used the system to his advantage and made a ton of money in the process. But those same characteristics could describe O'Neal as well. Merrill was on a roll through much of O'Neal's first four years as CEO, thanks in large part to rolling the dice in underwriting bonds packed with subprime debt. Having so many loyalists on the board allowed O'Neal to place himself among the top paid executives in all of Corporate America without much scrutiny to the amount of risk he was taking. Merrill's board amazingly never seemed to raise even the slightest concern about the firm's growing exposure to subprime debt on its balance sheet—that is, until 2007 when the world came crashing down on Merrill in the form of huge losses that lasted into 2008 and cost Stan O'Neal his job.

While Cayne's fall was long and painful, O'Neal's was a quick death—about as Darwinian as his management style; as soon as the losses began mounting, he faced innumerable foes. Former executives came out of the woodwork to point out his many flaws, including his addiction to risk, his purchase of a subprime lender at the top of the market, and how under his leadership the firm mislabeled the exposure and the losses due to risky bonds as manageable when they were burning a hole in Merrill's balance sheet.

Before the end of 2007, Stan O'Neal was out as CEO of Merrill Lynch, and no one shed a tear, especially not Grasso—that is, until he heard who would replace O'Neal. After a long search, the board announced that John Thain, the CEO of Grasso's beloved NYSE, would be the new CEO of Merrill. For Grasso, the appointment of Thain was a double-whammy.

Thain received most of his training at the hated Goldman Sachs. Moreover, Grasso loved to talk about how he was one of the few outsiders to be part of the insular corporate culture that ran Merrill for many years—the culture known as Mother Merrill. In the old days, if Merrill had to go outside the firm for CEO talent, Grasso would have been a shoo-in for the job given his relationship with former CEOs Dan Tully and Dave Komansky. Now he wasn't even considered.

Even worse was the guy who replaced Thain at the NYSE. Thain was succeeded by Duncan Niederauer, the former Goldman markets expert and current NYSE president, whose disdain for floor special-ists and Grasso's way of doing business was so obvious that Grasso had him barred from the building, particularly after he said he didn't want "five guys named Vinny" making markets at the NYSE.

"It could happen today, a month from today, or a year from today," Grasso got used to telling people about the status of the court case as the weeks and months dragged on with no end in sight. By early 2008, Grasso had done something his wife Lori had been urging for years: work. He had an office at Joe Grano's private equity firm and began showing up there with more and more frequency, helping Grano with deals and investments.

Friends of Grasso say he and his co-defendant Ken Langone dis-cussed throwing some big party once the entire mess was over. A really big one if they should happen to win. Grasso even discussed writing his own book, entitled *From the Pool Rooms to the Board Rooms*. Langone joked that his book would be called *Diary of a Serial Over-Compensator*.

Joking aside, waiting for the courts to make their decision wasn't easy for Grasso, but he did find it a relief not seeing himself in the newspaper every day, as the media obsession turned to more contem-porary bad guys like Stan O'Neal and Jimmy Cayne, and someone Grasso would have never guessed.

"We hear he has something going with a young girl," was Grasso's comment about the former attorney general and then governor of New York, Eliot Spitzer, when I began asking him sometime in early 2007 how he felt about Spitzer's investigation of his pay package, which now included a full inquiry into whether Grasso had an affair with his secretary and even fathered a love child.

Had Grasso and Langone fought fire with fire? That was the cen-tral question that arose in early March 2008, the same week that Bear Stearns imploded, when Eliot Spitzer exploded. Since becoming governor, the general consensus had swept through the state capital of Albany, New York, among both Republicans and Spitzer's fellow Democrats, that the governor didn't have the temperament for a job that demands a certain degree of compromise.

Spitzer's "reform" agenda was stalled. His budget was bloated with much of the same spending he attacked as wasteful during his campaign for governor. Spitzer was no longer the "enforcer" or the "fucking steamroller" he promised would wage war on the special interests. He was nothing more than a politician, only worse, because he couldn't even get along with people in his own party.

Now he was also embroiled in scandal. For months, Spitzer had been hounded by *New York Post* reporter Fred Dicker, the dean of reporters covering the governor, over a scandal dubbed by the paper as "Troopergate." Spitzer obviously believed what was good for Wall Street opponents like Grasso would be good for political enemies, like state senate majority leader Joe Bruno. Spitzer made unseating Bruno, the leading Republican in New York, a Grasso-like obsession. But now, his Grasso-like investigation of Bruno—using New York State troopers to dig up dirt and determine if Bruno was inappropriately using state aircraft for fundraising purposes—had landed Spitzer in deep trouble.

The new attorney general, Andrew Cuomo, who continued to pursue the Spitzer's pay case against Grasso, began pursuing Spitzer. In a highly critical report, Cuomo concluded that Spitzer misused his power by unleashing the state police to investigate Bruno's activities, which no matter how sleazy they might have looked, appeared completely legal. The report suggested it wasn't Bruno who may have broken the law, but Spitzer himself.

Spitzer was stung by the revelations. His once sky-high approval ratings began to drop like a stone. Even worse, Spitzer set himself up for further troubles: He told the press that he didn't know about the plot—it was the brainchild of aides, such as chief flack Darren Dopp, who had leaked what the troopers found to reporters. He made similar statements to the Albany district attorney, who soon learned that Dopp had a different story: Troopergate, Dopp said, was approved and vetted by Spitzer.

Spitzer, who as attorney general had so deftly spun the public and the financial press with tales of his tangles with Wall Street foes, found the political press less cooperative. Dicker continued to pounce, forcing Spitzer's allies in *The New York Times* to follow. Grasso hated *The New York Post* for how they covered his pay package—"Greedy

Grasso" was the paper's favorite line in discussing Grasso's salary and the case brought by Spitzer. But now he couldn't get enough of the aggressive tabloid. Troopergate became the biggest story in state government and Wall Street was cheering with every new revelation.

Grasso watched in awe as Spitzer's star fell from crusading investigator to incompetent public official almost in a blink. "Couldn't happen to a nicer guy," he said. But Spitzer's fall was far from complete. The run on the bank was underway at Bear Stearns with investors and customers pulling money from the firm, when *The New York Times* broke the story that finally broke Spitzer. Despite years of moralizing about the sins of Wall Street, Spitzer's own sins involved being a regular client of a call-girl service known as "Emperors Club VIP."

When the full story was told, Spitzer had used the name of a hedge fund manager and political supporter to become a client of Emperor's Club VIP. His call-girl friend was barely in her twenties. He allegedly liked "dangerous" sex, according to published reports. His name in the indictment of the call-girl ring and its executives was "Client No. 9."

Business reporters were shocked that someone with so much to lose would risk it all, but—given all of Spitzer's sleazy tactics against Grasso, his vows to put a stake through Langone's heart when Langone decided to fight the charges that he helped facilitate Grasso's allegedly improper pay, or Spitzer's threat to "come after" former Goldman CEO John Whitehead after he wrote a column Spitzer didn't like—they shouldn't have been. Spitzer was in many ways like a Wall Street Jimmy Swaggart, a man so seemingly moral and outraged by the excesses of humanity, he never saw those excesses in himself.

Meanwhile, Wall Street cheered. The few traders left on the floor of the stock exchange began to clap and holler when the news hit the tape. The real cheering occurred in e-mails between CEOs and top executives of the major Wall Street firms who had to deal with Spitzer for so long. Grasso, meanwhile, kept his composure and refused to comment, except for a brief statement about how sorry he felt for Spitzer's wife and children.

As was his custom, Langone showed no such restraint. That afternoon, the recipients of the Congressional Medal of Honor were at the exchange to ring the closing bell. It was a yearly tradition started by Grasso, who continued to hold a private dinner for the veterans and a small group of friends, even though he was no longer CEO of the exchange. That night he had reserved the Tribeca Grill in lower Manhattan.

Word soon leaked about Grasso's dinner to CNBC, which stationed cameras outside the restaurant. At around 7:30 P.M., Grasso saw the CNBC truck, the cameraman, and the reporter interviewing Wall Street types as they walked in. But the real money shots were Grasso and Langone. "I'm not saying anything," Grasso said. Langone muttered he was going to say what he felt.

It was as if Langone was waiting all day to tell the world how he really felt about his nemesis, now known as "Client No. 9."

"We all have our own private hells," he said, "I hope his private hell is hotter than anybody else's." Langone didn't stop there, adding "I had no doubt about his lack of character and integrity. It would only be a matter of time, I didn't think he would do it this soon or the way he did it. But I know for sure he went himself to a post office and bought $2,800 worth of mail orders to send to the hooker. . . . I know it. I know somebody who was standing in back of him in line. . . . "

Back at *The New York Times*, the statement brought the paper's reporting to a full stop; the conventional wisdom had been that Spitzer was snared because money transfers to Emperor's Club VIP touched off alarm bells at his bank, which, like all banks, monitors such maneuvers as part of its surveillance of possible terrorist money laundering. What gave the Langone angle salience was the difficulty of such a law enforcement operation. While it's certainly possible that Spitzer's bank transfers sent up red flags and led the feds to the prostitution ring, bank transfers of this kind occur every day without much notice.

In terms of Spitzer's involvement with the prostitute, so-called sting operations are incredibly burdensome, particularly one involving the governor. "Do you know how many detectives, how much surveillance would be needed?" said one *Times* reporter.

It wasn't long that an urban legend made its way around Wall Street and among reporters covering Spitzer that some combination of Grasso,

Langone, possibly another Spitzer hater, former AIG CEO Hank Green-berg, and private detective Bo Dietl had followed Spitzer, and brought the case to the Feds. The legend grew in stature after news reports that Republican consultant Roger Stone had himself alerted the Feds earlier to Spitzer's dalliances with prostitutes, and his fetish for having sex with his black socks on. Both Stone and Dietl worked for Joe Bruno, the New York State senate majority leader. Grasso, Langone, Dietl, and Green-berg all denied playing any role in helping the Feds snare Spitzer, though it appeared that with each denial, the urban legend grew.

"I had nothing to do with it; I think it's the Gambino's," Dietl in-sisted one afternoon while lunching at San Pietro, referring to the notorious New York crime family. Spitzer's hooker girlfriend, Ashley Dupre, apparently had some friendship with someone alleged to be one of the family's associates. Spitzer had made cases against the mob early in his career as a prosecutor, so in Dietl's mind, why wouldn't the crime family rat out a rat? In any event, Dietl said, it wasn't him. "I had nothing to do with it," Dietl said.

"No way Kenny is behind this," remarked Larry Fink, CEO of Blackrock and former NYSE board member who was seated at another table, now watching Langone walk the room in triumph over Spitzer's demise. Langone was basically being feted as a conquering hero at San Pietro in the days following the Spitzer news as executives in their dark suits took a moment from their power lunches to shake hands and thank Langone for having the guts to take on Client No. 9.

Fink may not have believed in Langone's involvement, but others did, thanks in part to Langone's smile whenever he was asked whether he was the source of the tip, particularly after what he told CNBC. Eventually, Langone had to publicly deny his involvement in the Spitzer sting. He said the statement to CNBC was merely informa-tion he received from a friend nearly the minute Spitzer's involve-ment with the prostitute became news. Maybe so, but when I confronted Grasso with his earlier statement—the one he made to me more than a year earlier that he knew about Spitzer's extramarital ac-tivities—he just laughed before hanging up the telephone.

In the end, it didn't matter who set Spitzer up or if he was set up, because he was now gone from public life. At the time of publication, it's still unclear if Spitzer will be indicted; his activities appear to constitute a felony because at one point, while testifying in Washington, D.C., on the credit crisis, he brought his call-girl friend with him, a violation of the Mann Act, which makes it a felony to bring prostitutes across state lines.

Just after the news hit the tape, Spitzer's office leaked that he might fight the case, not unlike former president Bill Clinton did after the Monica Lewinsky scandal. But Spitzer was no Clinton and his foes weren't just partisan. In the end, Spitzer managed to alienate both Republican and Democrats during his short stint as governor. So without a political friend in the world, just a few days after the hooker revelations first surfaced, Spitzer resigned as governor of New York, apologizing for his actions and the shame he brought to the state of New York, his family, and everyone else who believed his various attacks on the Street were anything more than a publicity stunt to gain higher office.

The media reaction to Spitzer was pretty much split; some believed that despite his personal foibles, he was still a great man for taking on Wall Street corruption. But others, looking back at his cases and his success rate, came to a different conclusion. He filed civil charges against Hank Greenberg over alleged accounting fraud, which as of mid-2008 have yet to be proven as the case languishes in state court. His research investigation may have been first rate—showing in e-mails how firms in their analysts' reports pumped up stocks of companies that hired them as investment bankers—but his remedies fell flat. The Spitzer "reforms" of Wall Street research haven't produced more critical stock recommendations; basically the same degree of sell ratings exists today as they did before Spitzer came up with his enhanced "Chinese Walls."

Then there's Grasso. The depositions of the top Wall Street executives, like Hank Paulson, and politicos, like Madeline Albright, demonstrated the power Spitzer had over the media. The common theme coming from Spitzer's press office and pushed through the business press was that Grasso, with Langone, had duped the board into approving his $140 million pay package. In other words, Grasso all but stole the money. The reality was far different. The depositions showed that these captains of finance either wanted to pay Grasso the money, were too lazy to show up to the meetings and didn't really care until the press made a fuss (i.e. Hank Paulson), or were too stupid to understand what they voted on in the first place.

Cuomo's office heard these arguments as well, and with Spitzer's demise came a wave of speculation from Grasso's friends that the case against him would fall apart as well. At first, it didn't. Cuomo refused to comment on his thinking, waiting for the appellate courts to rule before making a final decision. Grasso knew that Cuomo, like Spitzer, was at bottom a political animal. He wanted to be governor, like his dad Mario Cuomo, the long-time governor of New York.

The public impression about Grasso had always been a difficult one to understand. By now, even the people on Wall Street who hated Grasso believed Spitzer's case was a joke. But Wall Street wouldn't decide the next election for governor. As the economy turned sour in 2007 and 2008, as gas prices soared, as house prices declined, and as Wall Street imploded, the public had little patience for over-paid Wall Streeters, even those attacked by Eliot Spitzer. If the appellate courts somehow upheld the lower court's decisions against Grasso, Cuomo made it clear he would have no problem adding his name to the outrage over Grasso's enormous pay package.

Through the spring and summer of 2008, Grasso's attorneys told him to remain confident and patient. The appeals courts would be ruling any time now on a host of issues, including if he had to give back that very large check the NYSE mailed to him in 2003. Even if they lost, Grasso's lawyers said, they could appeal, because in the end they had a great case. Some friends of Grasso weren't so sure. They had been pressuring him to reach out to Cuomo's office, meet him halfway rather than risk losing in court. Several told Grasso's wife Lori to figure out a way to safeguard the family's savings. Grasso listened to no one but his gut, Langone, who never wanted him to settle, and his attorneys. "I'm not doing anything until I hear from the court," is all he would say.

In early July 2008, Grasso was seated in Joe Grano's office with Bo Dietl when he received a call from his attorney. It wasn't Brendan Sullivan, the name-brand lawyer Grasso thought he hired when Spitzer started to pounce four years earlier, but one of Sullivan's top attorneys, a man named Gerson Zweifach. A week earlier the state's court of appeals, the highest court, agreed with the middle court's ruling that threw out most of the counts against Grasso. There were now two counts left that Zweifach had argued should be thrown out as well. That case was before the appellate division, as were a host of other arguments and counterarguments from Cuomo.

But by the tone in Zweifach's voice, Grasso knew there was news—good news. "It's over," Zweifach said. He told Grasso that he had won.

The ruling went something like this: The appellate division threw out the entire case, including the charges against Langone stating that the attorney general's office didn't even have the right to press Grasso to give back the money. Remember, Spitzer sued Grasso under the New York not for profit law, which said the salaries of executives who run nonprofits must be reasonable. Forget that the NYSE was hardly a charity and the attorney general would be using taxpayer money representing a claim brought by the NYSE—a club of rich guys—it was still a nonprofit at least when Grasso was running it.

But the NYSE had ceased being a nonprofit about a year after the case was brought, and according to the court, at that very moment, the case was over. Four years and millions of taxpayers dollars later, the court was essentially saying that Spitzer should have dropped the case the minute the NYSE became a public company in 2005.

Cuomo, of course, could appeal the ruling to the state's highest court, the Court of Appeals, but the appeal wasn't guaranteed since it was a 3–1 decision. Even if Cuomo reinstated the case on appeal, he would have reinstated only two counts because the Court of Appeals had already thrown out the other four. Making the case even more difficult for the government: The two counts left against Grasso would be the most difficult to win in court. Basically Cuomo would have to prove malfeasance on the part of Grasso—that he hid key parts of the compensation package before the board voted. In effect, Cuomo would have to prove that Grasso intentionally lied, cheated, and stole his way to a $140 million pay package. Not even Spitzer was prepared to do that; he simply argued that Grasso made too much money, no matter how much state taxpayer money he wasted on investigating whether Grasso was alone in his New York City apartment with his secretary SooJee Lee.

Grasso was elated as he heard the news. He told Zweifach he had to hang up because he was now heading to San Pietro for a celebratory lunch. Bottles of wine were poured before he got there. Grasso took the back table, dining with Joe Grano, Dave Komansky, and Marty Kaplan, the former head of equities at Merrill and one of Grasso's closest friends through the entire ordeal. Grasso was clearly in his element. Former General Electric CEO and Grasso friend, Jack Welch, who was seated at a nearby table with *Today* show co-host Matt Lauer, stood up to shake his hand. Bo Dietl, the flashy, pugnacious private investigator, strolled in, hugged Grasso, and purchased him another bottle of wine, which Grasso and his crew quickly downed. CNBC waited outside for Grasso's first public statements since the ruling.

When he saw the camera, Grasso almost walked back into the restaurant. But he decided a few words were in order. Grasso could have done a victory lap, attacking Spitzer, John Reed, Hank Paulson, and all his critics in the press who for years jumped on every leak from Spitzer, all but convicting Grasso even before his trial began. But he didn't, and instead, just stated the obvious.

"From the get-go, there was never anything improper," he said, "It's important when you believe in the principle of integrity, and running your life and business honestly, that you never capitulate. . . . And that was my basic philosophy."

The mood up in Cuomo's Albany office was one of confusion. First, the new attorney general said he would review the ruling and then determine a response. It was an odd statement since the minute the ruling came out, legal opinion overwhelmingly sided with Grasso. No one, it appeared, but someone with the mind of a Spitzer would continue this case given all the obstacles. Just a couple hours after Cuomo's review, he proved he was no Spitzer.

"We have reviewed the court's opinion and determined that an appeal would not be warranted," Cuomo said in a statement. "Thus, for all intents and purposes, the Grasso case is over."

Grasso and Langone, who once spoke about throwing a party if they had won, possibly at their favorite restaurant in East Harlem, Rao's, decided to celebrate low key with family and friends. Then came the speculation: What would Grasso do next? The buzz around San Pietro that afternoon was that Grasso would do something Wall Street related—maybe work for an exchange, or maybe just continue to work for Joe Grano, who, like Marty Kaplan, was one of the few people who was there for Grasso from the beginning.

Indeed, much had changed since Grasso was King of the Club: The specialists were all but gone from the floor of the Big Board. The NYSE was now known as NYSE Euronext because of its merger with the pan-European exchange. But the battles with the Nasdaq and the other exchanges, those trading in commodities, those cropping up around the world, would remain.

Although the media assessment of Jimmy Cayne, the former CEO of the now defunct Bear Stearns, will no doubt be harsh, he did say something about Grasso that deserves attention. In assessing Grasso's ability as the head of the NYSE, Cayne said, "No one knew his product better." And he was right, as Niederauer and the new leadership at the exchange is discovering, Grasso was more than just a guy that lets the Vinnies run wild. During the Grasso era over 80 percent of the exchange-listed shares found buyers or sellers at the NYSE, not on some far-away trading desk; today it's 50 percent or less. The record shows that neither Thain nor Niederauer could hold a candle to Grasso's ability to convince companies to have their shares listed at the exchange. But Grasso's greatest achievement was turning the NYSE into a symbol of American capitalism. These days the Nasdaq "Wall" gets at least as much recognition.

When asked by CNBC what he would do next, Grasso just smiled, the same way he smiled when he was King of the Club, just before he was about to snare a big listing or orchestrate some elaborate show on the floor, and said, "Stay tuned."

ACKNOWLEDGMENTS

I could never have written this book without the support of friends, family, and many, many sources, most of whom do not want to be thanked publicly. For those who do, I would like to extend my sincerest gratitude for putting up with me during the past two years, particularly to my wife, Virginia Juliano, who believed not just in the book but in my ability to tell the story of Dick Grasso's life. Every writer I know experiences moments of self-doubt; thank God I had someone like Ginny to get me through each and every one of those episodes. She is my life, my love, and my rock. There is no one who believed in me more, and for that I am eternally grateful.

I would also like to thank my agent, Todd Shuster, who was there for me through all the ups and downs that come with any long project while keeping me focused on a story that he believed needed to be told. Marion Maneker, my editor, is among the most talented people I've worked with and deserves special thanks for shaping this story in a way that is readable to people beyond my sources on Wall Street.

I would like to thank the people at HarperCollins, Ethan Friedman, Sarah Brown, Joe Tessitore, and Steve Ross, for continuing to believe in this project even as the news cycle changed over the past two years.

My assistant, Ash Bennington, deserves much more than a simple acknowledgment. I met Ash at Elaine's one night. He wanted to be a writer, and I sold him on the idea that if I broke his chops for a couple of months that would be a step in the right direction. He agreed, and the job he's done has been invaluable. Leah Spiro, a friend and colleague, was hounding me for months to pitch a book on Grasso. Now that it's done, I would like to thank her for believing in the story and my ability to tell it.

Friends and sources are always behind the scenes lending a helping hand, and there were more than a few who came through for me in a big way. First, Pat Healy was more than a great buddy and drinking partner during the two years it took to write *King of the Club;* he was a source of information and inspiration. I don't think I could have finished it without his guidance. Eric Starkman and I have been friends for years and there is no one I know who understands the nuances of life better than he does. My brother-in-law Joseph DiSalvo is one of the smartest people I know; if I did one thing right in my life it was turning to Joe for help and guidance. He always has the right answers. My mother-in-law, Angela Juliano, was still my biggest fan, and I thank her for putting me above Oprah. A close second is my brother, Dr. James Gasparino, who has saved more lives than I can count on both hands. It wasn't so long ago that Jimmy and I were in our mother's house dreaming about making it big. We didn't exactly make it big, but we did all right. Better than that, we made our parents proud.

All of which brings me to my final acknowledgment. William and Joan Gasparino were interesting parents who produced two interesting kids. Like us, they were far from perfect, but they understood one thing that they made sure they passed on to their children: that there is a truth. It's not easily arrived at. It's not easily explained. But it's there if you dig deep enough. I hope this book lives up to their standards.

NOTES

In writing and reporting *King of the Club*, I relied on a number of sources for information. First, the subject of the book, Richard Grasso, agreed to a series of on-the-record interviews, as did his long-time head of marketing and public relations, Robert Zito, and many past members of the stock exchange board of directors, including Kenneth Langone, David Komansky, Jimmy Cayne, and Larry Fink.

Special thanks go to Lori Grasso for adding her perspective to the story about her husband, Jim McCarthy, spokesman for Ken Langone, and Richard Torrenzano, who both were invaluable in tracking down various details about Grasso's tenure as CEO of the Club and the controversy surrounding his pay package. Pat Healy, of the Issuer Advisory Group, was a virtual encyclopedia when it came to providing information about the battle between the Nasdaq and the NYSE, as well as the famous floor of the stock exchange and the traders who ruled there for much of the NYSE's history.

Many others, both friends and enemies of Grasso, spoke to me, though they asked that they not be identified by name. In the case of comments provided without attribution, I've attempted to verify them through documents and other on-the-record interviews. Where there's a discrepancy, as is often the case when people are describing events that transpired in years past, I have attempted to provide both sides of the story.

The case brought by the Office of the New York State Attorney General over Grasso's pay package produced a treasure trove of information, including depositions of top Wall Street officials who knew Grasso over the years. I have read most of those documents, and they have been instrumental in providing insight into the events portrayed in this book, particularly from the perspective of people who have refused to cooperate, such as the man who replaced Grasso after the pay scandal, former New York Stock Exchange chairman John Reed, and one of the people who knew the most about Grasso's pay package, former stock exchange human resources chief Frank Ashen.

My coverage of Grasso's pay package began in May of 2003 with a *Wall Street Journal* article (with co-bylines going to me and the reporters Kate Kelly and Sue Craig) that was the first to discuss in broad terms how much he was making and how much he had stashed away in his retirement account. Nearly a year later, New York Attorney General Eliot Spitzer filed his now-famous lawsuit against Grasso, saying the pay package violated state law governing the compensation of executives who run nonprofits (NYSE was incorporated as a nonprofit and has since become a public company).

Spitzer, now the governor of New York State, provided a single interview after many requests to check facts and speak with him about the Grasso controversy were initially denied. But since I have been covering the Grasso case, his chief investigator on the case, Avi Schick; his chief spokesman, Darren Dopp; and Spitzer himself have given me numerous interviews that were instrumental in the writing of my first book, *Blood on the Street,* and in stories I wrote for *Newsweek* and *New York* magazine about Grasso. Information from those interviews appears in this book as well.

In preparation for writing this book, I also read three books that provided me with historical perspective about the stock exchange and Grasso's early years there. They are: Tim Metz, *Black Monday: The Stock Market Catastrophe of October 19, 1987;* Chris Welles, *The Last*

Days of the Club; and John Brooks, *Once in Golconda: A True Drama of Wall Street, 1920–1938.* Without these books, I couldn't have gained a sufficient understanding of the New York Stock Exchange and its place in history, and information gleaned from these sources is cited in these notes. I hope I've done these authors justice.

I also relied on numerous articles from *The Wall Street Journal, The New York Times,* and *BusinessWeek* for source material, as well as Peter Elkind's exhaustively researched profile of Grasso that appeared in *Fortune* magazine in 2004. Again, I have cited these sources in the notes when appropriate, and again, I hope I've given those who deserve credit their due. Lastly, John Thain, the current CEO of the New York Stock Exchange, declined several attempts to provide his perspective on the story of Dick Grasso's rise and fall as well as the vast changes that have taken place at the exchange during his own tenure. But I have to thank his spokesman Richard Adamonis for providing valuable information and keeping an open ear in terms of fact-checking on the pre- and post-Grasso stock exchange as well as giving me access to NYSE documents that helped me in my reporting.

PROLOGUE

Page 2: Description of Grasso's office and final hours as chairman of the NYSE from author interviews and Susanne Craig, Ianthe Jeanne Dugan, Kate Kelly, and Laurie P. Cohen, "Taking Stock: As End Neared, Grasso Held On in Hopes Pay Furor Would Ebb," *The Wall Street Journal,* September 26, 2003.

Page 4: Description of Grasso as a "ward boss" from Gretchen Morgenson, "The Fall of a Wall Street Ward Boss," *The New York Times,* October 19, 2003; comparison to Jesse James from Landon Thomas, Jr., "Big Board Sets Aside $36 Million as Possible Grasso Payment," *The New York Times,* May 4, 2004.

–1–
IT'S GOOD TO BE KING

Page 14: Giuliani's whereabouts at the time of the 9/11 terrorist attacks from author interviews, various news accounts, and Rudolph Giuliani, *Leadership* (New York: Hyperion, 2002), pp. 6–7.

Page 14: Additional details on Giuliani during the initial hours of the terrorist attacks from Giuliani, *Leadership,* p. 12.

Page 17: General description of floor, and the financial background of its traders as well as Grasso's use of his role as chief regulator of trading activities to keep the traders in line from author interviews and Peter Elkind, "Fall of the House of Grasso," *Fortune,* October 18, 2004.

Page 19: Description of former police commissioner Bernard Kerik's lower-middle-class upbringing and background from author interviews and Alan Feuer, "After All the Ups, A Lawman's Life Has Many Downs," *The New York Times,* July 1, 2006.

Page 24: Description of what a floor specialist does at the NYSE in the context of John Mulheren's conversation with Bear Stearns CEO James Cayne from author interviews and Tim Metz, *Black Monday: The Stock Market Catastrophe of October 19, 1987* (Washington, D.C.: Beard Books, 1988), pp. 34–37.

− 2 −
THE EARL OF SANDWICH

Page 27: Grasso named honorary police commissioner and mother's comment about not becoming a real cop from author interviews and Jerry Capeci, "Italians Fight to Rise Above," *Daily News,* March 16, 1998.

Page 30: Grasso learning how to trade at Rosenbaum's pharmacy from author interviews and Sheridan Prasso, "The NYSE? Fuhgedaboutit," *Business-Week,* November 18, 2002.

Page 34: Some of my description of the history of the New York Stock Exchange, the functions of the various types of floor traders, and its building from Metz, *Black Monday,* p. 37, and from timeline on NYSE Web site.

Page 34: Description of NYSE's monopoly status and lack of regulation culled from Chris Welles, *The Last Days of the Club* (New York: E. F. Dutton & Co., 1975), and John Brooks, *Once in Golconda: A True Drama of Wall Street, 1920–1938* (New York: Harper & Row, 1969).

Page 35: Description of the federal response to the 1929 stock market crash from Brooks, *Once in Golconda,* pp. 210–216.

Page 37: Description of NYSE maintaining its monopoly status and ignoring pleas from institutional investors to modernize from Welles, *The Last Days of the Club,* p. 135.

Page 37: NYSE's incorporation as a not-for-profit in 1971 from interview with Grasso and testimony of former compensation committee chairman H. Carl McCall taken as part of the New York attorney general's inquiry into Grasso's pay package.

Page 38: Ethnic change on Wall Street and how it affected the floor of the NYSE from Brooks, *Once in Golconda,* pp. 50–55.

Page 42: Description of back-office crisis and its fallout on Wall Street from Welles, *The Last Days of the Club,* pp. 134–279, and interview with Grasso.

Page 47: Description of Phelan's "dark side" and his nickname "the undertaker" from Metz, *Black Monday,* p. 34, and Peter Elkind, "Fall of the House of Grasso," *Fortune,* October 18, 2004.

Page 53: Phelan's misgivings about Grasso and his "dark side" from author interviews and Elkind, "Fall of the House of Grasso."

Page 56: Description of the floor during the 1980s bull market when Phelan was chairman and the "ooh-rah"s from the large former Marine contingent among the traders from author interviews and Mark Potts, "Stock Trading Blasts Records: 275 Million Shares Trade, Dow Soars 36," *The Washington Post,* August 4, 1984.

Page 58: Description of 1987 crash and Phelan's handling of the media fallout from author interviews and Metz, *Black Monday,* pp. 123–226.

Pages 58 and 59: Description of Phelan's technology change on the floor that helped ease the pain during the crash from author interviews; Metz, *Black Monday*; and William C. Freund, "The Big Board Lives On," *The Wall Street Journal,* December 4, 1985.

– 3 –
"THE EMPTY SUIT"

Page 72: Description of Donaldson's messy personal life from author interviews and Andy Serwer, "Is Donaldson the Best Man for the SEC? Despite a glossy resume, William Donaldson's unimpressive track record has led critics to say that he used his establishment connections to 'fail up.' There are also questions about his personal life," *Fortune,* February 17, 2003.

Page 78: Description of Kappa Beta Phi fraternity party and Grasso's induction into the group from various author interviews with Grasso and James Cayne, and Landon Thomas, Jr., "If Only for a Night, Wall St. Fallen Idol Is One of the Boys," *The New York Times,* February 6, 2004.

Page 80: Donaldson's appearance at congressional hearings over the issue of payment for order flow from author interviews and various news accounts, including "AMEX, NYSE in Spat with NASD over Payment for Orders," Dow Jones News Service, April 14, 1993.

Page 92: Description of Donaldson's affair around the time of his wife's death, including his love child, is based on author interviews and Serwer, "Is Donaldson the Best Man for the SEC?"

Page 92: Description of funeral of Donaldson's wife Evan Burger based on various author interviews with attendees.

Page 95: Donaldson's marriage to Jane Morrison from Serwer, "Is Donaldson the Best Man for the SEC?"

Page 95: Description of the value of the Donaldson option package from Aetna from various author interviews and review of SEC disclosure documents when Donaldson was chairman.

Page 96: Description of Stanley Gault's new plan to attract and keep talent at the NYSE from author interviews, NYSE board minutes, and various news accounts, including Ben White and Alec Klein, "NYSE Documents Decisions on Pay; Directors Still Support Grasso," *The Washington Post,* September 11, 1993.

Page 96: Description of the size of the exchange during the early to mid-1990s from author interviews, NYSE annual reports, and Peter Elkind, "Fall of the House of Grasso," *Fortune,* October 18, 2004.

– 4 –
THE LITTLE GUY IN THE DARK SUIT

Pages 100 and 101: Description of Grasso and Zito's decision to give reporters access to the floor as well as details about CNBC and Maria Bartiromo from author interviews in "Extraordinary Popular Finance and the Madness of Crowds," *Institutional Investor,* April 1, 1998.

Page 104: Description of Grasso's listing of Republic Services and his meetings with its CEO Wayne Huizenga from author interview.

Page 106: Description of Grasso's head shave from author interviews and Erica Garcia, "Shaved by the Bell," *Daily News,* July 2, 1999.

Pages 106 and 107: Description of competitive battle between NASD chief Joseph Hardiman and Grasso, including the Il Mulino dinner with Joe Grano, from author interviews with both men and with Pat Healy, a former NASD marketing executive and current president of the Issuer Advisory Group.

Page 109: Description of new listings coming to the exchange from author interviews, statistics from the Issuer Advisory Group, and Aaron Lucchetti, "Spitzer Presses a Fresh Attack on Grasso Tenure," *The Wall Street Journal,* November 22, 2006.

Page 113: Incident at Lehman Brothers in which Billy Johnston and Cathy Kinney hear complaints about improper trading on the floor of the NYSE from author interview with a Lehman executive who was present.

Page 114: Listing stats from Issuer Advisory Group and Lucchetti, "Spitzer Presses a Fresh Attack on Grasso Tenure."

Page 115: Information about Grasso's and Sandy Weill's dealings with the Reverend Jesse Jackson from various news reports, author interviews, and Charles Gasparino, "Jesse Jackson Fund-Raiser Hits a Snag," *The Wall Street Journal,* January 8, 1998.

Page 115: Information on Jesse Jackson's lobbying on behalf of Sandy Weill to overturn Glass-Steagall from Monica Langley, *Tearing Down the Walls: How Sandy Weill Fought His Way to the Top of the Financial World . . . and Then Nearly Lost It All* (New York: Simon & Schuster, 2003).

Page 117: Description of Grasso's investigation of floor trader incident with Maria Bartiromo from author interview with one of the investigators.

Page 117: Description of Grasso's temper from author interviews and deposition of former board member Charles Bocklet in New York attorney general's civil case against Grasso and Langone.

Page 118: Description of incident involving Richard Simonelli from author interviews with Simonelli and Grasso, and Peter Elkind, "Fall of the House of Grasso," *Fortune*, October 18, 2004.

Page 119: Description of Grasso, Redstone, and Grammer getting "slimed" from author interviews and "It's Not Easy Being Green," *The Dallas Morning News*, April 9, 1999.

Page 120: Grasso's listing of AngloGold and bringing the lion onto the podium from author interviews and Lauren Chambliss, "US Seeking a Lion's Share of Listings," *Evening Standard*, August 26, 1998.

Page 121: Grasso's meeting with FARC leader Raúl Reyes from author interview and various news accounts.

Page 123: Data on companies switching their listings from the Nasdaq to the NYSE from Issuer Advisory Group.

Page 124: Seats selling at a then-record $2.65 million in 1999 from author interviews and Gaston F. Ceron, "Moving the Market: Seat Sale Hits $3 Million," *The Wall Street Journal*, August 4, 1999.

Page 124: Information on Grasso's salary from author interviews and civil lawsuit filed by the Office of the New York State Attorney General against Grasso and former NYSE compensation committee chief Ken Langone.

− 5 −
SUGAR DADDY

Page 128: Information on Ken Langone's background and his rise to power on Wall Street from author interviews, including several with Langone.

Page 134: Description of the newly created "Nasdaq Wall" from author interviews with former NASD chairman Frank Zarb and Paul Farhi, "Nasdaq 'Casino' Had Few Safeguards; Zarb Says Markets Did All They Could," *The Washington Post*, November 11, 2002.

Page 136: Rao's scene involving Bill Gates and Warren Buffett from author interviews with Grasso, Frank Pellegrino, and Buffett.

Page 137: Description of Oakford case and the NYSE handling of it from author interviews with Grasso; his attorney, Harvey Pitt; former SEC commissioner Harvey Goldschmid; and Gary Weiss, "NYSE: A Street Scandal That May Not Die," *BusinessWeek,* August 9, 1999.

Page 141: Grasso statement about SEC settlement after the settlement of the Oakford case from Greg Ip and Michael Schroeder, "SEC Assails Big Board for Failing to Dectect Illegal Trading on Floor," *The Wall Street Journal,* June 30, 1999.

Page 141: Description of Hank Greenberg's behavior regarding the work of his specialist and messages left with Grasso's secretary from author interviews and depositions taken for the New York attorney general's case against Grasso, particularly the deposition of SooJee Lee.

Pages 143–145: Grasso's battle with Morgan Stanley, Goldman Sachs, and Merrill Lynch, also known as "the MGM crew," over the implementation of the CLOB from author interviews and various news accounts, including Judith Burns, "Central Limit Order Book Declared 'Dead' by Critics," Dow Jones News Service, March 30, 2000.

Page 148: New-listing information between 1998 and 2000 from Aaron Lucchetti, "Spitzer Presses a Fresh Attack on Grasso Tenure," *The Wall Street Journal,* November 22, 2006.

Page 149: Grasso considering taking the NYSE public from author interviews and Matthew Goldstein, "What Makes You So Special?" *Smart Money,* February 9, 2000.

Pages 151 and 152: Former NYSE board member Charles Bocklet's description of what he did when he learned about Grasso's pay and that the floor would have "hung" Grasso if it had discovered how much he had been paid from author interviews, Bocklet's deposition in New York attorney general's case against Grasso and Langone, and Jenny Anderson, "N.Y.S.E. Executive Tells of Altering Documents to Hide Grasso's Full Payout," *The New York Times,* April 7, 2006.

– 6 –
THE SAVIOR

Page 157: Details of Bear Stearns meetings from various news accounts and author interviews with Grasso, Pitt, and Cayne.

Page 160: Damage assessment made during the Bear Stearns meeting by Verizon president Larry Babbio from author interviews and Christine Nuzum, "Verizon Says 9,000–14,000 NYC Businesses Lack Phone Svc," Dow Jones Newswires, September 17, 2001.

Page 160: Official reason for moving meeting from Bear Stearns to CSFB from Robert Dieterich, "Stock Markets to Reopen Monday: Testing Backup Systems," Bloomberg News, September 14, 2001.

Page 162: Grasso addressing reporters with the statement "Is this not just another one of those moments when America has been challenged, and will rise again?" from Alessandra Stanley, "Wall Street's Driven Steward Presses for Business as Usual," *The New York Times,* September 17, 2001.

Page 162: Dimensions of flag from author interview and Gaston Ceron, "Christmas Comes to Wall Street as NYSE Lights Holiday Tree," Dow Jones News Service, December 2, 2002.

Page 163: Description of CSFB meeting following 9/11 from author interviews and Dieterich, "Stock Markets to Reopen Monday."

Page 168: Description of former police chief Bernard Kerik as former mayor Rudy Giuliani's driver from author interviews and Karen Freifeld, "Kerik to Be Sworn In Today; Tradition-filled City Hall Ceremony Will Honor New Police Commissioner," *Newsday,* September 5, 2000.

−7−
THE LAST HURRAH

Page 178: Description of the unveiling of Grasso's 9/11 plaque from Landon Thomas, Jr., "Big Board Set to Take Down a Reminder of Ex-Chief," *The New York Times,* May 7, 2004.

Page 179: The descriptions of the salaries of top executives working under Grasso, as well as the salary of his former secretary, SooJee Lee, from Susanne Craig, Kate Kelly, and Theo Francis, "NYSE Lists Pay of Executives, Omits Details," *The Wall Street Journal,* October 13, 2003; Landon Thomas, Jr., "Officials Due $133 Million at Big Board," *The New York Times,* October 11, 2003; and Susanne Craig, Ianthe Jeanne Dugan, and Karen Richardson, "At the Big Board, Grasso's Secretary Made Big Bucks, Too—Executive Assistants Cheer Her $240,000 Salary; 'The Ultimate Gatekeeper,' " *The Wall Street Journal,* February 4, 2005.

Page 180: Technology glitch that temporarily shut down the NYSE during the summer of 2001 and caused Grasso to think he would get a pay cut in 2001 from author interviews and "General Accounting Office to Study Recent NYSE, Nasdaq Outages," Dow Jones News Service, July 13, 2001.

Page 180: Cuts in Wall Street bonuses and CEOs' pay, including the compensation of former Goldman CEO Hank Paulson and Bear Stearns CEO James Cayne, from author interviews and Charles Gasparino, "Rebuilding Wall Street: Bear Stearns Will Announce Big Staff Cuts," *The Wall Street Journal,* October 18, 2001, and Landon Thomas, Jr., "It's Bonus Season, and Even the Bosses Are Learning to Live Less Large," *The New York Observer,* November 19, 2001.

Pages 180 and 181: How Grasso's salary compared to Cayne's from "Bear Stearns CEO Takes Pay Cut of More than 50 Pct," Reuters, March 4, 2001.

Page 181: Langone's "lead pipe" quote from his deposition in New York State attorney general's case involving Grasso's pay package.

Pages 186 and 187: Many of the details of Grasso's dealings with New York attorney general Eliot Spitzer during the research probe as well as specific
quotes of their conversations are from author interviews with both men
and from Charles Gasparino, *Blood on the Street: The Sensational Inside
Story of How Wall Street Analysts Duped a Generation of Investors* (New York:
Free Press, 2005), pp. 258–317.

Page 192: Grasso's decision to begin the process of taking control of his retirement money in 2002 because of the corporate scandals can be attributed
to author interviews and two documents: Goldman Sachs CEO Hank
Paulson's deposition before Spitzer's investigators in the Grasso pay case
and his interview for the NYSE investigation into Grasso's compensation
conducted by Dan Webb.

Page 198: Vedder Price's analysis of Grasso's pay from author interviews, depositions in New York attorney general's case involving Grasso's pay package, and Peter Elkind, "Fall of the House of Grasso," *Fortune,* October 18,
2004.

Page 198: Cayne's worry that the seat holders would object to Grasso's retirement package because seat prices were declining in 2002 from author interviews and depositions in the New York attorney general's case against
Grasso; the actual decline in seat prices from "Price for NYSE Seat Sees
4th Consecutive Decline," Reuters, February 10, 2003.

– 8 –
STAR FUCKER OR SAVIOR?

Page 203: The timing of Grasso's desire to put Sandy Weill on the board of the
stock exchange as early as September of 2002 from Grasso's deposition
and deposition of members of the NYSE nominating committee given during the New York attorney general's investigation of Grasso's pay package,
and author interviews.

Page 205: The description of the "Cayne Mutiny," in which Bear Stearns CEO
James Cayne attempted to block the $1.4 billion research settlement, and
how Grasso outmaneuvered Cayne from author interviews with Cayne and
Grasso and from Gasparino, *Blood on the Street.*

Page 207: The amount of money Bear Stearns paid as part of the research settlement from Kevin Drawbaugh and Brian Kelleher, "Brokerages to Pay
$1.4 Billion in Research Settlement," Reuters, December 20, 2002.

Page 207: Details about the final outcome of the stock research settlement, including the NASD considering charging Sandy Weill, and the possibility
that Citigroup might then have dropped out of the deal from author interviews and Charles Gasparino, "The Stock-Research Pact: How Settlement
Train Kept on Track," *The Wall Street Journal,* December 23, 2000.

Page 209: Details of how NYSE board members are nominated and ultimately get approval to serve on the board from author interviews with Grasso and others as well as depositions in New York attorney general's case against Grasso over his pay package.

Page 210: Debate over Grasso's decision to place Sandy Weill on the NYSE board between supporters like Langone and those who opposed the move during a board meeting just before the matter became public from author interviews and Charles Gasparino and Randall Smith, "Behind Weill's Almost Directorship at NYSE," *The Wall Street Journal,* March 25, 2003.

Page 213: Spitzer's decision to attack Grasso over Weill nomination and their subsequent conversation about the merits of Weill's directorship from Gasparino, *Blood on the Street,* p. 213, and author interviews with Spitzer, during the time this occurred, and Grasso.

Page 213: Spitzer's belief that Grasso controlled stock exchange nominations from Brooke Masters, *Spoiling for a Fight: The Rise of Eliot Spitzer* (New York: Henry Holt & Co., 2006), pp. 176–178.

Pages 214–15: Grasso's decision to pull the Weill nomination following the attacks from Spitzer based on author interview with Grasso. His statement to the press from various news accounts, including Charles Gasparino, "Citigroup CEO Drops Candidacy for Seat on NYSE's Board," *The Wall Street Journal,* March 24, 2003.

– 9 –
THE UPRISING BEGINS

Page 218: Grasso's conversation with Ashen before the February 2003 compensation committee meeting where he said he wanted Ashen to alert the committee that his salary in 2002 should decline from the year before from Grasso's deposition in New York attorney general's case involving his pay package, and from an author interview with Ashen's attorney.

Page 219: Then–Goldman Sachs CEO Hank Paulson's 2002 compensation as described in passage comparing it to Grasso compensation that year from Susanne Craig and Jathon Sapsford, "Schwab CEOs Decline Bonuses, Give Up Options," *The Wall Street Journal,* March 31, 2003. Paulson's comment that Grasso "had a better year than I did" from author interviews with meeting participants.

Page 222: The general description of Paulson's rise to the top of Goldman Sachs from author interviews and Charles Gasparino, "Power Play: Goldman's Hank Paulson Won the Battle to Oust Dick Grasso over His Lavish Pay. But Will He Win the War?" *Newsweek,* June 7, 2004.

Page 223: The description of the meeting between Paulson and Ashen regarding Grasso's proposal to take his retirement money, including Paulson's comment that he "gasped at the numbers," in Grasso's pay package from author interviews, official NYSE documents produced during Dan Webb's investigation of Grasso's pay package, and Peter Elkind, "Fall of the House of Grasso," *Fortune,* October 18, 2004.

Page 225: Paulson's nervousness about the perception of Grasso taking so much money before retirement—"the optics"—and his decision to ask Langone if they could keep Grasso's pay package inside the compensation committee and away from the larger NYSE from Langone's and Paulson's depositions in the Spitzer case.

Pages 230 and 231: The controversy following the initial disclosure of Grasso's salary in May 2003 from author interviews. Its comparison to the salary of other regulators, like the chairman of the Federal Reserve, also from author interviews. The exact citation of the Fed chairman's salary in this passage from Caroline Baum, "Ex–Fed Chairman Remains a Force; Greenspan Has a Right to Talk, But We Don't Have to Listen to Him," Bloomberg Business News, March 16, 2007.

Page 232: Grasso's comment that SEC chairman William Donaldson was an "outstanding choice" for the job in the context of the congressional hearing that Grasso was attending with Donaldson and Spitzer when the pay package story broke from Michael Schroeder and Barbara Martinez, "Bush Nominates Veteran Financier to Head the SEC—William Donaldson Faces a Shaken Agency; A Mixed Stint at Aetna," *The Wall Street Journal,* December 11, 2002.

Page 233: Scene from the congressional hearing where Grasso and Spitzer discuss the *Wall Street Journal* story and Spitzer comments about Grasso's picture in the paper from author interviews and Grasso's deposition in New York attorney general's case over his pay package.

Page 233: Grasso's statement to reporters about *Journal* story on his salary from author interviews and James Toedtman, "10 Million Dollar Man Feels the Heat; NYSE's Grasso Testifies on Scandals but Is at Relative Loss for Words over Own Pay Package," *Newsday,* May 8, 2003.

Pages 234–238: Media coverage of pay scandal that ensued during the summer and early fall of 2003 and *New York Post*'s Grass-O-Meter from Yvette Kantrow, "The Grasso Watch," *Daily Deal,* September 22, 2003.

– 10 –

ONE BAD DAY

Page 244: Grasso responding to SEC chairman Donaldson's order to unveil corporate governance reforms, including disclosure of his compensation, from Kate Kelly and Susanne Craig, "NYSE to Disclose Grasso Pay Among Changes," *The Wall Street Journal,* June 6, 2003.

Page 247: Paulson's comments about compensation committee chairman H. Carl McCall not being "financially sophisticated" from Webb Report and Kimberley A. Strassel, "Behind the Spitzer Curtain," *The Wall Street Journal,* June 14, 2005.

Pages 248–255: Details of the August 7, 2003, compensation committee meeting and subsequent board meeting, including McCall's actions at these events and criticism of Grasso's move by Bill Harrison and Madeleine Albright, from the Webb Report, various press accounts, and Strassel, "Behind the Spitzer Curtain."

Page 256: Paulson's angry conversation with Grasso after he came back from Brazil and learned that Grasso was taking his retirement money from Landon Thomas, Jr., "The Winding Road to That Huge Payday," *The New York Times,* June 25, 2006, as well as author interviews with Grasso and a spokesman for Paulson.

Page 258: SEC's broadening the scope of its investigation into allegedly improper trading by NYSE specialists from author interviews; Nicole Maestri, "NYSE in Tough Spot with Specialist Trading Probe," Reuters, July 24, 2003; and Kate Kelly, Susanne Craig, and Deborah Solomon in Washington, "SEC Intensifies Inquiry at NYSE of Trading Firms—Move Comes as Big Board Names Reed Interim Chief; Regulatory Role Questioned," *The Wall Street Journal,* September 22, 2003.

Page 268: Cayne description of the firm Goldman Sachs as "Goldman Sucks" from author interviews and *The Wall Street Journal Guide to Who's Who and What's What on Wall Street* (New York: Ballantine Books, 1998), pp. 185–212.

Page 270: Grasso's statement to the press after he decided not to take the additional $48 million in his contract, "Some will say you waived $48 million in payments . . . ," from CNNfn transcripts of September 9, 2003, press conference.

Page 276: Information concerning the breakfast meeting at Goldman headquarters between Carl McCall and Hank Paulson just before Grasso's ouster from author interviews and September 26, 2003, *Wall Street Journal* article, "Taking Stock: As End Neared, Grasso Held On in Hopes Pay Furor Would Ebb—CEO Misread Depth of Anger on Floor, Insiders Say; Support from Giuliani—'I Didn't Offer to Resign,'" by Susanne Craig, Ianthe Jeanne Dugan, Kate Kelly, and Laurie P. Cohen.

Page 277: Details of Larry Fink's call to Grasso on the day of his ouster and Grasso's feeling of betrayal from author interviews with Grasso and Fink and from Craig et al., "Taking Stock."

Page 281: McCall's public statement following Grasso's resignation from "NYSE Says Chairman Richard Grasso Resigns," Reuters, September 17, 2003.

— 11 —
WITH FRIENDS LIKE THESE . . .

Page 286: Reed's decision to take the job as temporary NYSE chairman and CEO for a "symbolic $1" from Kate Kelly, "Painful Progress at the Big Board," *The Wall Street Journal,* August 27, 2004.

Page 291: Reed's comments regarding Grasso and how he should return his pay package from Patrick McGeehan and Landon Thomas, Jr., "Next for the Big Board: To Sue or Not to Sue?" *The New York Times,* December 21, 2003.

Page 293: The net worth of former Goldman Sachs president John Thain before he took the job as CEO of the NYSE from Susanne Craig and Ann Davis, "NYSE's New CEO Faces Tough Road," *The Wall Street Journal,* December 22, 2003.

Page 293: Thain's background as a protégé of former Goldman CEO Jon Corzine from author interviews and Ben White, "Goldman Sachs President Named Chief of NYSE," *The Washington Post,* December 19, 2003.

Page 294: Goldman Sachs market expert Duncan Niederauer's "five guys named Vinny" comment from Charles Gasparino, "The Seats of Power; Goldman Sachs Rules the Street with Smarts and Tough Tactics. But Has It Gone Too Far with the Big Board Deal?" *Newsweek,* November 28, 2005.

Page 295: Seat price information following Grasso's ouster in early 2004 from Kate Kelly, "NYSE Director Langone to Sell Exchange Seat," *The Wall Street Journal,* March 2, 2004.

Page 295: Information involving Todd Christie's handling of AIG shares and the government's probe of it from author interviews and depositions in the New York attorney general's case against Grasso. Alleged trading losses at Spear, Leeds & Kellogg resulting from its handling of AIG stock from author interviews and from Kate Kelly and Susanne Craig, "At Behest of AIG Chief, Grasso Pushed NYSE Firm to Buy Stock," *The Wall Street Journal,* October 3, 2003.

— 12 —
ENTER THE ENFORCER

Page 299: Details of Webb Report findings from the report itself.

Page 300: Spitzer's description of his meeting with John Reed concerning his decision to file a civil case against Grasso comes from his CNBC *Mad Money* interview with James Cramer; John Reed's description comes from his deposition in the case brought by the New York attorney general's office over Grasso's pay package.

Page 302: Spitzer's intention to settle the case with Grasso for $50 million from Charles Gasparino, "Street Fighting Man; Regulators Want Dick Grasso to Give Up a Chunk of His Controversial $139.5 Million Payday. But the Former Big Board Chief Says He Isn't Budging," *Newsweek,* May 17, 2004.

Page 302: Dave Komansky's conversation with Spitzer and his contention that the attorney general wanted $125 million from Komansky's deposition in the attorney general's case and author interview with Komansky and Grasso.

Page 302: Precedent for Spitzer's case involving former Adelphi University president Peter Diamondopoulos from author interviews and from Pradnya Joshi, "Suit over Compensation: Spitzer to Sue Grasso over NYSE Payout; New York Attorney General Looks to Take Back Part of the Former Exchange Chairman's $139.5M Pay Package," *Newsday,* May 21, 2004.

Page 303: Avi Schick's charity clothing store for children from Clem Richardson, "Helping's Their Style: New Clothes for Needy Kids Is Tribute to Grandmother," *Daily News,* September 29, 2003.

Page 303: Evidence uncovered about Grasso's spending habits, including his use of private jets, restaurant bills, and billing the exchange for pretzels and flowers to Langone's wife from author interviews, review of depositions, and John Crudele, "Dick Billed NYSE for Pretzels," *New York Post,* April 14, 2006.

Page 304: Avi Schick's case against Langone and his discovery of a worksheet that Spitzer says shows Langone misled board members over Grasso's compensation from author interviews and Kate Kelly, "Langone Says NYSE Wasn't Misled on Pay of Ex-Chief Grasso," *The Wall Street Journal,* June 15, 2004.

Page 305: Langone's warning to Grasso—"If you settle, Dick, I'll never speak to you again"—just before Spitzer filed his charges against both Grasso and Langone from numerous author interviews.

Page 306: Description of Eliot Spitzer's "playbook" that he followed when going after his targets from author interviews and Charles Gasparino, "Top of His Game: New York's Attorney General Is Reforming Yet Another Big Industry. His Secret? Inside 'Spitzer's Playbook,' " *Newsweek,* November 1, 2004.

Page 306: Accusations about Grasso's alleged relationship with SooJee Lee from May 2003 author interview with Spitzer and his staff before he charged Grasso in the case over his pay package.

Page 308: Spitzer's comment following the filing of his case against Grasso that Grasso "did nothing" when former SEC chief Harvey Pitt asked him to reform research from author interview with Spitzer at the time.

Page 308: The statement released by Spitzer when he filed his case quoting a former NYSE board member as saying, "Thank God I escaped that one," from Gaston Ceron, "Update: NY Attorney General Spitzer Sues Dick Grasso," Dow Jones News Service, May 24, 2004.

– 13 –
THE GOLDMAN SACHS EXCHANGE

Page 313: Spitzer's comments to Jack Welch that he wanted to "put a spike through Langone's heart" from Charles Gasparino, "Wall Street: This Case Is Personal," *Newsweek*, September 24, 2004.

Page 317: Langone's comments to Spitzer at Al Smith dinner from author interviews and Charles Gasparino, "Spitzer v. Grasso v. Langone: The Battle Between New York's Ambitious Attorney General and Two of Wall Street's Most Recognizable Figures Is About to Enter an Even Nastier Phase," *Newsweek*, December 15, 2004.

Page 318: The price of a NYSE seat after the Archipelago deal as well as the specialist Richard Wey's recollection of NYSE CEO John Thain's statement regarding NYSE plans to go public from author interviews and Aaron Lucchetti, "Former Seat Owner Sues NYSE, Thain over Remarks Before Deal," *The Wall Street Journal*, July 13, 2005.

Page 324: Post-Archipelago seat prices estimated from author interviews and Aaron Lucchetti, Susanne Craig, and Dennis K. Berman, "NYSE to Acquire Electronic Trader and Go Public—Archipelago Deal Signals Historic Shifts for Markets in Newly Competitive Era," *The Wall Street Journal*, April 21, 2005.

Page 327: Concerns raised by Merrill CEO Stan O'Neal over the Archipelago merger with the NYSE and Goldman's role in making it happen from conversations with NYSE officials, author interviews, and Charles Gasparino, "Big Board Bid; Could Former Wall Street Executive John Mack Be Joining Financier Ken Langone's Bid to Purchase the New York Stock Exchange?" *Newsweek*, April 25, 2005.

Page 331: Information about the status of the civil and criminal cases against the specialists, including the outcome of the case against specialist David Finnerty, from Chad Bray and Paul Davies, "Moving the Market: NYSE Ex–Floor Trader's Conviction Is Thrown Out in Latest Blow to US," *The Wall Street Journal*, February 22, 2007.

INDEX